REPORT ON THE AEGINETAN SCULPTURES

Report on the Aeginetan Sculptures

With Historical Supplements

Johann Martin Wagner
with F. W. J. Schelling

Translated, edited, and with an introduction by Louis A. Ruprecht Jr.

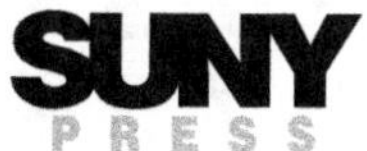

Cover image: The Temple to Aphaia on the island of Aegina, Greece (author's photograph).

Published by State University of New York Press, Albany

Printed in the United States of America

For information, contact State University of New York Press, Albany, NY
www.sunypress.edu

Production, Jenn Bennett
Marketing, Anne M. Valentine

Library of Congress Cataloging-in-Publication Data
Names: Wagner, Johann Martin von, author. | Schelling, Friedrich Wilhelm Joseph von, 1775-1854. | Ruprecht, Louis A., editor, translator. | Translation of: Bericht über die Aeginetischen Bildwerke im Besitz Seiner Königl. Hoheit des Kronprinzes von Baiern.
Title: Report on the Aeginetan sculptures : with historical supplements/by Johann Martin Wagner with F.W.J. Schelling ; edited and translated by Louis A. Ruprecht, Jr.
Other titles: Bericht über die Aeginetischen Bildwerke im Besitz Seiner Königl. Hoheit des Kronprinzes von Baiern. English
Description: Albany : State University of New York Press, 2017. | Includes bibliographical references and index.
Identifiers: LCCN 2016031492 (print) | LCCN 2016032160 (ebook) | ISBN 9781438464817 (hardcover : alk. paper) | ISBN 9781438464800 (pbk : alk. paper) | ISBN 9781438464824 (e- book)
Subjects: LCSH: Aeginetan marbles. | Ludwig I, King of Bavaria, 1786-1868—Art collections. | Aegina Island (Greece)—Antiquities.
Classification: LCC NB87.M8 G59 2017 (print) | LCC NB87.M8 (ebook) | DDC 730.74/495—dc23
LC record available at https://lccn.loc.gov/2016031492

10 9 8 7 6 5 4 3 2 1

This book is dedicated to my brother

CLIFFORD HOLT RUPRECHT

Οὐκουν, ἦν δ'ἐγώ, τὸ λεγόμενον, ἀδελφὸς ἀνδρὶ παρείη
"Then, I said, as the saying goes, 'Let a brother stand by a man' . . ."

Plato, *Republic* 362d

[On the island of Aegina] there are three temples (ναοὶ) very close to one another: one for Apollo, one for Artemis, and a third for Dionysus. Apollo is depicted by a nude wooden image (ξόανον γυμνόν) made in the local style, whereas Artemis is clothed (ἐσθῆς), as is Dionysus, who is also depicted with a beard. The sanctuary (ἱερόν) of Asklepios is located in another place, not here, and has a seated stone statue (λίθου δὲ ἄγαλμα καθήμενον). Of all the gods, the Aeginetans honor Hekate the most, and celebrate sacred rites (τελετὴν) for her every year, rites they say were founded by Orpheus the Thracian. Inside the sacred enclosure (τοῦ περιβόλου) is a temple (ναός) with a wooden image by Myron (ξόανον δὲ ἔργον Μύρωνος), stylistically similar (ὁμοίως) in the face and the rest of the body. It seems to me that Alkamenes was the first to make a statue with three images of Hekate attached to one another, an image that the Athenians call Turret-Round (Επιπυργιδίαν); it is set up near the temple of the Wingless Victory.

On Aegina, as you make your way up to the mountain of Panhellenic Zeus, there is a sanctuary (ἱερόν) for Aphaia, in whose honor Pindar composed an ode for the Aeginetans. The Cretans say (the story of Aphaia is a local legend) that Karmanor, who purified Apollo after he had killed the Python, had a son named Euboulus, and that Euboulos's daughter Carme conceived a child with Zeus, which was Britomartis. She took delight in racing and in hunting, and was the very closest friend (μάλιστα φίλην) of Artemis. Fleeing from Minos, when he was enflamed (ἐρασθέντα) for her, she threw herself into nets (ἐς δίκτυα) that had been cast out to gather fish. She was made a goddess (θεόν) by Artemis, and she is revered (σέβουσι) not only by the Cretans but also by the Aeginetans, who say that Britomartis herself also appears on their island. Her name according to the Aeginetans is Aphaia whereas it is Diktynna on Crete. The Panhellenic Mountain, except for the sanctuary (ἱερόν) of Zeus, does not have anything else worthy of mention (ἀξιόλογον). This sanctuary (ἱερόν), they say, was made by Aiakos for Zeus.

—Pausanias, *Guide to Greece* II.30.3–4

[S]o immature art, as we now see, has its own attractiveness in the *naïveté*, the freshness of spirit, which finds power and interest in simple motives of feeling, and in the freshness of hand, which has a sense of enjoyment in mechanical processes still performed unmechanically, in the spending of care and intelligence on every touch. As regards Italian art, the sculpture and paintings of the earlier Renaissance, the aesthetic value of this *naïveté* is well understood; but it has its value in Greek sculpture also. . . . In a sort of stiff grace, combined with a sense of things bright or sorrowful directly felt, the Aeginetan workman is as it were the Chaucer of Greek sculpture.

—Walter Pater, "The Marbles of Aegina" (1925)

CONTENTS

LIST OF ILLUSTRATIONS

A NOTE ON THIS TRANSLATION

A brief word of explanation may be in order regarding some of the translational decisions and strategies that have informed this work. I highlight the most important of them here.

First, the references to classical figures are not standardized. In general, I prefer to transliterate Greek names in ways that more closely mirror the Greek original. The exceptions are those figures whose names are so well established as to be virtually canonical; to change these names would, I fear, actually be confusing to many readers. So I will refer to Aiakos rather than Aeacus, Herakles rather than Hercules, and Pheidias rather than Phidias . . . but Achilles will not become Achilleus, Daedalus will not become Daidalos, and Crete will not become Krêtê.

The matter of names is complicated still further by the fact that both Wagner and Schelling Latinize all of their references to Greek divinities. So the sacred site on Aegina is consistently (and erroneously) referred to as the Temple of Panhellenic Jupiter, not Zeus, and the central goddess in the pedimental group is called Minerva rather than Athena. This is a very significant aspect of nineteenth-century classical scholarship—the filtering of Greek image through later Latin form—about which I have written elsewhere; it seemed important to me to maintain the Latin as it appears in the original texts.

In the copious notes accompanying this translation, however, it will often be otherwise. Neither Schelling nor Wagner make it a habit actually to cite their casual references to classical literature and history. The two most commonly cited ancient sources—Pausanias's *Guide to Greece* and Pliny's *Natural History*—tend to be cited by book number and chapter, but that is all. I have managed to track down all but two references in this book and felt that it would make a substantial contribution to the scholarly use of this volume if these texts were actually quoted in full in the accompanying notes. For ease of reference and in the interest of standardization, I have consistently used the Loeb Classical Library edition for all of the citations where such a volume has been published, and I include the relevant Greek and Latin terms in parentheses. I have occasionally emended the translation in order to highlight a semantic distinction of some importance to my reading of the text, and have indicated this in parentheses in the relevant notes. In all but a few cases, these emendations are relatively minor.

The use of the Loeb series, however, has the unintended consequence of creating some inconsistency in the names of classical figures as they appear on the page and in the accompanying note. In order to assist the scholarly reader who wishes to check the references I provide here, I felt that it was important to maintain the names as they appear in the Loeb translations, even in those cases where these differ slightly from the names as I transliterate them in the body of the text. There is no case in which this inconsistency creates a confusion about what figure is being discussed, but I want the reader to know that I am aware of the semantic twists and turns this creates.

The final judgment call—and it is stylistic as much as it is substantive—is when and in what manner to include the German text that I have translated here. I have included German terms, and occasionally longer phrases, in brackets in the body of the text of this translation, once again, to serve the interests of the scholarly reader who knows a bit of German. One of the major philosophical preoccupations of post-Kantian philosophy was the epistemological question of how to secure determinate [*bestimmt*] judgments, that is to say, a way of describing an object that sets it apart from all others and leaves no doubt about what we are discussing in all of its particularity. That kind of determination [*Bestimmung*] is not easily achieved however, especially since most of the judgments we wish to secure—in art and religion, as well as in philosophy, the three crucial arenas of spirit [*Geist*]—rely on linguistic and visual representations. Furthermore, *Bestimmung* in certain contexts clearly came to imply "destiny" for Hegel and his followers, as opposed to "fate" [*Schicksal*]; the reach of Greek thought was long indeed.

The two terms most prominently invoked in this regard are *Darstellung* (presentation) and *Vorstellung* (representation, or idea). Hegel famously argued that it was philosophy's task to become more scientific than art or religion could be, since both were still trapped in what he curiously referred to as "picture thinking"; philosophy's task, by contrast, was to work with a concept [*Begriff*] rather than with an image [*Vorstellung*]. The trouble is that art and religion, and the lusciously visual ways of thinking they embody, will not simply go away and stubbornly refuse to be transcended. Even Hegel's own first philosophy, *The Phenomenology of Spirit* from 1807, concluded by referring to phenomenology as a walking tour through a series of spirit-images, what Hegel calls "a gallery of images" [*ein Galerei von Bildern*], almost as if the phenomenological observer were walking through a museum.

Schelling, in this remarkable text, takes philosophy explicitly into this new world of the museum. One of the most interesting, and exceptionally creative, aspects of this text is the way in which it shows a philosopher and a visual artist utilizing the same vocabulary in relation to different subjects and disparate intellectual tasks. This text provides a marvelous point of entry into a particularly creative moment of real intellectual ferment in German scholarship, and we are meeting two remarkably self-conscious inhabitants of that intellectual formation, or culture [*Bildung*], here. I have therefore tried to give some indication each time a verb or adjective or noun form of these important terms has been used.

But I have included much else besides without, I hope, disrupting the flow of the reading. For all of their concern for determinate judgments, Wagner and Schelling utilize an art historical vocabulary whose terms tend to flow somewhat ambiguously into one another. The title refers to *Bildwerke*, and this is clearly a reference to sculptures in the round. But we will also meet references to "images" [*Bilder*] and "works" [*Werke*] in which the ambiguity of the term may or may not be intentional. Rather than answer that question definitively, I have included the terms referring to visual images wherever they appear in the immediate context.

I have done this with the citations from Pausanias as well (and, to a lesser degree, with Pliny). Pausanias appears to be working with a fairly technical vocabulary that clearly differentiates between a sanctuary or shrine (*hieron*), and an altar (*bômos*) or a memorial (*mnêmê*). He also seems to distinguish quite carefully between ancient wooden images (*xoana* or *daidala*) and statues (*agalmata*); he also makes reference to idols (*eidola*) and icons (*eikona*) in what may or may not have been a technical distinction to him. Once again, rather than answer that question definitively, I have made a point always to include these terms when they appear in his discussion in order to alert the reader to the presence of the question. I hope that this will enable the reader to gain some fuller sense of the rich semantic field in which those who ponder over the meaning of religious images, whether ancient or modern images (and the two overlapped at the Munich Glyptothek), were involved, a set of complex linguistic registers that could never be quite as determinate as they might have wished.

The longer I have worked with this text, the more I have come to appreciate the intelligence and self-consciousness with which both Schelling and Wagner approached these ambiguities. I hope this translation provides some sense of that appreciation.

TRANSLATOR'S ACKNOWLEDGMENTS

This is the third book that I have completed while working primarily at the Vatican Library and the Vatican Library's Secret Archives. The spirited cosmopolitanism of the place may come as a surprise to those unduly skeptical of things ecclesiastical, but it is precisely the Roman generosity, and I daresay the Roman *grace*, of this place that I have always found most sustaining while working there. Quite literally, this book could not have been completed anywhere else in the world.

I have been privileged by the opportunity to spend months at a time in the marvelous city that is Rome, each summer for more than a decade now, and in the past three years I have managed to be there in December as well, when the sparkle of the holiday season lends the city a new sheen, a new glitter, a new aura. My work in Rome has been supplemented by many other equally rich libraries and archives in which the city appears to take such pride: the Historical Archives of the Capitoline, the State Archives of Rome, the American Academy in Rome, the German Archaeological Institute, and especially the French School's vast Library, which is housed in the breathtaking vastness of the Palazzo Farnese.

Behind such institutions are people, of course, and it is the people who have made Rome home. Carolina Olcese arranged various apartments for me when I first began working here, each of them within a stone's throw of the Vatican Library. Wise in the ways of arts and of people, she has been a constant source of assistance, care, and insight. She has helped me deal with inconveniences, like missed travel arrangements, to genuine emergencies, like the theft of my computer with all of my supporting materials several years ago. And she has consistently made time in the evenings to sound me out on my research and to offer her guidance on interpretive matters in the visual arts. When Carolina invited me to visit her at her second home in Ischia di Castro, yet another mysterious ancient world was opened to me, Etruscan this time. I am ever grateful to her.

Similarly, for the past four years Mariasilvia Farci has made a lovely little green studio available to me; herself the editor of gorgeous and inspiring art books, she too has become a valued conversation partner and friend.

The Greeks and Romans we meet in antiquity kept lists, lots of lists. The matter of lists and how to read them comes up several times in the pages that follow. One senses that such people kept track of their hearts as well as their fortunes in this way. Since the strategy clearly worked for them, I approach the tending of my own emotional arrangements in much the same way here. Rome, by now, is mostly defined by the contours of friendships, new and old alike. My sense of Roman time spanning many years now has been animated and enlivened by the presence and care of Alice Bever, Ludovica Andrè Lanini, Tiziana Checchi, Elisabetta Calderoni, Mauro Corso, Chiara De Dominicis, Carmen Favre, Vania Felici, Cristiano Filadi, Pietro Filadi, Francesco Fiorillo, Marta Gentile, Donna Giulio, Lilia Ingallinella, Carmen Martino, Lea Messina, Gabriella Milea, Sara Millozzi, Emma Mintrone, Sara Moriconi, Marika Onofri and her son Milo, Nicola Pastino, Alice Rinaldi, Francesco Rocchi, Manuela Rosati, Mariaclara Samele, Corrado Sferragatta, Federica Sfoche, Irma Storti, Stefania Suetti, and Chiara Zanetti.

Greece serves to fill the emotional gaps and fissures that long periods away from home can make one feel, even in a place as lovely as Rome; as difficult as it is to leave this Eternal City, the island of Corfu has always been a marvelous hybrid, a Janus-faced point of embarkation, transition and arrival. It was so for Martin Wagner two centuries ago; it is for me still, today. By now, Corfu feels more like the point where my journeys begin and end, though of course such journeys rarely have static limits such as that. I had the rare good fortune to meet Maria Sartori-Dendias on my first visit to the island, where I had been invited to deliver a spring seminar at the Ionian University. We spent eight hours talking, without letup, on a rain-drenched boat crossing the Adriatic Sea; she has been the most spirited of friends ever since. Her husband, Spiro, and her son Alexi, have made Corfu feel as much like home as Rome does. While an unusual thing to say to Greek friends in 2015, I'm ever in their debt.

In Athens, Yianna Tzigounaki and Vangelis Kalambakas, accompanied now by their vivacious young daughter, Ariadne, have always awaited my arrivals patiently, with an open home and heart. It is often only when I talk with them about what I've been doing that I realize what the work that has occupied me in Rome has really been about.

Back in the United States, I am grateful to a great many of my university colleagues: Margo Alexander, Abbas Barzegar, Molly Bassett, David Bell, Hope Carter, Kate Daley-Bailey, Nick Demos, Christos Galileias, Jon Herman, Brian Kooy, Claire Kooy, Kathryn Kozaitis, Nadia Latif, Annie Latta, Ellen Logan, Dean William Long, Ashley Mastin, Kathryn McClymond, Pearl McHaney, Monique Moultrie, Gayle Nelson, Provost Risa Palm, Faidra

Papavasiliou, Gerard Pendrick, Esther Prince, Alessandra Raengo, Associate Provost Tim Renick, Susan Talburt, James Taylor, Felicia Thomas, Lela Urquhart, Cynthia Wilson, and Associate Dean Carol Winkler. Nedda Ahmed, our most remarkable research librarian, was the singular colleague without whom this book could not have been brought to a close.

Several of our uncommonly talented graduate students happened to arrive at just the right time in my research, and were essential in helping me bring this project to a conclusion. Sarah Levine has continued to work with me on professional projects long after she graduated from our master's program. Now a talented editorial presence at the American Academy of Religion, Sarah has gifted me with her editorial insights in ways too numerous to list. Karli Robinson-Myers brings her unerring charm and graciousness to everything, and everyone, she touches. She touched this work with her rare spirit in countless ways at a point when I was beginning to feel as if I'd never finish it. Mary Grace Dupree read this manuscript in its disheveled entirety, corrected my errors in six languages, and gifted me with her capacious intellect and her unerring sensitivity to matters human as well as historical. All of these remarkable women have become dear and trusted friends; that is not always the way academic life goes, but it is rare joy indeed when it does. What is good in this book belongs very much to each of them; much is still lacking, as I know.

In Würzburg, Drs. Damian Dombrowski, Tilmann Kossatz and Markus Josef Maier granted me access to the Martin von Wagner Archive, to his fascinating Greek *Reisebuch*, and to several of the finest images I reproduce here. In Munich, Dr. Astrid Fendt provided me with similar access to archival material and images in the Archives of the Antikensammlungen and Glyptothek Museums. Dr. Mathias Hofter made some of Ludwig's and Wagner's soon-to-be-published correspondence available for my consultation. I'm most grateful to them all.

In New York, the Frick Art Reference Library remains one of the most beautiful and one of the most congenial places in which I have ever been privileged to work. I have been especially grateful for the assistance over many years of Anna S. Covatta, Shana H. Fung, Suz Massen, and especially Elizabeth Lane, without whom this book would look very different indeed. The New York Public Library is a stunning warehouse of rare books in many languages that never ceases to amaze, and to save, usually at the last minute. Finally, Lucia Carbone, whom I originally met in Rome, has since moved to New York and recently completed a Ph.D. in Classics at Columbia University. A talented historian, epigraphist, and numismatist, Lucia shared her own abundant knowledge of the relevant historiography and archaeology on the island of Aegina as well as the history of Mediterranean trade. I am indebted to her for her friendship and for much more besides.

I owe an incalculable debt of gratitude to the family of William M. Suttles, formerly the vice president and interim president of my university; the gift with which he endowed the chair I currently occupy has enabled me to travel to Rome virtually any time when I am able to get away from my professional obligations in Atlanta. The chair has provided me with much more than a change of scenery; it has enabled me to re-conceive the scholarly responsibilities that ought to accompany such luxuries as scholarly freedom. I have learned a great deal about patience and the past, while working in various archives in what can seem like a deliciously, if not deliriously, ancient place. The Suttles Foundation has been essential in seeing my last four books into print. I hope the family knows how much they have both enabled and enriched my work.

There are many other friends and colleagues whose contributions to my life, both professional and personal, run far deeper than the form of a list can communicate; still, it is important to keep accounts. I am enormously grateful to Wesley Barker, Robert Bernasconi, Michael Bever, Peter Brown, Richard M. Carp, Timothy Craker, Shannon Dunn, Molly Farneth, Gregory Jusdanis, Vassilis Lambropoulos, Artemis Leontis, Michael B. Lippman, Katie Lofton, Roxani Margariti, Barbara Marston, Judith Miller, Shannon Mussett, Alexander Nehamas, Cynthia Patterson, Melanie Pavich, Dennis Schmidt, Michael Schwartz, Kathleen Skerrett, Larry Slutsker, Cornel West, David Williams, and Jim Winchester.

Jason M. Wirth, together with David Jones and Michael Schwartz, enriched my scholarly life by including me in the marvelous society that is the Comparative and Continental Philosophy Circle. Jason is a stunningly creative and original thinker, one deeply versed in Schelling's lifelong meditations on religion and myth. He offered a reading of this manuscript that has improved it in countless ways. Were I as versed as he in these matters, this would be a better book. I'm grateful for his ability to see what is good in this one.

Jeffrey Stout has been an uncommonly generous reader of my work for many years, and a deeply valued friend; I have recently attended two of his Princeton seminars—one on Hegel's *Phenomenology of Spirit*, and one on early modern political thought concerning republicanism and religion—and in addition to reminding me of the joy of being schooled well, both courses left an indelible mark on this book, and on me. The gift of a friend who is also a fellow traveler is a rare thing.

Lori Anne Ferrell has read more of my work, and with greater insight, than any friend I know. As marvelous at writing letters as she is at reading them, Lori Anne's mark—and not the red-pen variety—is all over this book as well. The kind of work I undertake here owes a great deal to her uniquely personal sense of what the craft of history entails, at its very best. Her book, *The Bible and the People*, provides me with inspiration and a model.

Back in Atlanta, I have been especially warmed by the close friendship of Paul Courtright, Jack Fitzmier, and Gary Laderman. Paul was the most gifted department chair for whom I've ever had the privilege to work, and Jack was the most extraordinarily creative and visionary dean I've been blessed to know. Gary and I are junior to these friends, and we have learned from them how to navigate the shoals of increasingly complicated professional careers. We meet regularly for meals, and occasional weekend retreats to Paul's cabin in the north Georgia mountains. These meetings possess far more than the power of ritual by now; they are how I stay afloat, how my life sustains itself in time. I have no other friendships with this capacious emotional range, dancing lightly from tragedy to comedy and back again. I have trusted them with this, and to know it.

This is the third book I have published with SUNY Press, and this experience matches my others for the efficiency and thoughtfulness they have bestowed on my work, and the generosity of their custodial care. I am especially grateful to Andrew Kenyon for shepherding the project to its completion, and to Jenn Bennett and Anne Valentine for their help with production and marketing.

This book proposes, and in a way it attempts to display, a *palimpsestic* view of images, of texts, and of history. In any such undertaking, the challenge lies in finessing a distinction which preoccupied the German idealists a great deal: the distinction between accidents and necessities, and the graceful art of accepting the transition from one state to another. A stunning collection of statues and fragments just so happened to be discovered by a group of traveling art students who just so happened to make it to the island of Aegina. Crown Prince Ludwig of Bavaria just so happened to meet Johann Martin Wagner, not long after his Grand Tour of Italy. Wagner just so happened to arrive on the island of Zakynthos (Zante) in time (barely!) for an auction. And so these statues just so happened to find their way ever so slowly from Aegina to Athens, then to Zante and Malta, then finally to Rome, and then on to Munich . . . making poignant stops at each complex step along the way. Berthel Thorvaldsen left his mark on the statues. Friedrich Schelling, who knew Thorvaldsen and Wagner both, left his mark on the *Report* that Wagner had been commissioned to produce.

Naturally, I am leaving a mark on this story and on this text as well. It has taken me twenty years, and a lot of scholarly retooling, to complete this project. It required long detours into the complicated world of art and art history, of papal patronage and early modern European politics, of neoclassicism and its role in the emergence of modern museums, of the French Revolution and its impact on classicism and on modern Greece alike, of German idealism, especially the sort branded by Hegel and Schelling. The work required a lot of travel, reading in a lot of languages, then a lot of sitting still to think it all through.

The challenge, as I came to see it, lay in distinguishing one historical layer from another, and then in pulling back a bit, to catch a glimpse of the new whole that had been created by these various layers lying artfully, if casually, upon one another . . . and so to perceive the way in which these subtle accidents of accretion are themselves the very stuff of history. Viewed this way, the seemingly accidental patterns created by addition, subtraction, and gradual transformation crystallize into new patterns of rare and sometimes staggering beauty. The Glyptothek Museum is one example of such a thing. Human lives are another.

My brother, Clifford Holt Ruprecht, took his doctoral degree in comparative religion before going on for a law degree at the University of Pennsylvania. He found both graduate programs equally challenging from an intellectual standpoint, and he has found his way into the practice of the law in ways that are as dazzling in their complexity and as replete with human drama as are the mystifying antiquities I am studying here. He was my first and my foremost childhood playmate, and the first person with whom I ever visited a museum. He is now a founding partner in a vibrant young law firm, a devoted husband and father who has seen one son, and soon a daughter, through their own palimpsestic transformations that culminate in college. It seemed a fitting time to dedicate a book of this kind to him. This one, then, is for Cliff.

LAR
Rome, December 2015

A BRIEF TIMELINE FOR THE AEGINA MARBLES

APRIL–MAY 1811

Charles Cockerell (1788–1863), John Foster (ca. 1787–1846), Jacob Linkh (or Linckh, ca. 1786–1841), and Carl Haller von Hallerstein (1774–1817) discover the Aegina Marbles at what they believed to have been "the Temple of Jupiter Panhellenius," but which we now know to have been the Temple to Aphaia.

JUNE–JULY 1811

The group of amateur archaeologists attempt a first reassembly of this collection of fragments in Athens. Georg Christian Gropius (1776–1850), the Austrian consul in Athens, is appointed as the agent for their eventual sale at auction.

JULY 30, 1811

The marbles are removed to Zante (latter-day Zakynthos) for safekeeping. The public auction is scheduled for November 1, 1812.

NOVEMBER 29, 1811

HMS *Paulina* plus one more brig o' war arrive in Athens's Piraeus Harbor. Cockerell convinces the ship's Captain Percival to remove the Aegina Marbles from Zante to Malta, in anticipation of a rumored French invasion of the island of Zante.

SEPTEMBER 1812–AUGUST 1813

Johann Martin Wagner (1777–1858), a visual artist and art collector from Würzburg, then residing in Rome, travels to Greece on behalf of Ludwig, the crown prince of Bavaria, to purchase the Aegina Marbles at auction.

NOVEMBER 1, 1812

Wagner purchases the collection on behalf of Crown Prince Ludwig of Bavaria, conditionally, pending inspection of the plaster casts in Athens.

JUNE 1–AUGUST 29, 1815

Wagner travels to Malta to arrange for transport of the Aegina Marbles to Rome.

1816–1818

Berthel Thorvaldsen (1770–1844), the noted neoclassical sculptor, "restores" the Aegina Marbles in Rome, carving new appendages to "complete" [*ergänzen*] the sculptural groups and discern their original placement in relation to one another. At the same time, Johann Martin Wagner prepares his *Report on the Aeginetan Sculptures* in Rome, after which Schelling prepares his additional notes and appendices in Munich.

OCTOBER 13, 1830

The Glyptothek Museum opens to the Munich public, designed by Leo von Klenze (1784–1864) specifically to house the Aegina collection as its centerpiece.

1845

The neoclassical *Ausstellungsgebäude*, directly facing the Glyptothek across the Munich Königsplatz, is completed.

1863

The *Propylaen*, a precise replica of the monumental gateway to the Athenian Akropolis, is completed at the head of the Munich Königsplatz.

1934–1936

The new Reichs-chancellor, Adolf Hitler, initiates a large building program to close off the eastern side of the Munich Königsplatz. He commissions his Munich architect, Paul Ludwig Troost (1878–1934), to design four buildings to this purpose: two *Ehrentempeln* (in which the bodies of the men killed in the failed 1923 beer hall Putsch were re-interred); as well as the Munich Chancellory and Nazi Party Headquarters.

JULY 16–21, 1944

Heavy Allied bombing in Munich, which began on September 21, 1942, and intensified in April of 1944, badly damages the Munich Glyptothek but leaves Hitler's newer Königsplatz relatively intact.

Many of Schelling's original manuscripts were lost; the Aegina Marbles had been removed for safekeeping.

MARCH 16, 1945

Allied bombing of Würzburg results in the destruction of some, but not all, of Johann Martin Wagner's letters and personal papers. The notes from his Greek trip, and his personal museum collection (left to his hometown when he died), survived the attack.

1948

The local Munich population and American occupation forces dynamite the two *Ehrentempeln*.

Occupying American forces refit the Chancellory and Party headquarters for their own administrative purposes, as well as to help coordinate the attempt to repatriate art stolen by the Nazis in the previous five years.

1962–1966

"De-restoration" of the Aegina Marbles is linked to the "De-nazification" of the Munich Königsplatz.

1972

The Glyptothek Museum reopens to the public, just in time for the Munich Summer Olympics.

1988

The "re-greening" of the Königsplatz, by the removal of the granite pavement stones, returns the Königsplatz more closely to its original nineteenth-century design.

Translator's Historical Introduction

NATION AND IMPERIALISM, OR, "ARCHAEOLOGY" AND THE GRAND TOUR

"Traveling outgrows its motives," notes the wizened world-wanderer Nicholas Bouvier. "You think you are making a trip, but soon it is making you—or unmaking you."[1] This introduction begins, necessarily, with a pause, a pause to cast our gaze briefly upon such travelers, on what they do, on what they make, on what they leave behind. You pack a bag with a few well-loved items, shed the rest. You bid some fond, and some not-so-fond, farewells. And then, as if in a flash, you are gone, given entirely to the care, and the curious rhythms, of the road. You make new friends, make new love, find yourself made and unmade in the process. There will be a great many other farewells built into the larger frame of departure and homecoming that define the contours of most travels—if you are fortunate, and if you make it home. You have to leave a place, or a person, even one you love, to get anywhere at all. So you pick up a stone, or a shell, or something more precious still, make room in your pack as well as in your heart, consider it a memento, an inoculation against loneliness, or a salve to prevent forgetting. Long periods of boredom, or else of quiet perseverance, are punctuated by overwhelming moments of such rare beauty that you are drawn quite suddenly to the realization that these constitute the reason you took to the road in the first place. Bouvier again: "In the end, the bedrock of existence is not made up of family, or work, or what others say or think of you, but of moments such as this when you are exalted by a transcendent power that is more serene than love. Life dispenses such moments to us parsimoniously; our feeble hearts could not stand more."[2]

Most of the people we will meet in these pages traveled, and most of them traveled rather widely. They did not travel in the way familiar to most of us in the twenty-first century; they traveled slowly, by sail or by coach, and so they tended to be gone for long periods of time. They communicated often quite elegantly by letter, thereby rendering each major port of call a sort of epistolary lifeline tying them more closely to absent friends. They never experienced jet lag or others of the indecencies of modern travel. They risked illness, and even death, very far from home, braving the indignity of anonymous burial, or worse. They engaged in what they imagined as a Grand Tour, not tourism. And what they brought home with them was often far more precious than the personal memento of stone or shell. This book is inspired at the outset by the dramatic discoveries of four itinerant artists who also made room, and time, to take what they'd discovered, to remove it from the island where they'd found it, to transport it no fewer than five times in ten years, and eventually to arrange for its public display in a remarkable new kind of traveler's clearinghouse: a public art museum. Here is how that happened.

Travel, specifically to Greece, often enough imagined as a sort of capstone to a proper education, was largely a fashion of the eighteenth and nineteenth centuries.[3] It was often framed, given the freewheeling spirituality of that Romantic age, as a pilgrimage.[4] And it was performed, as often as not, by self-styled children of the age, childlike and wide-eyed adepts like Lord Byron (1788–1824), whose own Tour was memorialized in the epic that made him famous almost overnight, *Childe Harold's Pilgrimage*.[5] Different as our own times appear to be, there are nonetheless subtle and suggestive parallels between these self-styled pilgrims and the student backpackers who flood the Greek islands each and every summer, even in times of fiscal crisis.

But Greece was not always the destination of choice for such would-be Tourists. Italy, especially Rome and Naples, had long been a magnet for British and German travelers especially.[6] Yet there was a very narrow window, scarcely twenty years in length, during which these Romantic pilgrims traded Italy in for Greece. It began in 1803 when a notorious edict from Napoleon effectively closed the Italian peninsula to British (and Prussian and Bavarian) travelers, forcing the would-be Grand Tourist further to the east. The new Tour came to a rather sudden end in 1821, when the Greek War of Independence broke out against the Ottoman Empire.[7] That war concluded with the Conference of London in 1830, and the dramatic creation of a quasi-European nation-state on the tip of the Balkan peninsula, within fairly narrow Peloponnesian borders,[8] with a constitution drafted by the British utilitarian Jeremy Bentham,[9] and with a very young Bavarian king by the name of Otto.[10] By the time travel to the eastern Mediterranean stabilized again, the age of steam had commenced. Trains and iron steamships fundamentally democratized such southern and eastern European traveling, such that an aristocratic Tour turned gradually to mass tourism.[11] There was no greater, nor more versatile, comic spokesperson for this sea change than Mark Twain, whose book *The Innocents Abroad* beautifully captured this shift in transit and in taste.[12]

Many of these older-style aristocrats on the Grand Tour were self-styled, and utterly amateur, artists or archaeologists as well. There was not yet a professional class of archaeologist, since the canons of such activity were being made up as they went along in their haphazard traveler's mode. When we think of the tentative beginnings of classical archaeology, we tend to focus on the dramatic discoveries of men like Heinrich Schliemann (1822–1890),[13] who bulldozed his way through stunning discoveries at Troy (1871), Mycenae (1876), and Tiryns (1884). But this kind of activity represented the culmination of a much longer historical trend born out of a mingled sense of aristocratic privilege and imperial entitlement. When French troops under Napoleon forced the papal states to sign a bruising peace, art historical looting was made an explicit matter of state policy for the first time. The Treaty of Tolentino (1797) is the first modern peace treaty in which works of art (one hundred in all) were explicitly listed for expropriation to Paris.[14] Napoleonic forces invaded Egypt next in 1798,[15] and that expedition included a veritable army of scientists as well as soldiers.[16] Given the Parisian taste for Egyptian as well as Greek and Roman art, the "excavation" of pyramids and temples created a vast traffic of artifacts—inscriptions, obelisks, mummies, and even the famed Rosetta Stone—that made their way back to Parisian museums, and later, to museums in other European capitals as well.[17] This set a precedent in which the venerable science of archaeology can seem almost indistinguishable from a relatively disorganized hobby, or else from imperial looting, whose primary aim was to boost the quality and quantity of the new national collections. The Greek mainland was to be infamously looted throughout much of the nineteenth century, such that many of her most precious treasures ended up in European capitals instead of Athens and its environs.[18] By contrast, the Roman papacy had established a bureaucracy to protect against such spoliation in Rome that dated back to the sixteenth century and that managed to survive the Napoleonic depredations.[19] In Ottoman Greece things were very different indeed. The Parthenon Marbles were taken by Lord Elgin to London in the first decade of the nineteenth century.[20] The Venus de Milo and the Winged Victory of Samothrace arrived in Paris shortly after the age of Napoleon.[21] The Pergamum Altar went to Berlin immediately after the formation of the modern German state in 1870–71.[22] And, of more immediate relevance to this book, through a complicated and fascinating series of at times bizarre events, the pedimental statues from the lesser-known Temple to Aphaia on the island of Aegina (located in the Saronic

Gulf just south of Athens) came to Munich and were installed in a brand new museum, the Glyptothek, that had been built specifically to house them. The Glyptothek Museum opened to public viewing in October of 1830.[23]

LORD BYRON AND THE ELGIN PRECEDENT

After three months in Turkey, and his storied swim across the Hellespont,[24] Lord Byron departed from Istanbul with his friend John Cam Hobhouse (1786–1869)[25] on July 14, 1810. Three days later, they landed at the island of Kea, just off the eastern coast of Attica. Here the two friends parted: Hobhouse returned directly to England; Byron moved on to the mainland. After traveling around the Peloponnese, Byron arrived in Athens on August 19, 1810. He and Hobhouse had lodged there the previous winter in the home of Procopius Macri (d. 1799), formerly the British consul in Athens. Macri's widow, Theodora (née Vrettos), would host British visitors throughout the first two decades of the nineteenth century; thanks in no small part to Byron's growing fame, her home became a necessary stopping point on this new-old Greek Tour after Byron immortalized her youngest daughter, Teresa, in a poem entitled "Maid of Athens, Ere We Part" (1810)—just prior to his Turkish excursion.[26] The poem did more than make the girl an object of continual fascination; it inspired the marital ambitions of the entire Macri household. And so when Byron returned to Athens, he felt the need to put some distance between himself and the three Macri daughters—Marianna, Katinka, and Teresa[27]—since his casual flirtations with all three threatened to become a more serious entanglement. Byron was installed in the Capuchin Convent, a famous Athenian landmark located at the foot of the Akropolis Hill, one that incorporated the famous Lysicrates Monument within its fortification walls.[28] The convent was to become an ever more popular hostelry until the outbreak of the Greek War for Independence, when it was dismantled (Lord Elgin and his team resided there as well, some years earlier). Only the Lysicrates Monument remains visible at the site today.

Byron spent the winter of 1810–11 in Athens, recalling it thereafter as one of the happiest periods in his life. There happened to be a remarkable circle of British and Continental expatriates living in Athens at the time, and so a continual circuit of dinners, excursions, and balls kept them engaged and in high spirits throughout the cool winter months. One of the main topics of conversation and controversy that year—apart from the possibility and the prospects of a Greek revolution—concerned the dismantling of the Parthenon, the work of Elgin's men being clearly visible from the Capuchin Hostelry itself. The work was nearly completed by the time Byron arrived in 1810, and was in fact to be completed that same winter. It had all been organized and financed by Thomas Bruce, seventh Earl of Elgin (1766–1841), a somewhat ill-fortuned career diplomat who was destined to lend his name both to this collection (the so-called Elgin Marbles) and to a notorious new French term for pillage (*elginisme*). After brief service in Brussels and Berlin, Elgin received the important assignment as British ambassador to the Sublime Porte in 1799. When the French suffered their reverses in Egypt the next year—harassed by the British navy as well as by Ottoman reinforcements on land—the British star was on the rise in Istanbul. Elgin leveraged this position to acquire a now-notorious *firman* that, when loosely interpreted (through diplomatic pressure or bribe), permitted his men not only to affix scaffolding to the Parthenon temple but much more besides:

> It is well known that the greater part of the Frank (i.e., Christian) Courts are anxious to read and investigate the books, pictures or figures, and other works of science of the ancient Greek philosophers; and that in particular, the ministers or officers of state, philosophers, primates and other individuals of England, have a remarkable taste for the drawings or figures or sculptures, remaining ever since the time of the said Greeks, and which are to be seen on the shores of the Archipelago and in other parts; and have in consequence from time to time sent men to explore and examine the ancient edifices, and drawings or figures. . . . [H]is Excellency the said Ambassador [Elgin] hath therefore engaged five English painters, now dwelling at Athens, to examine and view, and also to copy the figures remaining there, *ab antiquo*: And he hath also at this time expressly besought us that an Official Letter may be written from hence, ordering that as long as the said painters shall be employed in going in and out of the said citadel of Athens, which is the place of their occupations; and in fixing scaffolding round the ancient Temple of the Idols here; and in moulding the ornamental sculpture and visible figures thereon, in plaster or gypsum; and in measuring the remains of other old ruined buildings there; and in excavating when they find it necessary the foundations, in order to discover inscriptions which may have been covered by the rubbish; that no interruption may be given them, nor any obstacle thrown their way by the Disdar (or commandant of the citadel) or any other person: that no one may meddle with scaffolding or implements they may require in their works; and that when they wish to take away any piece of stone with old inscriptions or figures thereon, that no opposition be made thereto.[29]

That last line served the purpose. Presumably, the Ottomans anticipated Elgin's desire to make plaster casts of these pieces; Elgin, however, wanted the originals, originals that he was utterly determined to ship to England.

The work commenced in earnest in 1801, involving as many as four hundred laborers at a time. This sizeable team was under the direction of Giovanni Battista Lusieri (d. 1821), a Neapolitan artist who would always be Elgin's man in Greece. Elgin and his wife, Mary (née Nisbet, 1778–1855),[30] visited the site in the spring of 1802, remained in Greece from April to June, then returned to the Porte where they arrived in January of 1803, shortly before Elgin's recall to London. They made their way home slowly—via Athens, naturally, then Rome and Paris. Elgin just so happened to be in Paris on May 23, 1803, when Napoleon's notorious edict redefined him as an enemy of war and resulted in his imprisonment. His wife returned to England and worked tirelessly for his release, battling all the while with the depletion of the Elgin estate due to her husband's ongoing Athenian ventures. Elgin would be detained until 1806, at which point he was released on the promise that he would return if recalled by the French emperor. Shortly thereafter, in 1808, his wife left him to marry Robert Ferguson. The brief outbreak of hostilities between the British and the Ottomans further disrupted Elgin's activities in Athens; it was not until 1809 that the main work of the removal of the Akropolis marbles got under way. This was the dramatic phase of the work that was coming to an end when Byron arrived.

The notes first sounded in this debate have echoed ever since. The points that bore emphasis then, and still do, may seem relatively obvious today. The dismantling of the Parthenon seems as clear a case of pillage by aristocratic and political elites as that initiated by French forces under Napoleon, all of it animated by the marriage (happy or unhappy, depending on your political persuasion) of a strong sense of aristocratic privilege to an effusive neoclassicism. These things were simply in the air, defining cultural characteristics of the age. Lord Elgin clearly capitalized on his political position (along with flagging French fortunes in Egypt) in order to gain access to the Athenian Akropolis in the first place. But he paid for the work himself, and essentially consumed his family's fortune in the process (one might even say that he paid personally for it, with his own imprisonment and the failure of his first marriage). Moreover, Elgin accepted a sum from the British government that represented just half of what he spent on the project, despite the willingness of others—including Crown Prince Ludwig of Bavaria—to pay him more. Here was nationalism working hand-in-glove with fledgling archaeology and those nascent museums they helped to create.[3]

It was a point of national pride in Elgin's eyes that his collection would remain in England, *and* that it would remain intact. Moreover, the treasures would presumably have been looted by *someone* in these same acquisitive decades, Elgin's friends insisted; better that they fell into the hands of an empire with the resources and the will to display them properly.[32] The Elgin Marbles, so this argument runs, are in a far better state of preservation today than they would have been had they remained in Athens.[33] Others more inclined to the Greek claim remind us that the famed twentieth-century art dealer, Joseph Duveen—who gave his name to the Duveen Gallery in which the Elgin Marbles are housed today—ordered that these marbles be scrubbed with metal brushes and bleach in 1935,[34] suggesting that the opposite may in fact be the case. Geopolitically speaking, the return of the Elgin Marbles would set a precedent that might well signal the death knell of the modern Euro-American museum. Our main problem here is with nineteenth-century imperialism, and the generalized sense of aristocratic entitlement that inspired the most unregulated looting, yet it was of such sentiments that the modern museum was also born. Returning the Elgin Marbles alone will neither change, nor rewrite, nor rectify that history. And, given the Athenocentrism of most classical scholarship, this collection has come to be perceived as something different, something unique; so say the chief proponents of repatriation. Their opponents argue that they have ironically accepted the canons of empire in electing to see these statues in this way. The Parthenon Marbles have become symbolic of "the glory that was Greece" in the classical age of Pheidias and Perikles. Ironically enough, it was the obsession of neoclassical Europeans, and the prominent display of Elgin's marbles in London, that helped establish their reputation as such. And yet today, they could all be returned very easily; the New Akropolis Museum opened to considerable fanfare in Athens, and no little controversy, in 2010. Built at the foot of the Akropolis mount and boasting stunning views of the temple and its environs, this new museum is the last piece in the puzzle propagandizing for the Elgin Marbles' return to their long-suffering homeland.

Similar-sounding debates raged in the winter of 1810–11. Lord Byron, himself a quite self-consciously radical aristocrat, and one of the few Grand Tourists who seemed more interested in modern than in ancient Greece, was one of the first to understand the deeper paradoxes of British philhellenism. Other poets, like Keats, confined their reactions to aesthetic superlatives, ignoring the politics that landed this collection on British shores in the first place. A subtler issue concerned then-dominant ideas concerning origins and historicity. It became a commonplace among most travel writers in the early- to mid-nineteenth century to note that there was no connection whatsoever between modern Greeks and their illustrious ancient forebears. Theirs was a kind of philhellenism, Romantic at the root, that privileged antiquity *over* modernity, and this value judgment suggested that modern Greece—not even a country in 1810 but rather a somewhat peripheral Ottoman province—might be justifiably looted, since in doing so they were celebrating Greek antiquity, not violating the rights of her spiritual heirs. Those heirs had moved west—to Rome, to Paris, and now to London.

Byron spoke out vehemently against Elgin's work, which he saw as sheer rapaciousness, later on in his verse epic, *Don Juan,*[35] but he also composed a naughty little poem in that same winter, when he was still in residence with the Capuchins. That poem is "The Curse of Minerva,"[36] and in it, Byron imagines a tattered goddess, Athena herself, returning to protest against the spoliation of her most preeminent ancient temple. Now a sworn enemy of her former British friends, Athena lays an elaborate curse on Elgin's head as well as on the empire he served. Elgin, she warns, will suffer romantic and familial catastrophe: First, his children will all be idiots.

> My curse shall light,—on him and all his seed
> Without one spark of intellectual fire
> Be all the sons as senseless as the sire.

Second, his wife will leave him for another man, since he does not cut nearly as fine a figure as his marbles.

> While many a languid maid, with longing sigh,
> On giant statues casts the curious eye;
> The room with transient glance appears to skim
> Yet marks the mighty back and length of limb;
> Mourns o'er the difference between now and then;
> Exclaims "Those Greeks indeed were proper men!"
> Draws slight comparisons of these with those,
> And envies Lais all her Attic beaux.
> When shall a modern maid have swains like these!
> Alas! Sir Harry is no Hercules.

Third, in what was assuredly one of Byron's cruelest cuts to date, Elgin will eventually come to resemble the statues that bore his name (Elgin contracted a disfiguring disease in Istanbul, probably syphilis, and eventually lost his nose).

Yet still the gods are just, and crimes are cross'd:
See here what Elgin won, and what he lost!
Another name with *his* pollutes my shrine:
Behold where Diana's beam disdains to shine!
Some retribution still might Pallas claim,
When Venus half avenged Minerva's shame.

Politically, the goddess continues, the empire that Elgin has served will lose all of her colonies: first in the Baltic,

Look to the Baltic!—blazing from afar
Your old ally yet mourns perfidious war . . .

next in India,

Look to the East, where Ganges' swarthy race
Shall shake your tyrant empire to its base . . .

and on to Spain,

Look on your Spain!—she clasps the hand she hates,
But boldly clasps, and thrusts you from her gates.

To Byron's chastened eye, George Washington was simply the first of Britain's many neoclassical nemeses:

Yes—one—the first—the last—the best—
The Cincinnatus of the West,
Whom envy dared not hate,
Bequeathed the name of Washington,
To make man blush there was but one![37]

The ironies, however, did not come to rest when Byron set aside his pen. When he finally departed from Athens for England in April of 1811, he returned aboard HMS *Hydra*. Byron was carrying draft notes for *Childe Harold's Pilgrimage*, as well as the final text of "The Curse of Minerva" with him. And yet Giovanni Lusieri was also onboard that same ship. And below decks in the hold, presumably unbeknownst to Byron, was the very last consignment of Elgin's allegedly ill-gotten loot.[38]

FROM ATHENS TO AEGINA

While Lord Byron was making preparations for his final departure from Athens, a small caïque was seen leaving the Piraeus harbor. Spotting Byron aboard the *Hydra*, several sailors on the smaller craft swept up beneath her fantail and began singing one of Byron's favorite songs, badly out of tune. He invited the party of four men aboard, where they shared a round of port and a final, fond farewell. The men had all been part of the previous winter's social circle: Byron departed for England in the morning, whereas his four companions left that same evening for Aegina, a small island lying just twelve miles to the south of Athens. They arrived the following dawn.

One of the four was Charles Robert Cockerell (1788–1863)[39], a young man then twenty-four years of age, who had made his way to Athens along a slightly less privileged path than the one Byron and Hobhouse traversed. The third of eleven children and born to an extremely ambitious, savvy, and newly rich professional architect (Samuel Pepys Cockerell [1754–1817]), Charles R. Cockerell had secured the advantage of a public school education, enrolling in the Westminster School in 1802. He left three years later to take up an architectural apprenticeship under his father's direction. His first Tour of sorts, to the West Country and Wales, came in 1806 and, like most of his subsequent travels, was justified as an art-related trip designed to expose him to various architectural styles. After another year of training in the architectural office of Robert Smirke (1781–1867), Charles Cockerell determined that his next Tour would be Greek. Just five years Cockerell's senior, Smirke had recently returned from his own five-year Greek Tour (1800–05), and had spent some time working on the Akropolis with others of Elgin's men; he would later serve as architect to the British Museum (1823–47).

Cockerell got to Greece by a rather more circuitous route than Smirke's. Cockerell's father had arranged for his passage, as an unpaid courier bearing government correspondence to the British fleet in Cadiz, Malta, and the Sublime Porte; he met Byron and Hobhouse in Istanbul when he first arrived in May of 1810. The government dispatch was HMS *Black Joke*, equipped, as Cockerell later recalled, with "ten guns, thirty-five men, one sheep, two pigs and fowls."[40]

Just twenty-two years old when he left England, Cockerell had rapidly acquired the taste for travel so well attested in his journals from the period, *Travels in Southern Europe and the Levant*, published posthumously by his son, Samuel Pepys Cockerell in 1903.[41] The young man we meet in these charming notes and reflections was away for a number of years (seven in total),

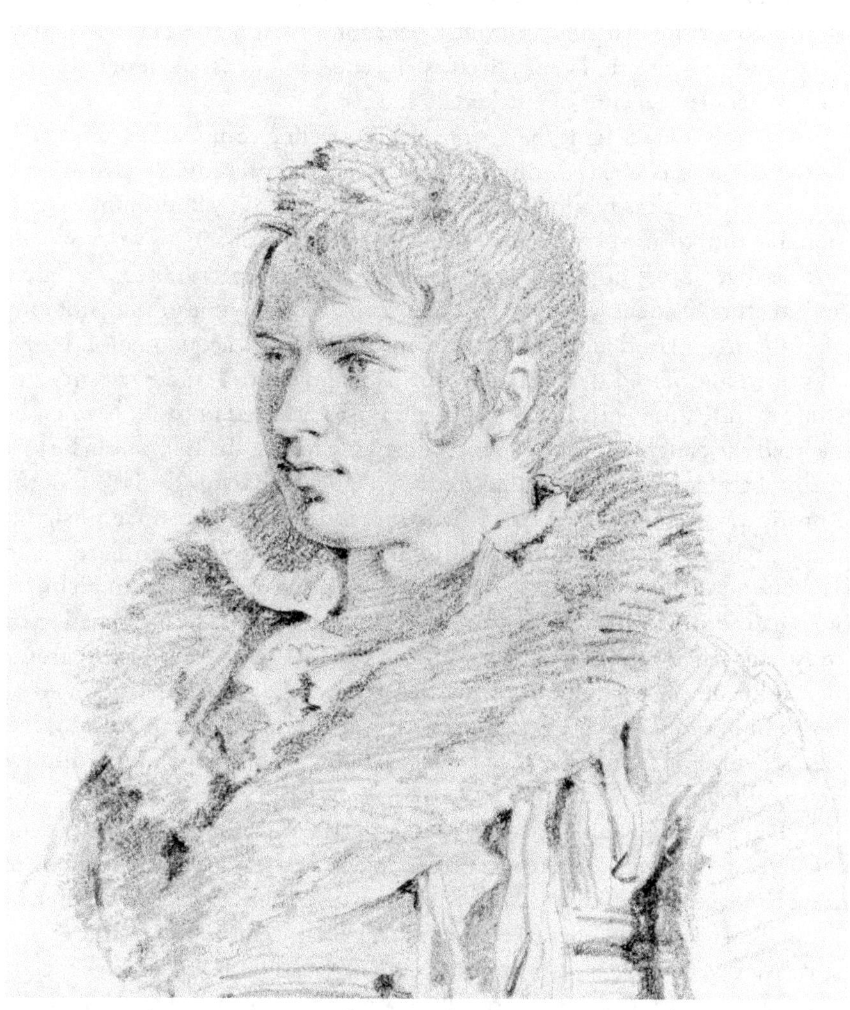

Figure I.1 Portrait of Charles R. Cockerell (1788–1863), ca. 1814, by Otto Magnus von Stackelberg. Photograph by Christa Koppermann. Printed with permission of the Munich State Collection of Antiquities and Glyptothek (*München Antikensammlung und Glyptothek* 15.016c).

and he spent time in many of the most popular locales that had emerged in the wake of the Napoleonic disruptions: Turkey, Greece, Crete, and Egypt. Italy beckoned, as it did for most architects of course, and so when Napoleon abdicated for the first time in 1814, Cockerell wasted no time. He settled in Rome just two months later (as well as Florence, and Paris; see appendix 1 for a more detailed account of Cockerell's travels).[42]

Arguably a lesser light than some of his traveling companions, Cockerell was by all accounts extraordinarily handsome and exceedingly charming.[43] He made friends easily and was a welcome addition to any impromptu excursion. He thus formed several extremely close attachments in his years of wide wandering,[44] most notably with John Foster Jr. (ca. 1787–1846),[45] a fellow architectural student whom he first met at the Porte in June of 1810, not long after he first arrived and shortly after making Byron's acquaintance. Foster was born and raised in Liverpool, but later moved to London in order to study architecture with Jacques Wyatt. His Tour lasted until 1814, when he married the daughter of the Russian consul in Smyrna (Izmir), whom he first met in February of 1812 (the affair required Cockerell to make his tour of the historic Seven Churches of Asia Minor on his own). The second most significant friendship Cockerell formed in his years abroad was with Baron Carl Haller von Hallerstein (1774–1817)[46], a somewhat older Bavarian architect who had studied in Nuremberg and Berlin, and who just so happened to be in Athens when Cockerell and Foster arrived. These three men were en route to Aegina on the evening they bade Byron farewell, and had been joined by Jakob Linkh (or Linckh, ca. 1786–1841),[47] yet another Bavarian artist, in this case a landscape painter seeking the cultivation of antiquity and its allusive archaeological remains.

Haller was the senior member of the party. An established architect and amateur archaeologist (there was no other kind at the time), he had obtained leave to move to Rome in 1808, where he remained until June of 1810, when he pressed on to Greece. There were a number of Bavarians in Rome at the time, since they were citizens of an empire not then at war with France; their access and freedom of movement were still relatively unimpeded. Haller departed Rome in the company of two fellow countrymen: Linkh, who hailed originally from Cannstadt, and Otto Magnus von Stackelberg (1787–1837),[48] who was originally from Estonia and had abandoned his career as a diplomat in order to become (what else?) a landscape painter and architect. Stackelberg—like Haller, Foster, and Cockerell—would remain in Greece for many years.[49]

Their reasons for traveling to Aegina had everything to do with their shared artistic ambitions. It is important to recall that these men were all

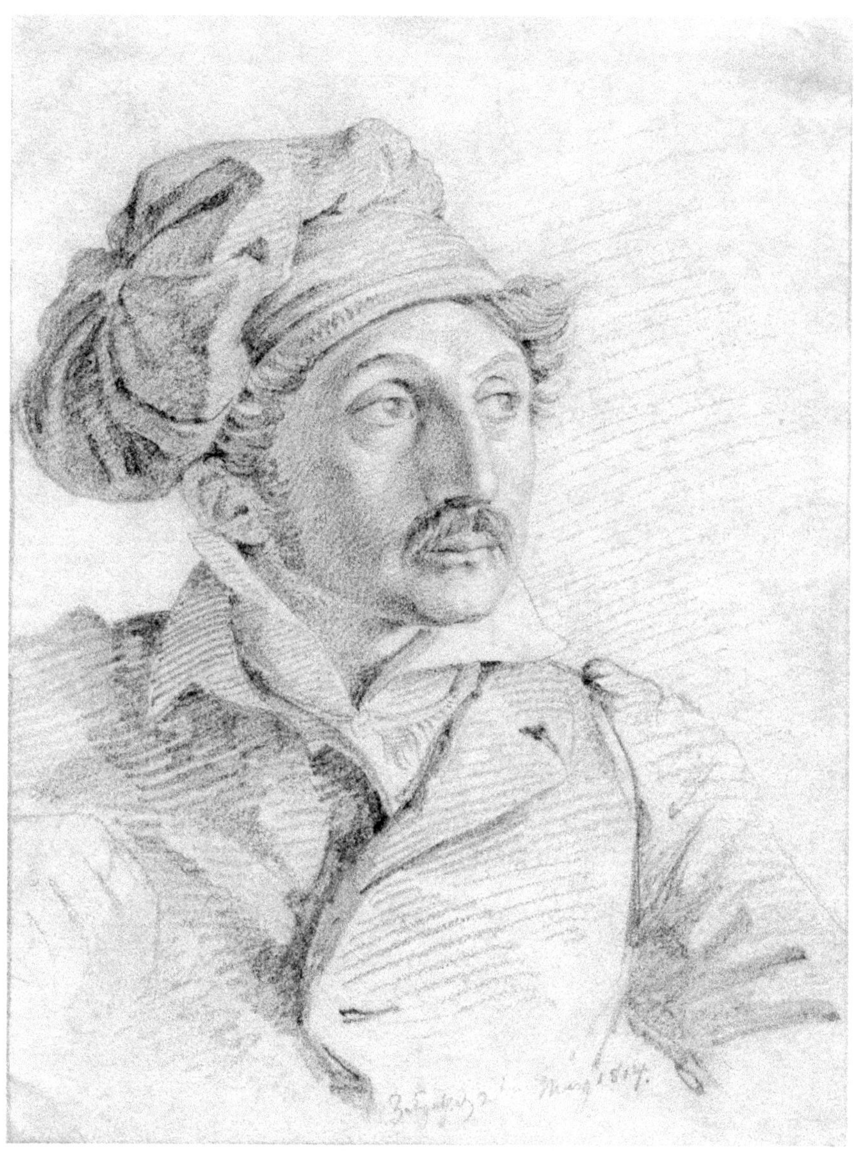

Figure I.2. Portrait of Carl Haller von Hallerstein (1774–1817), 1814, by Otto Magnus von Stackelberg. Photograph by Christa Koppermann. Printed with permission of the Munich State Collection of Antiquities and Glyptothek (*München Antikensammlung und Glyptothek* 15.016b).

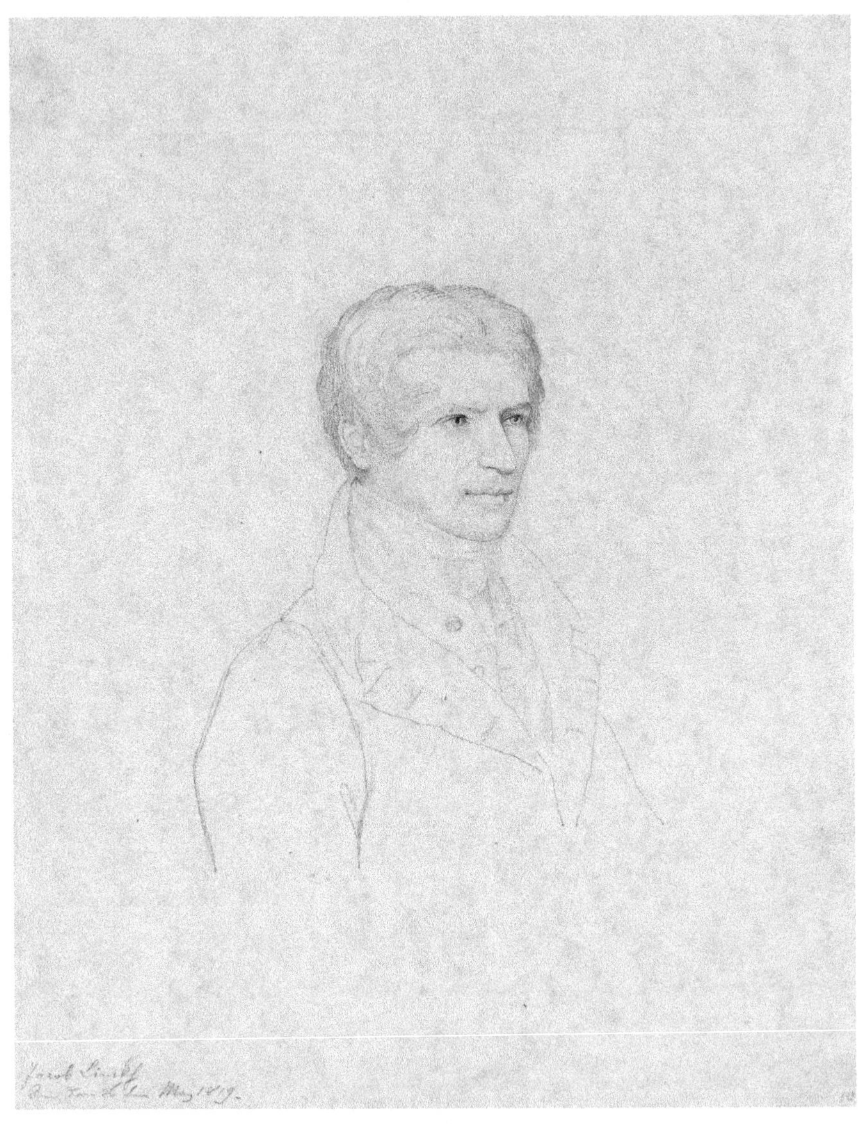

Figure I.3. Portrait of Jakob Linkh (ca. 1786–1841), 1819, by Carl Christian Vogel von Vogelstein. Photograph by Herbert Boswank. Printed with permission of the Dresden Collection of Engravings, State Art Collection (*Kupfertisch-Kabinett, Staatliche Kunstsammlungen Dresden* C 3193).

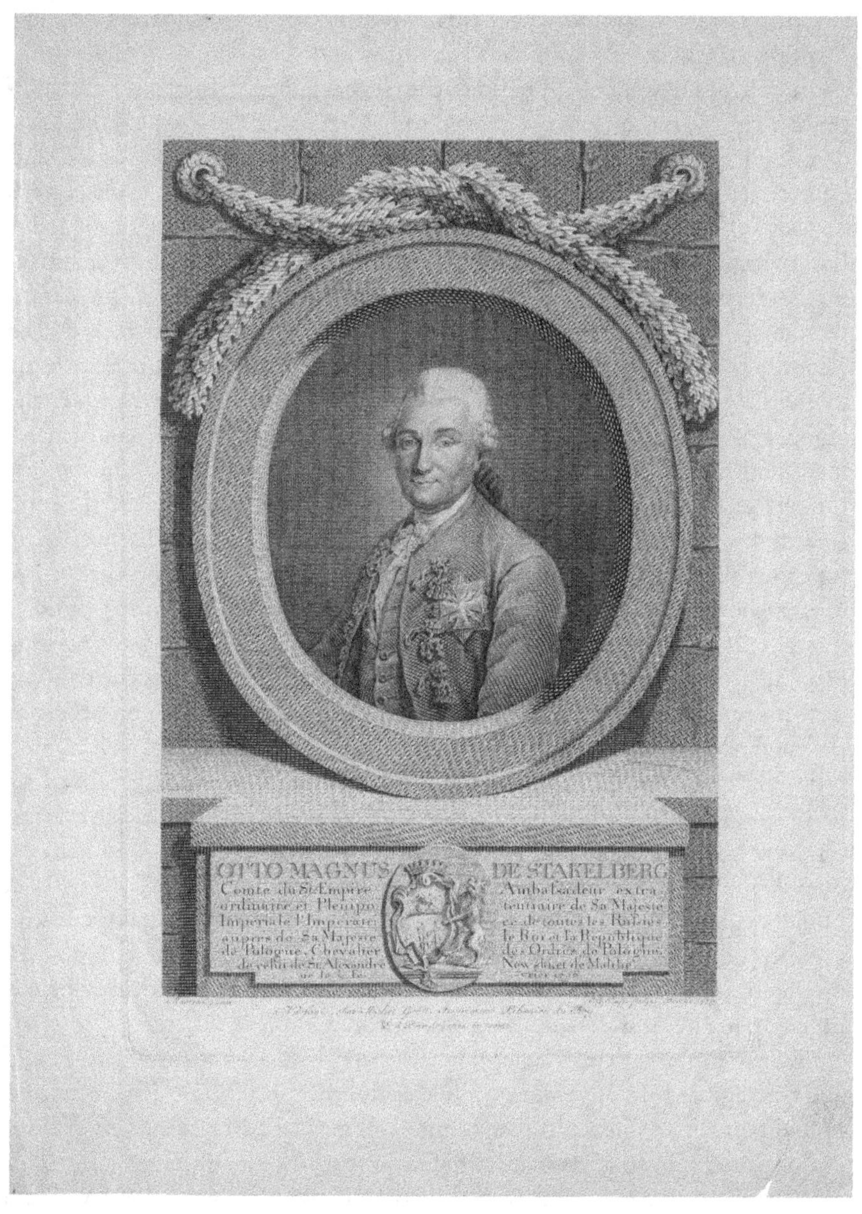

Figure I.4. Portrait of Otto Magnus von Stackelberg (1787–1837), ca. 1815, by Carl Gottlieb Rasp. Photograph by Herbert Boswank. Printed with permission of the Dresden Collection of Engravings, State Art Collection (*Kupfertisch-Kabinett, Staatliche Kunstsammlungen Dresden* A 143267).

artists, or at least aspired to be; their Mediterranean meandering was justified primarily as a time for the close study and sketching of ancient ruins, a sort of moveable apprenticeship to the classical ideal.[50] They were drawn in this case to what they falsely believed to be the Temple of Panhellenic Zeus, described appreciatively by Pausanias in a discussion of the only Greek island he included in his *Guide to Greece*,[51] an island clearly visible from Athens on a clear day. *Jupiter Panhellenius* is what they called him, in an instructive Latinizing of classical Greek religion. The four intended to produce an imaginative reconstruction of the temple, with elaborate sketches of the extant temple architecture and its decorative effects. To do so, they first needed to clear the foundation of the site. A richly illustrated painting of the site done by the Irish scene-painter Edward Dodwell (1767–1832) well illustrates the amount of work that would have been necessary to accomplish such a clearing—and why the statues underneath would not have been found before. On the second day of this "clearing," and no sooner than they had begun sinking shovels into the thin surface soil, they made their great discovery. The four men discovered a warrior's head carved in Parian marble on the second day; larger, more impressive finds followed almost immediately, most of them in far better condition than the Parthenon marbles that had been so long exposed to the elements. The same splendid accident would occur to some of this same fortunate group the following year at the Temple of Apollo at Bassae,[52] where they acquired the remarkable Phigalian Frieze that is housed today in the British Museum.[53] It would not be until 1860, well after the death of his three colleagues, that Cockerell would endeavor to publish his firsthand report of these discoveries.[54] That volume is impressively illustrated with his own sketches, but by then the tide of neoclassicism in the old Winckelmann mode was turning in England. At the time, however, the Aegina discoveries constituted a stunning collection of material from both pedimental groups[55] on the important temple that we now know, based on epigraphical evidence, to have been dedicated to Aphaia, the patron nymph of the island.[56]

By the time that this Aeginetan collection had been excavated, cleaned, and reassembled after five weeks of frenzied activity on the site (the men lived in tents on the mountain through most of April and May), the last of Lord Elgin's collection had made its difficult journey home. Some of the earlier cargo sank en route in 1802; it took two years for Elgin's secretary, William Hamilton, to arrange for its salvage, at a personal cost to Elgin of roughly £5,000. After two months of public hearings, a select committee in the House of Commons ultimately confirmed Elgin's rights to the acquisition and sale of the marbles, but recommended a purchase price of £35,000. This price

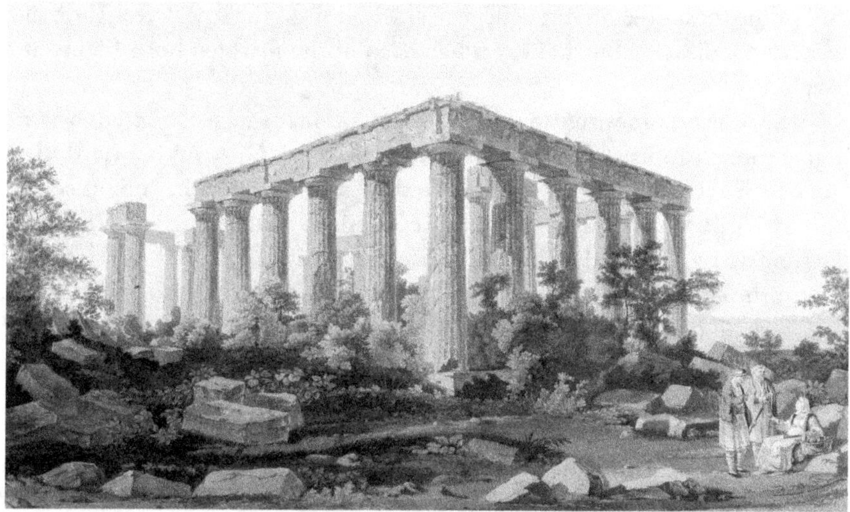

Figure I.5. Painting of the Temple of Aphaia at Aegina, prior to 1811, by Edward Dodwell. Photograph by Renate Kühling. Printed with permission of the Munich State Collection of Antiquities and Glyptothek (*München Antikensammlung und Glyptothek* 15.019a).

represented roughly half of the costs that Elgin claimed to have incurred in the removal and shipment of the marbles, as well as the undersea recovery of the lost shipment from Kythera.

The situation was literally unprecedented. Assessing the value of such an enormous collection of unquestionably original marble statues from classical Athens was made much more difficult by this absence of any reasonable precedent. Parliamentarians solicited the art historical judgments of some of the leading artistic lights of the day, most notably the neoclassical Venetian sculptor Antonio Canova (1757–1822).[57] Canova just so happened to be in Paris at the time, commissioned by Pope Pius VII to oversee the return of the Vatican treasures looted by the French in 1796.[58] Canova paid a visit to London and thought the pieces superb. He also encouraged his French friend, Quatremère de Quincy, to pay a visit to the marbles and then to offer his own judgments as to their value. Quatremère did so in June of 1816, just three months after Elgin's collection had been purchased by the Crown. He drafted his *Letters to Canova* at the time, while he was still in London; they were published in Rome two years later.[59] As we will see, the Aegina Marbles were also in Rome in that same two-year period, undergoing restoration at the hands of another one of the most preeminent neoclassical sculptors of the day, Bertel Thorvaldsen (1770–1844).[60] But I am getting ahead of the marbles, both Elgin's and Aegina's.

The Select Committee in the House of Commons was instructed to investigate three troublesome points of law and aesthetics: 1) whether Lord Elgin actually had the rights of ownership to this collection; 2) what might constitute an authoritative assessment of the collection's value; and 3) whether public funds might be used for the purchase of such a collection.[61] As to the first point, the committee concluded that Elgin was acting on his own authority, and with his own funds, rather than as an agent of the British government, and thus that the collection properly belonged to him. As to the second, expert opinions had varied widely (how could they not?) in the assessment of the collection's value, ranging between £25,000 and £60,000; the committee somewhat arbitrarily split the difference, albeit on the low end, and offered Elgin £35,000. As to the third matter, the committee concluded that this was indeed a legitimate use of public monies, but there was less in the way of argument here and more an assertion of a reigning neoclassical taste. For complex reasons that have everything to do with the discovery and sale of the Aegina Marbles at this same time, national governments were now in the business of competing with one another over the quality of the classical collections in their care. The complex and subtle relations between romantic nationalism, neoclassical aesthetics, and the rivalry of the European gunpowder empires are a crucial part of this entire story and the production of this report.[62]

The vote in the House of Commons was taken on March 25, 1816, and the result was 82-30 in favor of purchasing the marbles. Lord Elgin accepted the low offer when it became clear that there would not be another. He had the solace of being named a trustee of the British Museum, and the ironic assurance that the collection would always, if notoriously, bear his name. The entire collection—of friezework, metopes, and pedimental sculptural groups—was promptly installed in the British Museum in a room of its own, where Quatremère viewed it so enthusiastically just three months later.

Cockerell and his friends were determined to learn from Elgin's travails, and thus to avoid the financial ruin he endured. Since this group of erstwhile archaeologists was composed equally of citizens from Great Britain and Bavaria (two apiece), there could be no initial agreement about where the collection should go; both sides were engaged in a feverish correspondence with their respective governments, in the Bavarians' case, directly with their crown prince, Ludwig.[63] Cockerell, meanwhile, was lobbying British interests through family connections, which confused matters, as we shall see. In any case, after

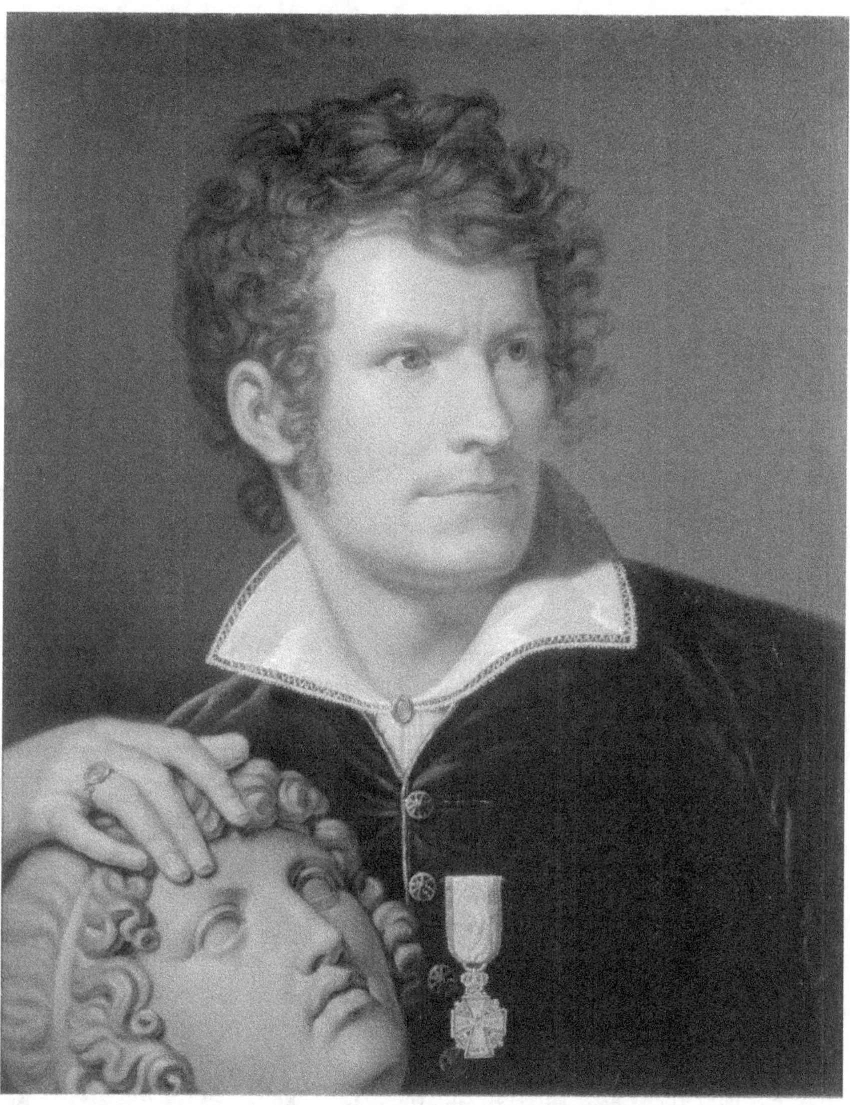

Figure I.6. Portrait of Berthel Thorvaldsen (1770–1844), 1810, by Rudolf Suhrlandt. Printed with permission of the Thorvaldsen Museum, Copenhagen (*Thorvaldsen-Museum* inv. no. B428).

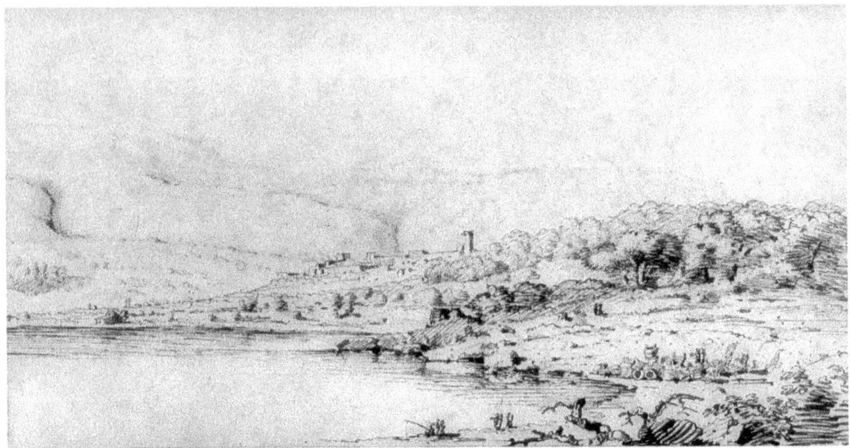

Figure I.7. Porto Germano During the Transport of the Aeginetan Marbles, 1811. Sketch by Jakob Linkh. Photograph by Christa Koppermann. Printed with permission of the Munich State Collection of Antiquities and Glyptothek (*München Antikensammlung und Glyptothek* 15.0923).

excavating at Aegina in April and May of 1811, Foster and Linkh transported the recovered marbles in secret to Athens for an initial survey and reconstruction, while Cockerell and Hallerstein remained behind to secure their purchase . . . for 800 Turkish piastres, or roughly forty pounds.[64] The collection was stored in the relatively new home of the French vice-consul in Athens (more on him below), where the four men oversaw the creation of plaster casts and intended to turn to the reassembly of this impressive collection—somewhere between fifteen and eighteen statues with abundant fragments from many more[65]—and estimated their value at somewhere between £6,000 and £8,000.

But there was little time. Fearful that the collection would fall into the hands of the reigning Ottoman officials, the four subsequently packed up the collection on a midnight mule train and hiked it overland to Porto Germano on the Corinthian Gulf, where they arranged for its shipment to the island of Zante (latter-day Zakynthos) in July of 1811.[66] Like the other Ionian islands, Zante had never been part of the Ottoman Empire; it had been an important Venetian outpost for centuries, but after Napoleon's dismantling of the *Serenissima* in 1796,[67] the island had been ceded to British control.[68] Charles Cockerell, in fact, was subsequently enrolled on the faculty of the fledgling Ionian Academy on the island in that same year—as professor, of all things, of archaeology.[69] The four friends decided to offer the collection for sale at auction, and were agreed that the entire collection must be sold together and kept together.[70] The auction was scheduled to take place on the island of Zante on November 1, 1812. Advertisements were posted in the major gazettes,[71] and Mr. Georg Christian Gropius (1776–1850), a painter from Berlin who had moved first to Rome and was then in residence in Athens, was appointed as director of the sale[72] in the anticipated absence of the four men who now "owned" the marbles. The four were, as I mentioned above, off to further adventures and discoveries on the Peloponnese—at Bassae and elsewhere.

JOHANN MARTIN WAGNER IN GREECE

The story then took a more complicated political turn. Britain, France, and Bavaria were art historical rivals, as we have seen. The crown prince, Ludwig of Bavaria (1786–1868, who reigned 1828–48), still smarting from the loss of the Elgin Marbles, was determined to have the Aegina collection at any cost. But at the same time, Cockerell's enthusiastic and emphatic letters home—not just to his parents in London but also to Elgin's former secretary, and now undersecretary of state for foreign affairs, William Hamilton—unwittingly led the Crown to believe that the statues were already theirs. When two British warships, one the brig o'war HMS *Paulina*, arrived in Athens on November 29, 1811, to purchase the group for £6,000 and then transport them to London, Cockerell had the unenviable task of explaining to the captain, Commander Westby Perceval, not only that the sculptures had been removed to Zante for safekeeping, but also that they were scheduled for public auction and could not be guaranteed to the Crown.[73]

And there was more. Rumors of an imminent French attack on the island of Zante were circulating in Athens, and so Cockerell requested that the British fleet remove the collection from Zante and move it to British Malta for safekeeping. (Most of Elgin's collection had laid over at Malta as well, and by then the fledgling Ionian Academy was linked to sister institutions on the island of Malta, as well as in Florence, Milan, Naples, Rome, and Venice.) It is a testament to Cockerell's charm, as well as his prudence, that the move was faithfully made by the British navy.[74] The shipment arranged, Cockerell departed for Crete and an abortive trip to Egypt.[75]

The auction was scheduled for the following year: November 1, 1812. It took place, as originally advertised, on Zante, where Gropius was presiding, and not on Malta, where the statues were now being held. This created an unusual situation in which collectors would be bidding on statues they could not see. The British representative, Taylor Coombe (1774–1826)—then keeper of antiquities at the Townley Gallery and the British Museum—had arrived earlier at Malta and could not be persuaded that the auction would be held away from the statues. Suspecting a ruse, Coombe stayed on Malta; thus the British delegation missed its chance to bid on the collection. Cockerell was incensed, blaming Coombe's "idiocy" for the lost opportunity. He returned to Zante in 1813 to attempt to redress the situation, to no avail. (A second auction for the Phigalian frieze from Bassae was held in May 1814, with a more favorable outcome to British interests . . . and the British Museum.)

In point of fact, only one representative, a Bavarian, appeared on Zante prior to the auction, and while French representatives communicated a written offer of 160,000 francs for the Aegina collection, it could not be guaranteed in the absence of the representatives themselves. The Bavarian Johann(es) Martin Wagner (1777–1858) is one more in an expansive list of contemporary aspiring young artists and Mediterranean expatriates.[76]

He trained in the visual arts first with his father, who was a successful painter in Würzburg, where he also apprenticed himself to the marvelous frescoes by Tiepolo that adorn the church and interior of the Würzburg Palace, or Residenz. In 1802, Wagner was awarded the first prize by the Vienna Academy for his study of "Venus and Aeneas," after which he returned home briefly to Würzburg. While there, he was awarded the first prize by the Weimar Academy for his study of "Ulysses and Polyphemus," solidifying his reputation for visually amplifying such mythological and classicizing themes.[77] Under the influence of an international circle of neoclassical painters including Jacques Louis David in Paris, Wagner was encouraged to move to Rome, as he did first in 1804/5. It was there that he conceptualized and completed his early masterpiece, "The Counsel of Greeks at Troy" ("*Der Rat der Greichen vor Troja*"), which won him considerable international attention, and now resides in the Wagner Museum in Würzburg.

When this monumental canvas was purchased by the Bavarian regime in 1808, Wagner accompanied the painting to Munich; it was en route, in Innsbruck, that he first met Crown Prince Ludwig.[78] He became one of the prince's primary agents in Rome, and the two men corresponded for the rest of their lives.[79] So Wagner returned, remaining in Rome for most of his life—excepting several extended trips, most notably to Greece and Malta. Wagner amassed an impressive personal collection of ancient art over the years, much of which is now also on display in the Würzburg museum that bears his name (Wagner donated most of his collection just one year before his death).[80]

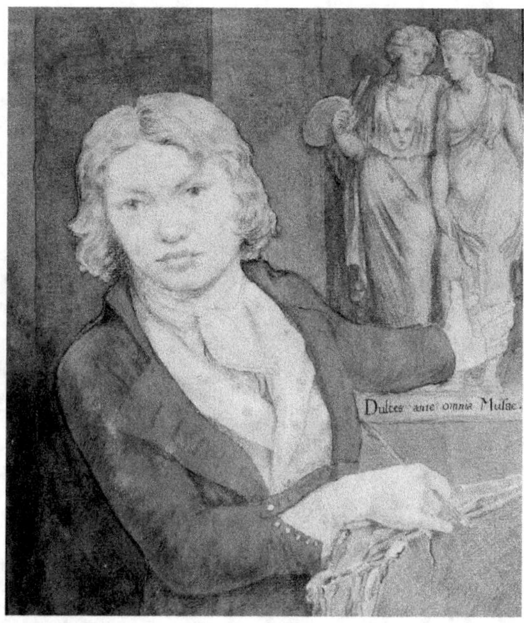

Figure I.8. Johann Martin Wagner (1777–1858): Self-Portrait, ca. 1793. Printed with permission of the Martin von Wagner Museum, Würzburg (*Martin von Wagner Museum* F442 [K504]; Catalogue #554).

And so, when news of the Aeginetan auction reached the prince some three years later, he drafted a letter from Salzburg on June 20, 1812, urging Wagner to make the trip to Zante as Ludwig's representative, and to arrive at the island no later than the middle of October (Wagner's annotation indicates that he received this letter on July 3, 1812).[81] Wagner attempted to get out of the trip: he spoke no Greek; he could not locate a good map of the country; and he would always prefer Rome to anywhere else (he was also in the midst of negotiating for the acquisition of several important pieces including the Barbarini Faun). But his prince was insistent. So Wagner hired an Italian guide, Pacifico Storani, and the two men took ship from Rome for Naples on September 8, 1812. (See appendix 2 for a detailed chronology of Wagner's long journey to Greece and back.)

It was a very difficult year for travel of this kind. Wagner was just three days outside of Naples when he was sent back without his luggage by French troops, in order to secure an additional letter from the French consul in Naples. Sea travel was especially difficult to arrange, with a British blockade of the eastern Mediterranean resulting in the seizure of boats of all kinds.

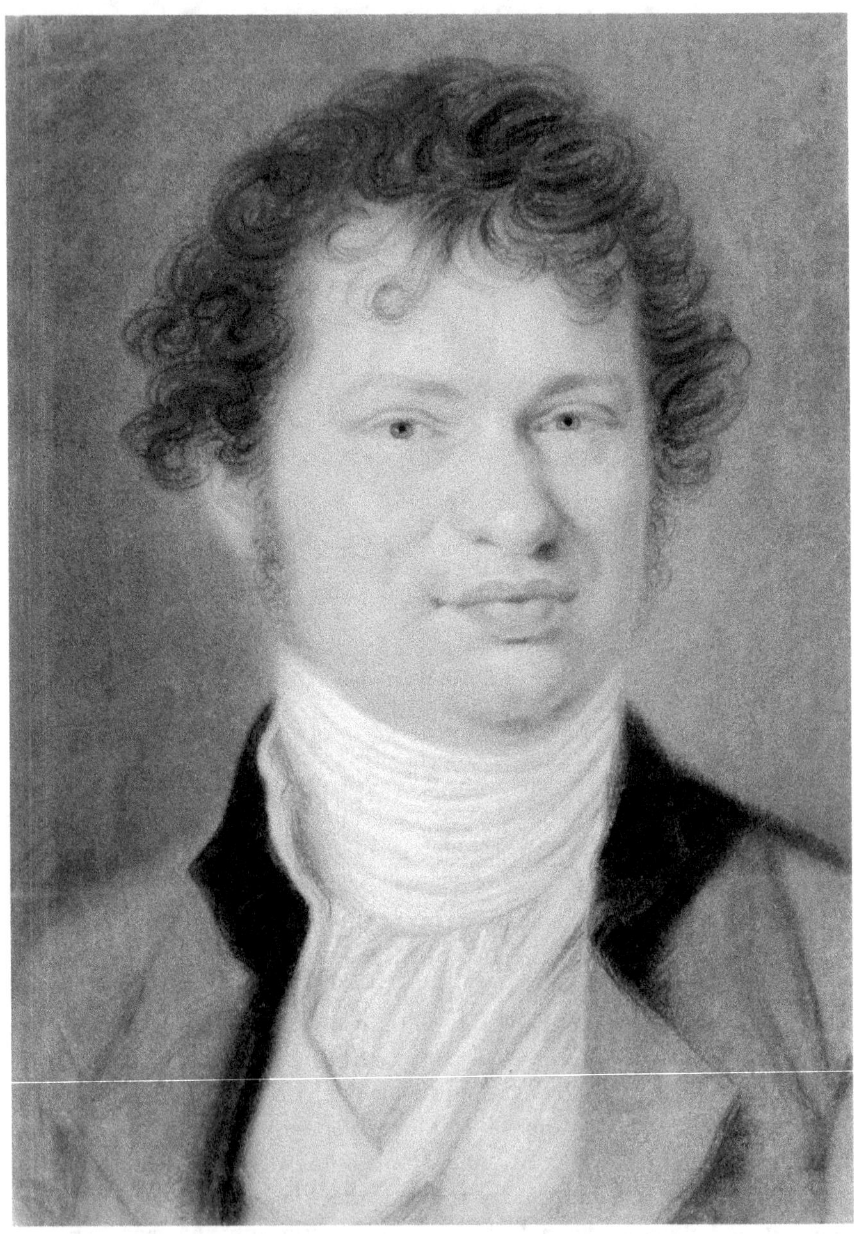

Figure I.9. Johann Martin Wagner (1777–1858): Self-portrait, 1804/5. Printed with permission of the Martin von Wagner Museum, Würzburg (*Martin von Wagner Museum* Z732; Catalogue #555).

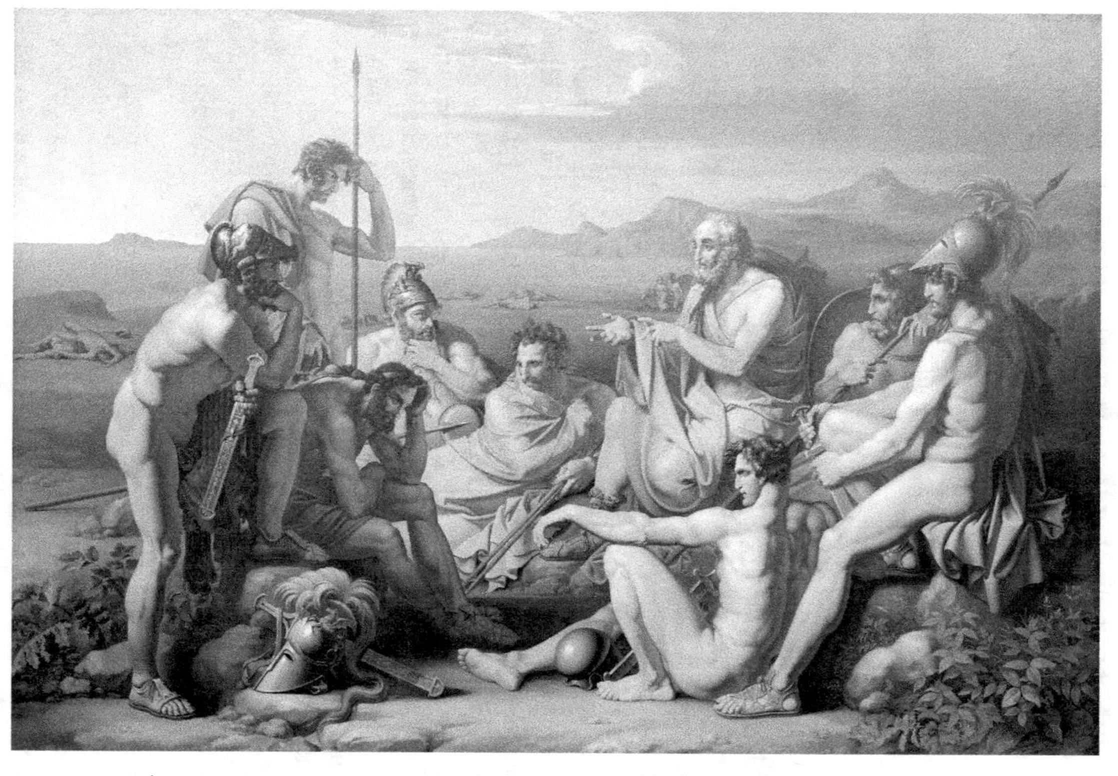

Figure I.10. Johann Martin Wagner, *Der Rat der Griechen vor Troja* (*The Counsel of Greeks at Troy*), 1807. Printed with permission of the Martin von Wagner Museum, Würzburg (*Martin von Wagner Museum* Z744; Catalogue #556).

On September 29, 1812, Wagner was in Otranto, where the French consul assisted with his arrangements for departure from Italy. Wagner's sleep was interrupted that evening by the sounds of a distant cannonade from several British warships patrolling these same waters. Wagner's Neapolitan captain, Saverio Castagnola (or Costajela), departed at dusk on the following day, successfully ran the British blockade, and arrived at French-held Corfu on October 2, 1812.[82]

Here Wagner was stuck yet again, for nearly two weeks this time, attempting to finesse his way from French-held Corfu to British Zante. Since, under the conditions of war, one could not travel directly from a French to a British port of call, Wagner was required to cross over to the Ottoman mainland first. After landing at four different islands and several mainland ports, Wagner finally departed from Prevesa without the proper documents, and headed for Santa Maura, from which point he intended to cross over the waterway to Zante. He just made it, and after bad weather delayed him for several more days, he arrived at Zante just two days before the auction.

While still held in quarantine, Wagner met with several members of the Bavarian party (Cockerell was then traveling in Sicily). Haller,[83] Linkh, and Stackelberg arranged for Wagner to have a meeting with Gropius, who informed Wagner that he was the only representative who had successfully managed the complicated passage to the island. The Bavarians agreed that the statues must be acquired for their prince, and that in any case Britain was too inaccessible a post for art historical treasures of such exceptional beauty and scholarly value (recall that the same argument had been made against Athens by the supporters of Lord Elgin). It was only now that Wagner learned that the statues were not on Zante but on the island of Malta instead (close, be sure to recall, to where Cockerell found himself at the time).

This placed Wagner in a most awkward position. He had been guaranteed nearly limitless credit from his prince, and he had made very careful arrangements with creditors in both Naples and Athens. But now he was being asked to purchase the statues, sight unseen. His new Bavarian friends assured him of their excellence and inestimable value, and so he agreed to purchase the collection as described in the manifest for 10,000 Venetian zecchini (a sum estimated in value as ranging from £4,500 to £6,000).[84] The agreement was conditional, and would be confirmed only after Wagner was able to inspect the statues. Given the ongoing difficulty of sea travel in those troubled years, the Bavarians suggested an overland trip to Athens, since the plaster casts of the essential pieces from the Aeginetan collection were being held by the French consul in Athens, the famed philhellene and art collector, Louis

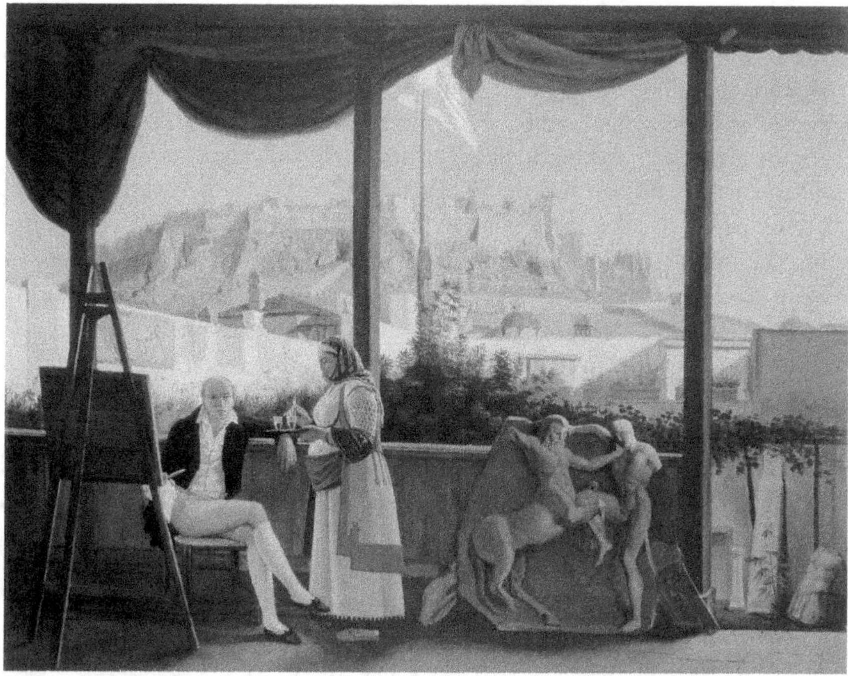

Figure I.11. Portrait of Louis François Sébastien Fauvel (1753–1838), 1819. Lithograph by Louis Dupré. Photograph (c) 2015 courtesy of the David and Alfred Smart Museum of Art, The University of Chicago (*Smart Museum of Art* 1980.33).

François Sébastian Fauvel (1753–1838), another European who had traveled extensively in Turkey and Greece since 1780, and who settled permanently in Athens in 1803.

Fauvel had observed Elgin's activities on the Akropolis at close hand, and was intent on keeping French interests alive in this complicated game of Greek spoliation. He had visited the Aegina temple himself after the original discovery of the marbles and secured a few additional pieces for himself. He did a good deal more of this kind of work until the outbreak of the Greek War of Independence in 1821 (his home, which housed many of his finds, was destroyed in 1825), at which point he moved to Smyrna, where he remained until his death.[85]

Wagner's itinerary between Zante and Athens maps, almost point for point, the one that Byron and Hobhouse had undertaken four years earlier.[86] When Wagner arrived in Athens on December 14, 1812, he presented himself to Fauvel since, as a resident of Italy, he was nominally subject to the French authority. Wagner remained in Athens for three months, and lodged at the Capuchin Hostelry, where Byron had also stayed not long before. He was delighted with the quality of the Aeginetan casts in Fauvel's possession, since they exceeded even his high hopes for them. He and Fauvel got on famously and spent a great deal of time together, but Gropius concerned him, since Wagner began to suspect him of overcharging his prince for the cost of shipping the marbles from Malta and Athens to Rome (arguments among the Great Powers' representatives concerning the legitimacy of the auction lingered for many months). Resolving these questions primarily with Fauvel's assistance, Wagner departed from Athens on March 15, 1813, and arrived back in Rome on August 4. In a letter sent to Wagner in 1813 and accompanied by the gift of a gold watch, Ludwig acknowledged the difficulty of the journey: "Like Odysseus you have suffered much, Wagner, on my account, and I will not forget it as long as I live."[87] The Aegina Marbles were to arrive in Rome a little more than two years later.[88]

FROM ATHENS TO ROME, AND THE PRODUCTION OF WAGNER'S *REPORT*

After traveling to Malta to retrieve the Aegina collection, between late 1815 and 1818 Wagner oversaw the "restoration" of this Aeginetan collection in Rome. Ludwig allowed him to commission his friend, the famous Danish sculptor Bertel Thorvaldsen, to do the work. Thorvaldsen had shown outstanding artistic promise at a very young age, and moved to Rome in 1797 to advance his artistic career. He was also to remain there for many years. Famous, among other things, for a marble bust of Lord Byron that he carved in 1831 (housed now in the Thorvaldsen Museum in Copenhagen), Thorvaldsen was considered, along with Canova, among the most preeminent neoclassical sculptors then living in Italy. He and Wagner met in Rome in 1811, and while Wagner seems not to have cared for him personally, the two men collaborated for two years (1816–18) on the final preparations for the crown prince's new collection.

Thorvaldsen was responsible for a kind of "restoration" that, in those heady romantic days, involved a great deal more intrusive activity than is artistically acceptable today.[89] It was not always so, of course; Canova and Quatremère had both advised emphatically *against* a similar "restoration" of the Elgin Marbles. With this Aeginetan collection, Thorvaldsen was confronted with countless

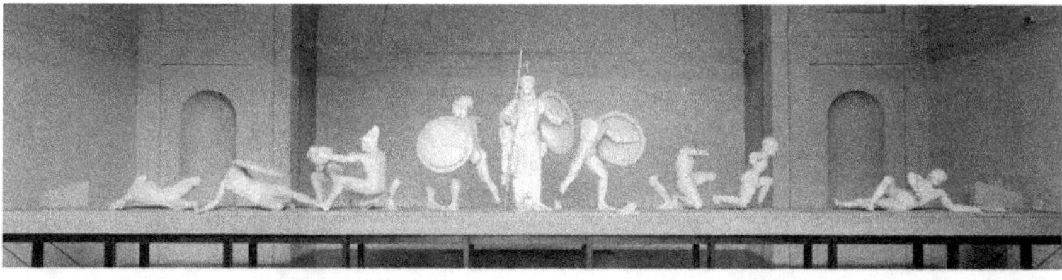

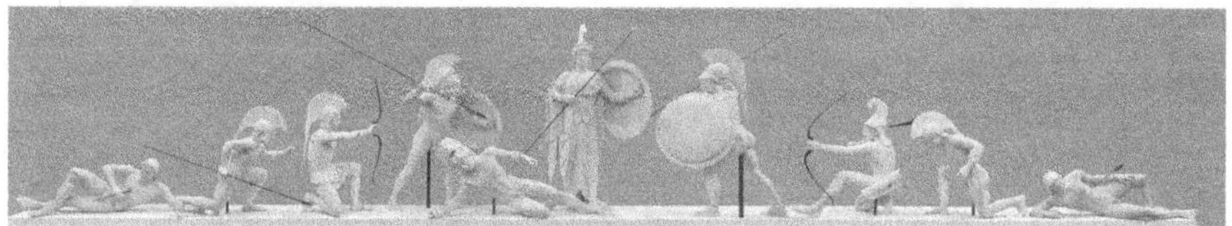

Figure I.12. West pediment, de-restored. Photograph by Renate Kühling. Printed with permission of the Munich State Collection of Antiquities and Glyptothek (*München Antikensammlung und Glyptothek* Abb. 242).

Figure I.13. West pediment, as restored by Thorvaldsen. Photograph by Renate Kühling. Printed with permission of the Munich State Collection of Antiquities and Glyptothek (*München Antikensammlung und Glyptothek* Abb. 243).

interpretive questions from the outset: how to size up the fragments, how to match heads and limbs to torsos, how to imagine the various figures' original relation to one another, how to pose them, and so on. Wagner occasionally disagreed with Thorvaldsen's aesthetic and scholarly choices, offering alternative interpretations, some of which were later confirmed when renewed excavations at Aegina under the direction of the Glyptothek's Adolf Furtwängler (1853–1907) recovered the statue bases for the pediments in 1901.[90] Still more surprising and remarkable, from a contemporary perspective, Thorvaldsen also carved *new body parts* to substitute for missing parts of the originals. The aesthetic goal was to "complete" [*ergänzen*] the collection, to make it appear whole again—and seamlessly so.

The philosophical and artistic goal was thus to make the gap between the past and present disappear, so that the viewer could not be sure what was ancient and what was modern. The resulting whole was decisively and unapologetically modern. Here was another ambitious aesthetic project with little precedent given the scale of the undertaking.

At the same time, Wagner himself was commissioned by his appreciative prince to write an art historical report on the collection, the first-ever

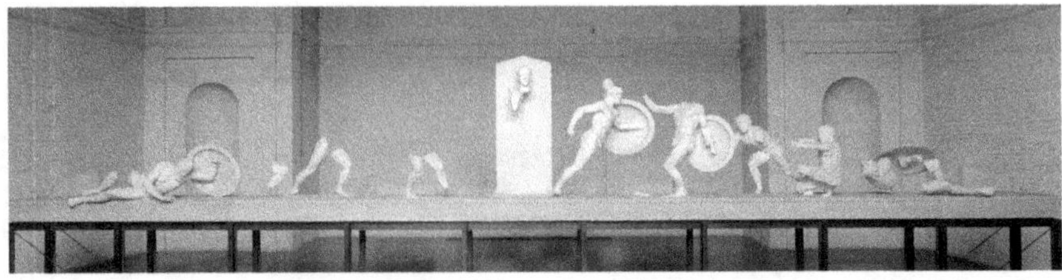

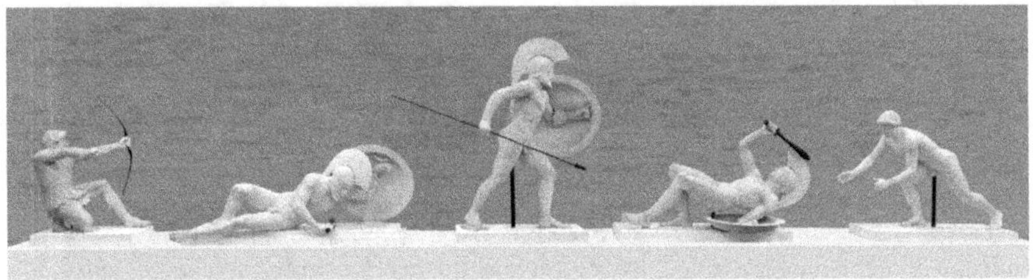

Figure I.14. East pediment, de-restored. Photograph by Renate Kühling. Printed with permission of the Munich State Collection of Antiquities and Glyptothek (*München Antikensammlung und Glyptothek* Abb. 244).

Figure I.15. East pediment, as restored by Thorvaldsen. Photograph by Renate Kühling. Printed with permission of the Munich State Collection of Antiquities and Glyptothek (*München Antikensammlung und Glyptothek* Abb. 245).

English translation of which I offer here. Wagner's *Report on the Aeginetan Sculptures* was to be edited by his friend, the Romantic philosopher Friedrich W. J. Schelling (1775–1854), and was first published in 1817,[91] just prior to the completion of Thorvaldsen's work of "restoration"; Schelling knew both men well.[92]

The text offers a remarkable example of early-nineteenth-century classicism, under the aegis of important new archaeological discoveries and the dawning era of the polychromatic public museum so well inscribed in the career of Antoine Chrysostome Quatremère de Quincy (1755–1849).[93]

On the one hand, Wagner provides a detailed description of each piece in the Aeginetan collection, no matter how fragmentary, as well as offering a careful description of how it appeared prior to Thorvaldsen's restorations. On the other hand, Schelling saw fit very nearly to "restore" Wagner's *Report*; his copious critical notes and appendices are often equal in length to (and sometimes longer than) Wagner's original text. They are also every bit as interesting in their own way and in their own right.[94] It is sometimes unclear when

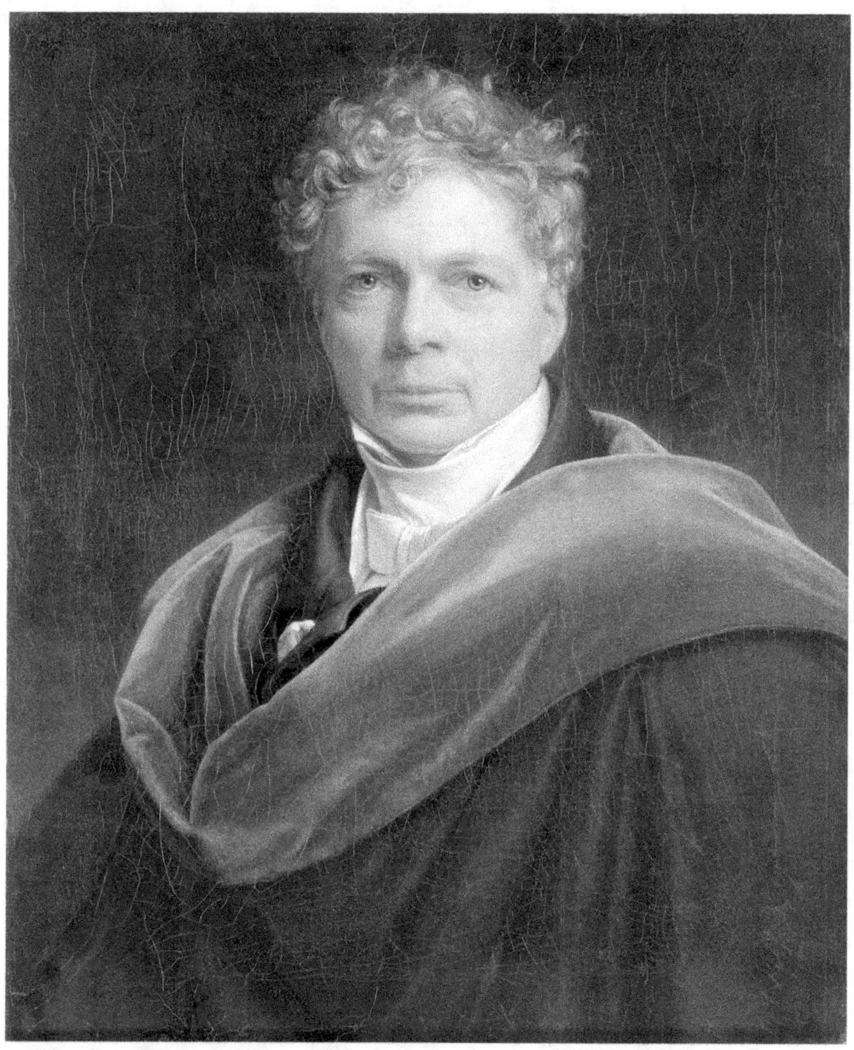

Figure I.16. Portrait of Friedrich W. J. Schelling (1775–1854), 1835, by Joseph Karl Stiele. Printed with permission of the Bavarian State Portrait Gallery (*Bayerische Staatsgemäldesammlungen, München* G0408).

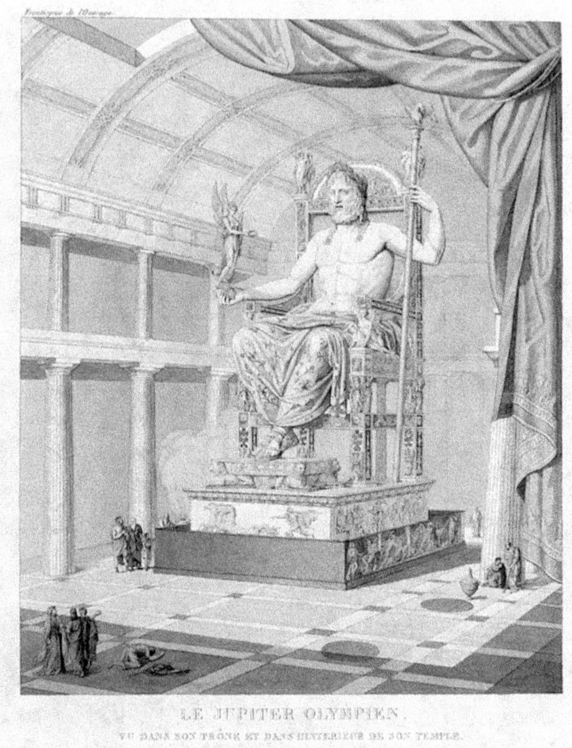

Figure I.17. Image of Olympian Zeus, from Antoine Chrysostome Quatremère de Quincy, *Le Jupiter Olympien* (1815). Antoine Chrysostome Quatremère de Quincy. Document in the public domain via Wikimedia Commons.

a note belongs to Wagner or Schelling and such ambiguities are endemic to all such nineteenth-century "restoration" and completion. (In this book, I will clearly identify each footnote in the body of the text as belonging to Wagner, or to Schelling, or to myself, since I am now ironically—or rather, palimpsestically—adding to the work of both men yet again.) In short, neoclassicism often hinged on a form of restoration designed to elide the temporal gap between then and now. Byron, we may recall, played humorously with this same idea in his condemnation of Lord Elgin's interventions.

Both Wagner and Schelling illustrate some of the areas of greatest neoclassical interest of their times, matters about which the Aeginetan collection had much to say. They both recognize the collection as an importantly transitional one, whose pieces amply illustrate the seismic shift from the Archaic to the Classical style. Both men freely acknowledge the Greek debt to Egyptian and Near Eastern sculptural precedents, while also speaking intelligently to the essential differences in Greek sculptural form (male nudity being only the most obvious aspect). The Greeks did not blindly copy what they borrowed; neither, for that matter, did neoclassicists or romantics.

Wagner is especially interested in discussing the surprising discovery of traces of painting on these statues; he devotes the final chapter of his book to the topic. These Aeginetan statues were decorated with brilliant reds and blues and greens . . . and must have looked for all the world like some of the medieval Catholic images one sees in Bavaria and in Rome, as he will wryly observe. Both Wagner and Schelling were also deeply interested in the existence of an "Aeginetan School" of sculpture, a school whose lusciousness and creativity are well attested by these statues and confirmed in later post-classical literary discussion. The existence of such a school was already well attested by Pausanias, for instance;[95] Quatremère made the careful delineation of the various schools of ancient sculpture central to the work of art history in the generation after Winckelmann, and Schelling makes great use of that work in his appendices here.[96] In short, this is an encyclopedic report in the best sense of that term, one that made sense of an exciting new discovery by situating it in its own times as well as within the canons of the classical scholarship of Wagner's and Schelling's contemporaries. And Wagner's *Report* was timely; we should recall that Charles Cockerell did not publish his own report on the sculptures and the temple until 1860. By then, virtually all of the protagonists in my story were dead and gone.

SCHELLING AS EDITOR

Friedrich W. J. Schelling's (1775–1854) scholarly career is perhaps most notable for its apparently shifting, episodic, and one might almost say its stop-start quality. He has been remembered as a philosopher who was unusual for the significant shifts in scholarly personality evidenced by the shifts in his primary scholarly and professional interests. These shifts have commonly been understood as involving four historically sequential sets of interests, roughly as follows: the development of a critical early philosophy of nature (1794–1800);[97] the overcoming of the early modern (Cartesian) model of philosophy, with its excessively narrow focus on the individual thinking subject, in the name of "idealism" and a more nuanced understanding of human freedom (1800–09);[98] a complex and unfinished investigation of time and reality that amounts to an extended philosophical meditation on the various biblical accounts of creativity (that is, history in the fullest and genuinely global sense of the term) to which he famously referred as "the ages of the world" (1810–15);[99] and what came to be known in later lectures in Berlin as his philosophy of mythology and of religion (this later work also involved Schelling in a far more explicit confrontation with Hegel's philosophy, and the long reach of Hegelian historicism, 1820–54). I would like to suggest that this intriguing range of interests is best imagined not as a sequence but as a palimpsest, one in which every new interest was inscribed over and upon its predecessors. Nothing was ever lost or foreclosed, in this view, but everything was serially transformed. And behind it all lay Schelling's perennial interest in things Greek.

One of the difficulties in assessing Schelling's intellectual development, and hence his true philosophical stature, stems from the fact that he failed to publish much of this later work.[100] He burst on the scene as a proverbial *Wunderkind*, the promise of whose early publications on nature and freedom was never fully realized later in his career. It is certainly the case that a great deal of his later work has been slow to receive its proper philosophical due. But renewed attention to Schelling's decisive 1809 essay on human freedom, by philosophers like Andrew Bowie,[101] Martin Heidegger,[102] Jason Wirth,[103] and Slavoj Zizek,[104] have helped to establish both his stature and enduring importance as much more than a mere appendage of (or appendix to) the story of Hegel's influence on German thought in the nineteenth century. For my purposes, Schelling's essay on human freedom is especially significant for reasons that relate Hellenism to religion in a subtle manner highly relevant to his reflections on the Temple of Aphaia on Aegina.

Schelling tasks himself in the essay with an intervention in one of the perennial questions of philosophy: the relationship between determinism, or fate, and freedom. If we take his early interests in "nature" as a placeholder for predetermined human conditions, then this essay serves as his attempt to secure the reality of human freedom, howsoever it is conditioned. It is a central question of *human* nature, then. Are we determined by our biological nature, or are we free to choose and to act at will? Schelling's answer is surprising in many ways, first of all because it announces itself as an intervention in the long-standing philosophical interest in theodicy, an early modern concern formally announced by Leibniz's influential *Essays on Theodicy*, published in 1710. From this perspective, the question of human freedom comes to this: is the source of evil to be located in the human or the divine realm?

Schelling's approach is to subvert such questions by showing how they rely on false dichotomies. As he put the matter in the stirring conclusion to his masterful 1809 essay, the true purpose of *dialectical* thinking lay in the overcoming of *dualistic* thinking. And now, here at the very end of this essay, one more time-tested dichotomy comes under surprising critical scrutiny: the distinction between pagan and Christian modes of thought. Here is how Schelling puts the point in the rousing final pages of that book:

> To transfer an absolute dualism of good and evil to history whereby either one or the other principle prevails in all manifestations and works of the human spirit, *whereby there are only two systems and two religions, one absolutely good and another simply evil*: further, the opinion that everything began in purity and simplicity and all subsequent developments (that were of course necessary in order to reveal the particular aspects contained in the first unity and thereby to reveal the unity fully itself) were only decay and falsification—while this whole view serves critique as a powerful sword of Alexander with which to chop the Gordian knot in two effortlessly everywhere, it introduces into history, however, a thoroughly illiberal and reductive point of view. There was a time that preceded this separation; and one worldview and religion which, although opposed to the absolute one, sprang forth from its own ground and not from a falsification of the first one. *Paganism is, taken historically, as original as Christianity and, although only a ground and basis of something higher, it is not derived from anything else.* . . .
>
> We have an older revelation than any written one—nature. The latter contains a model [*Vorbilder*] that no man has yet interpreted, whereas the written one received its fulfillment and interpretation long ago. If the understanding of this unwritten revelation were made manifest, the only true system of religion and science would appear not in the poorly assembled state of a few philosophical and critical concepts, but rather at once in the full brilliance of truth and nature. It is not the time to rouse old oppositions once again, but rather to seek that which lies outside of, and beyond, all opposition.[105]

At one level, this passage represents a brilliant play on Saint Paul's sacred history as laid out in the first chapter of his Letter to the Romans. The Greeks received a revelation in nature, Paul says, whereas the Hebrews received a revelation in scripture; both sides failed to attend to the religious truths made available to them. And yet the radicality of Schelling's mode of reasoning goes much further: he is out to subvert the very dichotomy—between Jew and Greek—that makes Paul's argument run. Schelling is calling us to go deeper, to come to Ground. And while he expresses *both* respect for the historical enterprise, *and* suspicion of how far such historical work can take us in philosophical terms, Schelling appears to be suggesting a whole new way of looking at Greek art and Greek religion, beyond "opposition." This may help to explain the apparent interruption of his philosophical publications after 1809. As the book that he and Wagner published makes very plain, what Schelling produced subsequent to the 1809 essay was a series of fairly specific case studies on the pagan world—its art and its religion—which he first attempted to rehabilitate here in the freedom essay.

After several highly influential years teaching in Jena, where he first offered his lecture course on the philosophy of art,[106] Schelling moved to Munich in 1806 and was to remain there for the most part until he was invited to take up the chair in philosophy at the University of Berlin that had been held by Hegel until his death in 1831. (Schelling left Munich once, for Erlangen, from 1820–27.) Schelling was thus in the city of Munich when news of the purchase of the Aegina Marbles was published, when Wagner began working on this *Report,* and also when the statues finally arrived (Schelling returned from Erlangen to Munich shortly before the Glyptothek Museum opened to the public in the fall of 1830). And so the philosopher elected to utilize this felicitous cultural event as a way to display the dialectical and palimpsestic way of thinking to which he appears to have become committed—by supplementing Wagner's observations with his own notes and appendices, much as Thorvaldsen was to supplement the ancient works of art with appendages of his own creation.

The palimpsests, as we shall see, were everywhere: in the history, in the statues, and in this text. That is a crucial point to keep in mind as we survey various strategies of modern neoclassicism and neo-Hellenism alike.[107]

Schelling can sound tendentious at times, quarreling with Wagner and other philosophers over the specific reading of classical texts. Of course the classics were a serious business in German intellectual life in the early nineteenth century, regardless of the field of specialization, and each new archaeological discovery resonated with the force of a revelation. The stakes in interpreting the ancient world were thought to be very, very high. As Schelling noted already in 1809, it will not do to write off Greek religion as evil, as pagan, or what have you. Greek religion was a religion of revelation too, just in a different way, a way that put a premium on visual representation. Schelling's fluency with classical literature in Greek and in Latin is impressive by any measure (Wagner's was as well), even if he occasionally strays from the text in the name of his own philosophical commitments. He possessed a keen eye for detail, and he was right to discern in Pausanias a special fondness for the work of an underappreciated Aeginetan sculptor named Onatas. But perhaps the most striking thing about Schelling's overall editorial interest in these statues and in this text is what we might call the "quest for origins" that haunts so much writing in the first half of the nineteenth century. Questions concerning the origin of human language, the origin of social inequality, the origin of religion, or the origin of species diversity, provided much of the essential intellectual furniture of the age. Schelling's later interest in mythology may seem to announce his break with this fixation since, after all, myths are notorious for nothing so much as providing ten different answers to any single question about origins. But in 1817, Schelling seems especially invested in origins, going so far as to suggest in his conclusion that these statues may be among the very oldest (i.e, the most original) of Greek artworks. Assessing why such a claim should matter as it did has something to do with assessing the merits of history and the use of historical periods to philosophical thinking. These statues were historical phenomena, and that was a central part of their appeal. I will have much more to say about this in appendix 3.

FROM ROME TO MUNICH, AT LAST

So great was Ludwig's excitement at having finally acquired a first-rate collection of ancient art, and this scholarly confirmation of its great importance, that he determined to construct a neoclassical museum for the express purpose of housing it. This is the Munich Glyptothek, which still houses one of the finest collections of classical and post-classical art in the world.[108] Ludwig's intention was to refashion his father's new capital in classical terms, rendering it an "Athens on the Isar," as it came to be known; the city was also designed to supersede, architecturally speaking, the old capital at Regensburg. Ludwig sponsored an architectural competition, soliciting designs for the entire project on the Königsplatz, or King's Plaza, well to the north of the city center. Carl Haller von Hallerstein submitted one of the unsuccessful proposals for this complex,[109] but the commission was finally awarded to Leo von Klenze (1784–1864), and the main idea was that the thing had to be Greek in inspiration.[110]

Klenze's plans called for an impressive program of new building on three sides of the Königsplatz. To the north was the Glyptothek, designed in the Ionic order and completed in 1830, when the Aeginetan collection was first made available to public viewing. Across the way to the south, the

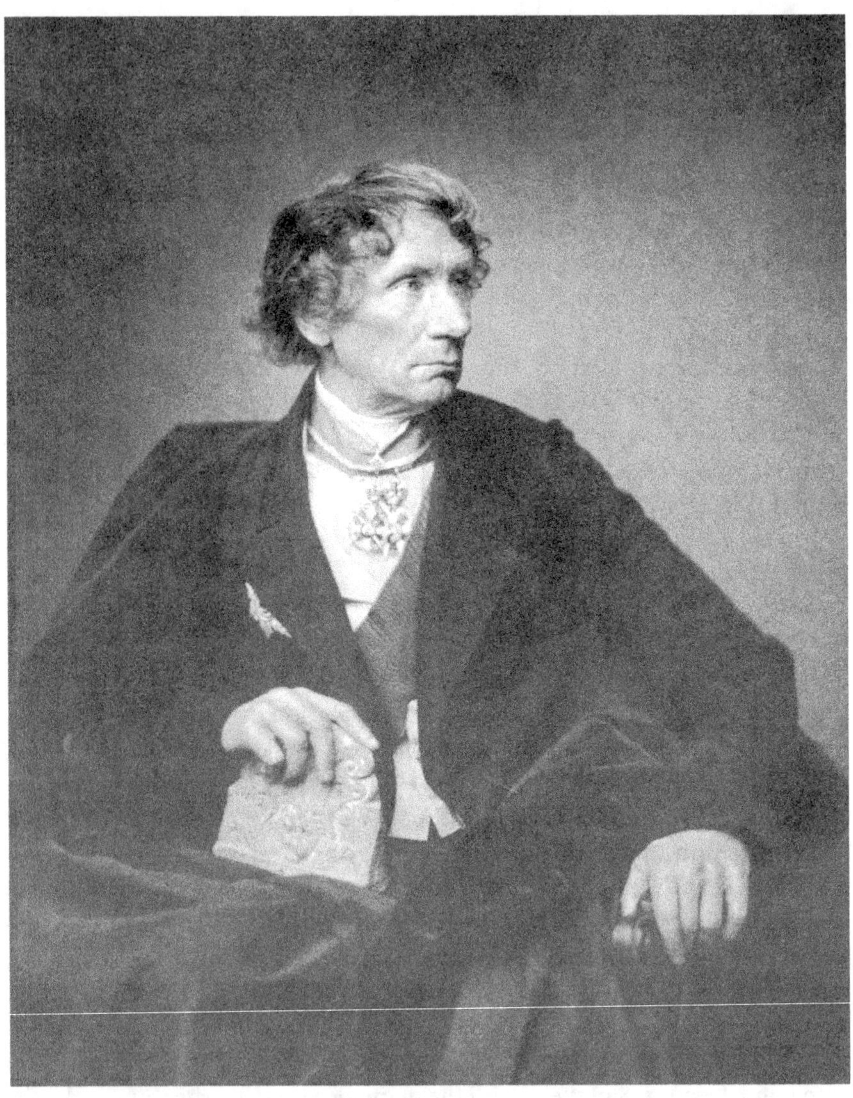

Figure I.18. Photograph of Leo von Klenze (1784–1864), 1856, by Franz Hanfstaengl (1804–1877). Printed with permission of the Munich State Collection of Antiquities and Glyptothek (*München Antikensammlung und Glyptothek* Abb. 135_Hans Haefstaengl).

Ausstellungsgebäude was designed in the Corinthian order and completed in 1845. It has served many purposes over the years, and now serves as a museum designed to house an impressive collection of ancient Greek and Etruscan works in ceramic, metal, and other materials. To the western entrance onto the Königsplatz, Klenze proposed a full-scale model of the Athenian Propylaia, the monumental gateway leading onto the Akropolis; this ambitious imitation in the Doric order was completed in 1863, one year before Klenze's death. By then, nearly all of the men who had made this venture possible were gone.

Carl Haller von Hallerstein remained in Greece as most of his friends gradually made their way back to Italy, mainly to Rome. Having acquired a taste for excavation on Aegina and at Bassae, Haller was excavating at Ampelakia, in the Tempe Valley not far from Delphi, when he fell ill with a repeated bout of malaria and died quite suddenly on November 4, 1817. His body was taken to Athens for burial.[111]

Jacob Linkh left Athens with Charles Cockerell on January 15, 1815. The two made their way slowly across the Peloponnese, then sailed to southern Italy, devoting most of their time to Naples and Rome. Linkh remained in residence in Rome until 1825, and then returned to Stuttgart, where he died on April 4, 1841.

Otto Stackelberg remained in Greece until 1816, but then he too returned to Rome, where he settled for twelve more years. Before shifting his interests to the study of art and archaeology, Stackelberg had intended to pursue a diplomatic career. He spent the rest of his scholarly life in several of the great capitals of Europe, researching and writing about his commingled interests in the ancient and modern Mediterranean, especially Greece. He was reunited briefly with Cockerell in Venice in 1816, and then he moved: first to Paris and London (1828–29), later to Dresden (1833–35), and finally to St. Petersburg, where he died two years later on March 27, 1837.

John Foster Jr. returned to Liverpool after his Grecian sojourn ended in 1814, where he settled into a long and prosperous life of commissioned architectural projects. He also secured several for his friend Charles Cockerell, who seemed loath to solicit work on his own behalf. Foster designed a great many of Liverpool's premier public monuments, most famously their new Customs House (1828–37, it was badly damaged in the Second World War). He retired from public life in 1835, and died a decade later at his home in Liverpool.

Charles Cockerell finally returned to England in 1817, after seven years abroad. He would think of himself, ever after, as "half a Mediterranean."[112] He returned to national acclaim for his archaeological activities and

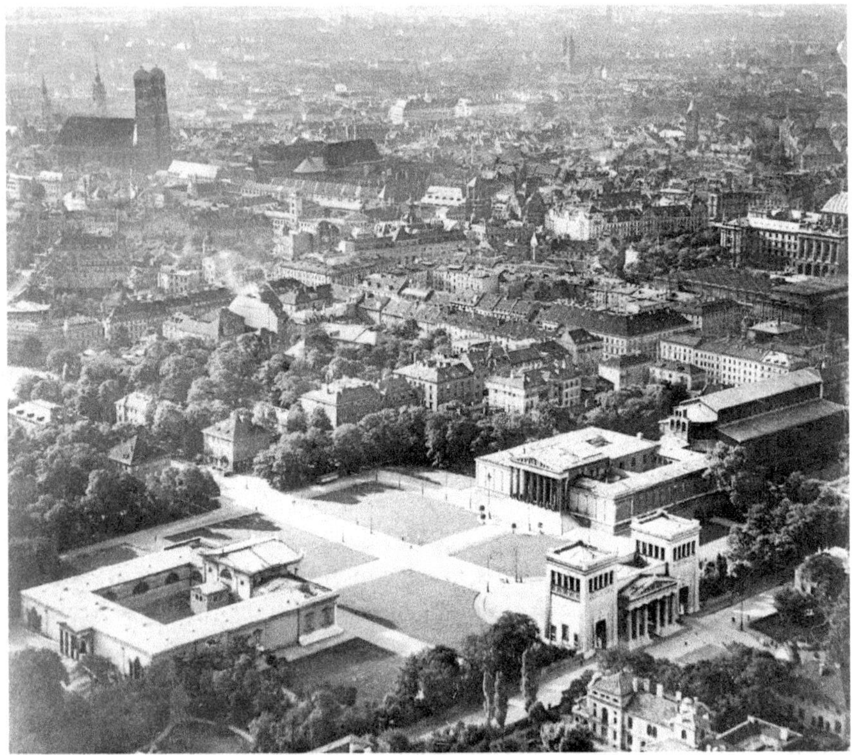

Figure I.19. Aerial photograph of the Königsplatz from the west, 1925. Printed with permission of the State Archives of Munich (*Stadtarchiv München* Stb-Luft-123).

acquisitions, but enjoyed more limited fame as an architect, though he did eventually receive several important commissions. Among his most notable architectural achievements were: additions to the Harrow School (1818) and Hanover Chapel (1838); the renovation of St. Paul's Cathedral in London (1821–22); one wing of the Cambridge University Library (1829–37); the Ashmolean Museum and Taylorian Institute, at Oxford (1839–45); the Branch Bank of London in Plymouth (1842); an addition to the University Library at Queen's College, Oxford (1843); the Fitzwilliam Museum in Cambridge (1846); the Flaxman Gallery of University College, London (1849–57); St. George's Hall in Liverpool (1851–54); and the Liverpool Free Library and Museum (1856).[113] Two things are instructive about Cockerell's long career. First, he was elected a professor of architecture at the Royal Academy

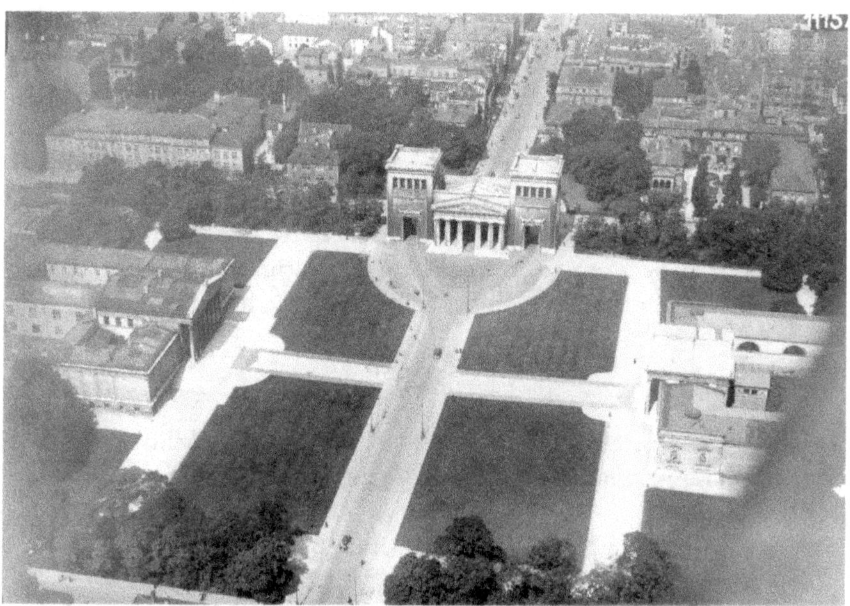

Figure I.20. Aerial photograph of the Königsplatz from the east, 1932. Printed with permission of the State Archives of Munich (*Stadtarchiv München* HB-II-A-0135).

in September 1839, and lectured extensively throughout the 1840s. It is all the more striking, then, how often his designs were refused; in his heyday, the neoclassical wave had crested in England, hence his designs were often rejected in favor of the new taste for Gothic architecture. Where Cockerell's neoclassical style clearly continued to have resonance was in the construction of *new museums*. This is an important detail to keep in mind in assessing the importance of Wagner's *Report* in the context of the newly emerging "museum era." Cockerell's own report, we will recall—sumptuously illustrated with his copious Aeginetan and Arcadian sketches and designs—was not published until 1860, after the deaths of his colleagues, and just three years prior to his own. Cockerell was laid to rest in London, at Saint Paul's Cathedral.

Johann Martin Wagner returned to Rome after fulfilling his Grecian duties for his prince in 1813; he remained there off and on for the rest of his life. Ludwig had a close circle of artists whom he especially trusted—Thorvaldsen, Canova, and Haller—among others, all of whom he commissioned to keep on the lookout for other examples of ancient art worth acquiring. With Wagner, Ludwig maintained a closer and more intimate relationship. Wagner was responsible for arranging the shipment of the restored collection of Aegina Marbles to Munich in 1828, after which Thorvaldsen oversaw their installation in a new building designed in tandem with his sculptural restorations. Wagner continued to acquire on Ludwig's behalf; most of what he acquired is housed in Munich and Würzburg today. In 1827, Ludwig made Wagner the curator of the Villa Malta in Rome (located at Via Porta Pinciana, 21), where he had long been in residence. Wagner remained there for thirty years, and died there on August 8, 1858; he is buried at the colorful and intimate Teutonic Cemetery located in the immediate vicinity of Saint Peter's Cathedral in Rome.

For the German text of Wagner's *Report,* I have used a lovely little (6½" × 4") leather-bound volume, which was very generously sent to me on extended loan by the Wesleyan University Library [5/WJ127/W 13]. That text is 246 pages in length, with a viii-page introduction by Schelling. The same text is now accessible at googlebooks.

I have included this edition's pagination in brackets throughout the text for ease of reference for any reader who wishes to consult the German original.

INTRODUCTION ENDNOTES

1. Nicholas Bouvier, *L'Usage du Monde* (Genève: Librairie Droz S.A., 1999), 10:

   > *Un voyage se passe de motifs. Il ne tarde pas à prouver qu'il se suffit à lui-même. On croit qu'on faire un voyage, mais bientôt c'est le voyage qui vous fait, ou vous défait.*

   This underground classic, originally published in 1963, has been translated into English as *The Way of the World*, translated by Robyn Marsack, with an introduction by Patrick Leigh Fermor (New York: New York Review Books, 2009).
2. Bouvier, *L'usage du Monde*, 110:

   > *Finalement, ce qui constitue l'ossature de l'existence, ce n'est ni la famille, ni la carrière, ni ce que d'autres diront ou penseront de vous, mais quelques instants de cette nature, soulevés par une lévitation plus sereine encore que celle de l'amour, et que la vie nous distribue avec une parcimonie à la mesure de notre faible couer.*

3. For some marvelous material on the Greek version of the Grand Tour and the literature it produced, see Helen Angelomatis-Tsougarakis, *The Eve of the Greek Revival: British Travellers' Perceptions of Early Nineteenth-Century Greece* (London: Routledge, 1990); Mark Cocker, *Loneliness and Time: The Story of British Travel Writing* (New York: Pantheon Books, 1992), 168–207; Robert Eisner, *Travelers to an Antique Land: The History and Literature of Travel to Greece* (Ann Arbor, MI: University of Michigan Press, 1991); Stephen A. Larrabee, *English Bards and Grecian Marbles: The Relationship Between Sculpture and Poetry especially in the Romantic Period* (Port Washington, NY: Kennikat Press, Inc., 1964), and *Hellas Observed: The American Experience of Greece, 1775–1865* (New York: New York University Press, 1957); R. A. McNeal, "Nicholas Biddle and the Literature of Greek Travel," *Classical Antiquity* 12, no. 1 (1993): 65–88; Richard Stoneman, *Land of Lost Gods: The Search for Classical Greece* (London: Hutchinson, 1987) and *A Luminous Land: Artists Discover Greece* (Los Angeles: The J. Paul Getty Museum, 1998); Hugh Tresgakis, *Beyond the Grand Tour: The Levant Lunatics* (New York: Ascent Books, 1979); G. Tolias, ed., *The Fever of the Marbles* (Athens: Oikos, 1996); and J. P. A. van der Vin, *Travellers to Greece and Constantinople: Ancient Monuments and Old Traditions in Medieval Travellers' Tales* (Istanbul: Niederlands Historisch-Archaeologisch Instituut, 1980). Far more critical accounts of this entire literary tradition may be found in: Duncan and Gregory, eds., *Writes of Passage: Reading Travel Writing* (New York: Routledge, 1999) and Mary Louise Pratt, *Imperial Eyes: Travel Writing and Transculturation* (New York: Routledge, 1992).

   Several highly influential early examples of such writing were: *The Voiages and Travels of John Struys through Italy, Greece, Muscovy, Tartary, Media, Persia, East-India, Japan, and Other Countries in Europe, Africa and Asia*, Done out of Dutch by John Morrison (London: Abel Swalle, 1684); *Voyage d'Itallie, de Dalmatie, de Grece, et du Levant, fair aux années 1675 & 1676 par Iacob Spon Docteur Medecin Aggregé à Lyon, & George Wheler Gentilhomme Anglois* (Lyon: Chez Antoine Cellier le fils, 1678), 3 volumes; George Wheler, *A Journey Into Greece in Company of Dr. Spon of Lyons* (London: William Cademann, Robert Kettlewell, and Awnsham Churchill, 1682); Richard Chandler, *Travels in Greece* (Oxford: Clarendon Press, 1776), *The History of Ilium or Troy, Including the Adjacent Country and Opposite Coast of the Chersonesus of Thrace* (London: Nichols and Son, 1802), and *Travels in Asia Minor, and Greece, or, An Account of a Tour Made at the Expense of the Society of Dilettanti* , 3rd Edition in 2 volumes (London: Joseph Booker, 1857; John B. S. Morritt, *A Grand Tour: Letters and Journeys 1794–96* (London: 1914, 1985); Edward Dodwell, *A Classical and Topographical Tour through Greece During the Years 1801, 1805, and 1806* (London: Rudwell and Martin, 1819), 2 volumes; John Cam Hobhouse, *A Journey Through Albania and Other Provinces of Turkey in Europe and Asia to Constantinople during the Years 1809 and 1810*, 2 volumes (London: James Cawthorn, 1813); John Cam Hobhouse [Right Hon. Lord Broughton, G.C.B.], *Italy: Remarks Made in Several Visits from the Year 1816 to 1854*, 2 volumes (London: John Murray, 1859); William Martin Leake, *Researches in Greece: Remarks on the Language Spoken in Greece at the Present Day* (London: John Booth, 1814), *Journal of a Tour in Asia Minor* (London: John Murray, 1824), *Travels in the Morea with a Map and Plans* (London: John Murray, 1830, available in a 1968 reprint by Adolf M. Hakkert Publisher, Amsterdam), 3 volumes, and *Travels in Northern Greece* (London: J. Rodwell, 1835), 4 volumes; William Turner, *Journal of a Tour in the Levant* (London: John Murray, 1820), 3 volumes; and Henry M. Baird, *Modern Greece: A Narrative of a Residence and Travels in that Country* (New York: Harper & Brothers, Publishers, 1856).

This tradition, while far more suspect in our own day, nonetheless had one of its finest representatives in the late Patrick Leigh Fermor, who died in the summer of 2011. On Greece, see his *Mani: Travels in the Southern Peloponnese* (London: John Murray, 1958) and *Roumeli: Travels in Northern Greece* (London: Penguin Books, 1966). For later recollections of his very first trip—"on foot to Constantinople from the Hook of Holland"—see *A Time of Gifts: From the Hook of Holland to the Middle Danube* (London: Penguin Books, 1977), *Between the Woods and the Water: The Middle Danube to the Iron Gates* (London: Penguin Books, 1986), and *The Broken Road: From the Iron Gates to Mount Athos*, Colin Thubron and Artemis Cooper, eds. (New York: New York Review Books, 2013). An excellent biography is Artemis Cooper, *Patrick Leigh Fermor: An Adventure* (New York: New York Review Books, 2012).

A superb supplement to such travel and travel writing is Artemis Leontis, ed., *Greece: A Traveler's Literary Companion* (San Francisco: Whereabouts Press, 1997).

4. It still can be. See Brian Bouldrey, ed., *Traveling Souls: Contemporary Pilgrimage Stories* (San Francisco: Whereabouts Press, 1999).
5. See *The Works of Lord Byron* (Hertfordshire: The Wordsworth Library, 1994), 174–244.
6. See Liliana Barroero and Stefano Susinno, "Arcadian Rome, Universal Capital of the Arts," and Christopher M. S. Johns, "The Entrepôt of Europe: Rome in the Eighteenth Century," in Edgar Peters Bowron and Joseph J. Rishel, *Art in Rome in the Eighteenth Century* (Philadelphia Museum of Art, 2000), 17–75, as well as Andrew Wilton and

Ilaria Bigliamini, *Grand Tour: The Lure of Italy in the Eighteenth Century* (London: Tate Gallery Publishing, 1996).

7. Several histories of that long war are: David Brewer, *The Greek War of Independence: The Struggle for Freedom from Ottoman Oppression and the Birth of the Modern Greek Nation* (New York: The Overlook Press, 2001); John S. Koliopoulos and Thanos M. Verenas, *Modern Greece: A History Since 1821* (Chichester: Wiley-Blackwell, 2010), 15-27, and *Greece, the Modern Sequel: From 1831 to the Present* (London: Hurst & Company, 2002); C. M. Woodhouse, *Modern Greece: A Short History*, 4th Edition (London: Faber and Faber, 1968, 1986), 125–56.

   See also Nina M. Athanassoglou-Kallmyer, *French Images from the Greek War of Independence, 1821–1830* (New Haven, CT: Yale University Press, 1989), and Gonda von Steen, *Liberating Hellenism from the Ottoman Empire: Comte de Marcellus and the Last of the Classics* (New York: Palgrave Macmillan, 2010).

8. See Woodhouse, *Modern Greece: A Short History*, 174.
9. See Edward J. Trelawney, *Recollections of Shelley, Byron and the Author* (New York: New York Review Books, 2000), 251.
10. Otto (1815–1867) was the son of the very crown prince, Ludwig of Bavaria, who commissioned this *Report* and who later became Ludwig I of Bavaria. Otto's dates coincide almost perfectly with the story of the acquisition, restoration, and installation of these statues that I shall relate in this introduction.
11. See Ian Littlewood, *Sultry Climates: Travel and Sex Since the Grand Tour* (London: John Murray, 2001), and Lynne Withey, *Grand Tours and Cook's Tours: A History of Leisure Travel, 1750 to 1915* (New York: William Morrow and Company, Inc., 1997).
12. *The Innocents Abroad, or, The New Pilgrim's Progress* (New York: Airmont Publishing Company, 1967), describes the new democratic sensibilities of such types of travel, in his case taking place on a transatlantic steamer in 1867–68. Twain's alternately hilarious and poignant descriptions of Athens, and of Greece more generally, appear at 225–37.
13. Schliemann's own record of his excavations of Troy on the hill of Hisarlik, originally published by John Murray of London in 1875, may be found in Philip Smith, ed., *Troy and Its Remains* (New York: Dover Publications, 1994).

    A highly critical account of Schliemann's career and its baser motives is David Traill, *Schliemann's Troy: Treasure and Deceit* (New York: St. Martin's Press, 1995). More balanced accounts are provided by Katie Demakopoulou, ed., *Troy, Mycenae, Tiryns, Orchomenos: Heinrich Schliemann, the 100th Anniversary of His Death* (Athens: Ministry of Culture of Greece, 1990), and Susan Heuck Allen, *Finding the Walls of Troy: Frank Calvert and Heinrich Schliemann at Hisarlik* (Berkeley, CA: University of California Press, 1999).

    It bears noting, given the topic before us, that Schliemann, who had married a Greek and settled in Athens, saw to it that most of the treasures from his mainland Greek discoveries remained in the country and may be viewed at the National Museum in Athens today. His work in Anatolia was less circumspect.

14. For more on this, see my *Winckelmann and the Vatican's First Profane Museum* (New York: Palgrave Macmillan, 2011), 109–17, 187–92.
15. See Juan Cole, *Napoleon's Egypt: Invading the Middle East* (New York: Palgrave MacMillan, 2007, 2008) and *Napoleon in Egypt: Al-Jabarti's Chronicle of the French Occupation,*

1798, translated by Schmuel Moreh with an introduction by Robert L. Tignor and an afterword by Edward W. Said (Princeton, NJ: Marcus Wiener Publishing, 1993).

For the art historical legacy of this Napoleonic looting, see Russell Chamberlin, *Loot! The Heritage of Plunder* (London: Thames and Hudson, 1983), 39–65, 123–48. An influential piece of travel writing that helped to inspire the French expedition was Constantin François Chassebouf, comte de Volnay, *Travels through Syria and Egypt, in the Years 1783, 1784, and 1785: Containing the Present Natural and Political State of those Countries, their Productions, Arts, Manufactures, and Commerce; with Observations on the Manners, Customs, and Government of the Turks and Arabs* (London: G. G. J. & J. Robinson, 1787), in 2 volumes, excerpts of which may be found in Tilar J. Mazzeo, ed., *Travels, Explorations and Empires, Writings from the Era of Imperial Expansion, 1770–1835*, Volume 4: The Middle East (London: Pickering and Chatto, 2001), 1–43.

16. See the related discussions from Edward Said in *Orientalism* (New York: Vintage Books, 1978), 76–92, and *Culture and Imperialism* (New York: Vintage Books, 1993), 33–35, 118–19.

17. The Rosetta Stone, of course, is now housed in the British Museum, not the Louvre. When Lord Elgin was still British ambassador to the Sublime Porte (Istanbul), he sent his personal secretary and famed collector, William Hamilton (1777–1859), on a diplomatic mission to Egypt, specifically to oversee the French evacuation at Alexandria. Hamilton discovered that the French, in violation of their treaty agreements, had already prepared to ship the Stone to Paris. Thus he organized an armed escort, boarded the French vessel, and (re)confiscated the Stone. It is striking how suddenly the European gunpowder empires were beginning to wage war with one another through this complex trade in antiquities. The following observations from Major General H. Turner, who accompanied the Stone from Alexandria to Portsmouth in January–February 1802, is telling: "[t]his artifact was a proud trophy of the arms of Britain (I could almost say *spolia opima*), not plundered from defenseless inhabitants, but honorably acquired by the fortune of war." Quoted in Brian M. Fagan, ed., *Eyewitness to Discovery: First-Person Accounts of More than Fifty of the World's Greatest Archaeological Discoveries* (New York: Oxford University Press, 1996), 89 (see also pages 170–75, "The Aegina Marbles," for an excerpt from Cockerell's posthumously published diary).

Finally, see Richard Parkinson, *Cracking Codes: The Rosetta Stone and its Decipherment* (Berkeley, CA: University of California Press, 1999), and John Ray, *The Rosetta Stone and the Rebirth of Ancient Egypt* (Cambridge, MA: Harvard University Press, 2007).

18. See Charles P. Bracken, *Antiquities Acquired: The Spoliation of Greece* (London: David & Charles, 1975), esp. 106–36, rehearsing the story of the acquisition, transport, and sale of the Aegina Marbles, as well as Neil Brodie, Jennifer Doole and Colin Renfrew, eds., *Trade in Illicit Antiquities: The Destruction of the World's Archaeological Heritage* (McDonald Institute for Archaeological Knowledge, 2001).

For a sophisticated and subtly nuanced analysis of the birth of Greek archaeology in tandem with the fledgling nation, see Yannis Hamilakis, *The Nation and Its Ruins: Antiquity, Archaeology and National Imagination in Greece* (New York: Oxford University Press, 2007, 2009).

19. See Ronald T. Ridley, "To Protect the Monuments: The Papal Antiquarian (1534–1870)," *Xenia Antiqua* I (1992): 117–54.

For a fascinating and roughly contemporary account, contrasting the Roman and Athenian situations, see Antoine Chrysostome Quatremère de Quincy, *Letters to Miranda and Canova on the Abduction of Antiquities from Rome and Athens*, Chris Miller and David Gilks, trans. (Los Angeles: Getty Research Institute, 2012). Quatremère's *Letters to Miranda* were published in 1796, in opposition to the French looting of the Vatican, and his *Letters to Canova* were published in 1816, expressing deep appreciation for the Elgin Marbles newly displayed in London. Quatremère himself published the two sets of letters together in 1836.

As we will see, Quatremère was one of the most important classicists and art historians of his generation, and a significant influence on Schelling. See my study, *Classics at the Dawn of the Museum Era: The Life and Times of Antoine Chrysostome Quatremère de Quincy (1755–1849)*. Here is a representative observation about the aesthetic state of things in 1796:

> [we enjoy] the general resurrection of the tribe of antique statues, whose population increases with every passing day. This world unseen by Leonardo da Vinci, Michelangelo, and Raphael, or which they saw only in its earliest infancy, will certainly exert an extraordinary influence on the study of the arts and on the genius of Europe. (*Letters to Miranda and Canova*, 99)

See as well Frederic Will, "Two Critics of the Elgin Marbles: William Hazlitt and Quatremère de Quincy," *The Journal of Aesthetics and Art Criticism* 14, no. 4 (1956): 462–74.

20. The acquisition and transport of the Elgin Marbles has of course generated an enormous bibliography in the past two centuries. I have found the following works especially helpful: Mary Beard, *The Parthenon* (Cambridge, MA: Harvard University Press, 2003), 155–81; Barbara J. Black, *On Exhibit: Victorians and Their Museums* (Charlottesville, VA: University of Virginia Press, 2000); John Boardman, "The Elgin Marbles: Matters of Fact and Opinion," *International Journal of Cultural Property* 9, no. 2 (2000): 233–62; Charles P. Bracken, *Antiquities Acquired*, 28–41; Russell Chamberlin, *Loot! The Heritage of Plunder*, 13–38; William St. Clair, *Lord Elgin and the Marbles* (New York: Oxford University Press, 1967); Eric Gidal, *Poetic Exhibitions: Romantic Aesthetics and the Pleasures of the British Museum* (Lewisburg, PA: Bucknell University Press, 2001); Jeanette Greenfield, *The Return of Cultural Treasures* (New York: Cambridge University Press, 1989), 47–105; Christopher Hitchens, *The Elgin Marbles: Should They Be Returned to Greece?* (London: Verso, 1997); Jacob Rothenberg, *Descensus ad Terram: The Acquisition and Reception of the Elgin Marbles* (New York: Garland Publishing, Inc., 1977); David Rudenstine, "The Legality of Elgin's Taking," *International Journal of Cultural Property* 8, no. 1 (1999): 356–76; Arthur H. Smith, "Lord Elgin and His Collection," *Journal of Hellenic Studies* 36 (1916): 163–372; Hugh Tresgakis, *Beyond the Grand Tour*, 44–50; and Theodore Vrettos's two books, *A Shadow of Magnitude: The Acquisition of the Elgin Marbles* (New York: G. P. Putnam's Sons, 1974), and *The Elgin Affair: The Abduction of Antiquity's Greatest Treasures and the Passions It Aroused* (New York: Little, Brown and Company, 1997); and Eleana Yalouri, *The Acropolis: Global Fame, Local Claim* (Oxford: Burg Publications, 2001).
21. See Antoine Chrysostome Quatremère de Quincy, *Sur la Statue Antique de Vénus Découverte dans l'Ile de Milo en 1820, Transporte a Paris par M. Le Marquis de Rivière,*

Ambassadeur de France a la Cour Ottomane (Paris: Chez Debure Frères, Libraires du Roi; de l'Imprimerie de Firmin Didot, Imprimeur du Roi, 1821). See also Bracken, *Antiquities Acquired*, 159–71.

22. Sebastian Prignitz, *Der Pergamonaltar und die pergamenische Gelehrtenschule* (Berlin: Arenhövel, 2008).
23. And coincided with the publication of a museum guide by the Museum's (and the entire Königsplatz's) chief architect: Leo von Klenze, with Ludwig Schorn, *Beschreibung der Glyptothek Sr. Majestät des Königs Ludwig von Bayern* (München: J. G. Cotta'schen, 1830).
24. For more on this swim, see Charles Sprawson, *Haunts of the Black Masseur: The Swimmer as Hero* (New York: Pantheon, 1994), 122–32.

    For more on Byron's time in Greece, see Stephen Minta, *On a Voiceless Shore: Byron in Greece* (New York: Henry Holt and Company, 1998), and Ruprecht, *Was Greek Thought Religious? On the Use and Abuse of Hellenism, From Rome to Romanticism* (New York: Palgrave Macmillan, 2002), 111–24.
25. Hobhouse published his own reminiscence of the two men's travels together as *A Journey Through Albania, and the Provinces of Turkey in Europe and Asia, to Constantinople, During the Years 1809 and 1810*, 2nd Edition in 2 volumes (London: James Cawthorn, 1813). Hobhouse later published two more Byron-inspired books: *Historical Illustrations to the Fourth Canto of Childe Harold* (1818); and *Italy: Remarks Made in Several Visits, from the Years 1816–1854* (London: John Murray, 1859), 2 volumes.

    Selections from Hobhouse's important first book may be found in Tilar J. Mazzeo, ed., *Travels, Explorations and Empires, Writings from the Era of Imperial Expansion, 1770–1835*, Volume 4: The Middle East, 183–223.
26. See *The Works of Lord Byron*, 59.
27. Byron would repeat this same domestic intrigue in Italy some years later, with yet another Teresa, the daughter of Amalia Gamba-Machirelli, in 1818 and thereafter, with lingering effects that were far more serious.

    See Maria Borghese, *L'Appassionata di Byron: con la lettere inedite fra Lord Byron e la Contessa Guiccioli* (Garzanti, 1949).
28. Some marvelous discussion, with images of the hostelry and the monument, may be found in Nicolas Revett and James Stuart, *The Antiquities of Athens, Measured and Delineated*, 3 volumes (London: Society of the Dilettanti, 1762, Arno Reprint, 1980), I: 26–35.
29. The text of this *firman* is quoted in full by Eugeneia Kefallineou, in *Byron and the Antiquities of the Acropolis of Athens* (Athens: The Archaeological Society at Athens Library, 1999), No. 192: 10–13, and more briefly by Tresgakis in *Beyond the Grand Tour*, 45.
30. A flattering portrait of Mary Nisbet, accomplished in part by placing her Lord Elgin in such unflattering light, may be found in an interesting (if overly ambitious) historical novel by Karen Essex, *Stealing Athena* (New York: Random House, 2008).
31. This legacy of modern nationalism is the issue upon which hangs my tale. The story of the acquisition of the Aegina Marbles that I am pursuing here very clearly illustrates the role that the imperialism of the new gunpowder nations, working in tandem with the neoclassicism and the sense of aristocratic privilege among those nations' social elites, played in the formation of a new discipline (archaeology) and a new institution (public art museums) in the first decades of the nineteenth century. These days, public consciousness has

been significantly advanced concerning the intimate connection between such cultural imperialism and an emerging museum culture in Europe.

Debates over the "repatriation" of unprovenanced or otherwise ill-gotten antiquities are one important result of this consciousness-raising, but they have become rather strident and highly politicized in their own right, with sometimes surprising results, depending on the power and influence of the *patria* making the demands. Italy has been most successful in demanding the return of "national" treasures; Greece less so. The recent decision by the Getty Museum to return some 160 objects to the Italian government was only the most spectacular example of the problem and one partial remedy. For more on the Getty's singular problems, see James Felch and Ralph Frammolino, *Chasing Aphrodite: The Hunt for Looted Antiquities at the World's Richest Museum* (New York: Houghton Mifflin Harcourt Publishing Company, 2011).

James Cuno, formerly president of the Chicago Art Institute and now CEO of the Getty Foundation, has been the most vociferous, and perhaps the most eloquent, critic of the new regime of repatriation that has emerged since UNESCO's 1970 convention on controlling the international trade in antiquities. Cuno observes that today most archaeologists seem to be critics of most museums' acquisitions policies, believing these overly acquisitive institutions have been tainted by the history of nineteenth-century imperialism and nationalism. Cuno's retort, defending his conception of what he calls the "encyclopedic museum," provocatively reminds the archaeological community that it is not that simple, and that archaeology is every bit as implicated in this colonial project as public museums have been. He rejects the simplifying morality tale in which archaeologists are critics of criminality and imperialism, since what he calls "nationalist retentionist cultural property laws" are themselves products of the very imperious nationalism they claim to oppose. See Cuno's books, *Who Owns Antiquity? Museums and the Battle over our Ancient Heritage* (Princeton, NJ: Princeton University Press, 2008), and *Museums Matter: In Praise of the Encyclopedic Museum* (Chicago: University of Chicago Press, 2011). Cuno has also edited two important volumes devoted to this topic: *Whose Muse? Art Museums and the Public Trust* (Princeton, NJ: Princeton University Press, 2004) and *Whose Culture? The Promise of Museums and the Debate over Antiquities* (Princeton, NJ: Princeton University Press, 2009).

Two excellent resources for the new norms regarding repatriation and the protection of cultural property are: Janet Marstine, ed., *The Routledge Companion to Museum Ethics: Redefining Ethics for the Twenty-First Century Museum* (New York: Routledge, 2011); and Lyndel V. Prott, ed., *Witnesses to History: A Compendium of Documents and Writings on the Return of Cultural Objects* (Paris: UNESCO, 2009).

Much depends on perspective, naturally. While the Vatican treasures were restored to Rome from Paris, and while calls for the return of the Elgin Marbles from London to Athens are perennial, no one is calling for the return of the Glyptothek's masterworks to the island of Aegina. Given the strange twists and turns I outline here, twists and turns that enabled their arrival in Munich in the first place, this can seem quite strange.

32. Ironically, Quatremère de Quincy made this point forcefully, concluding his 1816 *Letters from London to Antonio Canova* with effusive praise of the British Museum:

> In these few words—and in this reminder concerning the many treasures in the British Museum of which I have said nothing—my only purpose is to let you

> know what I think and indeed what anyone is bound to think of this collection. So let me tell you that, including as it does the greatest number of original pieces from the greatest period of Greece, it must henceforth be considered the foremost of all collections: the one to which science and history will go in search of classical models and of the most authentic materials for the salutary criticism of taste.
> (*Letters to Miranda and Canova*, 166)

33. Upping the art historical ante when he published his *Letter to Miranda* and *Letters to Canova* together in 1836, Quatremère de Quincy made this point explicit: "It has been abundantly shown that these sculptures, lost to the rest of the world, were in danger of complete destruction amid the ever-worsening decay of the Acropolis in Athens." (*Letters to Miranda and Canova*, 175).
34. See Meryl Secrest, *Duveen: A Life in Art* (New York: Alfred A. Knopf, 2004), 374–80.
35. See *The Works of Lord Byron*, 625–840, esp. 851, 855, and 859.
36. *The Works of Lord Byron*, 138–41.
37. This is the conclusion to Byron's "Ode to Napoleon Buonaparte," in *The Works of Lord Byron*, 74.
38. See Bracken, *Antiquities Acquired*, 45; Chamberlin, *Loot! The Heritage of Plunder*, 31; and Tresgakis, *Beyond the Grand Tour*, 105.
39. Cockerell appears in Bracken, *Antiquities Acquired*, 106–36; Chamberlin, *Loot! The Heritage of Plunder*, 28–37; Eisner, *Travelers to an Antique Land*, 109–110; and Tresgakis, *Beyond the Grand Tour*, 106–39.

    See also David Watkin, *The Life and Work of C. R. Cockerell* (London: A. Zwemmer Ltd., 1974), esp. 3–37.
40. Samuel Pepys Cockerell, ed., *Travels in Southern Europe and the Levant, 1810–1817* (London: Longmans, Green and Co., 1903), 2:

> On the morning following my arrival, viz. April 16th, I embarked on board the vessel which was to carry me. She was a lugger-rigged despatch boat, hired by Government, named the *Black Joke*. She was very old, as she had been in the battle of Camperdown in 1797, but I was charmed with her neatness and tidiness. We had ten guns, thirty-five men, one sheep, two pigs and fowls. The commander's name was Mr. Cannady, and we were taking 2000 young midshipmen to join the squadron off Cadiz.

41. The best sources for information about Charles Cockerell and his extended Tour are his own writings, all published much later: *The Temples of Jupiter Panhellenius at Aegina and of Apollo Epicurius at Bassae near Phigalia in Arcadia* (London: John Weale, 1860), and the posthumous *Travels in Southern Europe and the Levant, 1810–1817*, edited by his son.
42. The impact of Cockerell's Italian journey may perhaps be most clearly seen in this enthused expression from his later years, reflecting on the architectural genius of Michelangelo, which had moved him so years before:

> His religious, his moral, and his intellectual character have elevated the class [of art] to a dignity never before attained; he it was who raised the Beautiful

and the Sublime almost into a worship—the practice of them into a moral discipline, and success in them into an intellectual stimulant as eloquent and impressive as the accents of the orator or the poet.

[Charles R. Cockerell and John S. Harford, *Illustrations, Architectural and Pictorial, on the Genius of Michael Angelo Buonarroti* (London: Colnaghi and Co., and Longman and Co., 1857), 12.]

Visual art raised "*almost into a worship*"—this is precisely the romantic ideal Cockerell and his friends presumably first encountered at the Temple of Aphaia on Aegina.

43. Samuel Pepys Cockerell's note on his father's appearance is quite striking:

A man's career is immensely influenced by his personal appearance. My father's passport . . . gives, as was usual in those days, for identification, a description under several printed heads, as "stature, face, eyes, &c.," of the bearer. It is a large form printed in Italian. . . . At bottom is the description "*Stature, mezzana; viso, triangolare; occhi, negri e splendenti; naso, fine; bocca di vermiglia; fronto, di marmo.*" ("Height, medium; face, triangular; eyes, black and shining; nose, delicate; mouth of vermilion; forehead, of marble.") and below "*in somma Apollo lui stesso.*" ("In short, Apollo himself.") This . . . indicates that the bearer possessed a fortunate exterior, which had probably something to do with the good reception he generally met within society throughout his life.

(Samuel Pepys Cockerell, ed., *Travels in Southern Europe and the Levant, 1810–1817*, 38–39n)

44. Cockerell's son mentions three Bavarians [Haller, Linkh and Stackelberg], two Danes [Peter Oluf Bronstedt (1780–1842) and G. H. C. Koes (1782–1811)], and three British companions [Lord Byron, Sandford Graham (1788–1852), and someone named Haygarth, though curiously not John Foster], as well as the omnipresent Athenian noteworthies, the French consul, Fauvel, and Elgin's Neapolitan assistant, Lusieri.

See *Travels in Southern Europe and the Levant, 1810–1817*, 44–46.

45. See the entry for "John Foster" in *The Dictionary of National Biography* (London: Oxford University Press, 1885–1901) VII: 499.

46. The two best sources for nineteenth-century, German-speaking figures relevant to this study are: Frederick Noack, ed., *Das Deutschtum in Rom: Seit dem Ausgang des Mittelalters* [1927] (Darmstadt: Scientia Verlag Aalen, 1974), in two volumes, I: 233 (on Hallerstein), I: 361 (on Linkh), I: 370 (on Ludwig I), I: 569 (on Stackelberg), and I: 624–25 on Wagner), with cross references; and Hans Vollmer, ed., *Allgemeins Lexikon der Bildenden Künstler von der Antike bis zur Gegenwart* (Leipzig: Verlag von E. A. Seemann, 1929).

Bracken, *Antiquities Acquired*, also provides a superb biographical and bibliographical appendix at 185–204, and Anne Bordeleau, *Charles Robert Cockerell, Architect in Time: Reflections Around Anachronistic Drawing* (Surrey: Ashgate, 2014), 51–54, has real interest. Haller's correspondence with Charles Cockerell is housed in the Department of Antiquities in the British Museum. His diaries and other papers were published in several Leipzig publications, such as *Grenzboten* (1875, 1876), *Kunstkritik* (1875), and *Zeitschrift für Bildenden Kunst* (1877, 1883).

The best resources for Haller's career are Hansgeorg Bankel, *Carl Haller von Hallerstein in Griechenland, 1810–1817* (Berlin: Walter de Gruyter, 1986), and Hans Haller von Hallerstein, . . . *und die Erde gebar ein Lächeln: Der erste deutsche Archäologe in Griechenland, Carl Haller von Hallerstein, 1774–1817* (München: Süddeutscher Verlag, 1983), esp. 80–105, on the Aeginetan discoveries.

47. Linkh's journals from this period were edited by P. Goessler as "Jakob Linckh, ein Philhellene," in the *Münchener Jahrbuch der bildenden Kunst, Neue Folge* (1937/1938) Band XII: 149ff.

48. Among Stackelberg's own works, of special note are: *Der Apollotempel zu Bassae in Arcadien und die daselbst ausgegrabenen Bildwerke* (Frankfurt am Mein: Gedruckt mit Andreäischen Schriften, 1826); *Costumes et usages des peuples de la Grèce moderne* (Paris, 1825, no pub.), reprinted as *Trachten und Gebräuche der Neugriechen* (Berlin: Verlag von G. Reimer, 1831); *La Grèce: vues pittoresques et topographiques* (Paris: I. F. D'Ostervald, 1834); and *Der Gräber der Hellenen* (Berlin: Verlag von G. Reimer, 1837).

Of additional interest and value are: Carl Erich Gleye, ed., "Unveröffentliche Briefe des archäologen Otto Magnus von Stackelberg," in *Baltische Monatsschrift* (1913), Heft 6: 391–403, and *Aus Stackelbergs Nachlass* (Druck und Verlag Franzen und Grosse, 1859).

49. Hans Haller von Hallerstein, . . . *und die Erde gebar ein Lächeln*, 11–54.

50. For evidence of the strong importance of architecture in such Tours among men such as these, see Quatremère de Quincy's late works, *Histoire de la vie et des ouvrages des plus célèbres architects du XIe jusqu'a la fin du XVIIIe*, 2 volumes (Paris: Jules Renouard, Libraire, rue de Tournon, no. 6, 1830), and *Dictionnaire historique d'architecture* (Paris: Librairie D'Adrien le Clere et C.ie, Quai des Augustins, no. 35, 1832).

Quatremère famously referred to architecture as "an ocular music" (*une musique oculaire*) rather early in his career; see Jacques Daniel Guigniaut, "*Notice Historique sur la vie et les travaux de M. Quatremère de Quincy*," in *Memoires de L'Institut National de France, Academie des Inscriptions et Belles-Lettres*, Volume 25 (Paris: Imprimerie Nationale, 1877), Part One, 372, as well as Quatremère's *De l'état de l'architecture Égyptiennes, considérée dans son origine, ses principes et son goût, et comparée sous les mêmes rapports à l'Architecture Greque.* Dissertation qui a remporté, en 1785, le Prix par l'Académie des Inscriptions et Belles-Lettres (Paris: Chez Barrois l'aîné e Fils, Libraires, rue de Savoye, no. 23, An XI—1803), 215.

51. Pausanias, *Guide to Greece* II.29.6-30.5 (the other island is, curiously, Sardinia). Pausanias only mentions the highlights from the island of Aegina: the shallow waters that help protect the island from invasion; the so-called Secret Harbor; the major sanctuaries dedicated to Apollo, Artemis, Hekate, and Orpheus. He also discusses the local mythic hero, Aiakos, as the first man to supplicate Zeus as Panhellenic (τῷ Πανελληνίῳ Διὶ), in order to lift a curse from the island (*Guide to Greece* II.29.8).

Pausanias's account of the sanctuary dedicated to Panhellenic Zeus is somewhat confusing; I quote it in the frontispiece to this book. He informs us that "on Aegina, as you approach the mountain of Panhellenic Zeus (πρὸς τὸ ὄρος Πανελληνίου Διὸς), there is a Temple of Aphaia (Αφαίας ἱερόν)" (*Guide to Greece* II.30.3), then provides an elaborate account of her mythic origins on Crete. Pausanias seems to refer to the "Panhellenion" as if it is a place (unless he intends a reference to the mountain itself), which also contained "a Temple of Zeus (τοῦ Διὸς τὸ ἱερόν), but nothing else worth mentioning" (*Guide to*

Greece II.30.4). It is presumably this confusion between the two edifices that led our party of amateur archaeologists to identify this as the Temple of Panhellenic Zeus, rather than the Temple of Aphaia. Subsequent evidence from inscriptions recovered during later German excavation has shown the temple always to have been Aphaia's, and never Zeus's.

52. Pausanias describes the site as follows:

> Phigalia is surrounded by mountains, on the left by the mountain called Cotilius, while on the right is another, Mount Elaïus, which acts as a shield to the city. On the mountain is a place called Bassae, and the Temple of Apollo the Helper (ὁ ναὸς τοῦ Απόλλονος τοῦ Επικουρίου), made all of stone, including the roof. Of all the temples in the Peloponnese, this one may be placed next to the one in Tegea, for the beauty of its stone and the harmony of its design. Apollo received his name from the help he gave in time of plague, just as the Athenians gave him the name of Averter of Evil (Αλεξίκακος) for turning the plague away from them. . . . Ictinus, the architect of the Temple at Phigalia, was a contemporary of Perikles, and built for the Athenians what is called the Parthenon. (*Guide to Greece* VII.41.7V9)

While Cockerell was with his friends when they discovered the site, he missed the actual excavation of it; he was traveling in Sicily at the time and his place was taken by Bronsted and Stackelberg.

See Hans Haller von Hallerstein, . . . *und die Erde gebar ein Lächeln*, 179–201.

53. See Bracken, *Antiquities Acquired*, 139–58.

54. Charles R. Cockerell, *The Temples of Jupiter Panhellenius at Aegina and of Apollo Epicurius at Bassae* (London: John Weale, 1860).

55. The first reports of the discovery appear to have been published in the modern Greek journal *Hermes Logios*, but most relevant to my purposes, in the German journal *Allgemeine Zeitung*, no. 339 (December 5, 1811):

> *Weit unbezweifelter ist der Fund, der von deutschen Reisenden neuerlich auf der Insel Aegina unter den Trimmern des Tempels des Jupiter Panhellenios gemacht wurde. Man fand daselbst 18 Marmorstatuen, etwas unter menschlicher Größe, vom ältesten griechischen Styl, die auf den* Tympanis *oder Frontons gestanden hatten. Nur durch den Fall beschädigt, konnten sie leicht ergänzt werden. Außerdem grub man noch mehrere interessante Bruckstücke, und nach Wegräumung des e[]enhohen Schuttes selbst das nicht ganz erhaltene Paviment des Tempels aus. Der fränzosischer Konsul in Athen, Fauvel, eilte sogleich, nach erhaltener Nachricht bedeutend durch neue Entdeckungen und Ausgrabungen. Er hat viele Aschenfräge und in allen den Obolus gefunden. Auf einer* Vase in *Terra cotta, die sich in seiner Sammlung befindet, ist de Fabel von Charons Nachen abgebildet. Die oben erwähnten Statuen stellen alle Heldenfiguren aus dem trojanischen Kriege vor, Hector, Ulysses, Helena u.s.w.*

> Less in doubt is the recent discovery under the ruins of the Temple of Panhellenic Jupiter made by German travelers on the island of Aegina. Eighteen

marble statues were found there, slightly under life-size and in the oldest Greek style, which stood on the *tympanis* or pediment. Only damaged by the fall, they may be easily restored. In addition they have excavated more interesting fragments after clearing debris from the pavement which has not yet been completely uncovered. The French consul in Athens, Fauvel, hastened to the site after receiving reports of these new discoveries and excavations. He found a great deal of burnt wood as well as a cache of coins. A terra-cotta vase in his collection depicts the myth of Charon's Ferryboat. The statues mentioned above depict all the heroic figures from the Trojan War: Hector, Ulysses, Helen, etc.

56. The temple was excavated once again briefly by Greek archaeologists, under the direction of B. Staïs in 1894, and then more systematically under the auspices of the German School in Athens and by the following preeminent archaeologists: Adolf Furtwängler (1853–1907), who led the work from 1900 until his death in 1907 (he died of dysentery contracted at the site); Dieter Ohly (1911–1979), who returned in 1966 and worked there until his death in 1979; and Ernst Ludwig Schwandner and Martha Ohly, who supervised the remaining German work at the Aphaia Temple through 1989. In addition to important scholarly monographs by Furtwängler and Ohly, nearly annual publications of excavation results were published by the *Archäologischer Anzeiger* from 1970 until 1998.
57. Quatremère also wrote a book dedicated to the memory of his friend, *Canova et ses ouvrages, ou Mémoires Historiques sur la vie et les travaux de ce célèbre artiste* (Paris: Adrien le Clere et C.ie Imprimeurs-Libraires, 1834).
58. A nice summary of this Paris mission, and of Canova's role in it, may be found in Carlo Pietrangeli, *The Vatican Museums: Five Centuries of History*, translated by Peter Spring (Edizione Quasar, Biblioteca Apostolica Vaticana, 1993), 147–72. (Pietrangeli also notes that plaster casts of the Aegina Marbles were donated to the Vatican Museum in 1828, at page 170.)

    Abundant materials relating to this mission may be found in the Biblioteca Apostolica Vaticana (BAV), *Archivio della Biblioteca*, volume 102 , as well as in the *Archivio di Stato di Roma* (ASR), Camerale II, *Antichità e Belli Arte*, Busti 6, 7, 9, and especially 10.

    For more on Canova's Paris mission, see Christopher M. S. Johns, *Antonio Canova and the Politics of Patronage in Revolutionary and Napoleonic Europe* (Berkeley, CA: The University of California Press, 1998), 88–122, and especially 171–94.
59. Quatremère de Quincy, *Lettres écrites de Londres à Rome, et adressées à M. Canova; sur les Marbres d'Elgin, ou les Sculptures du Temple de Minerve à Athènes* (Rome, 1818); translated in *Letters to Miranda and Canova*, 126–67.
60. For my purposes two sources proved to be particularly useful: *Thorvaldsen in Rom: Aus Wagners Papieren* (Würzburg: 20ten Programm zur Stiftungsfeier des von Wagner'schen Kunstinstituts, 1887), and P. Kraeland and M. Nykjer, eds., *Thorvaldsen: L'ambiente l'influsso il mito* (Roma: L'Erma di Brentschneider, 1996).

    Finally, see: *Thorvaldsen's Ancient Sculptures: A Catalogue of the Ancient Sculptures in the Collection of Bertel Thorvaldsen, Thorvaldsens Museum* (Copenhagen: Thorvaldsens Museum, 2003), esp. 13–14; Bjarne Jørnaes, *Bertel Thorvaldsen: la vita e l'opera dello scultore* (Roma: Edizione De Luca, 1993), 81–113, esp. 92–96; and Raimund Wünsche,

"*Come nessuno, dai tempi fiorenti dell'Ellada,' Thorvaldsen, Ludovico di Bavaria ed en il restauro dei marmi di Egina,*" in E. di Majo, B. Jørnaes, S. Sussino, eds., *Bertel Thorvaldsen: 1770–1841, scultore danese a Roma* (Roma: 1989), 80–96.

61. The best source of information for this process is Arthur H. Smith, "Lord Elgin and His Collection," *Journal of Hellenic Studies* 36, no. 2 (1916): 163–372, esp. 340–45.
62. Smith, "Lord Elgin and His Collection," 332, and see note 31.
63. Carl Haller von Hallerstein apparently wrote to Ludwig directly about the collection in August of 1811. Though this letter is lost, see Richard Bergau, "Briefe an und von Carl Haller v. Hallerstein," *Zeitschrift für bildende Kunst* 12 (1877): 190–96, esp. 192, for a reference. Haller wrote to Ludwig again on December 23, 1811, including sketches of the Aegina Marbles this time (for which see Bergau, 193ff). A letter from either Haller or Linkh (dated June 12, 1811) describing the Aegina discovery was published in the *Morgenblatt für gebildete Stände* no. 244 (October 10, 1811): 975–76.

    See Hans Haller von Hallerstein, . . . *und die Erde gebar ein Lächeln*, 157–74 and 231–39.
64. Cockerell, *Travels in Southern Europe and the Levant*, 51–56.
65. Cockerell recalled them to be "no less than sixteen" in *The Temples of Jupiter Panhellenius at Aegina and of Apollo Epicurius at Bassae near Phigalia in Arcadia* (London: John Weale, 1860), 51–52. I will comment further on Wagner's estimate as to the final number in the body of his text.
66. Ibid., 65–67, and Hans Haller von Hallerstein, . . . *und die Erde gebar ein Lächeln*, 106–15.
67. For a mournful account of the Venetian Republic's decision to surrender without a shot being fired, see Mary McCarthy, *Venice Observed* (New York: Harcourt Brace Jovanovich, 1956, 1963), 5–6, and her evocation of the "finale" at 136–58.
68. Zante had been a Venetian holding (the name is Italian) until Napoleon dismantled what was left of the Venetian empire in 1797. The island passed to French control for two years, but was lost to the British in 1799. The French returned for two years in 1807–09, but then the British returned and organized the seven Ionian islands into a loose confederacy that lasted until Great Britain ceded the islands to Greece in 1864. The island of Zante/Zakynthos would subsequently be occupied by the French (1916–17), the Italians (1941–43), and the Germans (1943–44).
69. The *Academia dei Vigilanti Zacinthi* was established by the Venetians in 1625. It was reorganized as the Ionian Academy (literally called "The Academy of Free Ionian Islands," in Greek) in 1808, and ironically enough, it quickly became a clearinghouse for looted Greek antiquities. While ambassador to the Porte, Lord Elgin had been directly involved in discussions about the future reorganization of the Ionian islands. He arranged for some of the Parthenon metopes to be stored there, as Cockerell later made similar arrangements for his finds from Aegina and Bassae.

    Most of the archives of Zante were lost in a massive earthquake and fire in 1953. I was able to locate one vague reference to "the architect and archaeologist Cockerell," who was listed as a member of the faculty of the academy in 1811. I found this reference during a brief research visit to the island in the summer of 1995.
70. That point was nonnegotiable according to Cockerell, *Travels in Southern Europe and the Levant, 1810–1817*, 58, and is also the very first thing Schelling notes in the editor's preface.

71. While I have located a description of the Aeginetan collection in the *Allgemeine Zeitung* (dated December 5, 1811), I have not yet located any of the advertisements for the auction itself in the respective English or German literary journals, the French *Moniteur de Paris*, or the Italian *Gazetta de Rome*, for which see David Watkin, *The Life and Work of C. R. Cockerell*, 10–11, and Hans Haller von Hallerstein, *. . . und die Erde gebar ein Lächeln*, 112.

    That said, this was likely not how Ludwig learned about the collection or the auction; both Haller and Linkh wrote to their prince about their dramatic discoveries and the possibility of their purchase shortly after leaving Athens, just as Cockerell was writing to the influential and interested in London. As we saw in a previous note, Haller wrote directly to Ludwig in August of 1811 about the discovery. Either Haller or Linkh published another description in the *Morgenblatt für gebildete Stände* no. 244 (October 10, 1811): 975–76. And Haller wrote Ludwig another letter, with sketches of the Aegina treasures included on December 23, 1811. See Richard Bergau, "Briefe an und von Carl Haller von Hallerstein," *Zeitschrift für bildende Kunst* 12 (1877): 190–96, esp. 192–93, as well as P. Winfrid Frhr. von Pölnitz, O.S.B., *Ludwig I. von Bayern und Johann Martin von Wagner: Ein Beitrag zur Geschichte der Kunstsbestrebungen König Ludwigs I.* (München: Verlag der Kommission, 1929): Schriftenreihe zur bayerischen Landesgeschichte, Band 2, 61–64. Pölnitz (at page 67) also refers to an earlier description in the *Allgemeine Zeitung* dated June 20, 1811, which I have been unable to track down.

72. See: Pölnitz, *Ludwig I. von Bayern und Johann Martin von Wagner: Ein Beitrag zur Geschichte der Kunstsbestrebungen König Ludwigs I.*, 70–80, 215–30; Hans Haller von Hallerstein, *. . . und die Erde gebar ein Lächeln*, 109–112, and Raimond Wünsche, *Kampfe um Troja: 200 Jahre Ägineten in München, Ausstellungskatalog* (München: Kunstverlag Josef Fink, 2011), 32.

73. Remarkably, this same warship would be used to protect the fleet of nine or ten transport vessels sailing under various flags, including the ship used to remove the Aegina Marbles from Malta to Naples under Wagner's personal direction, in July of 1815. Wagner notes the irony of this in his letter to Ludwig written on August 10, 1815, from Naples. The fleet was bound for Genoa, but Wagner's ship lost sight of the British warship, and the entire fleet, off the coast of Calabria, and nearly sank in a terrible storm off the coast of Ischia; they eventually made landfall in Naples where, after a fourteen-day quarantine, they continued on to Rome.

    See Hubert Glaser, u.a., *König Ludwig I. von Bayern und Martin von Wagner. Der Briefwechsel. Band I: 1809–1815*, Bearbeitet von Mathias Hofter and Johanna Selch, Quellen zur Neueren Geschichte Bayerns, No. 5 (München: Kommission für Bayerishe Landesgeschichte bei der Bayerische Akademie der Wissenschaften, 2015), Dok. 225.

    I am especially indebted to Mathias Hofter, who made copies of the relevant letters from Wagner available to me prior to this important volume's publication.

74. See Cockerell, *Travels in Southern Europe and the Levant, 1810–1817*, 102–104, as well as Hans Haller von Hallerstein, *. . . und die Erde gebar ein Lächeln*, 146–57, for Haller's role in arranging the packing and shipment on Zante.

75. Cockerell, *Travels in Southern Europe and the Levant, 1810–1817*, 104–126.

76. A collection of Wagner's letters, with discussion of his Greek trip in particular, may be found in the *Bayerischen Staatsbibliothek* in Munich, as well as in his personal archive

located in the *Würzburg Institut des Kunsts*, in association with the Martin Wagner Museum at the University of Würzburg. The Wagner Museum also curated a show in 1989 entitled *Auf nach Hellas heil'ger Erde: Johann Martin von Wagners Reise nach Griechenland*. The catalogue boasts some interesting sketches Wagner made in the course of his journey. I am indebted to the late Diskin Clay of Duke University for providing me with a copy of this catalogue.

I was most illuminated by the edition of Wagner's diary from the trip, edited by Reinhard Herbig in *Johann Martin von Wagners Beschreibung seiner Reise nach Griechenland (1812–1813)* (Stuttgart: Verlag von W. Kohlhammer, 1938). My brief description of his trip comes primarily from this essay, although the faculty at the University of Würzburg were also extremely helpful in enabling me to consult Wagner's personal papers, and his Greek *Reisebuch*, in March and June of 2015 (see appendix 2). I am especially indebted to Professors Damian Dombrowski, Tilmann Kossatz, and Markus Maier of the University of Würzburg, as well as to Dr. Astrid Fendt of the Munich Glyptothek, for their kindness and generous assistance with my research.

Further helpful biographical materials may be found in Guntram Beckel, "Johann Martin von Wagner," *Fränkische Lebensbilder* 8 (1978): 228–56.

77. Tellingly, Schelling had accepted a call to Würzburg in late 1803, not long after he was married to his first wife, Caroline. That detail, and the proximity to the neoclassical artist Johann Martin Wagner, will be important shortly.

See Jason M. Wirth, ed., *Schelling Now: Contemporary Readings* (Indianapolis, IN: University of Indiana Press, 2005), 3–4.

78. For more on this important meeting and the long relationship it sealed, see Ludwig Hüttl, *Ludwig I: König und Bauherr* (München/Zürich: Serie Piper, 1986), Serie Piper, esp. 50–55, as well as Pölnitz, *Ludwig I. von Bayern und Johann Martin von Wagner: Ein Beitrag zur Geschichte der Kunstsbestrebungen König Ludwigs I.*, 25–31.

79. As noted above, the first volume of their correspondence (dating 1809–1815) has just been published: Hubert Glaser, u.a., *König Ludwig I. von Bayern und Martin von Wagner. Der Briefwechsel. Band I: 1809–1815*. I reiterate my thanks to Mathias Hofter for enabling me to see some of this correspondence, before its publication, in the summer of 2015.

See also Adrian von Buttlar and Bénédicte Savoy, "Glyptothek and Alte Pinakothek, Munich: Museums as Public Monuments," in Carole Paul, ed., *The First Modern Museums of Art: The Birth of an Institution in 18th- and Early-19th-Century Europe* (Los Angeles: The J. Paul Getty Museum, 2012), 305–26, esp. 311–12.

80. See Stefan Morét, "Wagner als Künstler und Kunstagent in Rom" (23–32), Christina Specht, "Die Antikenzeichnungen Martin von Wagners–am Beispiel siner Zeichnungen der Reliefplatten vom Cellafries des Apollontempels in Bassai" (39–52), and Irma Wehgartner, "Vasenzeichnungen aus dem Nachlass Martin von Wagners" (53–62), all found in Stefan Kummer and Ulrich Sinn, eds., *Johann Martin von Wagner: Künstler, Sammler und Mäzen* (Würzburg: Ergon Verlag, 2007), as well as Konrad Koppe, *Martin von Wagner Museum der Universität Würzburg: Gemäldekatalog* (Würzburg, 1986).

81. Mathias Hofter informs me that Ludwig first contacted Christian Daniel Rauch (1777–1857) and Johann Georg von Dillis (1759–1841) about making the trip on his behalf. The two men were unwilling or unable to do so, and Rauch (who then also happened to be in Rome) proposed Wagner as an alternative; it was he who first contacted Wagner on

Ludwig's behalf. See Hüttl, *Ludwig I: König und Bauherr*, 52–53, and Pölnitz, *Ludwig I. von Bayern und Johann Martin von Wagner: Ein Beitrag zur Geschichte der Kunstsbestrebungen König Ludwigs I.*, 68.

The Rauch letters are unpublished, but see Wünsche, *Kampf um Troja*, 37–48, esp. 38–39, and Friedrich Noack, *Das Deutschtum in Rom*, II: 470–71.

Ludwig also inquired about Wagner's requirements for cash, notes of credit, and passports for British and French territories, and recommended that he hire an assistant to accompany him to Greece (as Wagner did). This material corresponds to Letters 105 and 106 in the Martin von Wagner Museum's *Wagnerarchiv*.

See Hubert Glaser, u.a., *König Ludwig I. von Bayern und Martin von Wagner. Der Briefwechsel. Band I: 1809–1815*, Dok. 148.

82. The Historical Archive on the island of Corfu (Ιστορικο Αρχειο Κερκυρας) holds a great many Venetian, French, and British materials relating to the complicated task of Mediterranean port control. Most port business on Corfu continued to be conducted in Italian even after the French overthrow of the Venetian regime, which no doubt assisted Wagner greatly in his attempts to secure passage to Zante/Zakynthos in 1812.

The description of the ship, one of four that was reported to have arrived at Corfu on October 2, 1812 (two from Otranto, one from Barletta, and one from Venice), may be found in Υγειονομειο II, φ. 142, Libro 115, ff92r-v. The first of the ships listed was Wagner's transport, called a *spironera*.

2 8bre

Ottranto Cost Saverio Costajela Cap:ne di Spironera Nom:a la Madonna dalla Saluta con Band. Francese, [per]

adi: [R.e (i.e., "respondere")] Vengo da Ottranto partito di là gia due gioventier consentata di Tomasso Costaj[e]la al suo Cap:ne di Spironera Sta la Madonna del Rosario con Bandiera Francese anchi con la [rie.] di Grane il primo Tonno li quattrocento, ed il secondo trecento, uno anchi una Cassata uva filato per cadaca[n]. il tutte Effetuato a Barletta, destinati per qui, e toccano a farò donde sciolsimo in jeri a mezzogiorno.

add:t di Salute Of:e esser ottima

add:ti de Bastind: R.e non aver incontrato cercano Sono di Equi passaggio nella prima in tutti qui undeci, e li Passegeri: Stungiolbal Tent.e, S.e Giuseppe Francesco Choculx Inspetor Militara, S.e Martin Vagner, e Pacifico Storani, a nella 2 d:a in tutti Diecisette

Q. H. L. C. et Juravit [underlining mine]

It seems that two ships sailed together from Otranto, the first a 400-ton ship named either *La Madonna della Salute* or *La Vergine della Salute,* and the second a 300-ton ship named for the *Madonna del Rosario.* They were transporting a shipment of grain, along with some grapes, from Barletta to Corfu, as well as eleven French soldiers and two French military inspectors; Martin Wagner and Pacifico Storani are mentioned by name, along with two unnamed young men traveling with the permission of Tomasso Costajela (presumably their father and the captain's brother). Thus, excluding the captain, seventeen persons landed at Corfu on October 1–2, 1812; the Ministry of Public Health confirmed that everyone on board was in good health upon arrival.

According to Υγειονομειο II, φ. 63, f51v, the ship *Madonna della Salute e l'anime del Purgatorio* departed Corfu on October 21, 1812, with fifteen French soldiers and marines and seven paying passengers (six Italian, one French), bound once again for Barletta.

The materials in Υγειονομειο II, φ. 66 include letters from the (French) port confirming that boats newly arriving in Corfu had not come from English territories (the letters are written both in French and in Italian). The boat with which Wagner traveled (*La Vergine di Rosario*), along with its captain, "le Capitan Tommaso Costajolo," is mentioned several times in the later months of 1812, usually traveling from Barletta to Corfu and almost always with French soldiers and marines aboard.

Wagner's signature at his point of entry, also dated October 2, 1812, may be found in Υγειονομειο II.

While I have been unable to find the record of Wagner's and Storani's departure (since departing passengers were seldom named), the most likely possibilities are two Ottoman ships bound for Prevesa (one transporting six passengers and the other three), listed at Υγειονομειο II, φ. 63, 49v:

> a 11 8bre Francesco Rilanino Cap.e di Barca Ottemana, compagni in tutti sei per Prevesa senza carico di contenaria
>
> a d.o Gianni Cilanga Cap.e di Barca Ottemana a compagni in tutti trè per Prevesa senza carico di contenaria

83. Hans Haller von Hallerstein, . . . *und die Erde gebar ein Lächeln*, 202–17.

84. Wagner's letter to Ludwig, sent from Athens on February 28, 1813, confirms the down payment of 2,500 Venetian *zecchini,* and lays out the complicated process of converting Spanish *thalers* and Turkish *piasters* into Venetian coin. Wagner then instructed Ludwig to arrange the next three payments, of 2,500 *zecchini* each, to Gropius and his agents: on the 30th of October, the 30th of November, and the 30th of December, 1813.

    See Hubert Glaser, u.a., *König Ludwig I. von Bayern und Martin von Wagner. Der Briefwechsel. Band I: 1809–1815*, Dok. 165.

85. Some excellent resources for Fauvel's Greek career include: Christoph W. Clairmont, *Fauvel: The First Archaeologist in Athens and His Philhellenic Correspondents* (Zürich: Akanthus Verlag für Archäologie, 2007), 16–25, 158–79, 200–210, 218–26 (with abundant correspondence from Cockerell, Gropius, Hallerstein, Linkh, Stackelberg, and Wagner regarding the Aeginean acquisitions); John H. Kroll, "Dikasts' Pinakia from the Fauvel Collection," *Bulletin de Correspondance Hellénique* XCI/2 (1967): 379–96; A. and Ph. E. Legrand, "Biographie de Louis-François-Sebastien Fauvel. Antiquaire et Consul (1753–1838)," *Revue Archeologique* 30 (1897): 185–201, and *Revue Archaeologique* 31 (1898): 94–103; and Alessia Zambon, *Aux origines de l'archéologie en Grèce: Fauvel et sa methode* (Paris: CTHS: Institut National de l'Histoire de l'Art, 2014). Μανολης Κορρες, Οι πρωτοι χαρτες της πολεως των Αθηνων (Αθηνα: Εκδοτικος Οικος Μελισσα, 2010), 10–11, 82–84, 89, 188–89, contains some relevant material on Fauvel's interesting map of Athens, dated to 1787.

86. He traveled through Gastuni and Elis, Andravada and Lechaina, Achaia and Patras, Naupaktos and Vostizza, Delphi and Arachova, Chaironea and Livathia, Thebes, and finally on to Athens.

For a most helpful map of this itinerary, see the frontispiece to Stephen Minta, *On a Voiceless Shore: Byron in Greece* (New York: Henry Holt and Company, 1998).

87. This letter is quoted in Adolf Furtwängler and Hans Urlichs, *Greek & Roman Sculpture*, translated by Horace Taylor [1914] (Boston: Longwood Press, 1977), 10n1.

88. Remarkably, Wagner also secured a pass from the Papal Antiquarian in Rome, Carlo Fea, which allowed the statues to be unloaded in 1815 and then reloaded for later transport in 1818 at the *Dogana di Ripa* without payment of the customary fees. Fea was much impressed with the statues, and helped Wagner to maintain privacy during their restoration by discouraging visitors. Wagner reports this to Ludwig in letters written on May 19 and October 2, 1815, both from Rome.

See Hubert Glaser, u.a., *König Ludwig I. von Bayern und Martin von Wagner. Der Briefwechsel. Band I: 1809–1815*, Doks. 218 and 229.

89. Strikingly, Walter Pater spoke most appreciatively of Thorvaldsen's restorations, by distinguishing "antiquarian" from "aesthetic" interests:

> the latter, the aesthetic method, requires that, with the least possible addition or interference, by the most skillful living hand procurable, the object shall be made to please, or at least content the living eye seeking enjoyment and not a bare fact of science, in the spectacle of ancient art. The latter way of restoration—the aesthetic way—followed by the famous connoisseurs of the Renaissance, has been followed here.

See "The Marbles of Aegina" in Walter Pater, *Greek Studies: A Series of Essays* (London: Macmillan and Co., Limited, 1925), 258.

For a summary and analysis of the history of this restoration, see Raimond Wünsche, "Die Ergänzung der Ägineten," in *Kampf um Troja*, 57–143.

90. See Adolf Furtwängler, "New (German) Excavations at Aegina," *International Monthly* V (January 1902): 10, the relevant discussion in Adolf Furtwängler and H. L. Urlichs, *Greek & Roman Sculpture*, 6–17 (esp. 10–11), and especially Adolf Furtwängler, ed., *Ägina: Das Heiligtum der Aphaia* (München: Verlag der K. B. Akademie der Wisenschaften, 1906), "Die Giebelgruppen," 176–274, with remarkable plates at pages 204 and 224.

91. Schelling was in fact an enthusiastic promoter of Wagner's text, and an emphatic promoter of its art historical importance, as is evident in his correspondence with the book's publishers, the Cotta brothers (Johann Fredrich and Georg), with whom he engaged in a lifelong correspondence (beginning in 1803 and ending in 1849). See Horst Fuhrmans und Lisolette Lohrer, eds., *Schelling und Cotta Briefwechsel* (Stuttgart: Ernst Klett Verlag, 1965), 126–28 and 136–39.

I am most grateful to Jason M. Wirth for this reference.

92. See Arne Zerbst, *Schelling und die bildende Kunst: Zum Verhältnis von kunstphilosophischem System und konkreter Werkkenntnis* (München: Wilhelm Fink Verlag, 2011), esp. 253–65.

93. That is the overarching theme of my previous book, *Classics at the Dawn of the Museum Era: The Life and Times of Antoine Chrysostome Quatremère de Quincy (1755–1849)*, esp. xix-xxvi.
94. Friedrich W. J. Schelling, Hegel's precocious younger contemporary, is perhaps best known as a philosopher of nature, of subjectivity and of freedom. But Schelling also became deeply interested in mythology and religion in his later years, displaying a special (and perennial) interest in Greek materials, as we see very clearly in his notes and appendices to Wagner's *Report*. See, in addition: the important lecture, "The Deities of Samothrace," delivered to the Bavarian Academy of Sciences on October 12, 1815, and available in Robert F. Brown, *Schelling's Treatise on "The Deities of Samothrace": A Translation and an Interpretation* (Missoula, MT: Scholars Press, 1974); the unfinished dialogue, *Clara, or, On Nature's Connection to the Spirit World*, translated by Fiona Steinkamp (Albany, NY: SUNY Press, 2002); and the series of ten lectures he offered several times at the University of Berlin, published as *Historical-Critical Introduction to the Philosophy of Mythology*, translated by Mason Richey and Markus Zisselberger, with a foreword by Jason M. Wirth (Albany, NY: SUNY Press, 2007). To that list of significant writings, we should now add Schelling's supplements to this volume, here translated into English for the first time.

    Several other sources I have found helpful in establishing the connection between Schelling's philosophical interests and his work on Wagner's *Report* are: Edward Allen Beach, *The Potencies of God(s): Schelling's Philosophy of Mythology* (Albany, NY: SUNY Press, 1994); Jason M. Wirth, *The Conspiracy of Life: Meditations on Schelling and His Time* (Albany, NY: SUNY Press, 2003), and *Schelling's Practice of the Wild: Time, Art, Imagination* (Albany, NY: SUNY Press, 2015); as well as David Farrell Krell, "God's Footstool: A Note on the Source for Schelling's Description of the Olympian Zeus in the 1811 Draft of *The Ages of the World*," in Wirth, ed., *Schelling Now: Contemporary Readings*, 101–21, with its intriguing suggestion about Schelling's complex interest in Pausanias, and relatedly, in religious iconography. I will have more to say about Schelling's philosophy in relation to this *Report* later in this introduction as well as in appendix 3.
95. The major names in this "school" were Kallon, Onatas, Glaukias, and Anaxagoras. All four men seem to have been active between roughly 500–470 BCE, which is to say, right around the time when the Temple to Aphaia was erected on Aegina. Pausanias is our main source for information about these figures, and seems especially enthusiastic about Onatas, whom he believes "we should rate below none of Daedalus's successors, nor even below those of the Attic school" (*Guide to Greece* V.25.12).

    An excellent summary of this material may be found in H. Stuart Jones, *Select Passages from Ancient Writers Illustrative of the History of Greek Sculpture*, edited by A. N. Oikonomides (Chicago: Argonaut Inc., Publishers, 1960), 40–50.
96. This is clearest in what was to become Quatremère's most famous single work in his own day, *Le Jupiter Olympien, ou, L'Art de la Sculture Antique considéré sous un nouveau point de vue* (Paris: De l'Imprimerie de Firmon Didot, 1815), one much on Schelling's mind as he drafted his notes to this *Report,* as we will see. See also appendix 5.
97. To this early period we may assign the following important essays: an essay on Plato's *Timaeus* (1794); an essay "Concerning the Possibility of a Form of Philosophy in General" (1794); his "Philosophical Letters Concerning Dogmatism and Criticism" (1795); and his "Ideas Toward a Philosophy of Nature" (1797).

98. This interest was announced already in a 1795 essay, "On the I As Principle of Philosophy," but came into sharper focus in the 1800 "System of Transcendental Idealism." These interests culminated in his last published writing from 1809, the *Philosophical Investigations into the Essence of Human Freedom*, about which I will have more to say below.
99. Schelling's journals suggest that this project commenced in late 1810; three versions of the manuscript (dated 1811, 1813, and 1815, respectively) were produced, the latter two of which have been translated into English—the 1813 version by Judith Norman (in 1997), and the 1815 version by Jason Wirth (in 2000).
100. It is difficult to escape the impression that the death of his wife, Caroline, on September 7, 1809, changed Schelling's perception of his work (and its merely penultimate importance) forever. Schelling also became increasingly interested in silence and the unsayable, as he undertook his examination of "The Ages of the World." It is of interest to note that Johann Martin Wagner stayed with Schelling for six weeks after the death of his wife, and this intense period clearly cemented the two men's friendship.

    See Guntram Beckel, "Johann Martin von Wagner," *Fränkische Lebensbilder* 8 (1978): 238–39, and Jason M. Wirth, *The Conspiracy of Life*, 29.
101. Andrew Bowie, *Schelling and Modern European Philosophy: An Introduction* (London and New York: Routledge, 1993).
102. Martin Heidegger, *Schelling's Treatise on the Essence of Human Freedom*, translated by Joan Stambaugh (Athens, OH: University of Ohio Press, 1985).
103. Jason M. Wirth, ed., *Schelling Today: Contemporary Readings* (Bloomington, IN: University of Indiana Press, 2005).
104. Slavoj Zizek, *The Invisible Remainder: An Essay on Schelling and Related Matters* (London: Verso, 1996).
105. Friedrich W. J. Schelling, *Philosophical Investigations into the Essence of Human Freedom*, translated and edited by Jeff Love and Johannes Schmidt (Albany, NY: State University of New York Press, 2006), 74 and 77, translation slightly emended and italics mine.
106. This material is now available in English as *The Philosophy of Art*, edited and translated by Douglas W. Scott (Minneapolis: University of Minnesota Press, 1989).
107. I develop this point in greater detail in *Was Greek Thought Religious? On the Use and Abuse of Hellenism, From Rome to Romanticism* (New York, NY: Palgrave Macmillan, 2002), and utilize the idea of "palimpsestic history" for my investigations in *Winckelmann and the Vatican's First Profane Museum* (New York: Palgrave Macmillan, 2011), xv–xvi.
108. In point of fact, while the new Aeginetan collection was the chief inspiration behind the Glyptothek Museum, the museum guide that was produced to coincide with the museum's opening, written by Ludwig's Munich architect, Leo von Klenze (1784–1864), makes clear that it was already organized as what we would today call an "encyclopedic museum": with an Egyptian Gallery, followed by an Etruscan Gallery, followed in turn by the Aeginetan collection, and then moving on to rooms dedicated to Classical, Hellenistic, and Roman art, most of them named for their most important inhabitants, like Apollo, Bacchus, and Niobe, as well as gods and heroes.

    See Leo von Klenze, with Ludwig Schorn, *Beschreibung der Glyptothek Sr. Majestät des Königs Ludwig von Bayern* (München: J. G. Cotta'schen, 1830).

This guide was not updated for nearly forty years; see Heinrich Brunn, *Beschreibung der Glyptothek König Ludwig's I. zu München* (München: In Commission bei Theodor Ackermann, 1868). A second edition was published in 1870, with a fifth and final edition in 1887.

109. Hans Haller von Hallerstein, . . . *und die Erde gebar ein Lächeln*, 248–61.

110. See Peter Murphy, "Architectonics," in Johann P. Arnason and Peter Murphy, eds., *Agon, Logos, Polis: The Greek Achievement and its Aftermath* (Stuttgart: Franz Steiner Verlag, 2001), 218–19, and Franziska Dunkel, Hans-Michael Körner und Hannelore Putz, eds., *König Ludwig I. von Bayern und Leo von Klenze: Symposion aus Anlaß des 75. Geburtstags von Hubert Glaser* (München: Verlag C. H. Beck, 2006), especially: Reinhold Baumstark, "Klenzes Museen" (1–20); Hans-Michael Körner, "Paradigmen der Ludwig-I.-Forchung zwischen Kunst und Schönheit, Dynastie und Staat" (21–30); Bettina Kraus, "Ludwig I. und seine Kunstberater. Das Beispiel Johann Martin Wagner" (81–104); and Gabriele Köster, "Architektur als Bildträger. Klenze und die Bildausstattung seiner Bauten" (243–71).

There are also superb illustrations to be seen in *Der Königsplatz, 1812–1988* (München: Staatliche Antikensammlungen und Glyptothek, 1991), 16–25.

111. Hans Haller von Hallerstein, . . . *und die Erde gebar ein Lächeln*, 281–89.

112. As quoted by Walkin, *The Life and Work of C. R. Cockerell*, xxi.

113. See Watkin, *The Life and Work of C. R. Cockerell*, xix–xxiii, 249–53, and Jane Turner, ed., *The Dictionary of Art* in 34 volumes (London: Macmillan Publishers, Ltd., 1996), VII: 502–05.

Johann Martin Wagner
Royal Bavarian Professor of the History of Painting and Corresponding
Member of the Royal Academy of Fine Arts in Munich

Report

on the

Aeginetan Sculptures

in the Possession of

His Royal Highness

the

Crown Prince of Bavaria

With art historical observations

by

Fr. W. J. Schelling

Stuttgart and Tübingen
J. G. Cotta'schen Publisher
1817

EDITOR'S PREFACE

F. W. J. Schelling

[iii] When the artworks that are described in the following essay were first discovered, and their discoverers came to a unanimous agreement that the collection should be sold only in its entirety, then it was entirely possible that these works might have taken the comfortable and really the only safe journey by water, to England.[1] That this [iv] did not happen, that they have not come to rest under the foggy skies of London, as the figures of the Parthenon did, but rather to a proper[2] German capital where they will be accessible to all of us in a dignified environment best suited to them—for this we have only the Crown Prince of Bavaria to thank, with his magnificent taste for ancient art and his decisiveness when it comes to matters of quality.

The author of the following essay has long been known among the most respected German friends of the arts as a practiced artist of preeminent power and ability, one who has demonstrated an original grasp of the heroic spirit of the Greek past [v] through a great painting depicting the council of the Greeks before Troy, completed some eight years ago [Figure I.10][3] and inspired both by Homer and by the more general contemplation of antiquity. He was chosen by His Royal Highness to go, first to Zante, where the Aeginetan collection was then deposited, for an inspection of this collection of artworks, and then on to Malta, for the financial settlement with their legal owners.[4]

After this magnificent collection was brought safely and in its entirety to Rome, where he remained to oversee the reassembly [*Zusammensetzung*] and necessary restorations [*Ergänzungen*],[5] he now found himself with greater leisure to contemplate these works of high and awe-inspiring antiquity, [vi] examining them from all sides. This practicing artist, through whose singular efforts things had come to this point, was called upon to compose a report on these treasures—first and foremost for their lofty owner, but also printed and published in order to give the entire German art world a foretaste of the pleasure which awaited it someday through the actual confrontation with these works of art.

On account of our mutual and long-standing friendly relations, the author wished me, when the time came, to tend to this publication—a wish whose fulfillment [vii] laid upon me a higher commission of responsibility than mere honor or duty could ever have done.

While I am thus taking over the revision of this essay for publication, I do not think myself free to take liberties with editorial changes except as the considerations of style and composition might demand. In general I wish one to hear the practicing artist himself, to lose as little as possible of his peculiar eloquence, his artistic dialect and his humor. We have been afflicted for too long with dense and gloomy descriptions of artworks of all kinds. It goes without saying that nothing of significance in the expression nor in the general arrangement and progression of the whole [viii] could possibly be altered here.

However, since it is not possible to read so faithful and vivid and noteworthy a description regarding what are, in their own way, utterly unique works of art without having lively thoughts of one's own awakened, I must respond as an editor with that much more active and sympathetic interest in this author's research. I have therefore elected to include separate remarks, as well as several detailed appendices, in which I will concern myself independently with a discussion of the main differences and characteristics of Aeginetan art and to illuminate its relationship to some definitive Attic concepts, [ix] since ultimately the assessment of the profound historical importance of these artworks will be based upon such matters.

I hope in this way to introduce in a suitable manner a true artist to the world of German letters, one whose special talent for art unites within himself every general quality of spirit [*Geistes*] and of character, without which nothing of great or lasting value was ever brought to fruition. I add to this my hope that one may here find communicated, just as they are, a set of strictly preliminary thoughts and remarks upon works of art that are, on account of their entirely distinctive place of origin, [x] an historical and artistic enigma [*Räthsel*], ones that will remain genuine objects of the most serious and intensive research for some time to come.

Munich, December 1816
Schelling.

TABLE OF CONTENTS

Introduction

Johann Martin Wagner

[1] It is already widely known among the friends of art and of antiquity, how a team [*Gesellschaft*] of artists and amateurs from the German and English nations came together in the year 1811, among other things, in order to to explore and to record the architectural measurements of the temple of Panhellenic Jupiter[6] on the island of Aegina, which lies directly across the sea from Athens. It is also known how they, in the course of excavations undertaken with this scientific intention, happened upon an unexpected but spectacular collection of a large number of sculptures in varying states of preservation, all of which nonetheless represented invaluable works of art to be carefully recorded, sculptures that once adorned the eastern and [2] western pediments of this lofty building.

His Royal Highness the Crown Prince of Bavaria, inspired by the purest taste for everything grand and beautiful, purchased the entire collection from its discoverers in the following year (1812). In this way, he first of all managed an increase in his collection of antiquities, which may well exceed, without exaggeration, any other collection in our own time as well as in any previous period. These sculptures were acquired partly for art's sake, given their exceptional quality and distinctiveness as constituting the truest imitation of nature [*der treuesten Nachahmung der Natur*], and partly for history's sake, given their origin in an especially obscure period in the history of art [*dunkelen Zeit der Kunst*]. As such they are of incalculable importance for the entire field of classical studies [*Alterthumskunde*].

We gather from these works that the early Greeks borrowed [*entlehnt*] their art from the Egyptians. (1)[7]

[3] From them, it becomes clear to us what road art took from its childhood in order to achieve its highest fulfillment in the works of Pheidias and his contemporaries, works that move us to such wonder today. It is clear that

these great masters had merely to take a further step along the paths laid out so clearly for them by their predecessors. (2)

Through these works it will finally become obvious, one may say, that the perfect imitation of nature [*vollkommene Nachahmung der Natur*] is the only path to the highest achievement in art or, what amounts to the same thing, to what has been called the Ideal [*das Ideale*] in its final and most spiritual [*geistigsten*] appearance.

With regard to art historical knowledge, this discovery has brought into full consciousness what Winckelmann already suspected,[8] and what Visconti[9] sought out after him with greater confidence—namely, that what we had previously understood to be the *Etruscan* style in art ought actually to be called more or less the *Ancient Greek* [*altgriechisch*] style.

[4] As our concept [*Begriff*] of the Ancient Greek style in general is adjusted, so we gain through this important discovery information about what Pausanias and a host of others describe so appreciatively as the *Aeginetan* School—a school about whose distinctions and differences from the Ancient Greek school we could form no conception until now, or else only vague and uncertain ones, since we lacked any monuments with which to form a surer opinion.

What will be touched upon in only a few words here I will explain in the essay that follows, and I will seek to prove with concrete examples.

These conclusions, however, must be preceded by a precise description of the assembled figures so that the friends of art shall be made familiar, albeit in a preliminary way, both with the objects themselves and with their distinctive traits.

I consider this detailed description all the more important since the ongoing [5] piecing together [*Zusammensetzung*] of the fragments and their subsequent restoration [*Ergänzungen*], will require a great deal of time and must be completed before these same works will be accessible for open viewing and general evaluation. (3)

EDITOR'S NOTES

[6]

(1) The Editor would consider it entirely superfluous to show in a detailed way that this conclusion, insofar as it is derived from the quality of the Aeginetan images, is missing some of the essential intermediate links [*wesentliche Mittelglieder*] it would need to be established with greater certainty. Here as elsewhere it should be borne in mind that the author speaks as an artist, and generally speaking, can content himself unreservedly with his German perspective and German way of thinking, a perspective very much in line with the prevailing classical wisdom in Rome and Italy. Whoever would cast doubt [*läugnen*] upon this explanation [*Erklärung*] of the notable similarities between the Egyptian and the Greek style in the most ancient times, as the easiest and the simplest explanation, [7] ought to recall that there were many styles evident among the Greeks themselves, many of them passed on to the Egyptians. In ignorance of this pre-history it is as easy as it is natural for modern researchers to go astray.

Moreover, the generally accepted rule [*Gesetz*] concerning the relationship between the Egyptians and the Greeks—according to which the former [*jene*] is presented as the teacher [*Lehrmeister*] and the latter [*diese*] as the pupil [*Schüler*]—ought to be called into doubt, as should the term 'borrow' [*entlehnen*], and also the idea of material exchange or communication as the most suitable model for this relationship. Thus it is far more the interpretation and explanation of this relationship, rather than the relationship itself, that may well appear most objectionable from the standpoint of contemporary German research [*Forschung*].[10]

Since it is precisely among us that the entire world of antiquity is viewed more and more as a *whole* [*als ein Ganzes*], as a self-contained and integrated world, and since every day we appear to be [8] more convinced that Greek religion and culture represents the most vital development of all . . . because of this, the soil in which Greek culture grew and the ground in which it ripened—namely the religions and the cultures of other peoples—must be studied. Why should we not view Egyptian and Greek art in a living relationship [*lebendigen Zusammenhang*], indeed in one and the same line of development? The whole culture [*Bildung*] of Egypt bears the marks of a great reversal [*Umsturzes*], of the violent inhibition and postponement of a mighty principle in the course of its development. In the face of such repressive inhibition, must not the overflow of great cultural energy seek relief in the terrible [*Ungeheueren*], even in the desire to create the monstrous? And this same principle in Greece, beginning so to speak for a second time, but tending toward a freer, gentler and less repressed form of development, was it not able to achieve its highest possible perfection [*Vollkommenste*] through an inner necessity [*innern Nothwendigkeit*]?

It is indisputable, and even necessary [*nothwendig*], that [9] the most independent and contrasting forms, the ones that come to be most different in the end, are in their first beginnings really quite similar. As Mr. Quatremère-de-Quincy has charmingly observed, the seeds of a plant look much more similar than the plants which develop from them.[11] The application of this general observation will be even more determinative [*noch bestimmter*] in the present case, if we remind ourselves that it really was one and the same principle striving toward realization in both Egyptian and in Greek art, only it was pressed much further in the Greek case. Furthermore, whoever would comprehend the unity of cultural power [*die Einheit der bildende Kraft*], will he not most likely discover that this unlimited, continuous and irresistible drive [*Trieb*] already appears in the first mighty movement of the human spirit [*menschlichen Geistes*], that which the oldest religious beliefs of the people produce?[12]

We simply feel that there is no real place for such observations here, and would have limited ourselves accordingly since nearly every observation concerning this expression must go too far, [10] had not two considerations convinced [*bestimmt*] us otherwise.

The first concerns the oft-repeated opinion linking the Aeginetan sculptures to the appearance of novelty [*einen Schein von Neuheit*], such that these works are seen as providing a new confirmation of that idea. For these reasons we felt it necessary to observe that the Aeginetan artworks have nothing new to teach us regarding this historical hypothesis (namely, concerning the emergence [*Abstammung*] of Greek art from Egyptian art) and—taking this opportunity to contradict that partial attempt at explanation [*Erklärungs-Versuchen*]—these artworks, as popular as they now appear to be, can have no real use, since they actually obscure the way to a greater and more comprehensive theoretical explanation. Here then is the solution that we demand of the particular [*das Einzelne*] but may find only in great and universal relations [*grossen und allgemeinen Zusammenhange*], a solution whose depth we may not be able to discern given our present views.

[11] The other consideration was that this assumption regarding such a relationship between Egyptian and Ancient Greek [*altgriechischer*] art cannot fail to have an impact upon our perception and evaluation of the oldest Greek artworks. This assumption has gone so far that any occasional similarity is now treated as an actual and complete likeness. The art historical understanding of the Greeks must turn its attention to the very oldest Attic works of which we have as yet caught very few glimpses. They are decidedly unlike their Egyptian counterparts, as the following passage from Pausanias demonstrates, where he says of the Erythracian Hercules: "He is neither called Aeginetan nor similar to the oldest of the Attic sculptures (οὔτε τῶν Αττικῶν το℘ῖς ἀρχαιοτάτοις) but rather, if anything, Egyptian."[13] Such expressions should suffice to correct this false assumption. It is striking that the Aeginetan style and Aeginetan sculptures are mentioned [12] so often, when comparisons are made not only between them, but also between the Ancient Attic and the Egyptian, i.e., in one passage where Pausanias distinguishes between two statues according to whether they are *mostly* (though not perfectly) similar to Egyptian wooden images (τοῖς Αἰγυπτίοις μάλιστα ἐοίκασι ξοάνοις) and then continues directly as follows: the (third) figure, however, called the Archegetes (undoubtedly of the very greatest antiquity) is similar to the Aeginetan works (book I, chapter 42).[14] This recollection may be more subtle than useful. First of all, there is no doubt that there existed a closer relationship between Athens and Egypt, between the Attic and the Egyptian style [*Wesen*], as this passage also makes clear. Even so indisputable a point, however, cannot be extended to all of Greece and to all things Greek, as has too often been done. How far Attic and Aeginetan [13] art may be treated as similar is in no way a settled matter. Secondly, it is obvious that these explanations must be undertaken with the greatest precision so as not to be the cause of even greater confusion. In that spirit I tentatively offer the following stylistic categories following the example of the ancients—*Egyptian*, *Tyrrhenian* (*Etruscan*), *Old Attic*, and *Aeginetan*—merely as a way of distinguishing between them more precisely [*bestimmt zu unterscheiden*] and for general classification within the larger framework of an *Ancient Greek* style [*altgriechischer Styl*]. It is always the case that many works that are described as belonging to one style; i.e., the Etruscan style, might actually belong to some other.

(2) I recognize very well that it will strike anyone who begins with these notes [*Anmerkungen*] to the introduction that they take up more space than the text itself. This lamentable situation is unavoidable, since the introduction

[14] calls for critical and historical observations, and we deem it altogether necessary that the investigation should not become entangled in the kind of vagueness [*gleich in Unbestimmtheiten*] that there will not be time to clarify afterwards. Here the author considers the path of Aeginetan art to be the path of Greek art in general, a point that I do not wish to contradict insofar as he intended it. But I should like to clarify [*bestimmen*] the remark more precisely than it has been expressed here.

The relationship [*Verhältniß*] and the mutual lines of influence [*wechselseitige Einfluß*] between Attic and Aeginetan art is indisputably one of the most important points in the entire investigation to which these remarkable sculptures give occasion.[15] This relationship and this influence is, as yet, neither as clear nor as unanimously agreed upon as one might hope.

Whatever preliminary information we have already ascertained concerning this relationship, quite independent of the information that a close description of these artworks will provide, [15] we may be permitted to summarize briefly here.

Pausanias, in the seventh book and fourth chapter, says that Smilis of Aegina decidedly should not be ascribed the same level of fame which Daedalus enjoyed, even though he is ancient and perhaps was even a contemporary of the latter.[16] We concur with the objections that Heyne (*Opusc.* V. p. 344)[17] and Quatremère de Quincy (*Le Jupiter Olympien,* 175)[18] have made against this statement, according to which the statue of Juno [Hera] on Samos ought actually be ascribed to Smilis. We accord this statement no chronological or actual historical value. All that we can accept as conclusive is that, according to Pausanias, Smilis was the Aeginetan Daedalus, and thus that Pausanias described an *independent* [*unabhängigen*] founder of Aeginetan art (an intention that is confirmed even more clearly by the way he speaks of Smilis as contemporary with Daedalus). Generally speaking, this was an accepted and worthy [16] opinion: that Aeginetan art should not be traced back to an Attic origin, but rather should be considered independent [*unabhängig*] and as *similarly autonomous* [*selbstständig*] in its earliest origins.

This autonomy [*Selbstständigkeit*] was widely recognized in antiquity, i.e., the oldest Aeginetan works will be distinguished from Attic works as *a distinct type*, indeed even as opposed to them in a certain sense. A remarkable type, or a particular style of work (τρόπος τῆς ἐργασίας) will be observed in them, whereby one can distinguish them from all others and yet, at the same time, can make no meaningful distinction between them and their Attic counterparts in terms of the excellence of their rendering and composition.

All of this will be presented here as established fact, for which the evidence will appear in what follows.

After the political catastrophe designed for them by the cruelty of the Athenians, who forced the inhabitants [of Aegina] [17] to leave the island with their wives and children at the outset of the Peloponnesian War, a number of them were deported to a portion of land in Thyrea granted to them by the Spartans, while others were dispersed throughout the lands of Greece.[(1),19] How long after this political catastrophe Aeginetan art was subsumed into Greek art more generally is, as I say, no longer possible to determine [*bestimmen*] precisely. This much is certain: that shortly before this event the last of the Aeginetan artists were truly remarkable.

One might well wish to lend concreteness to this long-held assertion as to the distinctiveness of Aeginetan art, and to that end a report from Pausanias (book II, chap. 29) may serve us well. The first historical event that he mentions from Aegina is when a group of Argives who had occupied Epidaurus with Deiphontes [18] ferried across to Aegina and took possession of a portion of the island from its previous inhabitants [*Ureinwohnern*], thereby introducing Doric customs and the language as well (τᾀ Δωριέων ἔθη καὶ φωνὴν κατεστήσαντο ἐν τῇ νήσῳ).[20] Thus the Aeginetan dialect and customs were Doric, which helps to clarify its political relationship with Athens. Its art was also undoubtedly *Doric*—distinct [*bestimmt*] from the Attic in ways that are perhaps similar to the way in which Dorian poetry is distinct from Attic, which was originally Ionian. The concept [*Der Begriff*] of a distinctively Doric sculpture is in itself as natural as the concept of Doric poetry or architecture,[(2),21] and is presumably as evident here [19] as that which we meet everywhere else in the full range of Greek cultural expression [*Bildung*]. The assumption that this Aeginetan sculpture possesses a Doric character and no other, while preliminary, may serve to clarify the commonly asserted and widely recognized distinctiveness of Aeginetan art.

If however one wishes to move from this basic character to further explanation of the distinctive characteristics of Aeginetan art—i.e., their presumed attachment to an Archaic [*alterthümlich*] style, the achievement of a greater

1. SCHELLING'S NOTE: Thucydides book II, chap. 27.
2. SCHELLING'S NOTE: That the architecture of the Jupiter-temple [sic.] on Aegina was Doric is self-evident. What may not be so well known is that this temple, even now in its ruined state, should be counted among the loveliest examples of Doric architecture available to us.

excellence in execution, among other things—then we may simply accept these facts as tentatively established.

We have troubled ourselves to demonstrate, not only the difference in character of Aeginetan art, but also its original autonomy and independence [*Selbstständigkeit und Unabhängigkeit*] from Attic art. But we should not be taken to deny that, earlier or later, [20] both forms came to stand in a relationship of determinative mutual influence [*entschiedenen wechselseitigen Einfluß*].

Works by Aeginetans were disseminated throughout a large portion of Greece, with a particularly large number evident at Olympia. Aeginetan artists collaborated with others on mutual projects, albeit probably only at a later time. In earlier times a definite [*bestimmter*] relation between the two schools was acknowledged, such as when Pausanias (book II, chap. 32) describes *Kallon* of Aegina as a student of *Tektaeus and Angelion*, who were both in their turn trained by *Dipoenus and Scyllis*, themselves members of the *Daedalic* school.[22]

These facts are not sufficient to establish which of the two, the Attic or the Aeginetan, exercised the decisive influence [*entschiedenern Einfluß*] on the other, still less to determine [*bestimmen*] the specific details of this influence. A theory of mutual influence [*wechselseitiger Einfluß*] presupposes an exchange of distinctive traits, whereas a one-sided [*einseitiger*] model presupposes [21] either an elevation or an improvement of one's characteristics by the other. In order to know this, we would need to have a definite idea of the specific characteristics of each. This is the very concept [*Begriff*] we have lacked until now, requiring as we did the kinds of specific information that we now have for the first time in the following description of these confirmed Aeginetan works of art.

As for the following remark, however—"from these artworks it becomes clear to us what road art took from its childhood in order to achieve its highest fulfillment in the works of Pheidias"—we believe this is a necessary [*nöthig*] observation only insofar as it presupposes that Aeginetan and Attic art may be considered in the beginning as quite similar, and so to speak as one.

As for the other presupposition—namely that Aeginetan art, [22] such as it appears in these sculptures, pointed the way to that perfection achieved by the great later artists—we may leave that point undecided [*in der Unbestimmheit*].

(3) Not even drawings [*Zeichnungen*] of these Aeginetan figures have been available until now. Mr. Quatremère-de-Quincy has two of them at the end of his long and remarkable book on the Olympian Jupiter,[23] based on one

that Mr. Fauvel, the vice-consul in Athens, gave Croquis leave to print. These illustrations, however, when compared with the following descriptions by Mr. Wagner, have little in common with the originals. In the illustration [*Abbildung*] of Minerva all that is evident is her overall position and something of the character of the folds of her dress. The other female figure is represented with complete upper extremities, without the slightest mention [23] of her restoration [*Ergänzung*]. As the following description makes clear, the other two female figures lack both heads and hands.

CHAPTER I

Description of the Aeginetan Figures by Classification

[Wagner]

[24]
For a more accessible overview of these figures, numbering seventeen in all,[24] I will divide them into different classes, according to their position or their clothing, as follows:

I. Freestanding (Female) Figures
II. Advancing Figures, or Fighting Soldiers [*kämpfende Krieger*]
III. Kneeling Figures, or Archers
IV. Supine Figures, or Wounded Figures

This division seems so well suited to these figures that we are entirely [25] justified in using it, demonstrating as it does that a remarkable symmetry prevailed over the entire collection.

I.

Freestanding (Female) Figures

The freestanding and completely clothed figures are three, and they are all female.

A.[25]

The largest, not only of these three female figures but of all the figures in the group, is the Minerva. She is slightly less than lifesize, whereas the others are all smaller than she to a greater or lesser degree.

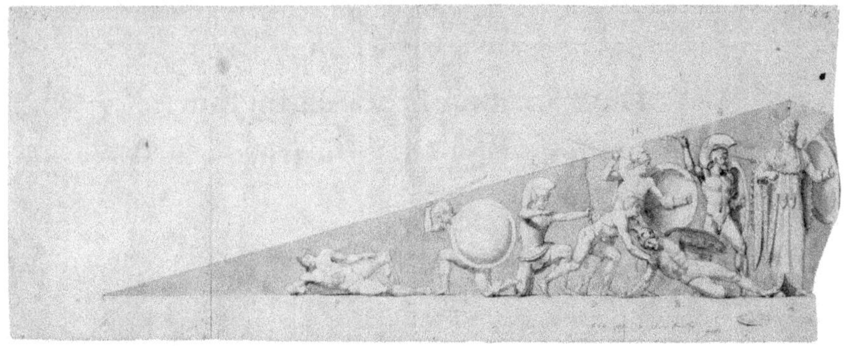

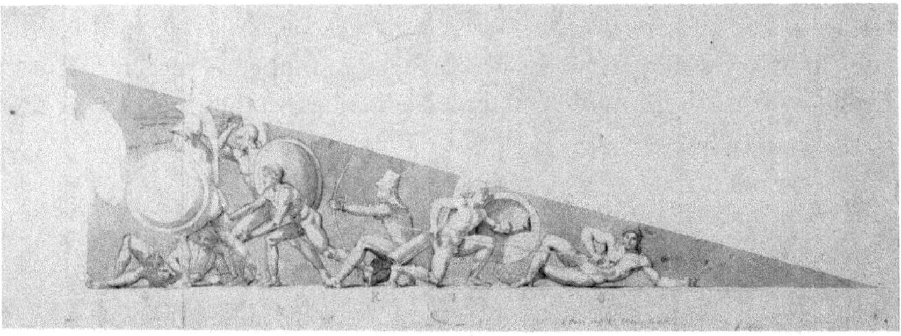

Figure 1.1a–1.1b. Wagner's reconstruction of the Aegina Pediments (1816). Printed with permission of the Martin von Wagner Museum, Würzburg (*Martin von Wagner Museum* Prints Hz4619 and Hz4620).

The posture of the Minerva, from the head down to the knee, is strictly forward facing [*en face*] in orientation, without the least suggestion of movement to either side. By contrast, the knees and lower parts are positioned entirely to the side [*en profil*]. [26] Viewing the upper body exclusively, one would never guess at the direction of the legs. Conversely, viewing the legs only, one might well believe that they belong to a figure depicted in an entirely sideways-facing position. It would be difficult to guess what motivated the artist to utilize this peculiar form.

The Minerva is clothed all the way down to the feet, in an entirely Archaic [*altgriechischen*] style, a style that has been mistakenly, or superficially, called Etruscan [*hetrurischen*], that is, with utterly conventional folds of clothing which seem to hang in a far more pressed and stylized than a natural way.

The head boasts a type of helmet that one customarily finds on vase paintings, but is entirely different from the helmet-form usually associated with this

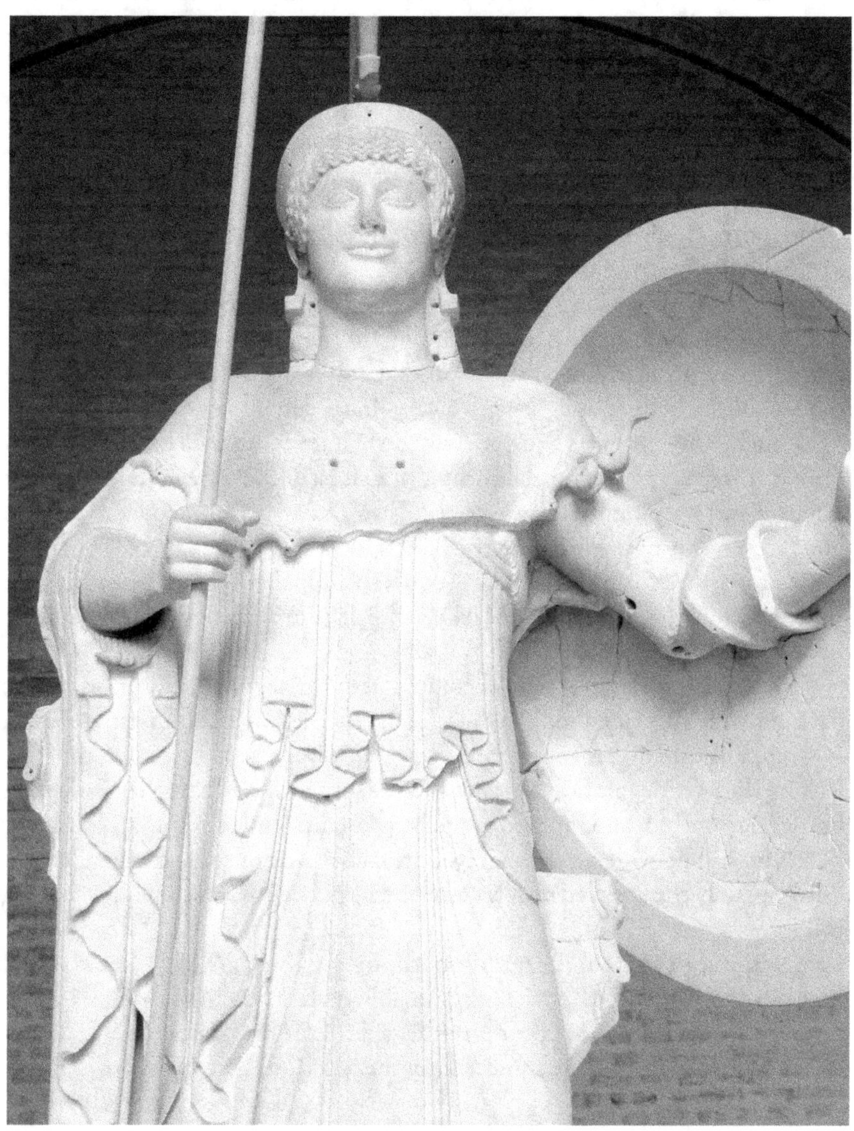

Figure 1.2. Statue of Athena from the Temple to Aphaia on Aegina. Glyptothek Museum. Author's photograph.

goddess. It surrounds the head very closely, in the manner of Roman helmets, and it lacks the high curvature that one usually finds in helmets of Minerva from later [27] times.[(1),26] In contrast, the helmet decoration and crest are more in line with what one finds on old Athenian coins. The entire surface is dotted with small-bore holes, none of which are more than one inch from another, and which presumably served to anchor some bronze decoration, such as one often finds indicated on vase paintings of Minerva's helmet. One may consult Tischbein's *Vases*, book I, page 1.[27]

Her ears are also drilled, doubtless for the purpose of attaching some type of appropriate earring or jewelry.

[28] The hair is, as far as its direction and form are concerned, most distinctive. One part runs across the brow; another part is drawn back at the temple behind the ears, and then comes forward again where, a little below the line of the helmet, it ends with a very linear cut.

Roughly one thumb's width below the helmet four more holes have been drilled. There is another hole in the middle, and a deeper one in the back. One might view this potentially as a continuation of an attachment for the hair, but I dare not propose anything with certainty.

As far as the form of the hair is concerned, little of it is visible, and it is similar in form to Italian pasta [*Nudeln*].[28] It is unremarkable, leaving little impression as to its finish or artistic value.

The breast of the goddess is decorated with the aegis, which runs from the back down across her shoulders [29] as far as the knees, and is rendered in its original, authentic form—that is, represented as a pelt. It appears smooth, lacking the later decoration of scales and the serpentine edging that served as a border decoration, and it possesses elevated, semicircular points and traces of blue wire still in evidence, probably for the fastening of some further decoration (possibly the knotted tassels with which the aegis was fastened, according to Homer).

On the aegis itself in the middle of the breast, there are likewise two small holes still in evidence that were presumably used to anchor a Medusa-head. Three other drilled holes appear on either side of the breast near the shoulders, due to which I will alter my conjecture in the description of the figure *Letter O.*

---

1. SCHELLING'S NOTE: The same form of helmet appears on a very old, and roughly life-size, head of a Minerva in the Florentine Gallery, which, thanks to its detailed description (see the notes to the 3rd volume of the Weimar Edition of Winckelmann's *History of Art*, p. 527f), may be considered the most certain example of Aeginetan workmanship among all the ancient sculptures known today.

She holds a shield on her left arm, and probably held a spear in her right hand.

[30] The form of the shield on this figure is similar to every other shield that survives intact. In a word, it is perfectly circular, in the form familiar from the Argolid [*argolischen*]. This shield would be worn on the left forearm, anchored with a strap through which the arm was placed. Along the border is a handle in the form of a half-circle. Such shields were completely smooth on both the inside and outside, lacking all decoration.

Only on the fragments of one unique shield do we find traces of a clothed female figure, in low relief. Otherwise, all these shields were similarly painted in red on the inside; only a finger-width band along the border remained unpainted. My guess is that this painting of the clothing or of the interior lining may well suggest a parallel to the ancient shields which were decorated with similar painting on the inside, as many passages in Homer suggest. [31] The outer surface of the shield bears traces of sky-blue coloring. What I have said for this shield goes for all of the others without exception.

Traces of blue coloring have also survived on Minerva's helmet and on the helmet of a warrior. The crest, or horsehair plume [*Haarbusch*], was painted red. Also on the lower hem of Minerva's robe one finds traces of red coloring. As to whether the entire robe was painted red, or just the hem, or all of the trim, one cannot say with certainty. But I am inclined to the latter interpretation.

The eyeballs of these figures were also painted, as undeniable traces of paint survive on the Minerva. I perceive similar traces on her lips, and most likely on the foundation [*Grunde*] as well. These portions have remained smoother and cleaner, like the eyeballs, and have not suffered as much from the acidity of the soil as the other portions of her face [32] whose encaustic pigments I have described.

The plinths [*Plinten*] of all these figures were also painted over in the same red color.

In the conception and execution of the marble, with its incredible attention to detail, this figure is perhaps the finest of all those that survive.

She is almost complete, in all her parts. Nothing of importance is damaged—not the head, not the hands, not the feet. All that is missing is a piece of the robe and her aegis.

B. C.

The other two female figures are the smallest of the group, roughly half-lifesize, and like the Minerva they are clothed in a conventional manner, a manner characteristic of all ancient Greek artwork. The folds of the clothing, so naturally and artistically arranged, are rendered with an indescribable grace and palpable affection.

[33] The most remarkable aspect of these two figures, with respect to their clothing and their pose, is that they are identical, but in mirror image. What one does with the right arm, the other does with the left. . . and so on, for the entire figure. This symmetry suggests that they both must have served as architectural decorations, positioned over the pediment on both sides—a façade whose peak has been recovered, but which otherwise survives only in fragments.

Since both of these figures lack heads and hands, it is more difficult to determine their character and attributes. Similarly formed and similarly clothed female figures appear much more often in ancient artworks from Rome. Until recently we took such women for Etruscan priestesses, since we did not know any better, and so we placed a *Sistrum* in their [34] hands, with how much justification I frankly do not know. I simply think it is possible to raise many objections concerning this restoration now.

The hair, which hangs down over much of the back, is depicted with a large number of small plaits, such as is still quite common for the female sex in Greece today, at least in Athens.

Under their feet one observes soles of the sandals, but no sign of the cords or straps with which they would have been attached to the feet. This is also the case with the Minerva, and several other female feet that lack bodies associated with them. I conclude from this that the straps were rendered with paint.

Likewise one observes three small holes on either side of both figures, between the breast and the shoulder, as on the Minerva.

The heads and the hands, all save one, are missing, as well as some portion of the robes. That which does survive is well preserved and rendered [35] with all possible diligence and loving attention.

Some few fragments of a third figure survive, which is similar to the two I have just described, only a little larger. This may serve as evidence that the group was originally composed of four figures, with two on either pediment.

In addition to the female figures just described, there are *three female heads*. There is nothing else from these figures worthy of description, save for a few feet and some minimal fragments of garment. The following may be said about the heads, however.

The one, which is the largest of the three and larger than lifesize, has a helmet, nearly identical in shape to the Minerva's. On top of this head is a quadrangular incision, a little more than one inch deep, in [36] which another piece of marble was attached. Perhaps it was designed to hold the plume. Incidentally, there is no evidence of hair on this head. Instead of hair, one observes a small, incised surface that runs across the brow with three small bored holes, designed for the attachment of another ornament. The ears are also drilled much like the Minerva's. I surmise that this head belonged to the other Minerva, which would have stood on the opposing facade. For the two pedimental groups, as it now appears from the fixtures at their bases that we have recovered, were quite similar.

The other female head has smaller proportions and lavish hair. The hair is gathered by a band, which, from the front to the sides, is rendered as a diadem. Earrings are observable on the ears, and some sort of decoration in little red roses, or rose-shaped florets, runs across the brow.

[37] As well preserved as the head I have just described is, so poorly preserved is the third. Only the shape of this head is discernable, from which one can determine that it was indeed female. From the way it appears, and as the hairstyle [*Haarputz*] suggests, it seems really quite similar to the others I have described. The proportion of the head is also exactly the same.

In summary, it appears that there were at least eight female figures in total, four smaller and four larger.

II.

Advancing Figures, or Fighting Soldiers

Next in the series come the standing or battling warriors, six of them in all. Here too, as I remarked previously, they are conceived two at a time [38], each group consisting of figures that appear very similar to one another, or rather, that appear to repeat a pattern.

D.

The youth, with whose description I begin, appears to be grasping at something, given his hunched posture, or perhaps he was conceived in the process of pulling a wounded figure out of the battle. He is striding forward boldly

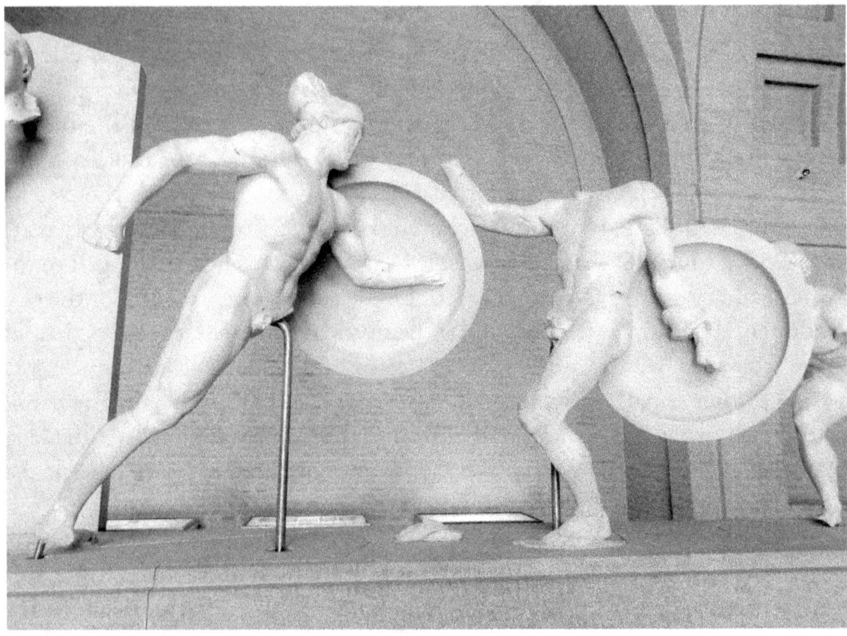

Figure 1.3. Two freestanding warriors from the Temple to Aphaia on Aegina. Glyptothek Museum. Author's photograph.

with his right leg, leaving the left leg extended behind him. The body, however, slopes sharply over that advancing right leg. Both arms are missing, but the preserved shoulders indicate that the arms were thrust forward in some type of exertion. There is no trace of weaponry or clothing on this figure; he is entirely naked. The head, which was never separated from the body, stands out most of all for its unique hairstyle [*seinen besondern Haarputz*]. Half of the head, from the crown forward, is decorated with the customary noodle-shaped hair [*nudelförmigen Haaren*]. This hair ends at the brow, running from one ear [39] to the other, in small, snail-shaped [*schneckenartige*] locks that lay on top of one another in three rows. The rear of the head, from the crown backward, appears to be entirely smooth and bald. Where the two halves of the head come together, there is another plait or twisted braid running from one ear to the other, under which a row of small locks of hair come to the fore. Over the brow, slightly above the coiffure [*Haarputzes*] and directly in the middle, is a single drilled hole. What use this served is impossible for me to imagine.

The body is well worked and well preserved. Both arms are missing, from the shoulders, as is the nose and both feet.

E.

Another figure is quite similar to the one just described, with respect to his posture. But he is the least well executed of all the pieces, and badly damaged.

His head is missing, including the neck, as are both arms including a portion of the [40] shoulders. The entire left leg is missing, from the middle of the thigh, as is the right leg from the knee downward. The abdomen and the thigh are fairly well preserved.

F.

The next two warriors are also rather poorly executed. I begin with the one that has acquired the nickname "Black," due to the black coloring the marble took on from the soil.

The figure is somewhat larger and clumsier than the previous figures in its proportions and form. In his left arm, which is extended forward, this warrior holds a shield of the well-known type described above. The right arm, which probably held a sword, is bent slightly backward.

Three small metal pins are visible above the genitals, for the anchoring [41] of the genital hair, which was attached separately.

The sculpting of this body is not of the best quality, appearing to me to be inferior to the others.

The head, both hands, and the thigh in its entirety are all missing, as well as the lower legs and feet.

G.

Although just as flawed in its parts, the next body is far more exceptional from the perspective of its composition. It depicts the body of a warrior rendered in the fullness of his masculine power.

We may suppose that he likewise carried a shield in his left arm, which was not carved from the same marble but rather must have been attached separately. He is distinguished from the previously described figures in that his right arm is extended forward whereas his left arm is withdrawn.

On the left knee, which survives intact, [42] one notes that he was equipped with leg armor. It is a shame that no part of the legs were found, so as to get a clearer sense of the shape and the quality of this leg gear.

There are two wounds, or scars, visible on the body, which appear to have been rendered with some care: one under the right breast, and the other under the left arm.

There is a metal pin visible on the left side, possibly for the attachment of a sword. These swords appear to have all been rendered in metal for these figures, as I will have occasion to make clearer in the discussion of the next figure.

The head, the entire right arm including the shoulder, as well as the left forearm, are all missing. The entire right leg from the abdomen down is also missing, as is the left leg from the knee down.

Although we appear to have some parts of the missing arms, which I take to be the originals, it is impossible to say [43] with certainty, as there are essential pieces missing between the fragments that we do possess.

H.

The next two warriors are, from the perspective of their position and other qualities, similar in their near perfection. The posture suggests an attacking warrior. The left leg moves forward in advance. The left arm, with the shield visible, is stretched out forward to protect the body. The right arm is raised and bent backwards, in a pose ready to strike, as if he were about to thrust a pike or cast a javelin at an attacker.

One of the figures, lacking a head, has the form of a youth and is well worked, nearly complete in all his parts, save for the right breast, which is somewhat damaged. In addition to the head, the entire right arm is missing from the shoulder, as well as the right foot.

I.

[44]

The other warrior with this same pose still has his head. He is bearded, with a high-crested helmet of the customary Greek type. Like the previous figure, he also holds a shield in his left arm. What survives of this figure is very well preserved. As for the head, only the nose and a small piece of the helmet are damaged. On his back there is a small projection of marble that probably served as an anchoring of some sort.

Both of these figures lack swords, as is the case for almost all of the remaining warriors, excepting the archers of course, but one can see a drilled hole on the right shoulder and several others under the left arm running front to back. That these holes served for the attachment of a belt to which the sword, probably made of bronze, was attached seems clear enough. [45] Upon closer examination of the points where the strap lay against the body, one can still see traces of the covering that gave greater protection to the marble against the elements, such that these portions are smoother even today.

The right arm is missing from the shoulder, as are both legs from the abdomen down. Among the fragments however, there appear to be portions of one thigh and one arm that might well have belonged to this figure. But the pieces do not fit perfectly, so we cannot say with certainty whether they belong to these figures or not.

III.

Kneeling Figures, or Archers

There are three kneeling figures, or archers. They all have, apart from slight differences, [46] a nearly identical pose—namely, with the right leg kneeling, and the left leg extended slightly forward. The left arm, which held the bow that was probably made of bronze, is also extended forward, with the right arm slightly raised and pulled back, so it would seem, in the manner of pulling a bowstring.

K.

One of these archers is most distinguishable for his uniform. He wears a sort of hat on his head, which, considering its form, appears to be in part rather similar to a Phrygian cap, and in part to that of a Persian Mithras. The very top of this hat is damaged and was, so it would appear, carefully worked and elaborately designed. Both earflaps are twined together crosswise on the back of the hat, so that one cannot be certain where they end. This hat comes to an end at the back in a fairly long and rounded cloth, and just below this cloth is a double [47] row of tightly bored holes, possibly for the attachment of artistically rendered locks of hair.

Under this hat in front, at the brow, there is another hood, which bears evidence of more metal pins.

His body is clothed with a tight-fitting jacket with sleeves, which extends all the way down to his hands. It is similar in design to the leggings, which extend all the way to the ankles. This uniform allows one to see the entire body with perfect clarity, without however being able to distinguish any particular musculature, and without so much as a crease or fold of fabric at the joints. This strengthens the conjecture that this uniform was made of thick, pliant leather. This conjecture leads me to a second: that this figure should be taken to represent a Persian archer. It is well known that the Persians were skilled archers, and the uniform of this figure accords [48] quite well with the observations of Herodotus (book I, chapter 7)[(2),29] who says that the Persians wore hose and clothing of thick leather, a material which served lesser warriors as armor, so to speak, or at least as protection against arrows.

2. SCHELLING'S NOTE: Perhaps V, '49. VII, '61?

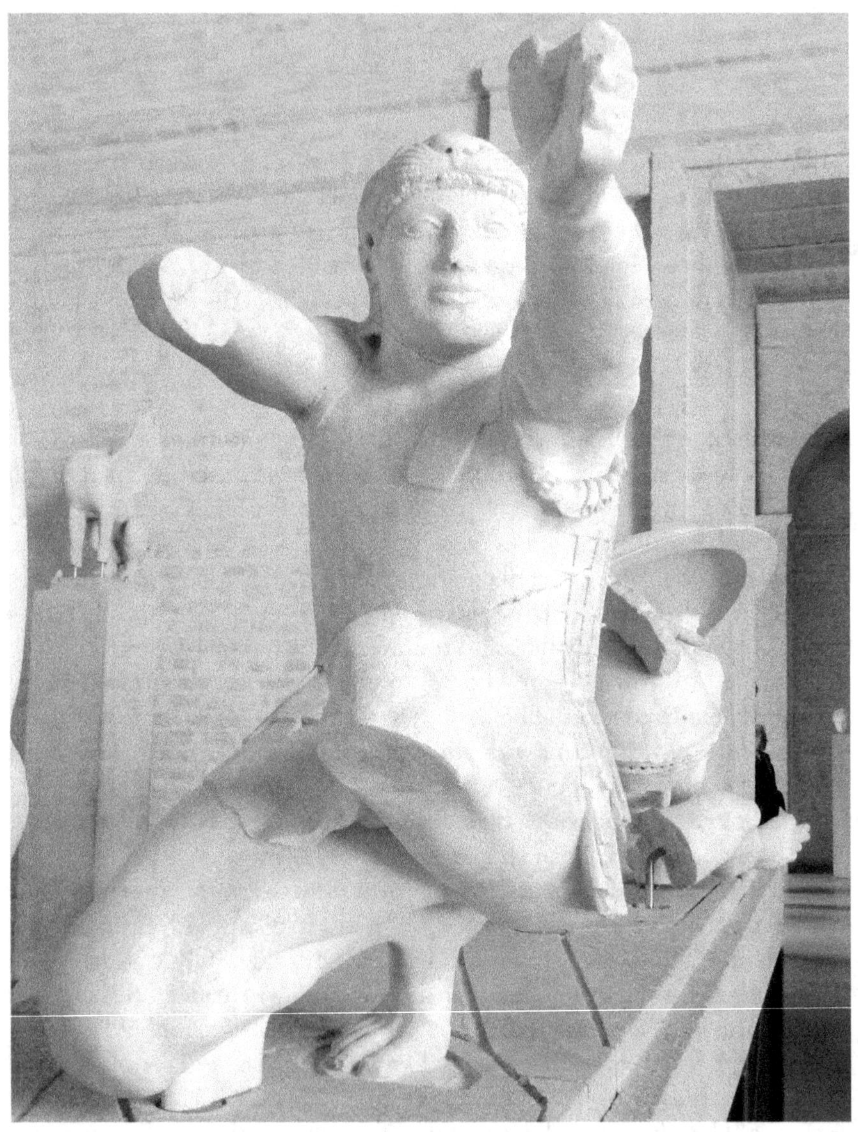

Figure 1.4. Kneeling archer (Herakles) from the Temple to Aphaia on Aegina. Glyptothek Museum. Author's photograph.

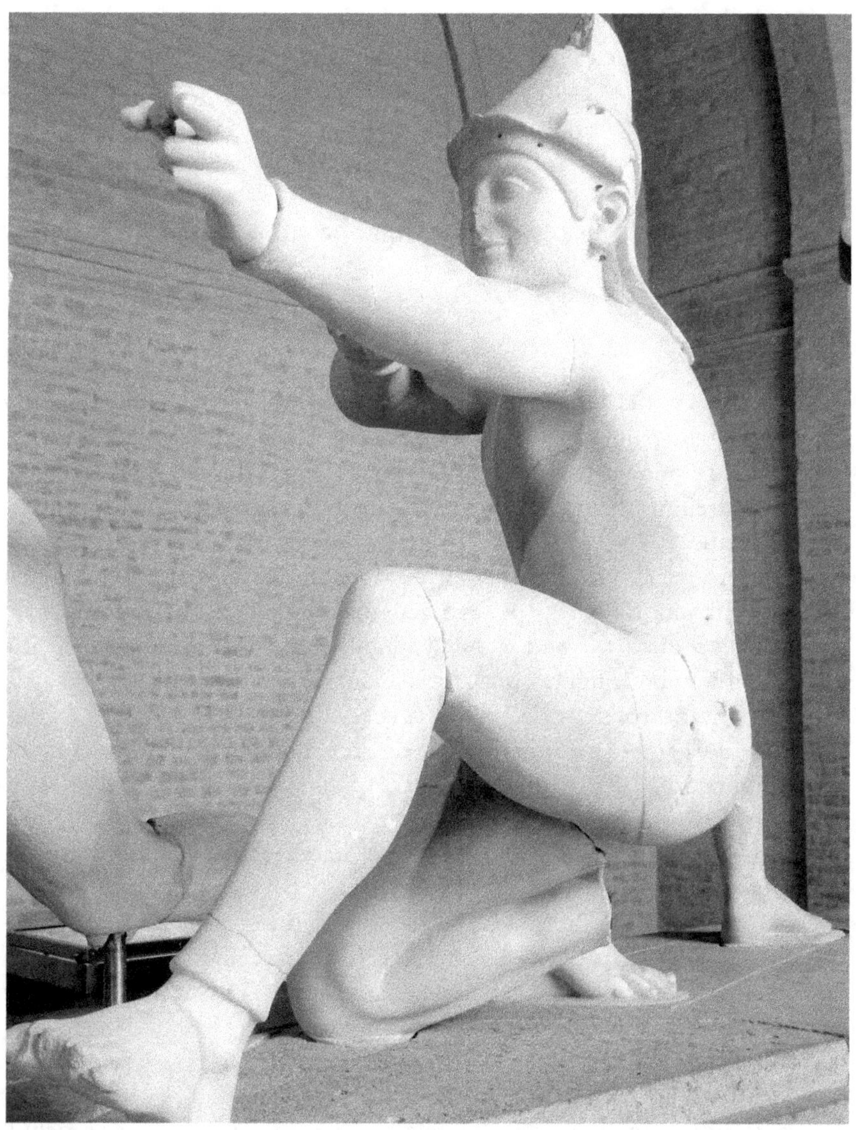

Figure 1.5. Kneeling archer (Paris) from the Temple to Aphaia on Aegina. Glyptothek Museum. Author's photograph.

This archer appears, from the position of the arms and the closed hand, to be about to draw his bowstring.

This figure is among the best preserved. Nothing is missing, save for one half of the left forefoot and two fingers. The nose and the left arm are somewhat damaged.

We also possess only the right arm, with the hand, and both feet of another similar archer.

---

[49] The two remaining archers are wearing armor of the sort frequently depicted in vase painting (see Tischbein, book I, page 4).[30] My guess is that this form of armor was originally Egyptian, which the Greeks borrowed. Herodotus tells us that the Medes took much the same form of armor from the Egyptians.

More specifically, they are cut in the same line all the way around, much like our contemporary breastplates or cuirasses, and not at all like the Roman form which comes to an end at the hip and thus protects the abdomen. The armor worn by both figures is, again like our own breastplates, rather stiff, with no indication of musculature and decorated with a double row of oblong, quadrangular patches in leather, attached to the shoulders with straps. On the left side under the left arm the buckle of the armor is rendered with [50] particular attention to its specific details.

Under the armor they wore a short coat that extended halfway down the thigh.

The uniform, like the armor, is rendered with the greatest care and meticulous accuracy, so that one can be certain that everything has been made in a most deliberate imitation of their real nature, omitting nothing, no matter how trifling.

L AND M.

One of the other two archers, who is missing a head and both forearms including the hands, as well as the left leg from the knee down, is depicted with youthful and delicate limbs.

The chemise that he is wearing under the armor is folded in the conventional way in the Archaic style [*altgriechischen Styl*].

[51] The other archer, however, appears to be physically robust and of the ideal manly age. As far as the armor and the posture are concerned, he is very similar to the one discussed previously, the only difference being that his underclothing beneath the armor is not rendered in the conventional Archaic style [*altgriechischen Styl*], but rather is entirely lacking in contours.

He wears a helmet on his head resembling a lion's head in front. The back side, however, is entirely smooth, much like the other helmets. This helmet's decoration, incidentally, is rendered with particular taste and attention to detail.

There are many distinctive qualities to observe here, but I omit them, since such a detailed description without additional illustration would be entirely inadequate to the task.

This figure lacks the right forearm, both hands, and the left leg from the knee down.

---

[52] Among the fragments belonging to the archers, there are two quivers, each of a different form and most carefully rendered. These were, in accordance with my previous argument, attached to the left hip with a pin, which was apparently held in place with a bolt. One of these quivers appears to belong to the headless archer [fig. L], but the other, which has a more Asiatic form, appears to belong to the Persian archer [fig. K].

There is one last figure to be placed here, since it is unclear whether he should be counted among the standing or the kneeling figures. He seems better suited to this heading, where I have elected to include him.

N.

Of all the masculine figures this is the smallest, represented as a youth [53] who appears to be in combat with another warrior who is already on the ground. His position is thus close to kneeling, as the youth appears almost to be touching the ground with his right knee. The left leg is extended, the left arm is extended forward, but the right arm is pulled back and downward, as if he is moving in to stab his opponent.

His entire body is naked, as are all the other warriors except the archers, and like them he wears only a helmet, a shield, and leg armor, with no other clothing or weaponry in evidence.

The helmet of this figure lacks all contour and is almost entirely smooth. It appears that it was originally decorated with a hairdress. One also notices, here as elsewhere, drilled holes on the front of the helmet for the attachment of some decoration.

The cheek-pieces on the helmets—which were separately attached to the marble in all other cases and which attached at the cheeks—were, [54] judging by the drilled holes on the helmet, open in this figure's case. That is to say, they stand open, such as one often sees in Greek vase painting, and as one sees also in a lovely example of a small bronze figurine in the Museum of Florence.

At the back of the neck, close under the helmet, there are likewise two rows of small, drilled holes for the fastening or the rendering of ornamental locks of hair that were composed of lead wire similar in form to our contemporary ball screws. As luck would have it, one of these locks of hair survived, and was actually found still attached to a head in the initial excavation, as Mr. Linkh has assured me. It might also be that this depicted a tassel that was visible on the aegis of the Minerva I have already described. That piece was also composed of lead wire.

[55] This figure lacks both hands and the left forearm, the entire left foot, and the toes of the right foot. Otherwise it is fairly well preserved.

IV.

Supine Figures, or Wounded Figures

There are four supine figures that are fairly similar in their general posture, but which differ to a greater degree from one another than those figures discussed in the previous sections.

O.

One of these supine figures depicts a youth pulling an arrow or spear from out of a wound under his right breast. His body is entirely naked, without a helmet or other armament.

[56] His hair, which is delicately rendered, moves in winding symmetrical lines from the center to the sides, and is bound up with some sort of rounded braid. The hair on the forehead, running from one ear to the other, comes to an end in small, snail-shaped locks that lie on top of one another in two rows.

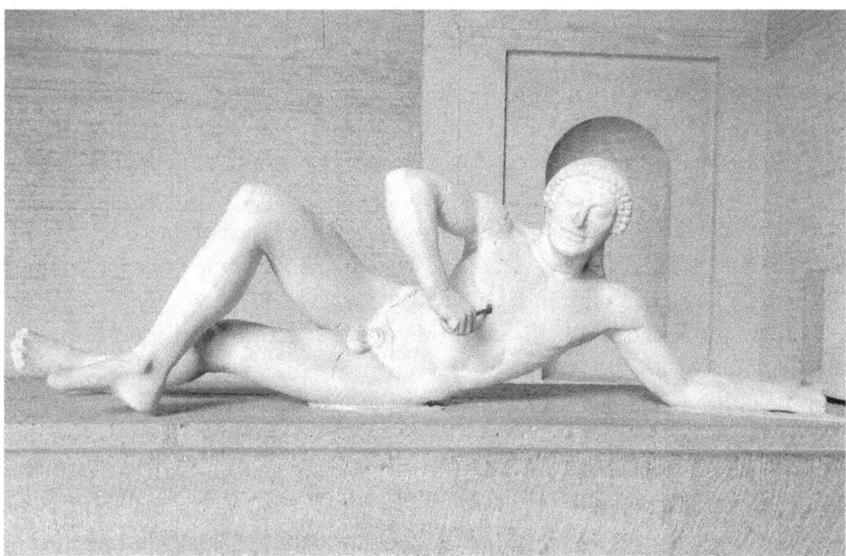

Figure 1.6. Twisted fallen warriors from the Temple to Aphaia on Aegina. Glyptothek Museum. Author's photograph.

The hair on the back, however, comes down to the middle of the back in wavy lines, ending in flamelike points. The hair, which is so conventional in form and arrangement, leaves nothing more to be desired from the perspective of its conception and the work's precision.

On both sides of this figure, between the chest and the shoulders, there are three holes drilled at small intervals one from another. This is a detail we have already observed on the statue of Minerva, and also on the two smaller female figures, B and C. The general interpretation of these holes is that they served for the attachment of some type of necklace. I cannot however [57] confirm this interpretation, for the following reason. If these holes really served this purpose, then one would expect them to appear in similar intervals all the way around the neck. That, however, is not the case here. There are only three holes grouped together on either side of the chest in front. Furthermore, I observe that it is only on this supine figure that the three holes on either side that are inclining toward the head are aligned sideways, which is to say, running toward the shoulders. From this I propose that these holes depended upon the position of the head for their placement, which was altered due to the distinctive position of this figure. I therefore conclude that these holes more likely served for the attachment or the anchoring of a band or braid, with which the hair was wreathed and which was visible once again behind the ears, than for the attachment of three small globes or tassels to the breast. I would be far more certain [58] of this conclusion if I had found another hole on either side behind the ears of this figure, as I did on the Minerva. This band was presumably made of metal and ran along the breast, anchored in these drilled holes. In the Greek vase drawings by Tischbein we frequently see these kinds of bands that end in two or three small balls or tassels. (See Tischbein's *Vases* book I, plate 38; book II, plates 34, 35, 43, 53; book III, plate 48; book IV, plates 16, 35).[31]

This figure stands out for its lovely rendering and good state of preservation, but also for its rather strange posture, with its two thighs crossed in a most curious manner. The wounded man lies on his left side, with his left forearm propping him up against the ground. The left leg is stretched out, but the right leg comes up over it, so that the right foot is actually closer to the left arm. He is using his right [59] arm to pull the arrow out of the wound.

Very little is missing from this figure: the right leg from the knee to the ankle, all the toes on both feet, all the fingers on the left hand, and one small piece of the right forearm.

P.

In addition to this supine figure, we have another one very like him but in mirror image, save that he lacks the strange crossing of the thighs and his arms are positioned differently. There is a remarkable lifelikeness and grace in the movement of this figure. It is thus all the more regrettable that its entire front surface has suffered as it has from the acidicity of the soil; the back side of the statue is much better preserved. This figure, like the previous one, had long hair running well down the back, but with this difference—that the plaits all [60] resemble noodles [*Nudeln gleichen*], lying on top of one another in narrow bands, and carved in linear shapes ending in flamelike points.

There is a small, drilled hole visible on the left leg that appears to be a wound, and in its immediate vicinity four barely perceptible extensions in the marble. I suspect that these are traces of the fingers and that the wounded man was depicted with his hand near the wound, which he received from an archer. Perhaps there was a metal arrow actually attached in the hole.

One also notices on this figure, as on most of the other warriors, a drilled hole on the right shoulder, and some others under the left arm, which probably served as anchoring for the strap on which the sword (*Parazonium*) hung. That strap was in all likelihood made of bronze.

The head, the entire left arm, and the right forearm are all missing, as are both [61] legs from the knee downward, including the feet and hands.

Q.

I now move on to the third of these supine figures, which is depicted as a somewhat older man. His entire body is characterized by strong musculature, but with a certain amount of fat such as is normal with advancing age.[32] This combination of the weakness of age and the evidence of lingering youthful strength is harmonized and combined by the artist with exceptional skill, and I have no hesitation is calling this figure one of the most excellent in the entire collection.

The posture of this older man cast upon the ground is somewhat violent but not at all exaggerated. He appears to have broken his fall with the shield he carries on his left arm and which has penetrated slightly into the earth. He appears to have held his sword in the right hand, given [62] the position and grip of his hand. Before this figure was properly reassembled, I was not opposed to the assumption that he seemed to be struggling with his right hand over an arrow penetrating the inner surface of his shield. A small opening on the inner surface of the shield led me to this idea. But the complete reassembly of the figure and repeated close investigation suggested that the hand did not lie in the necessary position relative to the opening on the shield, such as this assumption required.

He wears a helmet which is somewhat more highly crested than the Minerva's. Up over the eyes it has two semicircular incisions whose edges run parallel to the eyebrows. The middle piece between the eyes runs down to the point of the nose, protecting its entire length. The [63] helmet, moreover, had cheek plates, which were separately attached. One sees this most clearly on the side where the attachment is missing, and only the metal fastening remains. On top of the helmet in the middle, one notes a depression that, so it seems, served for the attachment of the plume. Apart from the beard, which is rendered in a peculiarly stiff manner, no other hair is visible.

This figure alone of the group shows evidence of an ancient restoration, or improvement, on the right buttock, which appears to be very similar to the original rendering of the statue. Perhaps the marble was faulty in one place, or perhaps a sculptor's mistake necessitated this alteration. Both here and in several other cases, one notes that the ancients did not use the so-called Greek or Calabrian pitch [*Pechs*] for their restorations [*Ergänzungen*] as we do, but rather an entirely different putty or cement unknown to us.

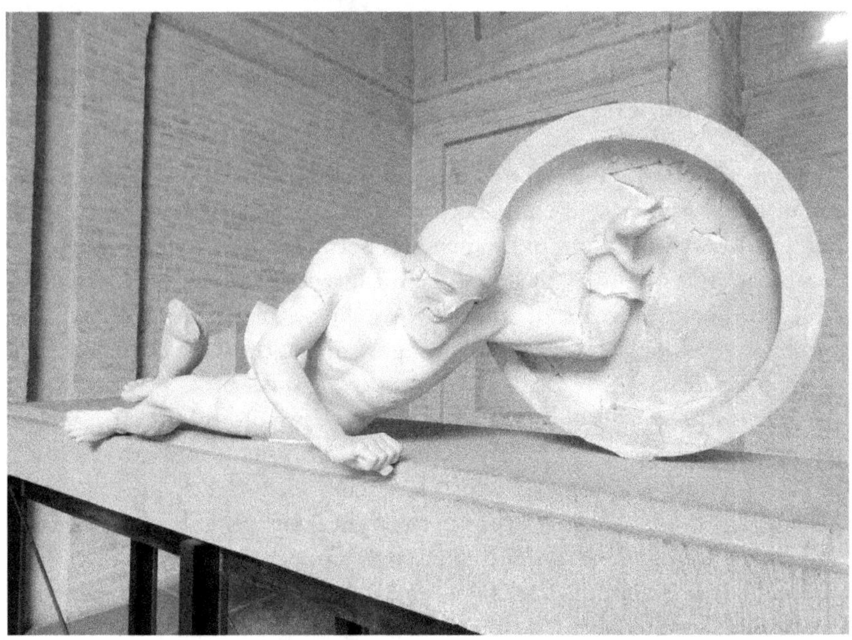

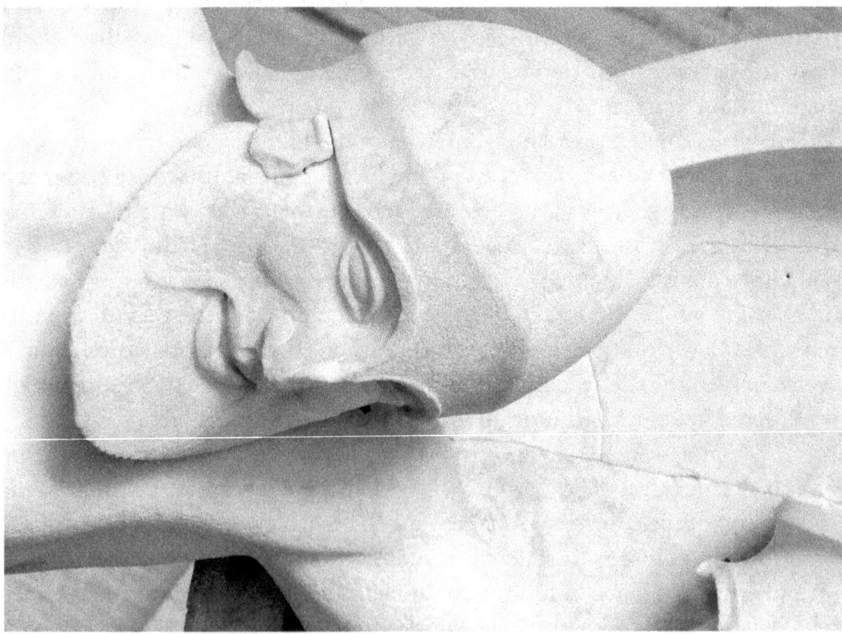

Figure 1.7a–1.7b. Bearded fallen warrior from the Temple to Aphaia on Aegina. Glyptothek Museum. Author's photographs.

[64] This figure lacks a right leg from the mid-thigh down, a few fingers from the left hand, and a few pieces of the left leg.

R.

The fourth of these supine figures resembles the first two in its youthful bodily composition. The posture or position of this warrior is more or less similar to that of the others, with this difference: this figure supports himself with a hand on the ground; the other two support themselves with an elbow. He carries a shield on his left arm, which appears to have been attached to the arm with a screw.

This figure has pride of place over all the others with respect to its superb execution and fine state of preservation, and might well have served as a source for the great artworks in the age of Perikles.

[65] Except for the head, which is missing, no significant part of this body is damaged. The fingers, toes, and a few cracked pieces are the only damaged portions of the whole. All the more pity, then, that the right breast and shoulder suffered from the dampness of the soil, or from general weathering, and are heavily pitted. The remaining portions of this statue are extremely well preserved, as fresh as they must have been when first they emerged from the hand of the artist.

Some fragments of legs and feet suggest that there may well have originally been a fifth supine figure.

CHAPTER II

Fragments that Belong Either to the Aeginetan Figures or to the Temple

[Wagner]

[66]
After I have attempted to describe the existing statues precisely, at least so far as can be done in words, it would be unthinkable to overlook the fragments in all forms that also may well belong to the images in this collection. They cannot be categorized with certainty, since they lack essential portions that would otherwise have linked them. When, however, we turn our hands to the restoration [*Ergänzung*], and examine each of these remaining fragments more carefully, then it becomes clear that [67] at least some of them belonged to one figure or another. For the present, we can only hope that at least some of these pieces will find their original places once again.

It would profit us little, and would also be far too lengthy, to describe every fragment independently. I speak thus only of the most excellent ones, which are as follows:

A.A.

Three Heads of Warriors

One has a high-crested helmet of the common Greek form with the visor, or eyeholes, and nose plate. It also has the similar remains of hair [*Ueberreste des Haarbushces*]. The helmet is pushed to the back of the head, so that the forehead is visible from the brow to the helmet as far as the hairline. It is a

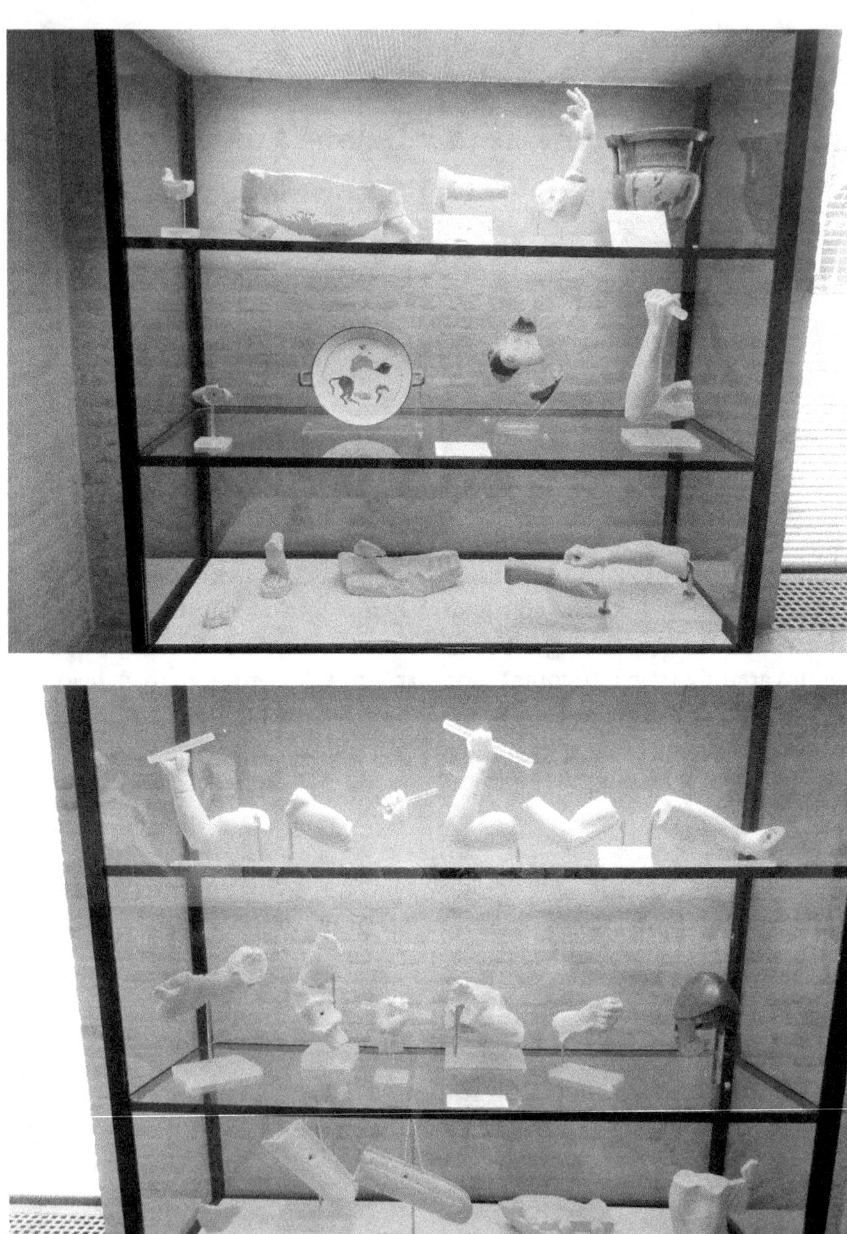

Figure 2.1a–2.1b. Fragment cases from the Temple to Aphaia on Aegina. Glyptothek Museum. Author's photographs.

source of wonder how elegantly and with what an eye for detail the hair on this piece is rendered, [68] although the position of the visor I have just described lends this rendering a certain unreality.

The hair is rendered in the same way as that on all the other heads—namely, with the shape of macaroni [*Maccaroni*]. The hair on the back of the head is covered, and there is an attached cord running along the length of the head from one ear to the other where the ear meets the hairline, ending in rows of snail-shaped locks. The head is very youthful and appears to belong to the supine warrior (fig. R). The proportion and character of this head correspond well with that figure, save that one half has suffered from the effects of moisture. The fracture line no longer fits, and so it must remain in doubt whether it belonged to that figure or not.

The other head likewise boasts a helmet, which nevertheless has a different [69] shape. It does not have the same high curvature or crest, but rather lies quite close to the head. It is not carved in a straight line in front over the eyes, but rather ends in line with the eyebrows in two semicircular cuttings. In between these two cuttings of the helmet, where the nose begins, a separate piece of marble is attached. I conclude that the helmet permitted this addition, which is preserved in its entire length in the figure (fig. Q.), and which also extended from the tip of the nose to the bridge. A similar design is to be found on the head of the figure (fig. N.).

That all of the helmets in this group were painted appears to be beyond serious doubt. I have discovered traces of sky-blue paint on most of them. This particular head appears to have been specially painted, since on one side a criss-cross pattern [70] is visible, like a string of pearls. This netlike string of pearls appears to have been painted, and the encaustic colors are preserved on the smooth surfaces of the marble, whereas the unpainted portions are somewhat pitted and rough due to weathering, creating a kind of *chiaroscuro* effect. Although a small section that was cleaned seemed to reveal hints of sky-blue coloring, the actual color is impossible to determine.

What I mentioned earlier regarding painted colors on the lips and eyeballs is supported by similar observations on all of these heads, thereby providing further confirmation. Even the head of the Minerva had visible traces of this painting.

The head is youthful and, like the others, very well preserved. There is no certain trace of hair on it, except on the back half, directly under the helmet, where one finds a small row [71] of drilled holes that served, as I have had several occasions to observe already, for the artful attachment of lead curls.

The third of these heads, whose lower jaw is damaged, also survives with a helmet of the more enclosed type. On the forward half of the helmet, running from one ear to the other, two incisions run in parallel, in which one may observe a double row of drilled holes. There are traces of lead wire still visible in the holes. The surviving lead ringlets may well have been found still partly hanging from a portion of this head, and thus seem to confirm my previous assumptions about this decorative trope. This head might well belong to the figure (fig. G.).

---

[72] One quarter-section of another head survives—namely, a portion of the helmet similar in form to the ones previously described, including the ear, which was beautifully worked with the greatest care and diligence.

B.B.

Fragments of Thighs, Legs, and Feet

Two thighs together with the lower leg portions. Both appear to go together. The right leg is extended, the left one is sharply bent. The feet are missing. My guess is that they belonged to a single figure in a pose similar to the figures (*lett. D.E.*) described above.

Two other thighs, without the legs. One notes traces of leg armor at the knees. They appear to have belonged to an armored figure rendered in a pose similar to that of the archers (figs. L. and M.).

[73] At the thickest part of the thigh there are traces of clothing, folded in the customary manner and style.

One leg from the knee down, together with the foot, which appears to have belonged to a supine figure. It is rendered in a deceptively naturalistic style, so that one might almost suppose it to be a living leg.

There are also a goodly number of other legs of every kind, some with feet and some without. There are also some other feet that survive independently, both masculine and feminine, more or less well preserved, with a few that are altogether excellent given their graceful rendering and delicate form.

C.C.

Fragments of Arms and Hands

Of the arms with shields attached, most are intact, a few are in pieces, and one is superb [74], both for its beauty and overall state of preservation. The shields themselves, although shattered into countless pieces, are still partly visible.

In addition to these limbs armed with shields, there are many more fragments of other arms—some of which may have belonged to supine figures, and some to fighting warriors. There is also one feminine forearm with a fragment of her robe. That fragment was specially attached, as the marble itself attests.

A great many more hands, more or less damaged.

Finally, an additional number of fragments of various sorts, large pieces that appear to belong to bodies that no longer survive, or perhaps to bodies that do survive but which cannot be determined with certainty, since in all likelihood the essential links or joints are missing.

[75] There are also a large number of fragments of helmet decoration—namely, the crest of hair on top, or the general structure of the helmet.

Comparison of these fragments with the surviving statues suggests that the original number of statues must have been considerably higher. According to my estimate, they may have amounted to thirty in all.[33]

D.D.

As for the griffins [or sphinxes] which stood on opposing ends of the façade, and which therefore probably were four in number (with one at the ends of each of the pediments), there are only some fragments remaining. It is regrettable that not a single head from one of these fabulous wolfish [*Arimaspischen*] animals survives. What do survive are a rear portion of the body, and more fragments of the legs, and the wings.

E.E.

---

[76]
A small round altar in limestone also survives, limestone being the stone out of which the entire temple was constructed, except for the roof tiles and the upper molding, which were all in white marble. There are some fragments of these roof tiles, and one tile that survives intact. The exposed sides of these roof tiles were painted, as one can clearly gather from the marble. There are many other pieces of architectural fragments, some in limestone and some in marble, as well as some roof tiles in baked clay, which were probably also painted.

F.F.

No less remarkable is one piece of a pilaster [*eines Pilestars*], which was made of white-green marble, and which is decorated with a Greek inscription. The upper portion is damaged, but it seems to have been a catalogue of artifacts [77] and tools that were stored in this temple.

The facing page contains an exact copy of this inscription. Judging by the script, this inscription comes from a later period than that of the construction of the temple.

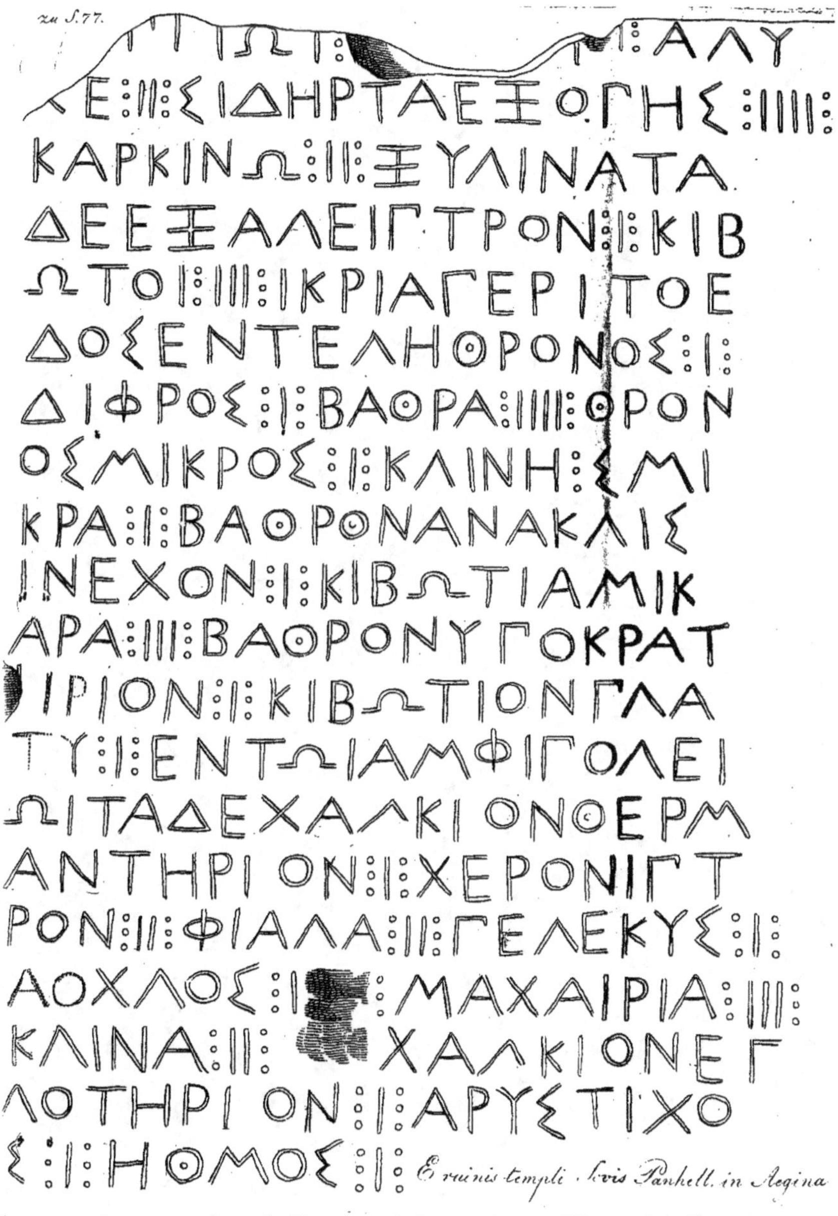

Figure 2.2. Inscription from the Temple to Aphaia on Aegina. Wagner/Schelling, *Report on the Aeginetan Sculptures . . .* (1817).

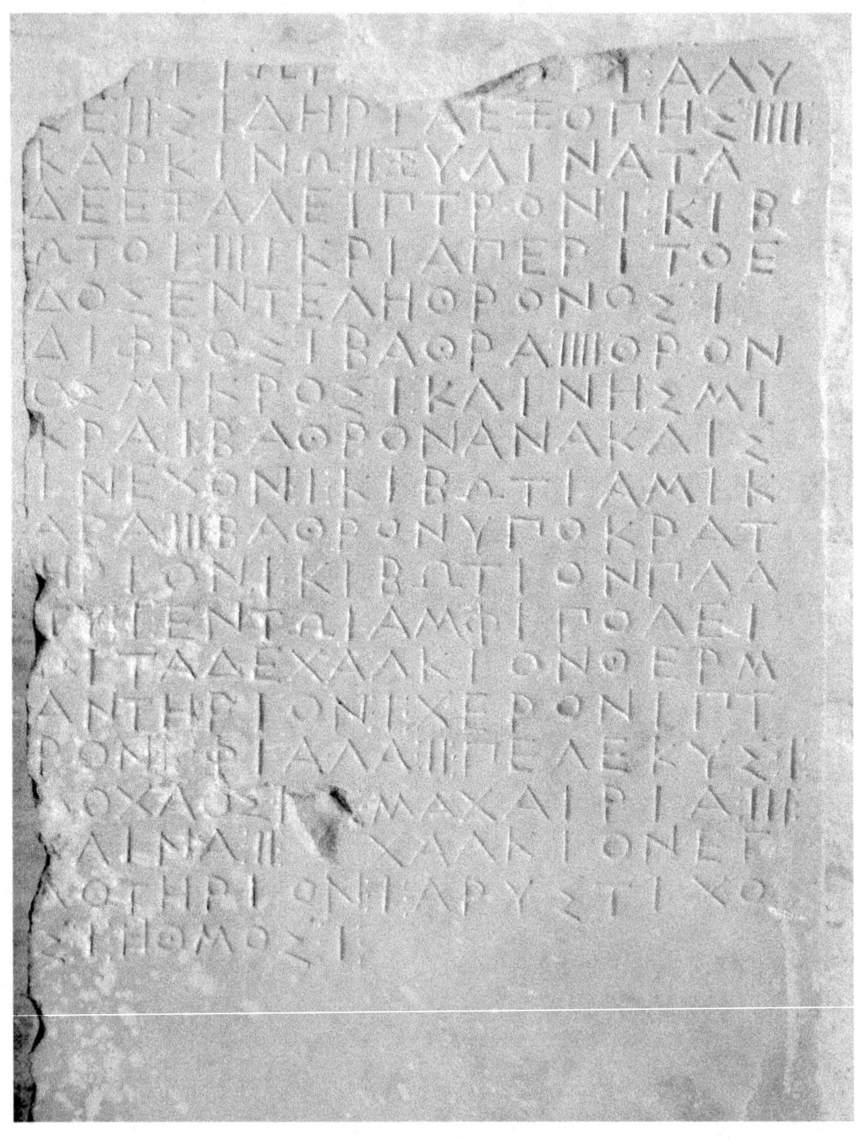

Figure 2.3. Inscription on the excavated stele from Aegina. Glyptothek Museum. Author's photograph.

NOTE FROM THE EDITOR

[Schelling]

If this inscription shall prove to be less important than some others from an epigraphical perspective, it will be dear to the hearts of antiquarians, who may take from it some pleasant evidence for the enrichment of their vocabularies. For this inscription appears to bring some heretofore unknown words to light. Readers who are inexperienced in working with inscriptions must content themselves with the mediation of a translation. And one must leave to the experts the reproduction of the damaged [78] first line and the continuation of one word onto the beginning of the second line. The numbers of the pieces catalogued may be found between the double row of three points ⁝, which also leave no doubt about the meaning of the many singular and dual forms used here.

Line of Inscription		Number of Pieces
2	Iron (weapons or tools) that are above ground	4
3	Tongs	2
	The following pieces are made of wood:	
4	Salve-box	1
	Cases	3
5,6	The scaffolding standing upright in position (for the temple, or statue?)	
6	Throne	1
7	Seat (sedan, or carriage?)	1
7	Frames	4
8	Small throne	1
	Small couch	1
9	Frame, which folds back	1
10	Small cases	3
11	Frame under a chalice	1
12	Wide case (or small chest)	1
13	In the Sacristy there are the following:	
14	Copper cauldron	1
15	Basin for hand-washing	1

	16	Bowls	2
		Axe	1
	17	Lever [μόχλος]	1
		Knives	3
	18	Couches [κλίνα, Dual.]	2
[80]			
		Copper Washbasin	1
		Bucket	1
	19	Leather Punch	1

[Wagner (cont.)]

No metal tools have survived. There remain only two pegs at whose function I cannot guess.

G.G. There are also many more fragments of Greek vases and small figurines in baked clay, which were found in the initial excavation of the temple. Especially noteworthy is the fragment of a cup [*Tazze*] of exceptional beauty. It is regrettable that the foot and [81] also the middle portion of the cup are damaged. On the inner surface there was a Europa, seated on a bull, rendered in color on a white background. Her arm buckle, necklace, earrings, and the hem of her garment, as well as her diadem, are all set off, gilded, and in high relief. The outside of the cup is decorated in the usual way, in red and black, with two winged genii who hold a cup in one hand and a lyre in the other.

H.H. Lastly I must mention *a colossal ivory eye*, which was also found in the excavation of the temple. It is just the white of the eye; the area of the pupil is slightly hollowed and was, so it appears, filled in with a different colored material. The length of this eye, from one [82] corner to the other, was one half of a Roman palm, or 4¼ inches (French standard). I cannot say whether this eye once belonged to some enormous statue, to which it was attached in the ancient manner, or whether it should be thought of as an *ex voto* offering. That it originally belonged to a statue is improbable for the following reason: the eye was found inside the temple, where one ought also to have found pieces of such a colossal statue; these were not found. In this respect, I consider the other assumption more likely—namely, that it was stored in the temple as a dedicatory offering [*Gelübde*].

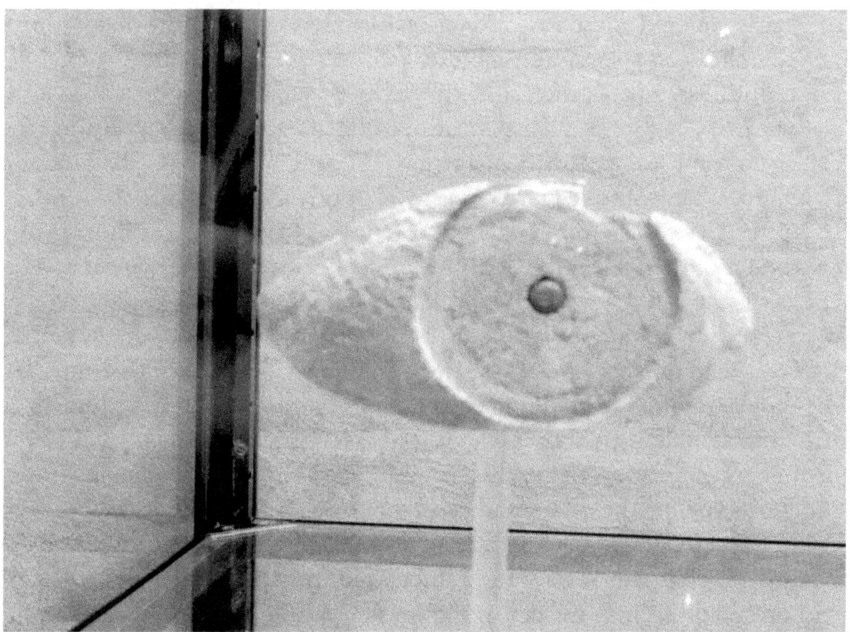

Figure 2.4. Incised eye from the Temple to Aphaia on Aegina. Glyptothek Museum. Author's photograph.

NOTE FROM THE EDITOR

[Schelling]

The following observations might well lead to a different conclusion. A [83] statue of the god must have been inside this temple. That it was colossal is historically impossible to prove, but was almost surely the case. That this colossus was made of ivory and gold is much less certain, given the absence of actual reported evidence, than Mr. Quatremère de Quincy (in the oft-quoted book, p. 306, note 4) supposes.[34] When one considers the great antiquity of this style of statuary in gold and ivory, and its nearly universal use in the major Greek temples, then this assumption achieves a much higher probability. And if this assumption is granted, then it clarifies why no small pieces of this colossal statue have been found. Such a statue of ivory and gold, which withstood the passage of time less well, had an entirely different appeal for barbarians and plunderers than a simple marble image. That no other portions of the image of Jupiter[35] have been found on Aegina is thus as [84] natural as the fact that every trace of the gold and ivory statue of Minerva in the Parthenon in Athens has disappeared. It was only the marble statues from both pediments that were relatively well preserved, at least up to the times of Spon and Wheler.[36] Indeed, when one considers the general similarity between both temples—the temple of Panhellenic Jupiter on Aegina and the temple of Minerva in Athens—as well as the general style and arrangement of the images in the pediment (see chapter VII of this report), then one can easily imagine one as the prototype for the other, and can more easily see the similarity between them.[37] There is thus no need to imagine this colossal eye as an *ex voto* offering, for which it would have been uncommonly large. Rather, and virtually without doubt, it may be seen as the former part of a colossal Jupiter in the temple of Aegina, and from this perspective it achieves its full significance. [85] The eyeball may well have been rounded out with a colored stone, but it is far likelier that it was painted, as the other statues were, since the incision on this piece is rather slight.

CHAPTER III

On the Style of These Figures

[Wagner]

[86]
After having described the exterior features of the Aeginetan sculptures, so far as that is possible, I turn next to their style, though I sense how difficult it is to provide a meaningful conception [*deutlichen Begriff*] or a vital image of such pieces merely with words. This can only really be obtained through an actual inspection of the pieces in their full and lifelike reality.

For those scholars and lovers of antiquity, for whom alone this report has been written, I include only as much information regarding art and antiquity as is necessary [87] to assist in drawing conclusions from one point to the other. So I dare now to apply my limited capabilities to a presentation [*Vorstellung*] of the style and the distinctive characteristics of these early artworks.

Before proceeding to the respective pieces and the distinctive aspects that characterize their style, I deem it necessary to begin with several more general observations. With these, the reader may place what I will say later on within a definite point of view, from which to understand what I am contending more easily.

I seek this point of view first of all through a recapitulation of the earlier observation, establishing that these figures, the naked and the clothed ones alike, are very similar in style. That style was previously called *Etruscan* [*hetrurischen*], but it is actually better to call it the Archaic [*altgriechische*] style, as I shall demonstrate a little later on.

However, when these similarities are read [88] in light of all the distinguishing features that were previously assigned to the Etruscan style, I freely admit that perhaps some of the small deviations from that style which are most obvious might be assigned to the Aeginetan School, which Pausanias, Pliny, and others[(1),38] spoke of with such praise, and which served to differentiate it from the Etruscan or the Ancient Greek style.

---

1. SCHELLING'S NOTE: For better or worse, Pliny does not reflect our knowledge of a distinctive Aeginetan style

Perhaps the naked figures in this group may be more clearly distinguished from so-called Etruscan works, since they are each and every one rendered with such natural realism. One seldom encounters this feature among the so-called Etruscan works. (1)

Except for the heads, which I will discuss further below, what prevails in all parts of the bodies is the most faithful [89] imitation of Nature [*die treueste Nachahmung der Natur*],[39] down to the smallest details and accidents of the flesh, which are rendered without the slightest trace of idealism or the tendency to idealize what we commonly refer to as Nature. Indeed, this felicitous imitation of Nature [*diese freue Nachahmung der Natur*] is neither tentative, nor wooden, nor unscientific [*wissenschaftslos*], such as we are accustomed to find in earlier works of the ancients as well as in contemporary art. Rather, it is a highly self-conscious imitation of natural beauty [*eine wohlverstandene Nachahmung der schönen Natur*], combined with the most complete knowledge of bones and musculature, which seems so effortless and self-assured that the lively form of the limbs appears almost to be a natural deception [*bis zur Täuschung natürlich erscheinen*], so much so that one experiences a sort of start, and even fear, when confronted with a few of the pieces whose naturalism borders on deception [*ihrer bis zur Täuschung gehenden Natürlichkeit*].

To be sure, this naturalism is not entirely free of conventions. Rather, one notices in a few of the poses or body parts certain peculiarities [90] and deviations from the standard human form, as I will endeavor to show a little further on.

In terms of *proportion* these figures are all slender, narrow at the hips, and the legs are rather a bit too long than too short. This is particularly noticeable on the Minerva, and the two small female figures B and C, both of whom, when observed from the back, have an upper torso and buttocks that are shorter than the legs are, extending below the buttocks. That relationship is clearly reversed in Nature. (2)

The *poses* are natural, often quite realistic if sometimes also a bit forced or twisted, as is the case with the supine older figure [*lett. Q.*] and with the legs of the Minerva. I do not mean to suggest that it is impossible to adopt such a pose or to represent one as such. Generally there is a great deal of liveliness in their movement, [91] although I can also say that they are not entirely free from the appearance of a certain stiffness.

It may well be unclear to some how a figure can be full of life and yet possess a certain stiffness at the same time. But do we not also find—in the pictures of Giotto, of Massaccio, of Pinturiccio, of Pietro Perugino, among others—for all of their easy grace, liveliness, and inimitable [*unnachahmlichen*] charm, also a certain stiffness? I should like to view this as the mark of innocence and childlikeness, since it manifests itself similarly in the early artworks of the Greeks as well as the aforementioned works of the fourteenth and fifteenth centuries.

The robes of these figures are, generally speaking, entirely conventional, fitting close to the body, especially at the thighs and legs. The folds do not fall naturally, but rather are artistically conceived and rendered, and normally end in straight masses of fabric with a [92] zigzag border. I do not consider a more precise description of the folds necessary, since they are well known from the Ancient Greek and so-called Etruscan artworks, and they are all entirely similar. I need only observe that these robes, howsoever conventional and stiff in the way they hang, are handled with extraordinary taste and are rendered with amazing detail, all of which clearly distinguishes them from customarily Ancient Greek and so-called Etruscan works.

I proceed now to a description of individual body parts and to some of their distinctive characteristics.

The *heads* of these figures, or at least the faces, appear from the perspective of their conception [*Bildung*] or style to be a good deal older than the surviving body parts, or at least to point to a much earlier artistic era. In them, one generally notes a transitional, imported form, from which one may assume [93] that the Greeks borrowed from the Egyptians.

The *eyes* are strictly front-facing, somewhat exaggerated in length, and occasionally rendered in a vaguely Chinese manner.

The *mouth* has strong, full lips with sharply defined edges, and in a few cases the corner of the mouth is pulled up slightly higher, which gives the appearance of a laughing or grinning expression.

The shape of the *noses* and *ears* are unexceptional. The former appear somewhat flat, whereas the latter are seen to be rendered with the greatest fidelity and clarity of conception.

The *chin* is rather strong and full, so that the portion of the face running from the nose to the end of the chin is overly long in relation to the rest of the face.

What I observe here in relation to the faces goes for every figure without [94] exception. From the Minerva to the last of the warriors, all look quite similar and appear to be a flesh-and-blood [*leiblich*] assembly of brothers and sisters, without the slightest expression of emotion [*Leidenschaft*]. Between besiegers and besieged, between divinity and humanity, there is not the slightest difference to be seen.

The *hair*, from the standpoint of its presentation [*Darstellung*], is every bit as conventional as the garment folds, and is so far removed from the natural and unaffected shock of hair as to seem almost like the stiff, powdered wig of an abbot. As I have already had the opportunity to observe on several of these figures, the hair flows in long running lines, rendered in the form of thick strands or macaroni [*Maccaroni*], from the crown of the head downward; it falls in wavy lines down the back, but in the front, from one ear to the other, it ends in small snail-shaped locks that are very delicately and artistically rendered. The hair of the Minerva is really [95] the strangest and most bizarre of all. But all of the hair is rendered in a conventional manner to one degree or another.

Just as strangely conventional is the handling of the hair over the genitals. It is all carved in a certain way, very carefully curled in alternating portions and with carefully regulated form. The form of the carving is almost identical in every case, although with slight individual differences and deviations, to be sure. This artistically established form, the careful way in which the hair is depicted flowing in one direction or the other, as well as the scrupulous execution and conscientious presentation [*Darstellung*] of the same—all this suggests to me, without doubt, that the men of that time used to curl the pubic hair, and associated a certain preciousness or value to this fashion. This would have been most clearly the case with the youth who, in public ceremonies, games, or military exercises, [96] would have appeared naked. Thus, I do not think that the manner in which the hair on the head is represented on these figures is a caprice of the artist or even a fixed artistic norm [*eine festgesetzte Norm in der Kunst*]. Rather, I believe that it was an actual custom [*Sitte*] of that time to wear the hair in this manner.

I hold a similar opinion about the conventional form of the robes, with their well-pressed artistic folds, such as we see on all surviving Ancient Greek and Etruscan artworks. (3)

The bodies are rather small above the hips, and the appearance of the ribs and the associated muscles (*dentati*) is also a bit leaner and nondescript, but still entirely conventional in form, save for a few peculiarities and differences, which I will note here. The sword-shaped chest cartilege (*ensiformis*) is more or less well defined on all these figures, [97] such as would be the case only when the body is bent sharply backwards, but is the case with all the figures here, even those lacking the motion that would cause the cartilage to protrude. Furthermore, the definition of the *pectoral muscles* on all these figures, which run perpendicularly from the chest to the navel. deviates from the otherwise customary manner of their rendering. We consider it normal in all later artworks that the definition of the upper muscles is deeper than the lower ones nearer the navel. But in this case it is the reverse; the abdominal muscles are more defined, or at least as well defined, as the upper musculature. I note these deviations from the otherwise standard form, because these peculiarities seem to be a characteristic of this style.

The *arms* have nothing remarkable about them, or at least nothing that deviates from the usual form, save that they perhaps appear to be rather too short [98] than too long. The bones, muscles and veins, and even the accidents of the flesh are all, here as in all other portions of the body, presented [*dargestellt*] with such truth and reality [*Treue und Wahrheit*] that many portions appear to be Nature itself, or at least formed so as to appear directly taken from Nature.

The *hands* are every bit as natural in their movements as in their several parts. Nothing is overlooked, no wrinkle of the skin, no trace of the nails. Of course, one finds hands among the fragments that appear to have been rather carelessly worked. This may have been due to their original position, such that they were probably placed so as to be invisible, or at least made far more difficult to see.

The *legs* are slender and well shaped, especially the *knees*, which are handled with great mastery and tremendous anatomical awareness. These also have a unique characteristic however, which is all the more [99] remarkable since they appear to be due, not to the unconsciousness of the artist, but rather as the result of a deliberate choice.

It is well known to both the visual artist and the trained eye that the knee, when it is sharply bent, loses its rather sharp and well-defined form and becomes rather blunt. The reason is that, with sharp bending, the thigh bone (*Femur*) and the shin bone (*Tibia*) move apart, and the kneecap drops down into this previously closed opening or gap. These natural changes in the knees, in direct relation to the degree of the bend, are visible primarily among those of our figures that are at rest or kneeling. In all the others, however, where the knee naturally forms such a bend, no artistic notice is taken of the fact. Generally speaking, the knees are formed far more as they naturally appear when [100] the leg is not at all bent or bent only slightly. This distinguishing feature is most notable in figures N and R. The rest of this part, like the rest of the body, is rendered with such profound anatomical knowledge that one must assume such an experienced master would have deviated from the natural form only by intention and not unconsciously. I doubt this even less since one observes the same thing, or at least something very similar, in other later artworks and even from the latest periods of [Greek] art, for example, the world-renowned Laocoön Group, where it is easy to see a similar issue in the right leg—namely, that the knee does not have the form it should have, given the way it is bent.

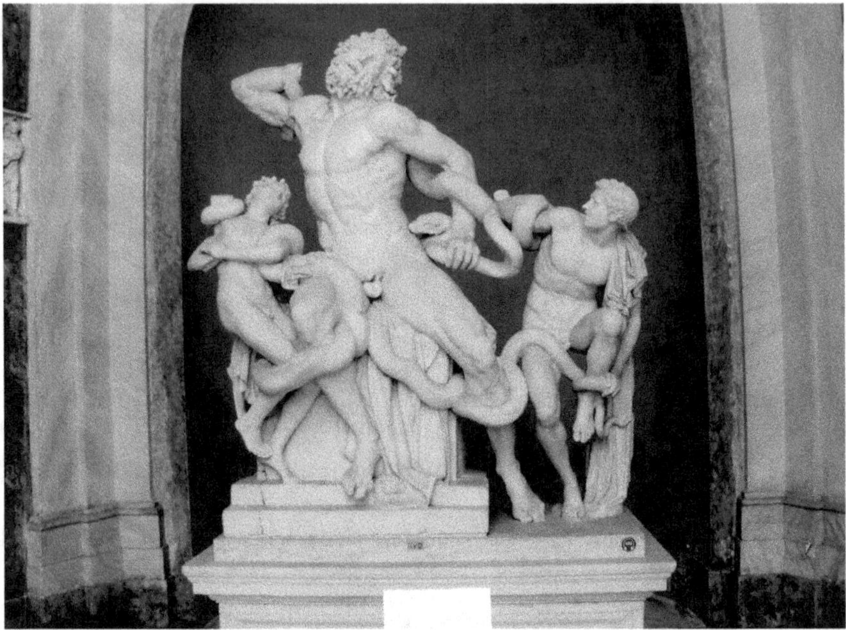

Figure 3.1. The Laocoön Group, the Vatican Museums. Author's photograph.

I have also to observe another peculiarity of the legs: that the so-called Achilles tendon is almost always rendered as very wide and angular where it attaches to the heel bone, such as I [101] have never found on any other work of art.

The *feet* are, like the hands, among the most beautiful and generally rendered in a very delicate manner.

What is all the more striking, therefore, are the toes, which are rather long and which run strictly parallel to one another, deviating from the rendering of the feet of statues from later times where the toes are drawn inward slightly, i.e., bent or curved toward the middle. It is also to be noted that both middle toes (I mean the first and second after the big toe) are of the same size on most feet, whereas the third toe is sharply pulled back and the smallest of all. It is doubtless the case that these feet, shaped in this manner, have tremendous affinity to Ancient Egyptian figures, which also have very long toes that run in parallel, but with this difference: that they have a more barbaric [102] form, and are much inferior in terms of workmanship. The veins on the feet are rendered with the greatest realism and care. Even on the feet that are not walking, but are rather freestanding, one observes a callous beneath the ball of the big toe, which is customary for those people who go everywhere barefooted.

Finally, it remains to be said that these figures, actually all quite similar from the stylistic point of view, and all appearing to have been completed at roughly the same time, nonetheless display significant differences in appearance depending upon whether they were more or less fully worked. This leads us to conclude that these figures were doubtless all made at the same time,[40] though not all by the same hand, but rather by the different hands of artists of greater or lesser skill.

[103] So much for what may be said regarding the generally prevailing style as well as the distinctive traits of the various parts of these figures. (4)

EDITOR'S NOTES
[Schelling]

[104]

---

(1) We ask the reader to keep the author's explanation clearly in mind in the discussion that follows. As carefully restrained as his language is, he nonetheless asserts that, as far as the *naked figures* are concerned, the style of these figures distinguishes itself remarkably and unmistakably from the so-called Etruscan style. This point can be combined with a second assumption: either that Aeginetan sculpture first turned away from the arid, stiff, and uniform style of so-called Etruscan art, and then later toward a greater naturalism; or that Aeginetan art strove from the very beginning toward a closer imitation of Nature [*die Natur nachzuahmen*] than did Etruscan art. In the first [105] instance, one may observe a style advanced far beyond this oldest style, despite the heavy clothing. This is similar to the way one may discern the school of Perugino still in the works of Raphael, in which there is far more of Nature than the works of his teacher, or the way in which one can feel the masters of the thirteenth century still in the works of the fifteenth, which are not at all comparable so far as science [*Wissenschaft*] and the perfect imitation of Nature [*vollkommene Nachahmung des Naturs*] are concerned. But if one takes up the second assumption, then the older works of the Aeginetans could be *duriora et Tuscanicis proxima*, as Quintilian[41] described the works of Kallon the Aeginetan, in which hardness and stiffness are necessarily combined with a faithful, if more tentative and uncertain and lifeless imitation of Nature [*Nachahmung der Natur*]. How this is related to the present figures, however—whether the style of the naked figures is actually reminiscent of the Etruscan style, or whether this is said simply on account of [106] generally accepted theory—one should presume to judge only after a careful review of the sculptures themselves. We content ourselves, therefore, by recalling the judgment of the author regarding one figure (*lett. R.*): that it might possibly have stood beside works from the age of Perikles, which accords well with our own thinking. That is, he does not wish to compare the style of these works in any way to the form and feeling of the Etruscan style, as Quintilian was the first to have done, by linking the works of such leading artists to Tuscan [*tuscischen*] works.

(2) This proportion is well known, but then the question becomes this: if this proportion does not have a place in the most beautiful physical specimens, or in Nature, then to what degree may it have a place in statues of the most beautiful style?

(3) That these folds and the entire artistic rendering of the robes will be found in such a wide variety of artworks that are assuredly not all from the same time period, is explained by the author as follows: namely, that [107] *the customs of the time* [*Sitte der damaligen Zeit*] which were used here are not entirely adequate as an explanation. Moreover, Mr. Quatremère de Quincy (p. 21) argues against this explanation with further reasons.[42] This is not entirely applicable to these Aeginetan figures since, as the following [paragraph] demonstrates, in these figures most of the forms are not original or freely rendered, but derive rather from an earlier time whose conventions they maintain. As for the last point regarding these artistically rendered and folded robes, one may approve the advice of this distinguished author, namely, that a more precise examination and general discussion should be undertaken here.

(4) It is doubtless the case that this masterly description of the style of the Aeginetan figures will be received with the liveliest gratitude in the service of art historical knowledge and general curiosity. Of course now, after the precise observations of the author and his most accurate and graphic representation [*Vorstellung*] of [108] the style of such works of art, one important matter remains for those who have not seen them. The author's description justifies us in pursuing the next question: whether these distinctive features or characteristics of the Aeginetan School, which Pausanias recognized and presumed with such certainty [*Bestimmtheit*], could have existed. In addition to the many peculiar details that the author has so carefully laid out, one must also find that overarching general characteristic, or else the school is not to be found.

If one accepts the opinions expressed up to now, then one shall return to the differences of Aeginetan art as evident in the following qualities.

1. Hardness of style, leanness of the forms. One identifies with the judgment of Quintilian (*Inst. Orat.* XII, 10), who, as was mentioned, called the works of Kallon *duriora*.[43] However, despite the fact that what applies to a single artist may also be applied to a school, it does not follow that the distinctive qualities of this school can be determined [*bestimmen kann*] for all time. Thus this same commentator adds that they were *Tuscanicis proxima*; and if Quintilian finds the works of these Aeginetans close to the Etruscan

style, then Strabo speaks against this[44] in the previously cited passage from Winckelmann (Stelle B. XVII, p. 806, Casaub. Ed.),[45] where he finds figures of the Egyptian temple to be similar to the Etruscan and the very oldest Greek style. All of this demonstrates that the Ancient Greek, or Attic, the Etruscan, and the Old Aeginetan works of art, from the perspective of their stiffness and general similarities, yield us nothing.[46] Indeed, another teacher of rhetoric, Demetrius of Phaleron, cited leanness and unity of design (ἡ ἰχνότης και ἡ συςτολή)[47] as the chief characteristic of the works of Pheidias. And who would dispute the truth of this, with whatever slight qualification?

2. An affected style, unnatural movements, [110] stylized smiles, slightly angled eyes. This last feature, similar to what Mr. Wagner also observed on the first figures that were discovered, is also clearly visible on other pieces, on which basis it was first possible to prove that these sculptures belonged to the Aeginetan School. Since the upturned eyes and corners of the mouth have long been recognized as characteristic features [*Merkmale*] of the oldest works (see the notes in the Weimar edition of Winckelmann's *History of Art*, volume III, page 531),[48] giving an impression of being the original style [*des ursprünglichen Stils*] and not strictly an Etruscan feature, so one should not call everything in this style Aeginetan either. The distinctive qualities just cited are more or less common [*gemeinschaftlich*] to the taste of all the very oldest works.

3. The unnatural folds, the artistically rendered garments, the spiraling and layered strands of hair reminiscent of balled twine. The same holds true for these features. The oldest of these are also Etruscan and Attic [111] alike. Pausanias, for his part, certainly did not distinguish Aeginetan works on the basis of these folds. To these features Mr. Quatremère de Quincy added the following,[49] namely:

4. Contrast between style and execution, the former [*da jener*] conveying the impression of an as yet imperfect period, while the latter [*diese*] suggests the very highest degree of mastery. A similar contrast does indeed reveal itself among these newly discovered figures—namely, the effect rendered by the head, the face, the hair, and the garments. So it is natural [*so liegt es in der Natur der Sache*] that this feature [*dieses Merkmal*] may be assigned to a specific moment in the history of Aeginetan art, but not to the Aeginetan style in general. It would also first be necessary to prove that this contrast was not simply a natural necessity such as one observes more or less in the works of every developing school [*jeder fortschreitenden Schule*]. It is evident that the artist begins by perfecting himself at first, before he dares to alter the established

traditions that have been handed down to him [112] through many previous works of art. A mere exaggeration of this feature is

5. Inflexibility of taste, perpetuated by the force of routine and custom. As simply given, this force did not express itself so decisively in other schools until a certain point in time. So the actual figure [*das Eigentliche*] evades the very feature [*Merkmal*] one most needs to know about—namely, just what was unchanging, what remained always the same.

As little as these statements will serve to establish something about Aeginetan art *as such*, with all its peculiarities and distinctive characteristics, just as little will one be able to determine such a distinctive character from the details enumerated by the author in his description, i.e., the anatomical particulars.

It is evident that these characteristics, which served always to distinguish the Aeginetan works as such, must lie in a quality or property that [113] goes deeper, to something living and immediate [*lebendig und unmittelbar*], a quality that conferred upon these works a definite [*bestimmte*], marvelous, and unmistakable physiognomy, yet which at the same time could remain essentially the same through every alteration.

Among the many remarkable things the author mentions concerning the style of these recently discovered figures, the most remarkable is surely what he describes as a true and perfect imitation of Nature [*treuen und vollkommenen Nachahmung der Natur*]—which, as he notes, comes close to deception [*Täuschung*], and yet at the same time to a certain reserve, however lively and excited its naturalism. Taking this as a given, I believe that I may now assert that the characteristic aspect of Aeginetan art, unaltered *from the very beginning*, was precisely *this true and exact imitation of Nature* [*treuen und genauen Nachahmung der Natur*].[50] I confirm [*bestimmen*] that claim primarily on the following grounds.

1. The real imitation of Nature alone [*wirkliche Nachahmung der Natur allein*] confers a truly distinctive, unmistakable, [114] and virtually indestructible impression that does not fade—like artistic conventions, how so often and however long they are used—but rather becomes deeper with the passing of time.

2. This impression is especially keen, even when imperfectly expressed and even if a bit too preciously, only if the imitation of Nature [*Nachahmung der Natur*] is diligent and sincerely intended in each work, distinguishable from any other only if it appears to be grounded in a spiritual (or ideal) type [*geistige (idealen) Typus*]. Or, as Winckelmann put it, if it is made according to a system of rules, discernable at first glance—and the oldest Attic and Egyptian

works were almost certainly of this latter type. For this very reason Pausanias, who is often errant in details but most reliable on the main points, often compared these (the Attic) works, but never the Aeginetan, with Egyptian works, which were as far removed as possible from any awareness of Nature.

3. This assumption seems to me also [115] entirely in keeping with the expression of Pausanias, ὁ τρόπος τῆς ἐργασίας ὁ Αἰγιναῖος (καλούμενος ὑπο Ἑλλήνων).[51] There, he interprets neither from the purely external fact of an imperfect work (the pure execution), nor from a purely spiritual [*geistige*] principle, but rather from the work [*Arbeit*] itself, which is at the same time the more spiritual type [*geistiger Art*].[52]

4. There is no extant work of Attic sculpture, just as there is none mentioned by any historical writer, in which an imitation of Nature [*eine Nachahmung der Natur*] of the type described by the author in these newly discovered figures may be recognized or revealed. Not a single one. I speak specifically, as I said, of works from ancient times. I also speak only of *such* an imitation of Nature [*einer solchen Nachahmung der Natur*], namely, one which borders on deception [*bis zur Täuschung geht*], such that the individual limbs seem formed according to Nature, indeed almost as if they were living and part of Nature itself. The clearest proof that one does not find anything similar [116] in Attic art is that the prerequisite of *such* an imitation of Nature [*einer solchen Nachahmung der Natur*] is foreign to all contemporary theories of art history, and even stands in contradiction to them, since examples of true excellence were taken almost entirely from the Attic works. I compare this to the following far-from-perfect analogy, as follows: Dutch industry and Dutch talent in imitating natural objects to the point of deception [*Naturgegenstände bis zur Täuschung nachzuahmen*] was never given to the Italians, but rather an imitation of Nature *which above all else pursued the Ideal* and which, as this Aeginetan report describes, was never a part of the spirit or character [*niemals im Geist und Charakter*] of the Attic artist.[53] In addition, such a true imitative diligence accords very well with the Aeginetan essence [*Wesen*], since the art on this island stood in very close relation to business and craftsmanship. The great expansion of its foundries is well known. Aeginetan bronze and Aeginetan candelabras for which the island [117] became famous not only in the time of Pliny, are viewed by Mr. Quatremère de Quincy[54] as the probable prototypes for the marble candelabras with so-called Etruscan figures in relief. The characteristic in Aeginetan illustration and imitation of animal forms must have been no less important, as we see in Pausanias X, 17,[55] where he compares the appearance of Sardinian she-goats to the wild

rams of Aeginetan visual artists in clay; all of this was a general and widely recognized type.

5. The author of this essay says explicitly: there is nothing dry, lean, or artless in the works of Natural imitation [*Werken die Nachahmung der Natur*] that we see in the works he describes, but rather a well-conceived, powerfully felt, and well-integrated effect achieved with broad knowledge. Imagine the time it took for an artistic school to bring the imitation of Nature [*der Nachahmung der Natur*] to such a degree of mastery. Thus one cannot help [118] but believe that, from the very beginning, as Aeginetan art set out on this path, with whatever degree of conscious thought, that if it had taken a different path from that same point of origin, it could have moved in the same direction toward such an agreement with Nature [*zu solche Uebereinstimmung mit der Natur*].

In any case we accept the fact that the imitation of Nature [*Nachahmung der Natur*] was from the very beginning the distinctive direction and chief characteristic of the Aeginetan School. It is very hard to say, when we look around at other schools, whether this distinctive physiognomy was derived from universal properties that the Aeginetan School in the most ancient times might have had more or less in common with the others.

Perhaps this is the place to return to what the author observed in the introduction: "These Aeginetan artworks show the way which Greek art took from its beginning in order finally [119] to achieve the high-point which was achieved by Pheidias."[56]

It was not so long ago that we viewed the chief merit of Pheidias as the creation of the Ideal, an Ideal that somehow excelled and even surpassed Nature. We state, against that view, that this complete freedom and power of art ought not to be thought of as an excelling or a surpassing (which would amount to the purest emptiness), but rather as a conquest [*Ueberwindung*], an overthrow [*Ueberwerfung*], and a total penetration [*Durchdringung*] of Nature. This conviction frees us to agree with the spirited [*geistvollen*] artist whom we have to thank for this essay, as well as with several other men of deeper insight than our own. It is clear that such a mastery [*Bewältigung*] of Nature, here as elsewhere, is not the result of blissful ignorance (as might almost seem to be the case for a few talented artists), but is rather a genuine achievement through effort [*eines wirklichen Angreifens*], that is, the result of an ever-deeper and fuller imitation [120] and an ever-more complete study, which almost goes without saying.

Today it is thought that the purity, the freedom, and the liveliness of art with which one generally begins, was the distinctive achievement of Pheidias and his school, simply the result of such a conquest of Nature [*Ueberwindung der Natur*], and thus also the imitation of Nature [*Nachahmung der Natur*] achieved simply through such penetrating insight into Nature herself. Furthermore, it is a truism in contemporary art history that the mastery of art [*Herrlichkeit der Kunst*] we meet in Pheidias simply appeared miraculously, admitting no really satisfactory transition from that which preceded him. On the other hand, these newly discovered works of art display this imitation of Nature [*jene Nachahmung der Natur*] at a point of perfection, from which the latter freedom and full potential of art [*Freiheit und Allvermogenheit der Kunst*] is really nothing more than a further step taken. The relationship seems to be as follows: that it is not only conceivable but more than likely that, [121] developing historically from the emulation of Nature to Nature herself, so to speak, Aeginetan art showed Attic art the way forward—from the abstract to the lifelike, and from systematic to natural form. Thus Aeginetan art is actually the hitherto missing link [*vermißte Mittelglied*] between the Ancient [*ältern*] style of Attic art and the later style [*spätern*] that appeared with Pheidias.

Such a development [*Gang der Dinge*] is entirely in agreement with the customary processes of Nature. When she intends to bring forth perfection [*das Vollkommene*], Nature first develops the individual qualities out of whose confluence perfection emerges, each element first developing on its own, until they recognize themselves as mutual [*gegenseitig*] elements belonging together and each one takes up the other into itself.

A similar interpenetration [*Durchdringung*] is necessary for the development of that highest form of poetry, Attic tragedy. For this is as rare as the art of Pheidias, which came forth out of a purely Attic, but originally Ionian [122] style [*Wesen*], without the attraction of foreign elements. This is perhaps clearest in Aeschylus, but more integrated in Sophocles, and it appears in a diluted form among others. In Pheidias, as in Aeschylus, art limits itself to pure necessity [*das rein Nothwendige*]. This principle, which is equally at issue in the elevation [*Erhebung*] of art and poetry, appears here in its sheer magnitude. In Sophocles, as in the successors to Pheidias, the same principle is already weakened [*gekränkt*] and involved in a lovers' quarrel between itself and a supposedly higher principle. It is more and more overwhelmed, and finally brought to naught. Naturally, the loveliest, the most beautiful and the tenderest things are first born of this decline [*Untergang*], just as in Nature pure beauty and charm emerge only after the originally great and powerful decline [*untergehet*].[57] Despite the charm of the loveliest and most perfected things we should not forget that art, [123] in its own bringing forth, is always ready to take another direction, and no longer to remain within this original, ascending movement.

From this standpoint we should say that Aeginetan art emerges from a truer and more austere imitation of Nature [*Nachahmung der Natur*], more or less in contrast to Attic art, securing that principle which would later provide the real basis for greatness in Attic art, namely in the art of Pheidias. Perhaps not very long before him Attic sculpture had noticed Aeginetan sculpture, from which it borrowed this principle. Pheidias elevated it to complete and equal importance with the higher principle, the Ideal. It should be generally recognized that the imitation of Nature [*Nachahmung der Natur*] appears as such only so long as art has not itself become Nature, that is, independent and autonomous, and consequently art in the highest sense, such that one can no longer distinguish between the two, and the work [124] belongs just as much to Nature as to art—because art became Ur-art, that is, Nature, and Nature became art.[58]

As was already mentioned in the second note to the introduction, any trace of authentic Aeginetan art disappeared at precisely the same time that the works of Pheidias were completed. It is possible that this flickering out, or extinction, of Aeginetan art was the result of the subsequent political overthrow of Aegina. Who would deny any influence to this tumultuous change? Their art survived only among the exiles, and this very fate [*Schicksal*], which scattered one part of the inhabitants throughout all of Greece, was to become, as in other cases, the means [*das Mittel*] to the most powerful and widespread dissemination of their most distinctive characteristics. But this did not happen, and this proves that this cessation had a different, and a deeper, reason. What better reason than this: [125] that Aeginetan art, in the highest sense that Pheidias created, did not really perish, but rather was raised to a spiritual [*geistigern*] life? Henceforth there was no Attic style in the older sense, nor an Aeginetan style, but rather a single perfect form that spread with irresistible force over the whole of Greece.

If through these suggestions we have been successful in communicating the meaning [*Bedeutung*] and the destiny [*Bestimmung*] that Aeginetan sculpture had in the totality of Greek artistic culture [*Kunstbildung*], then this sheds some light on our investigation: that the recently discovered sculptures stand to fill an empty place, a veritable black hole in contemporary art history, as well as to bring to light a long-hoped-for and long-suspected link in the art historical chain. We may delight especially for these reasons in their worth and their value for Germany, where one may well expect a welcoming reaction to their appearance [126] through further teaching and study.

Perhaps it is permissible to say the reverse as well—namely, that these works were transplanted to our fatherland not without a kind of Providence [*Schickung*], prompted by a German prince's passionate love of art.[59] Here, where the concept [*Begriff*] of a true art history—not merely external but internal—is entirely at home. . . . Here, where the essence [*Wesen*] and the true way [*wahren Weg*] of art have provided the principles [*Grundsätze*], the first presentiment of which sprang half-consciously from the pens of English artists studying the works of Pheidias.[(2),60] In this country [*Lande*], where one is accustomed to delight in perfection [127] only insofar as one has also conceived it in the course of its development [*Werden*]—here these works of art are surely already at home [*eigentlich zu Hause*], and must, once we have been able to breathe soul and consciousness [*Seele und Bewußtsein*] into them, come to feel themselves at home among us [*einheimlich*].

It may be that the exceptional impression made by these Aeginetan works is due to the fact that, in them, art has reached the pinnacle, in which such works of art achieve their fullest freedom and liveliness, with remarkable clarity and consciousness, and do so without such freedom being misused or such clarity being muddied by free will, in which case their innocence would be lost. Still we must admit, with all due sense of wonder—precisely because the process [*das Werdende*] is generally more important than the actual results [*das Seiende*] for the scholarly researcher committed to understanding [*Verstand*] and the spirit of enquiry [*Forschungs-Geist*] that works such as these Aeginetan masterpieces attract our attention since here we meet art not yet conscious of the pinnacle, but rather in the pure course of its development [*Bewegung*]. [128] These Aeginetan works are of the type that, even if we have not set eyes on them, their mere description enables us to form a judgment [*Urtheil*].

2. SCHELLING'S NOTE: One finds their remarks in the printed Report [English in original], or *Bericht*, which was filed away like so much garbage in the British Lower House [of Commons], after the purchase of Lord Elgin's collection, remarks that would be well served by being translated independently in a German journal.

CHAPTER IV

On the Conflict of Opinion Concerning the Relationship Between the Heads and the Leftover Body Parts from a Sculptural Perspective

[Wagner]

[129]

The previous discussions of these Aeginetan works illustrated that the naked figures are fashioned [*bearbeitet*], or conceived [*dargestellt*], with the greatest realism and the truest imitation of Nature [*der treuesten Nachahmung der Natur*], whereas the heads, the hair, and the robes are, by contrast, handled in a conventional manner characteristic of ancient Greek works.

As far as the form of garments and the hairdo are concerned, it stands to reason that they [130] accurately reflected the actual customs [*Sitte*] of that time. As to what might have prompted the artist to set the heads—which, as described, were depicted [*darzustellen*] in an entirely conventional way—in contrast [*Widerspruche*] to the surviving body parts that are, save for a few details, entirely free of such conventions, is another question that will have to be resolved here.

There are various opinions concerning this question. Some believe that certain specific persons [*gewisse bestimmte Personen*] may have been portrayed [*vorstellen*] in these statues, and that they should accordingly be viewed as portraits. Others suppose, by contrast, that this was a specific [*bestimmte*] and established [*festgesetzte*] design, sanctified according to the established taste [*Vorurtheile*] of that time, which the artist was prohibited by certain law from altering. Still others go so far as to think that the people of that time, or [131] at least the people on Aegina, actually had faces that looked this way.

This last opinion seems to me too frivolous to warrant refutation. Thus I will take into consideration only the first two of these hypotheses.

That these were portraits of certain specific persons [*gewisse bestimmte Personen*] does not seem likely to me, since one looks very much like another, and there is little in the way of distinctive characteristics in the faces. Even if it were the case [*Gesetz*] that the original models through some accident of nature were so very similar, then at the very least the Minerva, as a divinity [*Gottheit*], should bear a different demeanor from the others, or in any case should bear some exceptional expression to distinguish her. But even this is not the case. The Minerva is not in the least different from the rest, but rather entirely similar to one and all—if not literally [132] like peas in a pod, then at the very least as similar as only brothers and sisters can be. There is one and the same facial form, modified only in accordance with age and gender. And if one wishes to ignore even this observation, and to blame it on the inadequacy of the art of that time, then this same art, the way in which the surviving body parts are rendered with the highest degree of naturalism and truthfulness, gives the lie to that opinion as well. Are we to suppose that an artist who betrays so great a knowledge of the human form, and who was able to render [*darzustellen*] all the other body parts with such truth and natural realism, was not able to carve a better head? I reject this opinion as woefully untenable.

The contrasting opinion—that a certain widely accepted and securely established facial type prevailed among the ancient Greeks, [133] which the artists were forbidden by custom [*Gesetze*] to violate—seems far preferable to me. Only it must first be proved that the ancient Greeks actually had such a rule [*Gesetz*], since to assume or assert such a thing as pure conjecture seems much too risky to me.

It will be difficult in any case to provide a definitive reason [*gewissen Grund*], and therefore whatever is provided by way of explanation must remain only a hypothesis. In the meantime, I shall be permitted to present my opinion here, and to lay it before friends of the arts [*Kunstfreunden*] for further examination.

I am of the opinion that the basis [*Grund*] for this contrast between the faces and the other body parts may be found from the perspective of their culture [*Bilding*], and should be sought out strictly in the times when these statues were completed. As the form of the faces, the feet, [134], and many other features makes apparent, these statues were completed in the time when Greek art was just beginning, when it was breaking free of its original old-fashioned forms, forms which derived, in my opinion, from the Egyptians.

The artists of that time, it would seem, began with the body, freeing it from its formal stiffness, and conferring on it motion, life, and realism [*Bewegung, Leben und Wahrheit*], whereas the head, and the inherited ancient form of the face, remained largely the same. It was perhaps too great a feat of daring for the people of that time to seek to alter the forms they had inherited from their elders and which were sanctified by custom and religion. One would naturally have viewed such an attempt as a cavalier, even wicked, attack on the inherited norms and customs [*Sitte und Gebräuche*] of the fatherland, and even against religion itself. Art in these times was still [135] too tightly bound to religion and not yet sufficiently independent to allow an artist sufficient boldness to alter forms that were so closely tied to the religion.[61]

Just how long such old-fashioned and Gothic faces may remain in favor among the common people [*bei dem gemeinem Volk*] may be understood by comparison with examples from our own times. In similar fashion and in many cases, even today, the artist may not be permitted to make changes of this kind.

This, it seems to me, is the key to solving our riddle, and here is to be found both reason and cause for this apparent artistic contradiction. This was the fetter by which the artists' hands were bound, which prevented them from altering facial forms that had been inherited as sacred [*geheiligt*] from the Heroic Age. At long last, they seized the freedom with which they finally subjected the conventions and prejudices [136] concerning the representation of body parts to their will [*Willkur*], and so to present [*darzustellen*] art and Nature in a contemporary manner.

Here however, the artist was obliged by no formal law [*Gesetz*], but rather by his own circumstances and by popular opinion itself, which imposed this tacit command [*Gebot*] upon him.

EDITOR'S APPENDIX

[Schelling]

The strange contrast that one finds between the heads and the rest of the bodies of these figures will doubtless give rise to considerable speculation and debate. The editor recognizes that he, after long and repeated consideration of all possibilities, doubts whether any further examination or any other explanation beyond those provided by the author will add anything of value. For the author appears not only to have [137] seized the truth in general, but he has also hit upon the right measure and the true lines of interrogation, over and beyond which one would only fall into error.

Generally speaking, there can only be either internal or external reasons that explain this apparent artistic paradox [*Inconsequenz*]. By internal I mean those reasons that lie within the artist himself. These can be ignorance and inability, or else an entirely voluntary self-imposed limitation. But what could possibly inspire an artist to the last of these? And the first has already been refuted by the author, and virtually refutes itself, since these heads and faces, however uniform, are all worked with the same art and care [*Kunst und Liebe*] as the remaining parts. Thus it appears to be an entirely appropriate conclusion that the artist who knew how to present [*darzustellen*] the other body parts truly and according to Nature would also have been in the position to make better, [138] by which I mean less conventional, heads and faces. There remain, therefore, only the external reasons. And here, it seems to me that the author is precisely right in identifying the reason [*Grund*] for this artistic limitation of the rendering of heads and faces. He locates the reason neither in an established artistic type [*Kunst-Typus*], nor in a religious or political law [*Gesetz*], nor in the two together, but rather and much more simply in a perfectly natural popular taste [*Volks-Empfindung*]. This taste would not permit the appeal of old-fashioned custom to be lost, in accordance with the simple and sincere attachment to inherited traditions which, generally speaking, are promoted [*bildet*] in small republics, and which had taken deep root in the volatile Attic people. Indeed, even after the Persian Wars, it lived on for a considerable time in the breasts of common men who lived on meal and grain.

Who does not recall many such passages in the comedies of Aristophanes? Who does not recall especially that powerful spokesman [139] for law and ancient custom [*Recht und alte Sitte*] who, in *The Clouds,* with his sour seriousness in which every member of the audience would have recognized the mind of the poet himself describing the voice, the cadence, the clothing, the walk, the posture, the movement of the young men of that time which emerged from the warriors of Marathon—a description to which the spokesman for his more fully enlightened times can only reply as follows:

> Ol'fashioned it is, the smell from the Dipolieia and
> the cicadas in his hair,[62]

This refers back to a time when the most ancient offerings to Jupiter were introduced, and our forefathers adorned their locks of hair with golden grasshoppers. What Thucydides I.6 observes is remarkable,[63] namely that it was only shortly before his own time that this hairstyle had gone out of fashion.

The old-fashioned sense here refers to the customs and art [*Sitte und Kunst*] of an older and still respectable time, what may also [140] appear more or less conventionally in the clothing, the hair, the demeanor, the features, in short everything associated with our Aeginetan figures. In point of fact, if this Aristophanic spokesman for an older time feels so strongly that the introduction of more artistic changes and an effeminate modulation into the older and more manly ceramic arts is to be seen as decadence and decline [*Verderb und Untergang*], then how much more sensitive should we imagine the citizen of a Greek free state [*Bürger griechischer Freistaaten*] to have been, especially the hard-working Aeginetan of pure Dorian lineage, when it comes to sculptural presentation [*bildliche Darstellung*]? Was it not natural, since they followed the accustomed and beloved ways of the ancestors and of their ancient images of the gods, to demand this in the cut of the hair and the form of their clothing, even at a time when art was ready to admit diversity in character and facial expression, and in general to create freer and more natural forms? If one is inclined to ask why these artistic demands [141] were extended also to the figures of Persian or generally barbaric warriors, then the simple answer is that the naturally creative artist would do nothing to disturb the overall unity of the whole.

Perhaps it will appear to some that this entire explanation would have greater consistency if one could assume that the sculptures described here had other, still older antecedents, through which one could place them in an already flourishing artistic epoch. On this assumption, the retention of old-fashioned facial features would be no less natural than the contemporary retention of facial coloring on a so-called Black Madonna [*schwarzen Mutter Gottes*], or the conventional shaping of the face in certain images of saints or miracles, which must always be manufactured anew. The author, however, as I gather from one of his writings, is not [142] inclined to this assumption. Since everything, he says, is made with such naiveté, care, distinctiveness, and innocence, I cannot think it possible that this is a work of imitation [*Nachahmung*].[64] If one wishes to imagine this imitation [*Nachahmung*] in less material and more spiritual [*geistig*] terms, then we come full circle back to the first explanation, with which the matter will probably have to rest.

CHAPTER V

On Mechanical Matters, or the Working of the Marble

[Wagner]

[143]
From the standpoint of their technical treatment, the Aeginetan figures are even more remarkable than for those merits we have already discussed. From this perspective also they inspire astonishment [*Erstaunen*] in anyone with knowledge or an understanding of art. Everything is rendered with the same care, nothing is neglected, not even the portions which could not have been seen and which would have been for the most part impossible to approach. Even the most insignificant detail is completed with the greatest care and loving attention [*der größten Sorgfalt und Liebe*], [144] such that one searches in vain for a similar perfection among the finest modern works.

All the figures are rendered with the same art from all sides, both front and back, and are materially and truly completed, so that one cannot determine [*bestimmen*] with certainty which was actually the main, that is to say the forward-facing, side of the figure—unless the treatment or the posture offers a clue, or else the difference in weathering of the front and back indicates which was which.

What astonishes one with artistic understanding the most, however, is that there are no marble supports for any of these figures, such as were normally provided to secure their position, whether in the form of a tree trunk, a piece of rock, etc. These figures for the most part stand alone on their feet without any extra pieces and without any reinforcement of the marble. In addition, the vast majority [145] of these figures held shields, most of which were made out of a single piece of marble, usually 2½ French feet in diameter and with a thickness of one inch at their thickest point. These shields, completely independent of the figures, were carried on the outstretched arm without any additional support and must have significantly increased the weight of the whole as well as complicated the position of the outstretched arm; it is incomprehensible how this could have been achieved without breakage. One may thus conclude that these statues were originally anchored with iron from the back. But no matter how hard I have looked, I have been unable to locate a single trace that might confirm this opinion.

Is it thus all the more strange that these figures, [146] so grossly top-heavy and lacking any independent support or assistance save for the thin and inordinately narrow bases on which they stood, were rendered freestanding on their feet. The thickness of the base was two inches at its thickest. One notices that as much superfluous material as possible was cut away, presumably in order to set the figures that much closer to each other, or to allow them to be combined with greater ease.

The tools or instruments which were used for the working of these pieces may be determined from the features and traces remaining on the marble. The tools were much the same as those our contemporary sculptors use today: namely the drill, the iron awl, the iron claw, the flat iron chisel, and the file. The final completion or polishing of the statue was done with pumice stone, as one may conclude from the better-preserved parts of these figures.[147] The marble is the same for all the statues—namely Parian marble, small-grained, which one would call *grecchetto* in Rome.

CHAPTER VI

On the Epoch in Which These Figures Were Probably Completed

[Wagner]

[148]

According to the report of Pausanias (book II, chaps. 29–30),[65] this temple to the Panhellenic Jupiter was built by Aiakos. The manner in which Pausanias reports this suggests that he took it to be more of a folk tradition [*Volkssage*] than an established historical fact [*geschichtliche Thatsache*]. One may reach back to this faraway time of the first founding of the temple dedicated to Panhellenic Jupiter on Aegina in the following way: by ascertaining the time in which [149] the sculptures described here were completed, which I believe can be proved with sufficient certainty.

According to Diodorus Siculus (book IV, chap. 61),[66] Aiakos was a contemporary [*Zeitgenoß*] of Minos and thus of the older Daedalus. That makes them part of a time that was, according to common tradition, the childhood of art [*der Kindheit der Kunst*], when art took the first step toward free and lifelike movement. Previously, as Diodorus reports (book IV, chap. 76),[67] one saw only statues with their feet drawn together, the arms hanging straight down at the sides, and with closed eyes. Daedalus was the first to dare to depict standing figures with their legs apart and extended, the first to lend his figures some movement or action, and the first to open their eyes. Whether one elects to view these stories about Daedalus as pure history [*lauter Geschichte*], or as history mixed with fable, it is clear that our Aeginetan sculptures cannot belong to this time-period in which we meet the very first [150] beginnings of art [*allerersten Anfänge der Kunst*], and when sculptures were made strictly out of wood, not marble. In these Aeginetan figures, there is only the faintest and most distant trace of the original Egyptian stiffness that Diodorus describes. They are all full of life and full of movement, rendered with a complete knowledge of muscles and bones, and of the human body in general. Here we see the greatest perfection of the material working of marble, such as is only attainable through long practice.

All of this points to a later period of art. If we simply consider the distance between the condition in which art stood in the time of Daedalus, and the time in which the Aeginetan figures were produced, and if we calculate the time necessary for such progress to have been made, then three hundred years seems a sufficient length of time in which to move from such a beginning to this [151] degree of perfection. Consequently, if we take the period of Daedalus to have been one hundred years before the Trojan War, then the epoch of our Aeginetan sculptures may be taken as being in the third century after the Trojan War. This is my opinion concerning the latest point in antiquity [*das höchste Alterthum*] that can be assumed.

That these statues were completed after the Trojan War and not before it may be demonstrated on various other grounds—for instance, the tools that were used in the working of these figures.

Pausanias tells us (book I, chap. 26)[68] that Callimachus, nicknamed *Kakizotechnos,* was the first who discovered how to drill marble. Now there are frequent traces of drilling on the Aeginetan sculptures. But Callimachus lived, as is well attested, a long time [*eine gute Zeit*] after the Trojan War. Later on in Pausanias (book V, chap. 10) we meet Byzes, an artist from Naxos,[69] [152] who was the first to discover the art of sawing marble, and to use it for roof tiles. This Byzes lived in the time when Alyattes reigned in Lydia, and Astyages, the son of Cyarares, reigned in Media. Consequently, our temple to Panhellenic Jupiter must have been built after that time, since it was fitted out with marble roofing, as the fragments that are a part of this collection attest.

Another proof comes in the form of the weapons with which our heroes were depicted. Winckelmann, *Monumenti inediti* nos. 17 and 109 (pp. 18 and 144) sought to prove, especially in light of Homer's silence on the matter, that in the time of the Trojan War shields were not yet fitted with a handle so as to be carried on the left arm such as we see in our figures. Rather, they were fitted with a strap that was worn around the neck.[70] The Carians were the first, according to Herodotus (book 1, chap. 171),[71] to have made shields [153] fitted with a strap or handle. Before that time shields were worn, as he says, on the left shoulder and attached by the same leather strap fastened to the middle of the shield. It is unclear whether this Carian discovery came before or after the Trojan War. Winckelmann sought to prove the latter on other grounds.

On the one hand, I have endeavored to demonstrate that one should not locate these statues in the time of Aiakos, nor in the time of the Trojan War; on the other hand, I have to defend my own opinion against situating the origin of these Aeginetan heroes in that later time of flourishing, that is, the very highest artistic epoch [*der höchste Kunst-Epoche*], which draws them too close to the times of Perikles.

There are indubitable traces, or remains, of the Egyptian style on parts of our figures, and which resemble [154] the ancient Greek style. The extremely antiquated parts of the face, the distinctive manner of the curls of hair, the conventional fall of the garments, and finally the general manner in which the various parts are handled and placed together—all of this provides incontrovertible evidence of a great antiquity [*eines hohen Alterthums*], justifying our assumption that these artworks are among the earliest examples of the time that Pausanias and Pliny so often mention as the period of the Ancient Greek style.

EDITOR'S APPENDIX

[Schelling]

In a previous section we were in the admirable position to acknowledge the correctness of the author's artistic judgment, but here, by contrast, we must confess that he has entangled himself in a side issue [*Nebensachen*] of chronology. Three hundred years after the Trojan War is more than eight hundred years prior to our [Christian] calendar [*Zeitrechnung*]. Alyattes in [155] Lydia, who reigned at the same time that the art of sawing marble was discovered, according to the arguments reported by Pausanias—roughly from 620 to 560 [BCE]—thus, dating from the midpoint of his reign, some six hundred years after the Trojan War. This date coincides fairly well with the period in which, according to Pliny (book 36, chap. 4), Dipoenus and Scyllis first distinguished themselves through the working of marble. Pliny's statement (*Marmore scalpendo primi omnium inclaruerunt*) seems entirely unambiguous to me.[72] Not to exclude some earlier failed and imperfect attempts, these two artists [*Künstler*] were the first famous sculptors [*Bildner*] in marble who mastered this craft. It is as clear as it is certain that the Aeginetan images which so distinguished themselves by the consummate working of the marble, could not have preceded the time of Dipoinus and Scyllis. The author can simply cite Pausanias, according to whom (book II, chap. 15)[73] both artists [156] were not merely spiritual heirs [*geistige*] but actual [*sondern leibliche*] sons of Daedalus. Pliny's dating [*Bestimmung*], however, deviates significantly from this, when he says that they were both born on the island of Crete in the time of the Median Empire, before Cyrus came to the Persian throne—that is, in the fiftieth Olympiad (580 BCE). This dating also accords well with what Mr. Quatremère de Quincy observes (p. 179),[74] namely, that this epoch was attributed by Pausanias to the aforementioned students, Tektaeus and Angelion, an attribution that remains, even if one reverses it, an apparent anachronism. It was easy for this perceptive author to perceive the contradiction; it proved less easy for him to delete it from the text, especially when he wished to maintain a portion of it. His opinion regarding the great age [*hohen Alter*] of these Aeginetan works must remain tentative—based as it is on the singular reporting of Pausanias or Pliny, concerning the discovery of how to saw marble, or [157] the first application of the drill to marble, or the first sculptors to work in marble at all, statements whose meaning and degree of certainty are all equally unclear. It is for precisely this reason that we suspect the author came to his opinion concerning the possibility of such great antiquity [*so hohen Alters*] for the Aeginetan artworks, not through such specific historical circumstances, but rather through the irresistible impression of great antiquity [*der unwiderstehliche Eindruck des Hochalterthümlichen*] that the works themselves confirm [*bestimmt*]. In assessing the cogency of his judgments, no one would deny them who has himself had the experience, so often emphasized by the author, of their spiritually rich and exceptionally lively presentation [*die geistreichste und lebendigste Darstellung*]. Here once again, our judgment and enthusiasm depend upon the general view of antiquity that we have formed [*gebildet*]. Up to now, two contradictory inclinations have been prominent in classical studies [*Alterthumskunde*]: on the one hand, to play down as far as possible the primitive period in their [158] culture, religion, and science [*Kunst, Religion und Wissenschaft*]; and on the other hand, to play up as much as possible the period of high culture [*Bildung*]. Clearly, we have erred more in the former direction than in the latter. And though most may find unthinkable what may only now be considered as a possibility—namely, that works like our Aeginetan artworks may have been created scarcely a century or century and a half later than Homer—then we come to a competing question. If these pieces come after the period of the Homeric poems, as is generally accepted, then there is a great value in the evidence which these same Homeric poems provide concerning the fine arts in general [*die bildende Kunst*], such as his description of the shield of Achilles, the statues in the palace of Alcinous, and so on. He describes these works like a god, and could not simply have pulled them out of the air. And so with respect to the more general question concerning the state of Greek culture [*Bildung*] in the first century after the Trojan War, [159] the unanimous received opinion can hardly be accepted any longer, given the author's contrasting opinion as laid out here.

We must admit, however, that when the author simply asserts that these sculptures cannot possibly be assigned a date earlier than the third century after the Trojan War, then we feel free to make a similar assertion from the other direction, as it were, no less convinced than the author as to its accuracy. We assert that these sculptures must have originated quite some time [*eine gute Zeit*] before the Persian Wars, and an even longer time [*und eine noch längere*] before the loveliest period of Attic art [*der schönsten Epoche der attische Kunst*] in the age of Perikles.

It would be possible to assert, however, against the reasons the author provides to contest such a late date of composition, that soon after the Persian Wars, Attic art had already attained a high degree of perfection, whereas

Aeginetan art clung to the same [160] old style, which it quite possibly never abandoned.

We therefore take up the task, as far as it can be done, to counter this assertion, and to investigate, as far as it is possible, the state in which Aeginetan art found itself in and around the time of Pheidias. At the same time, this will provide us with the opportunity to bring our previous investigations into the history of Aeginetan art to a close.

Around the same time that the high style [*die hohe Styl*] originated with Pheidias, the following Aeginetan artists were alive:

1. *Anaxoragas*, by whose hand came the Jupiter that was dedicated at Olympia (Paus. V, 23)[75] and was the common offering of all the Greeks who had struggled victoriously at Plataea (479 BCE). The fact that an Aeginetan artist manufactured a work that was dedicated by the Lakedaimonians, the Athenians, the Corinthians, and all the other most esteemed [161] Greek peoples [*Völkern*] is a sure sign that in the time of the Persian Wars Aeginetan art was held in the very highest esteem.

2. *Simon of Aegina*, by whom the dedicatory offerings for a certain Phormis was made, and who achieved notoriety for his works under Gelon and his brother Hieron (roughly between 480 and 470 BCE) in Syracuse.[76]

3. *Glaukias*: from him we have a chariot and an image of a certain Gelon, whom Pausanias[77] took to be a private citizen, and who competed in the 73rd Olympiad.

4. A fourth person must be named here, about whose dates and *floruit* serious doubts remain: the previously mentioned *Kallon of Aegina*. According to the first statement by Pausanias (book II, chap. 32),[78] he was a student of Tektaeus and Angelion, who manufactured wooden statues (ξόανα). In a second discussion, Pausanias places him (book VII, chap. 18)[79] in the time of Kanachus of Sicyon, whom [162] Pliny (34, 8)[80] dated to the ninety-fifth Olympiad. But who today would assign any value to this designation [*Bestimmung*]? Better than Pliny would be to rely on the judgment of Cicero, who states in the Brutus, or the book *De clar. oratt.*, chapter 18: "*Quis enim—non intelligit, **Canachi** signa rigidiora esse, quam ut imitentur veritatem? **Calamidis** dura illa quidem, sed tamen molliora, quam **Canachi: nondum Myronis** satis ad veritatem adducta, jam tamen, quae non dubites, pulcra* [sic] *dicere*."[81] From this standpoint, especially when it is joined to the previous discussion, it is at the very least evident that Kanachus was, in Cicero's opinion, closely related in terms of both date and style to Kalamis, as Kalamis was to Myron. But Kalamis belongs indisputably to the age of Pheidias. Quintilian appears simply to have borrowed [*nachgeahmt*] this dating from Cicero, with the

single change in detail of substituting [163] Kallon and Hegesias for Kanachus: "*Nam duriora et Tuscanicis proxima* ***Callon*** *atque* ***Hegesias,*** *jam minus rigida* ***Calamis,*** *molliora adhuc supra dictis* ***Myron*** *fecit.*"[82] From this statement it is clear that in Quintilian's opinion Kallon was earlier than Kalamis, and therefore he should not be placed in the ninety-fifth Olympiad, and certainly not in the eighty-seventh Olympiad, as Pliny has done. On the other hand, it is also clear that Quintilian, who substituted Kallon for Kanachus, as Cicero had done, takes them to be not only stylistically related as artists, but actual contemporaries.

So it seems impossible to separate Kanachus from Kallon. But it is still an open question as to what period the two belong. From either perspective, whether Cicero's evaluation of Kanachus, and even more Quintilian's assessment of Kallon (particularly the reference to *Tuscanicis proxima*), one might well conclude that both must have belonged to an early [164] period. Arguments from analogy, rather than from the works themselves, are used to assign these works to a period closer to Pheidias's, if not actually to the same time. But how can we know what would have appeared stiff (*rigidum*) and hard, or similar to the Etruscan style, to these Romans, who took the charm, tenderness, and delicacy of the later arts as their standard [*Maßstab*]? Might not even Pheidias, for all of his greatness [*seiner reinen Großheit*], have appeared somewhat hard [*herb*]? It is certainly striking that Cicero, for his part, is entirely silent about Pheidias and does not include him in a discussion which ends with Polykleitus, whose works alone are deemed absolutely perfect (*jam plane perfecta, ut mihi quidem videtur*). Quintilian, however, who ventures the following statement about Polykleitus, *nihil ausus praeter leves genas*, assesses them as follows: Pheidias was a better artist for gods than for human beings (which is indisputable, since it seems legitimate to render the divine nature on a massive scale, and to [165] dismiss anything accidental or imperfect). If under such conditions a proof by analogy does not prove much, then we are driven back to strictly historical arguments. It should be noted first of all that Pausanias speaks strictly from his own scientific perspective and opinion. And in the second place, he merely reports what the inhabitants of Patras assume or conjecture (τεκμαίρονται), namely, that the artist who completed the statue of Diana Laphria, which was presented to them by Augustus, could not have been very much younger than Kanachus of Sicyon and Kallon of Aegina. From this association we may see that the good people of Patras were especially interested in ascribing as great an antiquity as possible [*ein so hohes Alterthum als möglich*] to their statue; Pausanias also calls it ἀρχαῖον. We therefore accept the first report by Pausanias; that is, we assume Kallon to have been a student in the second generation of Dipoinus and Scyllis. But at the same time we take [166] these men's dates from the aforementioned passage in Pliny: 580 BCE. Thus, Kallon would have been active roughly in the year 516 (BCE), and Kanachus with him.

There is also an epigram from the Greek Anthology (*Brunck. Anal.* vol. II, p. 15, no. 35)[83] which sings the praises of a group of Three Muses that were carved by Kanachus, Aristokles, and Agelades. This same Agelades, however, also made the chariot for a certain Kleosthenes who was the first (Paus. VI, 10)[84] of all victors in the chariot race to erect his statue at Olympia. Kanachus's dates are thus confirmed by this notation. Kleosthenes competed in the sixty-sixth Olympiad; the difference between this and the fiftieth Olympiad in which Pliny claims that Dipoinus and Skyllis lived amounts to roughly four-times-sixteen years, that is, two generations. The year 516 BCE falls within the first year of the sixty-sixth Olympiad. According to such calculation, the opinion of the men of Patras concerning [167] their statue accords well with the first statement by Pausanias. The only thing it does not confirm is the great antiquity [*das hohe Alter*] of Dipoinus and Skyllis, which we have already rejected on other grounds. Thus we may now be permitted to state that Kallon lived in the sixty-sixth Olympiad, at the very latest, and thus a long time before [*eine gute Zeit vor*] the age of Pheidias. It should not be overlooked that there is also a *third* statement from Pausanias that once again calls the date of this artist into doubt, namely book III, chapter 18.[85] But this passage is corrupt according to the unanimous opinion of all the critics, and its meaning may be restored best if we do not take the dates of Kallon from Pliny. For he places a certain Kallon, without ascribing him a homeland, though it was probably Aegina, in the eighty-seventh Olympiad—in the well-known passage (34, 8)[86] where he lumps together so many names of so many artists with so little comment and so little precision in dating. It is [168] hardly surprising, then, to find an oversight in such a compilation, such as when he places Skopas here, even though he himself later says that Skopas collaborated in a funerary monument for Mausolus in the 106th Olympiad. In both cases the difference is roughly the same: nineteen Olympiads on the one hand, and twenty-one on the other. I am thus perfectly willing to assume that Kallon actually lived between twelve and eighteen Olympiads closer to the artists who created our statues than Pheidias did (insofar as one can determine [*bestimmen*] this with precision, given the unequal lifespans of the various individuals), whoever they may have been.[87]

5. *Onatas of Aegina.* If what Pausanias reports (V, 25)[88] can be confirmed, that Onatas completed certain dedicatory offerings at Olympia for the tyrant

Hieron—after his death and at the bidding of his son, Deinomenos—(there is little doubt of this, since Pausanias includes inscriptions to this effect), then Onatas [169] achieved his greatest fame in the second year of the seventy-eighth Olympiad (467 BCE), at the end of the reign of Hieron. This is made even more certain given the testimony of Athenaeus in Pausanias (VIII, 42),[89] which confirms Onatas as a contemporary of Hegesias and Agelades; given his part in the decoration of the temple of Minerva Area at Plataea (Paus. IX, 4),[90] he was thus a contemporary and stylistic partner of Pheidias. About this Onatas, Pausanias (V, 25) expresses himself as follows: "This Onatas however, who is Aeginetan, we will assign a place not lower than the successors of Daedalus or of the Attic School."[91]

First of all, I make the following of this remarkable statement: *who is an Aeginetan* (in Greek: ὄντα Αἰγινήτην, which communicates a great deal more than simply Αἰγινήτην). Clearly, Pausanias wishes to suggest that Onatas belonged to the Aeginetan School, and should be held [170] in no less regard than someone from the Attic School.

If one were to take these words simply to be referring to a homeland or birthplace, then one might also draw the opposite conclusion, namely, that Pausanias assigned Onatas more to the class of Attic artists. A simple homeland is not intended here, although there is one inscription that claimed he lived in Aegina; the other clearly states that he was born there. So, homeland and birthplace in one!

One should bear in mind, however, that Pausanias uses no other expression than this to assign an artist to the Aeginetan School; for instance Kallon (7, 18),[92] who, as we know from other evidence, was also of the Aeginetan School. Furthermore, given Pausanias's customary economy of expression, this addition of an inscription at the end is unusual, as two inscriptions regarding the artist's homeland [171] will attest. They had an entirely practical sense, then, where the name "Aeginetan" [*Aeginet*] refers to an artist of the Aeginetan School, and contrasts him with artists originating in the Daedalic or the Attic schools. So one has to prefer the first interpretation.

Thus Onatas is named as an artist of the Aeginetan School, or at least it was understood that he came from an Aeginetan workshop, which was at this time in no way inferior to the Attic School (οὐδενὸς ὕστερον θήσομεν). From this comment stems my own conclusion, that Aeginetan art had unquestionably achieved a similar degree of distinction [*Höhe von Vollendung*] in no way inferior to that of Attic art. Thus it seems wholly arbitrary for Mr. Quatremère de Quincy (p. 176) to suppose that this comparison should be confined to the Old Attic School.[93] At the same time, it also seems implausible, partly on account of the dating [*der Zeit*] (which is admittedly not very precise, given that this same scholar places Onatas [172] in the seventieth Olympiad), and partly on account of the terminology (Pausanias's terminology in any case), that he should add the phrase "from the Attic workshop," if the phrase "from Daedalus" had already implied the same thing. And he would have had even less need to link the two terms, as they are linked here, ἀπὸ Δαιδάλου τε καὶ ἐργαστηρίου τοῦ ' Αττικοῦ, which here clearly means: "not only from Daedalus, but also from the Attic School in general."

Should this judgment of Pausanias be taken as established fact? And even so established as to include [the later figure of] Pheidias? In fact, and I hope to prove this with another passage from the same author, he has not exempted Pheidias. Onatas also competed with Pheidias in the composition [*Bildung*] of colossal figures. One of these, which was mentioned by Pausanias (book 8, chap. 42),[94] was a bronze Apollo in Pergamum which he described as among those works "ranking among the very greatest [*die es am meisten sey'n*] [173] (θαῦμα ἐν τοῖς μάλιστα) as much for its size as for its artistry." These expressions are too precise [*zu bestimmt*] to refer to any other works except the colossal works of Pheidias. For these were certainly intended by reference to "the very greatest" [*am meisten*], that is to say, the ones surpassing all others in size and artistry. This connection will become more obvious when it is noted that Pausanias happily equated Onatas with the Attic artists, as he did in reference to that same colossus, the Hercules at Olympia.

This I take to be a complete refutation to the objection that Aeginetan art did not seize upon the style represented in our figures until a later date. For Pausanias certainly would not have placed Onatas on a par with the Attic artists, had the Aeginetan School not already possessed in those days a style and artistry resembling that of our statues.

[174] Indeed, the aesthetic heights [*Maßstab der Höhe*] that the art of Aegina had attained, after the Persian Wars and not long before the beginning of the Peloponnesian War, is attested even more clearly shortly before it flowed into the universal stream of Greek art, which was the reward it earned for such strenuous effort. At this point Aegina produced an artist whose works may be placed among the very greatest works of art [*das Höchste der Kunst*]. He was both a sculptor and a painter, not unworthy of his great contemporary Pheidias, and he has left us one of the wonders of his time: the Ceres of Phigalia, which he completed through a kind of divine inspiration vouchsafed to him in dream visions.

This Ceres was destroyed after just a few generations in Phigalia, or else it was lost, probably within six hundred years of the artist's death, and after everything that had happened to the old faith. Pausanias [175] describes his visit to that place to pay his respects to her and to consecrate her with the customary bloodless offerings. This calls to mind what Quintilian aptly, if subtly, said about the Olympian Jupiter, *cujus pulcritudo adjecisse aliquid etiam receptae religioni videtur*.[95]

That the Aeginetan School continued as a distinctive school only up to a certain point in time is natural enough [*liegt in der Natur der Sache*], but it may also be demonstrated with the following historical observations.

1) The Aeginetan works, as described by Pausanias (book 7, chapter 5)[96] from the outset, were only mentioned with the very oldest Attic works.

2) The Aeginetan τρόπος τῆς ἐργασίας was mentioned by Pausanias only in reference to works of the greatest antiquity: such as book 8, chapter 53, for a wooden statue probably made of ebony;[97] and book 10, chapter 36, for a [176] statue in black stone, representing [*vorstellend*] an Artemis Diktynna.[98] That this style is identifiable in our figures no one will deny, yet it belongs to an even earlier period.

3) Mr. Quatremère de Quincy is of the opinion that it is not easy to determine from the ancient authors if these Aeginetan artists and sculptures came before or after the events that led to the loss of Aegina's political power.[99] We hold the opposite opinion. We are convinced that Kallon is the oldest of all the Aeginetan artists mentioned by name in Pausanias (after Smilis), that his dates may be fixed between the sixtieth and seventieth Olympiads, and that all the others mentioned by him came between the seventieth and eightieth Olympiads. We doubt if there is any artist named by Pausanias who is younger than this. Are we to assume, after the loss of their political freedom, and the subsequent return of [177] the inhabitants at the end of the Peloponnesian War, that Aegina's power [*Herrlichkeit*] and creative spirit [*schöpferische Geist*] were never rejuvenated, or that they simply expired?

We must leave this question open. As opposed to the uncertain circumstances concerning the end of this school, we believe that the Aeginetan influence over the Greek, or at least over the Attic, world of art began first with Kallon, who may be more firmly dated now before the seventieth Olympiad. The earlier masters, like the creators of our figures, may be known only through the impression left by their surviving works; their names are lost. The sole figure from this distant age [*Vorzeit*] who was to be named is the father and founder of this art, Smilis.(1)

---

1. SCHELLING'S NOTE: Among the many things confirmed by these investigations, one cannot doubt—given the very first mention of Kallon as a student of Tectaues and

[178] 4) There might have been later Aegina-born artists who distinguished themselves (who would doubt it?). But the Aeginetan School as such could not continue, once a mighty genius had broken through its limits. *Onatas* is the last one to be named in contrast to Attic artists, and he is also the one whose works received praise for standing unarguably on a par with the finest [*der höchsten Zeit*] Attic works. So in him we come to the limit [*Gränze*]. He was still Aeginetan [*noch Aeginet*], but as a type, he was like Pheidias. I believe that I have sufficient reason [*Grund genug*] for asserting that he represents the pinnacle [*Gipfel*] of the Aeginetan School, and completes it, from an art historical point of view.

[179] This intensification of Aeginetan art, the last appearance of which we find in Onatas, is made more probable and conceivable by what we claimed in the last note from the third chapter, concerning the fusion of Ancient Attic and Aeginetan in the later, perfected Attic style. No further comment is necessary here.

We remind the reader only that we imagine this not as a one-sided [*einseitige*] effect of one on the other, but rather as a mutual [*gegenseitiges*] development taken up by both. Aeginetan art elevated itself through the attraction of the Ideal in Attic art, just as Attic art perfected itself through the attraction of naturalism in Aeginetan art. In this way both, while starting from opposite sides, could, and indeed had to, merge at such a summit [*Gipfel*].

Angelion—the first trace [*Spur*] of a connection and [178] reciprocal influence [*gegenseitigen Einflusses*] between Attic and Aeginetan art. Whether Kallon was actually instructed by the two Daedalus's is another question. But this much is clear: from this time forward, Attic art began to take up Aeginetan techniques [*Kenntniß*].

CHAPTER VII

How and Where These Figures Were Originally Arranged

[Wagner]

[180]

That these figures once belonged to the Temple of Panhellenic Jupiter on the island of Aegina is well known, and commonly attested.[100] Thus, the topic here shall be simply how and in what manner they were placed in this temple.

The number of surviving figures is seventeen. That there were originally many more can be discerned from the surviving fragments, from which we may estimate their original number to have been closer to thirty.[101]

[181] Two of the surviving figures—namely, the two small, clothed, and freestanding female figures B and C—stood above the pediment to either side of the floral decoration, which adorned its peak. These figures were simply a part of the architectural design and had no relation to the arrangement [*Vorstellung*] of the other figures.

I have already explained in an earlier description that these small female figures were originally four in number, with two to either side of the peak of each pediment.

The fifteen remaining figures were placed inside the two pediments, i.e., inside the interior of the enclosure created by the obtuse triangle itself, an enclosure that was deepened more than usual to serve this purpose.

The surviving figures were arranged in the following manner: there were nine in the front pediment, and six in [182] the back.[102] The figures that were in the front pediment are those to which I have assigned the letters A, H, I, K, L, N, O, P, and R. Of those figures that belonged to the rear pediment, and which appear to have been somewhat more extended in their arrangement, only six remain: namely, D, E, F, G, M, and Q.[103]

In the middle of the pediment where the interior space is highest, stood the Minerva, since she is the tallest of the group. She stood almost completely straight and appears to have had little part in the battle in whose midst she stood and that she, so to speak, divided in two parts. To her right and left, the engaged warriors confronted one another, armed with shields and helmets. The kneeling archers took their places further out, where the pediment slopes downward and begins to be lower; they were entirely [183] symmetrical and faced one another in the same position. At the extreme end of the pedimental recesses on both sides, where they come to a point at the corner, there lay a wounded warrior, who in this manner filled out each corner.

What I have said here for one pediment holds in the same way for the other. The figures were symmetrically arranged in both. Thus, in the middle of both stood a Minerva. The warriors were placed in similar fashion and set one against the other. At the place where an archer was placed in one pediment, another was placed in similar position in the opposite pediment, and that is how it went with all the surviving figures.

If we have spoken with great certainty [*mit vieler Bestimmtheit*] about the assembly and arrangement of these figures, then it is natural that an objection may be made, as to the grounds on which one can establish this sort of assembly or [184] prove such an arrangement of the figures. This is especially the case since they are no longer in their original places [*Stelle*], but rather were found buried under the rubble.

To this objection I can do little more than answer with a description of these figures' recent discovery. The manner in which these statues were found beneath the two pediments during their excavation confirms [*bestimmt*] an order of placement [*Ordnung der Lage*] that enables this kind of reconstruction [*Zusammenstellung*].

The Minerva, for example, was found in the middle under the pediment. The standing warriors were next to her, the archers a little further to the side, and the supine figures at the very end of the pediment. In other words, these figures fell in the collapse of the top portion of the temple, which was probably caused by a strong earthquake,[(1)] in a way which [185] necessarily mirrors their original position in the pediment.

The conclusion [*Schluß*] I draw from these facts seems natural and appropriate to me, and sufficient in themselves to establish this beyond any reasonable doubt. If one considers such evidence unreliable and does not wish

1. WAGNER'S NOTE: That this temple was not intentionally destroyed by human hands, but rather must have collapsed through [185] the force of a great earthquake, is easily proven. There is no trace of deliberate injury to these figures. Whatever is damaged or broken was clearly due simply to the fall. And if the temple had been destroyed by fire, then one would see traces [*Spuren*] of this in the marble, which always suffers through fire, especially with respect to its brittleness.

to depend upon it, then one may come to precisely the same arrangement, in my view, from the varying heights of the figures in relation to the pediment. This proves that they could only have been arranged in this way and no other [*nur so und nicht anders*], since the varying height of the pediment will not allow another [186] arrangement. One might just as well doubt whether these figures stood in the temple pediments at all.

That they did indeed stand inside the two pediments and nowhere else is easily proven on other grounds. Since these statues were found in part under the front pediment, and in part under the rear pediment, only two cases are possible: either they stood inside the pediments themselves, or else they stood under them. If they had been located under the pediments, that is, under them and in front, then certainly one ought to have found their anchoring points or pedestals in the original excavation. It is highly unlikely that they would have been set up at ground level without such support. Since no trace [*Spur*] of this has been found, we are left with the first explanation—namely, that they stood inside the pediments themselves.

Furthermore, we see from the figures themselves, with their shortened bases [*Platten*], [187] that they were originally arranged in close order, and the effect of the whole was a tightly connected arrangement [*Darstellung*] or group. How can we assume that this crowded mass of figures might have stood across from the temple, where it would have entirely blocked access to the temple itself?

The one serious objection to be made counter to our assertion would be this: Why were these figures worked on all sides equally, front and back, as they clearly [*bestimmt*] were, if they were to be set up inside the pediments where their backs could never be seen?

I admit that this circumstance is striking, and that it certainly [*bestimmt*] runs counter to later artistic practice. But this does not seem to me a sufficient condition to prove the contrary. For ancient artists [*die alten Künstler*], especially those from earlier times [*der frühern Zeiten*], diligently worked their statues from all sides, without regard for placement, [188] and completed them with the greatest care, of which we possess other indisputable examples. The most important examples of this type come from the pedimental figures on the Parthenon, some fragments of which remain in the front pediment to this day. Of even greater significance are the complete figures that Lord Elgin removed some years ago from the pediment and which are currently housed in a collection in London that bears his name. These statues are, much like [*gleich*] our Aeginetan sculptures, symmetrically and fully worked, both front and back.[104]

Since this commendable artistic custom [*Kunstsitte*] survived into the flourishing age [*jene blûhende Zeit*] of Pheidias, we have still less reason to wonder that this custom was also in force at an earlier time [*in jenen frühern Zeit*]. Even without this, it is the custom in the first flowering of art to carry out and complete every small detail with the greatest diligence, care, and attention.

[189] What finally establishes these matters beyond any reasonable doubt, however, is the fact that the architect, Mr. Cockerell, who so professionally conducted this excavation with the greatest care and precise measurements, found certain traces of incised holes [*Spuren von Vertiefungen*] at the interface of the cornice on which the plates for these figures must originally have been set. This discovery goes some way toward explaining how these figures, which were so freely rendered without any external support, could have stood upright on such a narrow base, which was only two fingers thick, without being anchored at the back with iron.

I believe that I have also sufficiently proved that these Aeginetan figures stood inside the pediments, despite the fact that they were worked on all sides, as was doubtless the case with the figures from the Parthenon, as well as those from the Temple of Theseus in Athens, where one finds similar holes [190] at the interface of the cornice such as are evident here on the Temple of Jupiter at Aegina.

I would also add that Pausanias's description of the Jupiter temple at Olympia permits one to assume that the works in both of these pediments also were not worked on only one side [*halbenhobener Arbeit*], but rather completely in the round [*völlig rund gearbeitet*], much like the pedimental figures from the Parthenon and our Aeginetan figures.

The effect created by such a crowded assembly of figures, all worked fully in the round [*rund gearbeiteter*] and in a single pediment group, must have been favorable and intense, I should think. The whole group [*Das Ganze*] must have appeared more lifelike and closer to Nature than any figures worked on only one side [*halberhobenen Werken*] can appear. For this type of arrangement of figures in the round [*runder Figuren*] not only guaranteed a stronger and more natural impression [*Beleuchtung*], together with its original and deceptive effects [*entspringenden tauschenden Wirkung*], but also [191] achieved an entirely natural perspective [*Anblick*] from every standpoint and when viewed from any distance, an effect that half-carved figures with their necessary artistic limitations can never achieve.

That similarly arranged sculptural groups of figures more or less in the round were common in open or public spaces among the ancient Greeks may be proven by countless other examples. I cite just a few of the most excellent.

Thus in the so-called Altis, the space in Olympia sacred to Jupiter, a sculptural group of Greek heroes from the Trojan War was set up and paid for by all the Greek peoples; it depicted them casting lots to determine who would engage in single combat with Hektor, who had challenged them.[105] They stood near the [192] temple, armed with shields and javelins. Over against the heroes on a separate pedestal stood Nestor, who threw their lots into the helmet. Eight of these figures survived. The ninth—namely, the statue of Ulysses—was taken by Nero to Rome. This was a work of the sculptor Nikon of Aegina[(2),106] (Paus. book 5, chap. 25).[107]

Further along, in the sacred Hippodamium at Olympia, there was a semicircular stone platform in the center of which stood Jupiter together with Thetis and Hemera, or else Aurora, who pleads on behalf of her son. The two sons, Achilles and Memnon, stood at both ends in battle pose along with four Greeks facing off against as many Trojans: Ulysses against [193] Helenus; Menelaus against Paris; Diomedes against Aeneas; and Ajax against Deiphobus. These were masterworks of Myron from Lykia (Paus. book 5, chap. 22).[108]

There was a similar group at Delphi, depicting the quarrel [*Streit*] of Hercules and Apollo over the tripod. The two are both represented, as it were [*wie im Begriff*], on the verge of coming to blows. Leto and Diana attempt to calm Apollo, as Minerva does Hercules. The statues of Minerva and Diana came from the hand of Chionis; the Hercules, the Apollo, and the Leto were completed by Diyllus and Amiklaus working together (Paus. book 10, chap. 13).[109]

Here also may be included two surviving works, the sculptural group known as the Farnese Bull [194] in Naples, and the Niobe in Florence.[(3),110]

---

2. SCHELLING'S NOTE: Actually by Onatas, son of Micon, as an inscription on the shield of Idomeneus makes clear.
3. WAGNER'S NOTE: Mr. Cockerell tried briefly to assemble these figures of Niobe, which are now in Florence, on account of their number and various sizes, into a single group, and then to imagine them as a pedimental adornment similar to the collection of Aeginetan heroes. He attempted to illustrate this fascinating hypothesis in a specially prepared incised print, and sought to defend the reconstruction with an accompanying discussion.

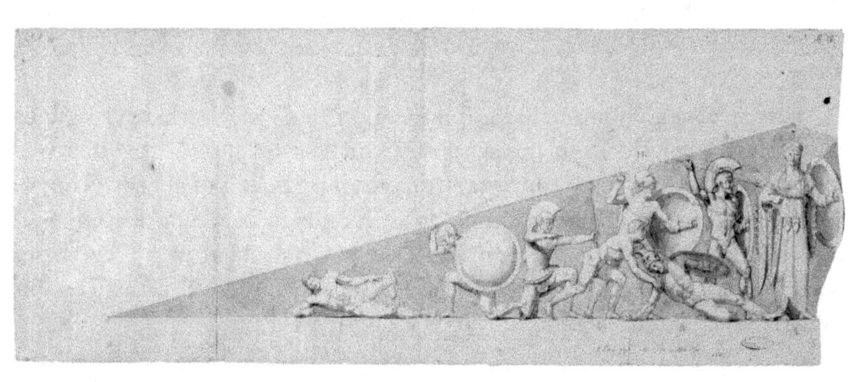

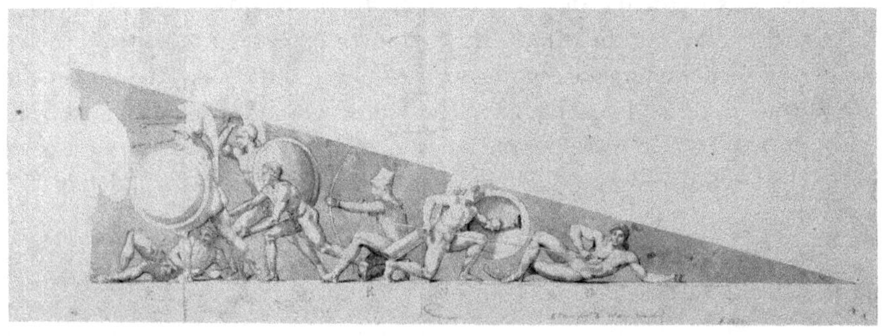

CHAPTER VIII

On The Meaning or Idea [*Vorstellung*] of These Figures

[Wagner]

[195]
The description I have provided of each one of these figures makes sufficiently clear that the whole group must have depicted [*vorstellen*] a battle between heroes or warriors, all of them under the particular supervision of Minerva. What specific battle was intended to be depicted [*vorstellen*] is a question not easily answered, and probably must remain a mystery. On the one hand, Pausanias deals with this temple to Jupiter Panhellenius [196] in piecemeal fashion; and on the other hand, the figures themselves have no distinguishing characteristics with which one might draw conclusions about their identity or the situation in which they find themselves. The Minerva and the Phrygian archer are the only figures who have anything exceptional about them: the Minerva because of her aegis; the archer for his tight-fitting clothing and his half-Phrygian, half-Persian cap. Apart from these two figures, the others have nothing in their clothing or weaponry that might justify an historical conclusion about them.[111] The helmets are more or less in the Greek form, although each one is different and none are entirely the same. The shields of all the figures are generally the same, including that of the Minerva. They are all circular with a sharp curvature and a wide border, that is, in the Argolidian form. The two surviving [197] quivers are dissimilar: the one which appears to belong to the Persian or Phrygian archer has a more Asiatic form than the other. As for the swords, bows, and other weapons, which were probably made of metal, nothing has been recovered. No name or sign was to be found either painted or incised, neither on the shield nor on anything else, despite the great effort I made to discover something of this sort.

If, then, nothing is to be concluded either from the character of the figures or from the types of weapons they possess, and if there is no other evidence that would assist in drawing a conclusion about the historical situation or the meaning of these assembled figures, then nothing remains save to turn to the original purpose [*Bestimmung*] and first construction [*Entstehung*] of the temple.

What we learn from Pausanias in [198] this regard consists solely in the fact that Aiakos must have built this temple, and for the following occasion. Once, when there was a great drought throughout the whole of Greece, the Greeks sought advice from the oracle at Delphi, which directed them to turn to Aiakos, through whose intercession they would receive rain from Jupiter. Aiakos made his offering in the name of all the Greeks and this had the desired effect. On account of this,[(1),112] Aiakos built a temple to *Jupiter of all the Greeks* [*Jupiter aller Griechen*].

There is nothing, of course, in this story that relates directly [199] to the statues from this temple. On this matter, as on the matter of the quality of the temple itself, Pausanias maintains a frustrating silence. So, we must leave this issue to the side.

Since there is no surer point on which to base a conclusion, nothing is left but to make do with conjectures based on long-standing, ancient practices.

Assuming that the collapsed temple in whose environs the figures were found is indeed this temple of Panhellenic Jupiter, a hitherto worthy assumption,[113] then what relation [*Beziehung*] might there be between the figures associated with this temple and Jupiter or Aiakos, its alleged founder? It is well known, and confirmed by other examples [*Beispiele*], that, as far as their temple decoration went, the ancients did not always expect a very close relationship [*strenge Beziehung*] between the actual images depicted [*Gegenständen ihrer Darstellung*] [200] and the sites [*Orte*] upon which they were erected. How else might we explain the conflict between Centaurs and Lapiths, or the battle of the Amazons, on the shield of Minerva or the throne of the Olympian Jupiter, and other similarly selected scenes? Thus I do not think there is any particularly close relationship [*strenge Beziehung*] that provides an absolute or determinate explanation [of these Aeginetan figures]. Nonetheless it is possible to conjecture that the display [*Darstellung*] of these figures on the temple under discussion was not entirely arbitrary, but rather was conceived in some relationship [*Beziehung*] to it. We might suppose that some military engagement [*Gefecht*] was the intended representation [*vorgestellt*], in which the Aiakides achieved their exceptional fame under the general protection of

1. SCHELLING'S NOTE: This, of course, is not stated explicitly in Pausanias, neither in book 1, chap. 45, nor in book 2, chap. 29. The real reason is reported by Isocrates (*Evag.*, chap. 5), but those who built the temple were the leaders of the assembled Greek city-states who initially requested Aiakos's intercession before Jupiter.

Minerva. Similarly, on the other pediment, we might suppose that the figures of the Phrygian and Persian archers were intended to recall [*vorgestellt*] some engagement [*Gefecht*] in which the Phrygians or [201] the Persians had a part, or else that a war of the Aiakides against these peoples was intended.

Many are the praiseworthy achievements of the Aiakides, which have come down to us from the histories and poems of the ancients. In particular, two great wars [*grosse Kämpfe*] are well known: the one, in which the Aiakides fought personally against the barbarians for the common good of all Greece; and the other, whose positive outcome was attributed at least in part to their invisible assistance. These two wars are *the Trojan War* and the common *war of Greeks against the army of Xerxes.*[114]

In the Trojan War the most praiseworthy deeds of the Aiakides were those of Achilles, Telamonian Ajax, and Neoptolemus. In the Persian War, Herodotus relates that the Greeks, before the naval engagement at Salamis, which [202] actually decided the continued independence of all Greece, thought it best to call upon Ajax and Telamon for aid, and that a boat was actually sent to Aegina for this purpose, to pick up Aiakos and the Aiakides (whether this referred to their statues or to their ashes remains unclear). This ship bearing the Aiakides returned to the Greek fleet in the precise moment when the call to battle was given.[(2),115] The Greeks attribute the happy conclusion of this decisive battle, in which the Aeginetans [203] excelled all the other Greeks, for the most part to this supernatural assistance.

It would not be impossible that the Aeginetans—in order to glorify the Aiakides, their local heroes, and to commemorate their own valor, which was proved in this conflict—would have wanted to depict [*darstellen*] precisely these events on the two pediments of this temple, of which Aiakos himself was believed to have been the founder or builder.

Only the style of these figures does not appear to be in unison with the time in which the battle of Salamis took place, that is, the style appears to belong to an earlier time, as I endeavored to show in some detail in my stylistic discussion of these figures. It also seems to me that the figure of Minerva had no part in this design [*Absicht*], since the result of the battle at Salamis was due to the presence and assistance of the Aiakides, according to [204] Herodotus.

---

2. SCHELLING'S NOTE: That the author's interpretation of the meaning of Herodotus is justified is confirmed in part by the phrasing of Thucydides VI. 93 (ἐπὶ χρήματα καὶ ἱππεῖς) and in part by Herodotus V.80, with the accompanying note by Wesseling. A later Greek writer says: "the ship brought the house (the family) of the Aiakides to Salamis."

This belief must have called, not for the Minerva, but rather for Aiakos and the Aiakides as the overseers [*Vorsteher*] of this battle.

Taking all of these contradictions into consideration, which counsel against the supposition [*Meinung*] that this arrangement [*Darstellung*] could have represented the battle of Salamis, I am inclined to believe rather that our group may have depicted [*darstellen*] the great deeds of the Aiakides at Troy. According to this interpretation, the figure of Minerva would be entirely appropriate in this position [*Stelle*], since she provided the most prominent support of the Greeks in the hard fighting before Troy.

As for what particular battle [*Gefechte*] before Troy was intended by this arrangement [*Vorstellung*], this will be difficult, if not impossible, to guess at, since the individual figures, as discussed above, lack any distinguishing characteristics.

The opinion that this group might have referred to the sea battle of Salamis is considered worthy of refutation by the author, only because it had actually been asserted, likely in Italy. Much as the theme [*Vorstellungen*] in the pediments of the Parthenon only made reference to Minerva, so generally speaking it is most likely that these recently discovered sculptures from the pediments of the Jupiter temple of Aegina should have represented [*vorstellten*] none other than the Aiakides. For Jupiter, Aiakos, and the Aiakides together were the patron deities [*Schutzgötter*] of the island, as this invocation of Aegina, the mother of Aiakos, from an Ode by Pindar makes clear: "Dear mother Aegina, safeguard the city on its journey of freedom, together with Zeus and king Aiakos, with Peleus, noble Telamon, and Achilles" (Pyth. VIII, at the conclusion). Pindar also mentions [206] "the Aiakides' well-founded place" on another part of the island, from which their images [*Bilder*] were doubtless removed to be taken to this decisive sea battle. For none of the sons of Aiakos remained on the island. Peleus and Telamon were in exile, after the death of Phokus, and there is no mention anywhere that their ashes were brought back to their homeland. Therefore there were *images* [*Bilder*] of these heroes on Aegina, but probably not in the Aiakeion (Αἰάκειον). According to Pausanias's description (II, 29) this was a simple *peribolos* made of marble. At the entrance were the images [*Bilder*] of the men dispatched by the Greeks to Aiakos in the time of the drought. Inside the *peribolos* itself were very ancient olive trees and an altar raised not far above the ground, which was in all likelihood the grave monument for Aiakos. This, in any case, was preserved as one of the secrets of the place [*des Orts*].[116] Not far from the Aiakeion, however, was the grave of Phokus. Apart from the funerary monument to Aiakos, this district appears to have had [207] no other sanctuary to speak of. Pausanias mentions no other temple in which the images [*Bilder*] might have been displayed. They were doubtless housed in the temple of the ancestors, where they were venerated by all, and the household of the Aiakides would have been brought to Salamis from the temple of Panhellenic Jupiter. Since there were objects of veneration inside the temple, it is to be expected that the portrayal [*Vorstellung*] of one of their great deeds would have adorned the exterior of the temple, just as the portrayal [*Vorstellung*] of the birth of Minerva and her contest [*ihres Streits*] with Neptune over the possession of Athens adorned the pediments of the temple consecrated to her. That the scene represented [*vorgestellte*] was in fact some scene from the Trojan War is likely, primarily due to the presence of Minerva. But it is less than certain, simply because we do not know the entire mythic cycle [*Fabelkreis*] surrounding [208] the heroic lives of the Aiakides. It is even less certain that we should look for the battle represented here [*das vorgestellte Gefecht*] in a description from Homer, since the discussions of the Trojan War were so very different in different traditions [*Stämmen*], and nothing is less certain than that these images [*Bilder*] originated at the same time, or in an even earlier time, as our current version of Homer did.

As it stands, the absence of historical references in the whole arrangement [*Vorstellung*] is a point that must be taken into consideration alongside the assessment of the ancients themselves, as is the striking similarity in the arrangement [*Gleichförmigkeit in den Vorstellungen*] of these two pediments in contrast to the great variation that may be observed between the forward and rear pediments of the Parthenon.

CHAPTER IX

On the Painting [*Bemalung*] of the Figures and of the Temple

[Wagner]

It was already noted in the previous description of these figures that they were partially painted. The traces of color [*Spuren von Farbe*] that appear here and there are quite faint and are now half gone, due to weathering and the moisture of the earth into which the collapse of the temple deposited these figures. Still, the few remaining traces [*Spuren*] present irrefutable evidence as to their original painting [*Bemalung*].

The colors that are still visible here and there on these figures are pure *red* and [210] *sky blue*. The red appears to be both a dark vermilion, or a shade of vermilion similar to red clay; the sky-blue colors appear to be the ordinary blue made from ground cobalt [*Smalte*]. As for other colors or mixed pigments such as yellow, green, etc., no trace [*keine Spur*] may be found on these figures, but there are indeed traces on portions of the temple architecture that I will treat in greater depth below. It may also be the case that certain other colors were less resistant to the effects of weathering and soil acidity than the reds and blues were. One also observes that the red coloring [*die erstere*] survives in more vibrant and lively a fashion than the blue [*die andere*] has done.

The parts on which traces of color [*Spuren von Farbe*] survive are the following.

First, almost all of the accompanying military equipment, such as the helmets, which possess some traces of sky blue, or the plumes and strands of hair, which were all painted in shades of vermilion red.

[211] The shields were painted over their entire inner surface in a dark red that seems closer to red clay than vermilion. This red color, as observed, decorated only the interior hollow of the shield as well as one part of the interior border, running to roughly a finger-length from the outermost edge where an incised line is visible that defines the borderline of this red coloring. On the exterior surface or curvature there is virtually no visible coloration any

longer; just a few fragmentary pieces of the shields bear clear traces [*deutliche Spuren*] of sky blue on the surface. This coloring did not cover the entire exterior surface, however, but rather was similarly confined within incised, circular lines. If, as I suggested earlier, this red coloring on the interior should be taken to represent [*vorstellen*] the lining [*Fütterung*] of the shield, then it is also possible that real Greek shields were sometimes painted on their interiors instead of having the usual inner decoration [*Bekleidung*], [212] as this passage from Pausanias (book 6, chap. 9) makes clear. He says there "that in one of the so-called treasure-houses of Olympia, in addition to a helmet and greaves, there is a shield which is covered in bronze *and painted on the interior*, which was a portion of war-booty dedicated by the Myanians."[117] However, the way in which this is described suggests that it was unusual, or at least that it was not the general practice.

In addition to the shields and helmets, there are traces [*Spuren*] of the former painting, or at least a colored hue, on both surviving quivers. There is a trace [*Spur*] of sky blue on the one that belonged to the Phrygian or Persian archer; on the other there are clear signs [*deutliche Zeichen*] that it was partially painted with red coloring.

On the armor or cuirasses I have thus far been unable to discover any trace [*keine Spur*] of color.

The bases [*Plinten*] of these figures were painted entirely [213] in red, as is quite clear from the traces that are still detectible on most of the fragments. The sandals [*Sohlen*] on the feet of the female figures were decorated with the same color. The feature that we have already observed—namely, that the straps or belts with which these sandals were attached to the feet were not rendered in the marble—leads to the supposition that they were rendered in paint, although there is no clear evidence of this. It is also probable that the robes of the three freestanding female figures were partially, if not entirely, painted, although I have been unable to discover a clear trace [*deutliche Spur*] of this anywhere save on the Minerva, where, along the hem of her robe just above the right ankle there is a clear trace [*deutliche Spur*] of vermilion. Whether this color extended over the entire robe or should be taken to have decorated [*vorgestellen*] strictly the hemline is uncertain, since, as I observed, no further remains of it are visible.

[214] I could find no trace [*nirgends eine Spur*] of color on the naked portions of these figures, save for some vermilion visible on the shoulders of figures L and R. I consider these traces to be incidental [*zufällig*], rather than describing them as the result of intentional painting, in which case one would have to accept the idea that this red coloration must have represented [*vorstellen*]

blood flowing out of the wounds that were so often depicted on these figures. What has been said concerning the painting of the weapons indicates that they were *multicolored*, i.e., painted partly red and partly blue, so it is unlikely that the naked parts of the figures were, themselves, painted vermilion.

I have already clearly stated [*bestimmt ausgesprochen*] several times that the eyes and lips were painted. For almost all of the heads display the same general structure of clear, well-rendered eyes and lips, which enabled the application of encaustic colors, and serves as proof of what I have already mentioned regarding the netted patterning which is so clear on one of the surviving helmets. This decoration appears almost as a sheen on the surface of the marble. From this we developed the idea that the spaces that were not covered with paint suffered the effects of weathering and became rougher, whereas the other spaces were pure and smooth due to the encaustic coloring. That this explanation for this sort of light and dark [*Helldunkel*] pattern is correct, through which one can clearly determine the original decoration even if the coloring has been completely lost, is confirmed by the fact that this light and dark [*Helldunkel*] pattern is visible on only one side, certainly the side that was exposed to weathering. The same pattern suggests the earlier presence of paint on the lips and eyeballs [*Augäpfeln*] of all these figures. Indeed, with closer attention, especially to the eyes of the Minerva, [216] it is possible to discern just a whisper [*Hauch*] or trace [*Spur*] of color along the entire outline of the eyeball.

As to whether the *hair* of these figures was originally painted, I must leave that issue to one side, since no trace [*keine Spur*] survives. Since so many other portions of these figures were painted, it would be strange if they neglected the hair, all the more so since it was entirely common among the ancients to paint the hair red on their marble statues, their figures in half-relief, and especially their works in baked clay, even when the other body parts lacked color entirely. This custom [*Gewohnheit*] of painting the hair red has continued from ancient times to the present day in Greece, where even now it is a general practice [*allgemeine Sitte*] among the female sex to give the hair a red coloring.(1),118

[217] Now a few short words regarding the painting of the temple itself, in particular the various parts and architectural joints!

1. WAGNER'S NOTE: The plant that the women in Greece use for this purpose, as was reported to me, [217] is the *Lawsonia inermis. Linn.*, which dye does not give the hair the same shade of red that is common among us in Germany. This plant, when applied to naturally black hair, which is almost universal in Greece, creates rather a pure reddish luster, i.e., black hair plays with the light to create a purple hue that creates a most pleasing effect to the eye, and which is worlds away from the sorrel hair color common among us.

The various decorations, foliage, and such, things that are usually carved into the stone, are to be seen here simply in color. All portions of the cornice, as well as the lower entablature, were painted. Surviving fragments of the architrave show that a continuous band of red color ran beneath the triglyphs [*Dreischlissen*], whereas the protruding element beneath the triglyphs was decorated [218] with spots of sky blue. The entablature running continuously over the exterior colonnade was decorated with painted foliage in alternating greens and yellows.

The interior space of the pediment in which our group of figures once stood was painted sky blue.

The cella of the temple, as the fragments confirm, was vermilion, whereas the interior walls themselves were coated with a thin, lime stucco [*Kalkbewurf*], which was spread smooth and also painted red.

Even the marble roof tiles were decorated on their exterior face with a type of flower whose patterns have likewise survived.

It remains to be said finally that the temple, including the columns, was not constructed with marble, but rather with a type of yellow sandstone. Only the roof and the upper [291] cornice were made of marble. Probably this was done to protect the rest, which is to say the underside of the building, from the harmful effects of weathering.

It will likely strike us as quite strange, given our contemporary tastes and modern views, to behold statues worked entirely in marble that were also painted at least in part. It is similarly strange to behold temples that were colored on the inside and the outside, and whose decorations were not carved, but rather were painted in many colors. We wonder at this apparently bizarre taste, and judge it to be a barbaric custom [*Sitte*], a crude survival from an earlier time.

It seems to me that our situation is no different from that of the man in the gospel who wished to pull the mote [*Splitter*] from someone else's eye while having a beam [*Balken*] in his own. If we were first [220] to clear our own eyes of prejudgment, and if at the same time we had the good fortune to see one of these Greek temples in its original state, then I wager that we would happily withdraw our rash judgment, and would praise the very thing we now condemn.[(2),119]

2. SCHELLING'S NOTE: No one will hesitate to give full approval to this author's judgment, which is considerably strengthened by the more detailed discussion and explanation

[221] That this painting of temples and works of art was not merely a crude survival from an earlier time in Greece, but rather was the custom in the period of the very highest development [*in den Zeiten der höchsten Ausbildung*] of Greek art, of this the Parthenon provides the most eloquent example. This temple, one of the most perfect works of architecture, was as everyone knows erected in the time of Perikles by the architect Iktinus, and probably under the specific direction of Pheidias who, as we are justified in concluding from the testimony of ancient writers, even if he did not complete all the statues himself nonetheless [222] arranged for them to be completed according to his design. The Parthenon also bore the stamp of his school.[120] On this building, which was erected in the greatest period of Greek art, or indeed of any art,[121] one observes that both the architectural pieces and the works in relief [*halbheroben Arbeiten*] that ran around the exterior of the *cella,* were all painted to one degree or another.[(3)]

That this custom or tradition [*Sitte oder Gewohnheit*] of painting statues and other works in relief, entirely or in part, survived into the period of the Roman Caesars, and on until the ultimate deterioration [*Verfalle*] of art, may be demonstrated by other artworks of every age, of which I will cite only a few examples. We find [223] two female figures in the antiquities collection in Naples, portraits from the period of the Roman imperium, which had painted red hair. We also find in the recent excavations near the ancient Volscian city of Veii, in addition to other artworks of great interest, one statue that appears

---

in that lovely work by Mr. Quatremère de Quincy. I take this opportunity to note that this published *Report* was composed in the beginning of this year (1816), and thus the author could make no use of the valuable work of this French scholar. To pursue the judgment of the author further would lead to important observations concerning the necessary deterioration [*nothwendigen Verfall*] of art through the isolation, and eventually the complete separation, of the mutually [*gegenseitig*] reinforcing arts of architecture, painting, and sculpture. It has now devolved to such a point—as it had to do, once painting and sculpture, rather than serving a public function, became purely the objects and the hobby of private persons. Each of these three arts [221] in their contemporary abstraction must remain unable to satisfy the ultimate demands of feeling. And it is probably safe to say, especially given the subordinate condition of the arts, for which there is scarcely room in the world any longer, that we can barely have a concept, much less form a judgment [*keinen Begriff noch weniger ein Urtheil haben können*], concerning the true glory of a Greek temple, which originated out of the unification and combination of both form and color [*von Form und Farbe*].

3. WAGNER'S NOTE: On this work of carved relief [*halberhobener Arbeit*], which depicted [*vorstellt*] the Panathenaic Festival as a traditional religious ceremony, the background is painted sky blue. The hair of the figures as well as other devices were gilded, and one finds traces [*Spuren*] of green color in some other places.

to be *Julia Soemia* depicted [*vorstellen*] as a Venus, whose robe was similarly painted with vermilion. I also observed, as they removed the bas-relief [*Bassorelievi*] from the casino of the Villa Borghese, that beneath it was another fragment in relief [*halberhobener Arbeit*] from the later years of the Roman imperium on which may be seen a warrior with red-painted hair and beard.

It appears, then, that the vermilion or red color was a favorite among the ancients, and served for the painting of both statues and buildings. Vitruvius testifies to this with respect to architecture, and Pausanias mentions a great many similarly [224] painted red statues. This color was preferred for images [*Bildern*] of Bacchus, Priapus, and the Faun.

As to what was the primary reason or instigation [*erste Ursache oder Veranlassung*] among the ancients for painting their statues and temples, I offer the following opinion: namely, that it was not only their inclination toward color that led to this practice, but rather the main reason derived from the necessity imposed upon them principally by the materials they used in the very earliest times.

As is well known, all the oldest carvings [*Schnitzbilder*], or at least the vast majority, were made of wood, and were referred to by the general name of *Daidala*, according to the testimony of Pausanias (book 9, chap. 3).[122] So too were the oldest temples built of wood, as is confirmed by the essence [*Wesen*] and origin [*Ursprunge*] of architecture.

[225] Wood, as is well known, is by nature always impure and grainy in appearance and not particularly pleasing to the eye. Thus it was natural that people came to the practice of coloring the wood, which served at the same time to protect it against the effects of weathering and moisture. So began the custom of painting carved images [*Schnitzbilder*] as well as temples, whether in one color or many.(4) They later began to use harder materials than wood, and eventually marble took the place of wood. So this tradition [*Gewohnheit*] of painting statues and temples carried over to the marble, since the people were already [226] accustomed [*gewöhnt*] to seeing these objects colored.(5)

4. WAGNER'S NOTE: A similar situation exists with the sculptural works and altars in our churches in Germany. Are we not required, on account of the material—the wood—either to paint them or else to gild them?
5. WAGNER'S NOTE: That we have done something similar in modern times (and perhaps for similar reasons)—that is, painting or gilding stone statues—is apparent from the many

This manner of painting temples must naturally have improved to the same degree as taste in general and as the various branches of art approached nearer and nearer to perfection. And thus it may be concluded that this union of color and form [*diese Verbindung der Farbe mit der Form*] came to its highest point in the time of Perikles when the Parthenon was built, that is, to its purest and most satisfying harmony [*Einklang*].

---

examples in our Gothic churches and churchyards. The statues of the Apostles in the Dome at Cologne are also partially painted and partially gilded. There is a similar example in the Chapel to Mary [*Marien-Kapelle*] in Würzburg, whose pillars and attached figures of the apostles are all in sandstone.

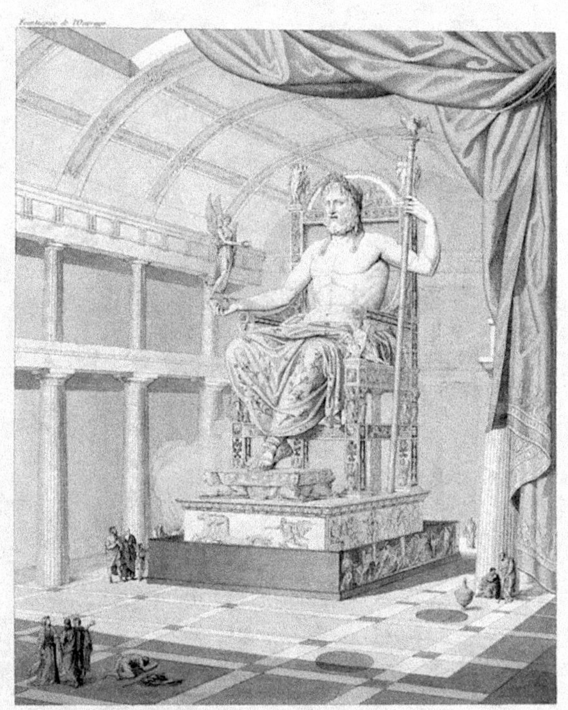

LE JUPITER OLYMPIEN,

VU DANS SON TRÔNE ET DANS L'INTÉRIEUR DE SON TEMPLE.

CONCLUSION

[Wagner]

So much may be said about these remarkable works of early sculpture, as they now appear to us and in their current condition. Time will provide the occasion for further observations when one will be able to inspect and investigate them with greater ease [*Bequemlichkeit*] from *all* sides.[123] Since the plinths or pedestals [*Plinten der Fußgestelle*] for these figures were missing, this was impossible until now. Some things are touched upon very briefly here, and some other matters that warranted attention may have been passed over in silence. This *Report* [228] should suffice simply as a preliminary description of what one may expect from these statues [*Bildwerken*]. Words [*Worte*], in any case, do not suffice to call up the idea [*Begriffe*] of things [*Dinge*] that have not been seen, and that may only be understood perfectly with actual observation [*Anschauung*]. Were one able to supplement this writing [*Schrift*] with the actual preview [*Umrisse*] of these figures, then much would be gained, and the experience of the reader [*die Sache der Leser*] would be much livelier [*anschaulicher*]. This simply was not possible given the current condition of these works.

I conclude these lines with the expectation that they will be similarly welcome to the friends of art and antiquity. For I am convinced that the appearance of these works opens the door to some new perspectives and will provide new information concerning many things about which we have remained in darkness and doubt until now.

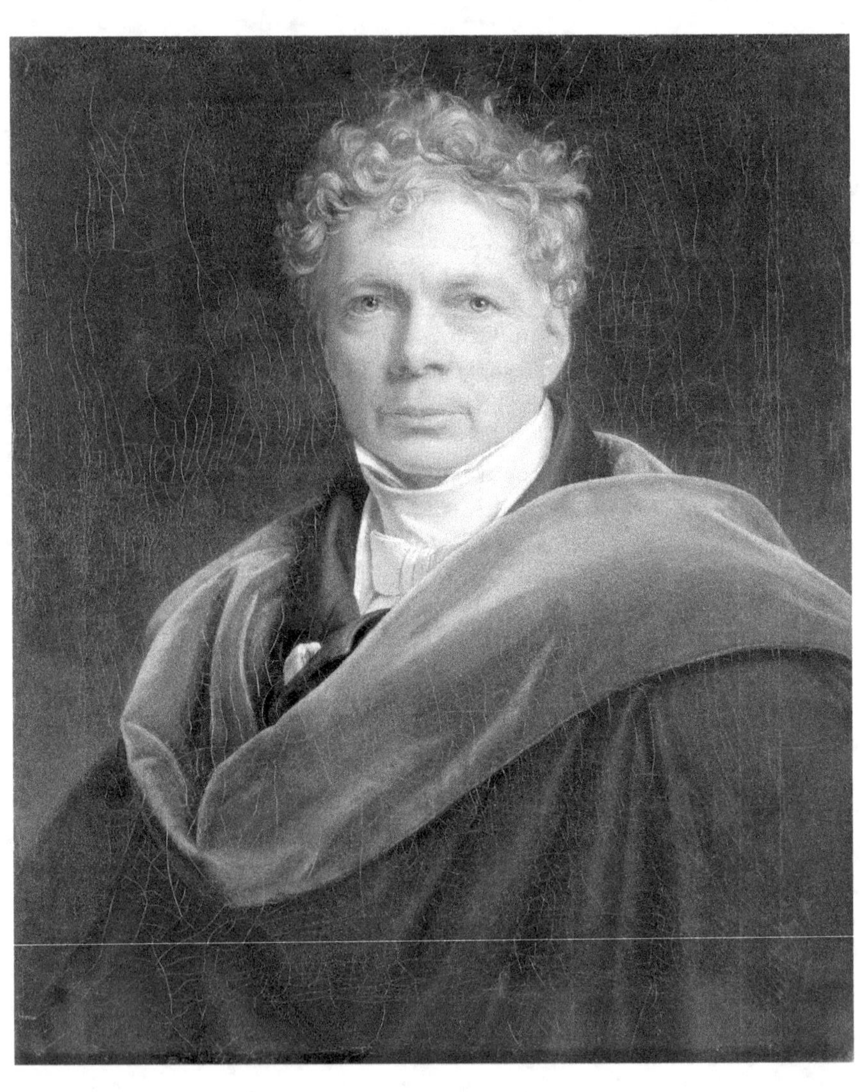

EDITOR'S CONCLUDING REMARKS

[Schelling]

The editor should be allowed to add his own remarks to this conclusion, in which he may set out a few things that either had no proper place earlier in the text or else may have been overlooked.

At the outset it stands to mention our gratitude to *Winckelmann*, who was a pathbreaker in so many other ways and was also the first to discern from the reports of Pausanias the existence [*Dasein*] of a distinct and very ancient school of art on Aegina. One may consult the *History of Art*, Volume IV, part 1, p. 13, Weimar Edition.[124]

[230] *Lessing*, in his "Notes on Winckelmann's Art History" (*Writings*, part 10, p. 252) wished to contest this conclusion [*Schluss*] by means of a general, but rather arbitrary, concept [*Begriffs*] of such schools of art [*Kunstschulen*]. "We cannot think in terms of Schools until art attains a certain degree of perfection, that is, until the masters begin to work according to established principles and *each according to his own*."[125] Lessing himself speaks, in fact, in the same connection, and according to a classification of schools of painting found in Pliny, of a Helladic school that split into the Sicyonian and Attic schools. According to this statement, one can speak just as little of an Attic or Sicyonian school as of an Aeginetan one. Rather, one may speak of a school of Daedalus, and later of Kanachus, of Pheidias, and so on, thinking in terms not of schools but of masters. He who is familiar with the manner and the context in which Pausanias uses the phrase ἐργαστήριον ἀττικόν will see at the very least that [231] Lessing's concept [*Begriff*] is not that of the ancient writer's. One may speak of a school when speaking of a circle of artists among whom a tradition of distinct and established traits is in use, or else whose works demonstrate a certain family resemblance [*Familien-Aehnlichkeit*]. That this was the case among the ancient Aeginetans we have demonstrated with the testimony of the ancients themselves.

According to his own determined explanation, Lessing asserts that "the naming of an Aeginetan style was used simply to distinguish certain ancient works which had been made long before the establishment of the Schools."[126] Such works were really called Attic, *or* Aeginetan, *or* Egyptian, he believes, and to prove this he cites the passage quoted above at page 11 (Pausanias, book 7, chap. 5), in which this contrast is most apparent.[127] It is impossible that Lessing consulted the Greek text of this passage; he follows the Latin translation, which in this case has it completely backwards [*völlig verkehrt*].[128]

[232] It should be recalled, however, that these notes were not published by Lessing himself, and were only made in passing, as a sort of postscript or marginalia to Winckelmann's brand of art history, intended as suggestions for further investigation in the future.

The discovery of the works described in this essay must surely draw the attention of scholars and art historical researchers anew to this Aeginetan School. But it is preferable always and everywhere that the new and the unknown lead us back to the old and the known. So we ought not be surprised if one presumes to find in the style of these figures merely a new example of that which we have previously thought of as the Etruscan, the Ancient Greek, or the Egyptian style. If, however, the sharp-eyed author of the descriptions in this *Report* does not arrive at this conclusion, if he himself wishes to conceive of the Aeginetan within earlier categories, [233] then his excellent descriptions nonetheless give us the means, despite certain general similarities with Etruscan and Ancient Attic works, to see Aeginetan art as different and distinctive in its way from the very beginning [*ursprünglich*].

Here, where the proposal is made that we consider Aeginetan sculpture to have been actually Doric, we are happy to recall a remark by the Weimar publisher of Winckelmann's *History of Art*, a remark that recently came to our attention, namely the seventy-sixth note to Volume IV, which reads as follows: "All new discoveries of older monuments, and all previous comparisons, have not yet assisted researchers in acquiring a more precise knowledge of the peculiar differences between the various Schools of art [*Kunstschulen*]. That such differences existed—in works of painting, as in works of sculpture—and that they were noticeable to the practiced eye, is clear beyond any doubt by virtue of the reports, and also *by virtue of* [234] *the profound distinction in customs, manners, language and way of life between its Ionic and Doric lines of influence.*"[129]

We should include Doric poetry and architecture, as well as *Doric music* [*Tonkunst*], in this same connection.

Pindar was personally familiar with these kindred Aeginetan works. As evidence we cite the song to Aphaia (*Diktynna*, *Britomartis*), which he composed for them (Αἰγινήταις ἐποίησεν, Pausanias II, 30),[130] as well as the many songs for Aeginetans who were victorious in the athletic contests [*Wettkämpfen*]. One allusion to the blossoming art of visual representation [*Bildnerkunst*] on Aegina is the beginning of the Fifth Nemean Ode.[131]

In order to establish the meaning of the expression τρόπος τῆς ἐργασίας beyond any reasonable doubt, it must first be mentioned that Pausanias used the word ἐργασία in most cases with reference to the architectural orders [of classification]: [235] for the Doric, for example, see book V, chapter 10, which says τοῦ ναοῦ δὲ Δώριος μὲν ἐστιν ἡ ἐργασία,[132] which means that the architecture of the temple was Doric. So too in the same book, chapter 16, at the beginning.[133] It is clear and indisputable here that the word does not refer only to *execution*, but also refers to the material objects themselves and their distinctively articulated [*bestimmt sich aussprechenden*] character which, when one is speaking of sculpture, can refer to nothing other than the manner in which Nature is taken and depicted [*darzustellen*].

As far as the strange posture of the Minerva is concerned (p. 25)—in which she is turned to the side from the knees down, whereas the head, the breast, and the entire upper body face straight forward—it should be noted that this contrast *in posture* [*Stellung*] might have had similar reasons as the contrast *in style* one notices between the heads of these figures and the rest of their bodies.

This Minerva would be especially valuable if one may take her as an example, [236] and thus also as an explanation, of the term σκολιὰ ἔργα. mentioned by Strabo (book XIV, p. 532, Tzschuck Ed.).[134] Winckelmann supposed in the first edition of his *Art History* (I, p. 90)[135] that they had placed under this category only such figures that, unlike the very oldest images, imitated [*nachahmten*] various postures and activities [*Stellungen und Handlungen*] in a completely rigid and motionless manner. It is certainly a strange expression, to call these same [rigid] works completely *twisted*! A later explanation may be found in the text of the Weimar Edition, page 20.[136] The expression should only be taken to indicate the exaggeration that necessarily accompanied those first attempts to lend variety to the postures and activities [*Stellungen und Handlungen*] of the figures. Even allowing for this necessity, the expression [*Ausdruck*] nevertheless remains significantly overstated in terms of what is allowable in the appearance of images of the gods [*Götterbilder*].

Nevertheless it cannot be denied that our Aeginetan Minerva was [237] correctly identified as a σκολιὸν ἔργον. Works of *this* sort may also be contrasted with ancient wooden images [*Holzbildern*] in every detail. Since most of these were images of gods [*Götterbilder*], if not actual idols [*Idole*], they gazed straight ahead without looking to one side or the other. Given the strict regulations which applied even to the space in which divine images were arranged, art could only deviate from the norm by slow degrees, as we see here in our Minerva; it was to this form and to this transitional moment that σκολιὰ ἔργα belonged.

To grasp this idea [*Vorstellung*] was in any case impossible before such a work was known. But the idea was rendered unlikely by what Winckelmann (page 20 of the new edition) quoted from Strabo: "that there were *many temples in Ephesus* both from the greatest antiquity and from later times; the former contained very old wooden statues (ἀρχαῖα ξόανα), [238] but in the others there were σκολιὰ ἔργα." If the report [*Bericht*] was really so general, then the σκολιὰ ἔργα must also have referred to something rather general too. In contrast to the ancient wooden statues, they were far more artful images [*überhaupt künsterliche Bilder*]. The broader context of this sentence suggests something else however, as the following passage demonstrates.

> Somewhat higher above the sea (than the city of Ephesus) lies the sacred grove called Ortygia, in which Leto was born with the assistance of the wet-nurse Ortygia. Mount Solmissus looms over this grove. In this place (ἐν τῷ τόπῳ) there are other shrines [*Capellen*] (that ναοῖς are to be understood here is made clear by the following). Some of them are ancient and others were built later. In the older ones there are ancient wooden statues, whereas in the later ones there are σκολιὰ ἔργα—namely, Leto holding a scepter, and Ortygia who holds a child in each hand.[137]

Images [*Bilder*] from later times [*aus neuerer Zeit*] were generally never [239] present in these shrines [*Capellen*], but only those from the most ancient [*alleraltesten*] times or from times just slightly later [*nächstältesten*]. This serves as a proof of their great antiquity, or even better, of the later obsolescence [*Veraltung*] of this unique cult, which is also evident on other grounds. Namely, these little temples [*Tempelchen*] were, as Strabo later reports, the central site [*Mittelpunkt*] for the annual youth festivals, which were especially extravagant; in addition, the College (*Collegium*, ἀρχεῖον) of the Kouretes arranged banquets there as well as secret offerings (μυστικὰς θυσίας).

It is clear that this language [*Rede*] does not refer to statues in general or works of a general [*unbestimmter*] type, but rather to the specific images [*bestimmten Bildsäulen*] of Leto and Ortygia, which were housed in ancient shrines [*Capellen*] in a specific district not far from Ephesus, where they were venerated in a distinctive and partially secret cult. Based on this observation, *Tyrwhitt's*[138] emendation—reading Σκόπα (a work of Skopas) instead of Σκολιά—loses all plausibility. [240] As to whether Lessing's theory (*Writings*, volume X, p. 236)—according to which the ancient wooden images refer to works *from the finest and most ancient era* of art, whereas the σκολιὰ ἔργα denoted *miserable works from a much later period*—is better suited to the context of this description, as well as the otherwise generally accepted meaning of the expression ἀρχαῖα ξόανα, we do not wish to speculate. We hope only that our remark will inspire a more thorough examination by classical scholars [*Alterthumsforscher*].

We simply add, so as to avoid misunderstanding, that it cannot be our opinion [*Meinung*] that the Aeginetan Minerva and the other figures assembled with her, should be dated to this time period in which the twisting of images of the gods [*Götter-Statuen*] first originated or was becoming an established custom. We are far more inclined to suggest that this rotation of the Minerva bears a similarity to the heads, faces, etc., which [241] all appear to belong to a much more ancient period [*viel alten Zeit*], than the sculpting of the other parts, which simply goes to show that these distinctive qualities are no longer to be viewed as evidence of the archaizing [*alterthümlichen*] style. Rather just this: that one may be inspired to see in these distinctive qualities the surviving remnants of the most ancient [*uralten*] style, which also suggests an extremely distant date of origin.

As far as the unique treatment of the *hair*, it should be noted that the hair was generally neglected for the longest time and handled in an entirely conventional way. Pliny (XXXIV.19.4)[139] names Pythagoras of Rhegium as the first artist who rendered the hair in a more precise manner, and his *floruit* [*Kunstzeit*] cannot have been much before that of Pheidias. This is even less remarkable if we consider the colossi of *Monte Cavallo*—which we now may regard as an *Opus Phidiae*, according to the most convincing argument of the worthy publisher of Winckelmann's *Art History*—[242] whose hair is not handled naturally, much less freely or with close detail. Moreover, according to Pliny (Ibid., sect. 3) even Myron was called to reproach, *capillum et pubem non emendatius fecisse, quam rudis antiquitas instituisset.*[140]

In the age of Aeginetan art (between Smilis and Kallon), when no names of specific artists were given, one may be tempted to situate those sculptors according to what Winckelmann *op.cit.* says: "A specific Aeginetan sculptor [*Bildhauer*] is known, not by name, but rather by his designation as an Aeginetan artist [*Bildner*]," in support of which he quotes Pliny XXXV, 40.41.[141] Only the expression, *fictor Aegineta*, probably did not refer to a specific sculptor, but rather had the meaning of the Greek πλάστης, since the Αἰγιναῖα πλαστική (Paus. 10.17) we discussed earlier[142] referred to Aeginetan ceramic artists [*Thonbildneren*] and their considerable range of export.

[243] Henceforth, as we become more versed and more precise in our knowledge about the distinctive traits of the Aeginetan style, one important task will be the study of Greek ceramics [*Vasen-Kunde*] to identify examples

of Aeginetan vessels or their copies [*Nachahmungen*], and to distinguish them from other styles. To that end, the unique piece, which is mostly intact and is discussed on page 80, *Lett. G.G.*,[143] has redoubled value.

From the description of the (so-called black) Ceres of Phigalia[144] it may be seen how far the art of that time had already broken free of received tradition, as well as in some circumstances from superstition (and how much more so in others!). The belief [*Meinung*] that Onatas made *most* of his work based on an image he received in a dream vision, demonstrates on the one hand that we have here to do with a *Vera Icon* of the goddess, and on the other hand that the artist did not utilize the ancient idol [*das alte Idol*] in any way as a model [*Vorbild*], but rather [244] conceived it as a work of utterly free [*völlig freier*] creation. Thus Onatas's decision to complete the image [*Bildes*]—at any price, as Pausanias reports—is a clear sign that they believed *him* to be in a position to excite the sacred awe associated with the most ancient and naive divine images [*uralter unförmlicher Götterbilder*] through his own stylistic grandeur and the sheer power of art [*Macht der Kunst*].

Whoever reads the various remarks by Pausanias concerning Aeginetan art attentively and in context cannot help but notice that he discusses this art with a certain affinity and inclines to it with special fondness. The silence of other writers ought not incline us to mistrust Pausanias's reports; on the contrary, this very silence serves as just one more proof of how far Pausanias excels, in terms of accuracy and expertise, the other ancient authors upon whom we rely for our knowledge of ancient art history. That Pausanias [245] did not invent or imagine the concept [*Begriff*] of an Aeginetan style all by himself, in much the same way that a contemporary researcher may more or less arbitrarily distinguish between various artistic schools, confirms the central place [*Hauptstelle*] of the Aeginetan style: when he says "*among the Greeks,*" whom he names in general, even as he mentions the Aeginetan works as distinct, and *names* them as such (τοῖς καλουμένοις Αἰγιναίοις).

Given this preference [*Vorliebe*], it is all the more to be regretted that Pausanias, in his description of Aegina, surveyed the Mountain and Temple of Panhellenic Jupiter strictly from such a distance, instead of eliminating so many of our uncertainties and doubts with a few well-chosen words, as he might well have done.

Moreover, whoever observes the way in which Pausanias distinguishes the foundation of Aeginetan art from Attic art, in part to elevate [*heraushebt*] it, and finally with what interest he attempts to establish the excellence [*Trefflichkeit*] of Onatas, [246] even in comparison to Pheidias, he will scarcely be able to avoid the following conclusion: Pausanias, for whom the works of Aeginetan art themselves were considered to be the high art of antiquity [*als hohe Kunst-Alterthümer*], had come to something like our own opinion [*Meinung*] considering its relation to Attic art . . . namely, that Aeginetan art led Attic art on the way to its true perfection. Beyond that, a more or less well-founded opinion [*Meinung*] is not available through such investigations, and we ought not expect a probability to be derived from a single case study [*von dem einzelnen Grund*]. Everything, down to the smallest details and relationships, must be considered together, and pondered thoroughly in the spirit [*im Geist*], in order to reveal the theory that brings everything together in the most natural fashion, and thus finally comes to a satisfactory conclusion [*Schluß*].

ENDNOTES TO THE WAGNER/SCHELLING TEXT

1. RUPRECHT'S NOTE: At the time of the sculptures' discovery, transport, and later acquisition (1811–12), the British had placed the eastern Mediterranean under naval blockade, in support of their Napoleonic campaigns. This made travel by sea for any non-British ships a complicated and dangerous affair, as Johann Martin Wagner was to discover on his complicated and harrowing trip to Zakynthos.
2. RUPRECHT'S NOTE: While the word "proper" does not technically appear here, this term communicates the real thrust and purpose of Schelling's remark. As I will note several times in subsequent notes, one subtext of this *Report* is the emerging rivalry between England and Bavaria, more specifically London and Munich, a rivalry which now takes on an important aesthetic dimension. Schelling here not-so-subtly suggests that these Aegina Marbles are artistically superior to their Parthenon counterparts in the British Museum, and that a German university town is a more suitable location for such a classical collection than the mercantile capital of an empire.
3. RUPRECHT'S NOTE: As we can see, Wagner's massive canvas, *Rat der Griechen vor Troja,* depicts the scene (from *Iliad* book VII: 120–99) where the Greek elder, Nestor, instructs seven of the nine greatest Greek military leaders (Diomedes and Odysseus are seen approaching from a distance over a corpse-strewn field) in response to Hektor's challenge to single combat. The painting was completed in Rome in 1807 and was designed to establish Wagner's reputation as well as to secure his financial position in the city he hoped to make his home. In this he was most successful. The painting was praised not just for its stylistic virtuosity, but also for its keen psychological insight. When this monumental canvas was purchased by the Bavarian regime in 1808, Wagner accompanied the painting to Munich; it was then, in Innsbruck, that he first met the Bavarian crown prince Ludwig, who would later utilize his friend as one of his chief agents in Rome, later supplying him with an apartment in the "Villa Malta" in northern Rome. The two men carried on a robust lifelong correspondence; the canvas is now housed in the Martin von Wagner Museum in Würzburg.

   An excellent composition history of this complex and densely psychological painting may be found in Heinrich Ragaller, "Martin Wagner's *Rat der Griechen vor Troja*: Die Entstehungsgeschichte eines klassizistischen Bildes," *Kunst in Hessen und am Mittelrhein* 3 (Darmstadt, 1963): 107–20. See also Monika Meine-Schwahe, "Johann Martin von Wagner: *Die griechischen Helden vor Troja* und Neues zur Kunstlerbiographie," *Aus Weltkunst* 73, no. 6 (2003): 863–64.
4. RUPRECHT'S NOTE: This was presumably the original commission Ludwig gave to Wagner; as we have seen, it was not the way the trip worked out. Wagner went to Athens rather than Malta to examine plaster casts and to arrange for Ludwig's payment, and then returned to Rome. For more on Wagner's return from Greece without continuing on to Malta (he eventually went there in June–August of 1815), see Reinhard Herbig, ed.,

"Johann Martin Wagners Beschreibung seiner Reise nach Griechenland (1812–1813)," *Würzburger Studien zur Altertumswissenschaft* 13 (1938): 44.

5. RUPRECHT'S NOTE: Schelling appears to assume that Wagner remained in Rome strictly on account of the Aeginetan collection. In point of fact, Wagner returned to Rome in 1808, intending to remain there . . . as he did, save for brief trips to his German homeland and longer trips such as the one he made to Greece. Wagner died in Rome on August 8, 1858. See Friedrich Noack, *Das Deutschtum in Rom: seit dem Ausgang des Mittelalters* (Berlin und Leipzig: Deutsche Verlags-Anstalt Stuttgart, 1927) II: 624–25.

6. RUPRECHT'S NOTE: As I noted in the preface, this "team of artists and amateurs" misidentified this temple as the Temple of Panhellenic Zeus, based on an ambiguity in the description of the site by Pausanias. Based on inscriptions that were excavated later, we now know this to have always been the site of a Temple for Aphaia on Aegina.

   See, for example: Adolf Furtwängler, ed., *Aegina: Das Heiligtum der Aphaia* (München: Verlag des K. B. Akademie der Wissenschaften, 1906), Volume I, iv, 1–9 ("Der Name des Heiligtums") and 367, and Volume II, Tafel #25; Adolf Furtwängler, *Die Aegineten der Glyptothek König Ludwigs I. nach den Resultaten der neuen Bayerischen Ausgrabung* (München: A. Buchholz, 1906), 11–13; Adolf Furtwängler, *Beschreibung der Glyptothek König Ludwigs I. zu München* (München: A. Buchholz, 1900), 77; A. Maiuri, "L'iscrizione del tempio di *Aphaia* in Egina," with L. Savignoni, "Nuove osservazioni sull'iscrizione e sul tempio di Aphaia" (Roma: Loescher & Co., 1910), 197–220; and Dyfri Williams, "Aegina, Aphaia-Temple IV. The Inscription Commemorating the Construction of the First Limestone Temple and Other Features of the Sixth Century Temenos," *Archäologischer Anzeiger* 97, Heft 1 (1982): 55–68.

7. RUPRECHT'S NOTE: As Schelling observed in the preface, his additions to Wagner's text take two forms. Sometimes, as here (and also in chapter 3), he includes actual notes [*Anmerkungen*] in the text, notes that are printed at the end of the chapter. In other cases (chapters 4, 6, and 8) Schelling attaches an appendix [*Zusatz*] after the chapter with which to engage in a more sustained scholarly discussion. Both types of entry can be quite long.

8. RUPRECHT'S NOTE: The relevant discussion may be found in Winckelmann's *History of the Art of Antiquity*, Harry Francis Malgrave, trans. (Los Angeles: Getty Research institute, 2006), 301–02, with a telling reference to an Aeginetan "school." Many of the terms Wagner uses here, such as "the imitation of nature" and "the ideal," were first enunciated by Winckelmann in his seminal 1755 pamphlet, *Reflections on the Imitation of Greek Artworks in Sculpture and Painting*, bilingual volume edited by Elfriede Heyer and Roger C. Norton (La Salle, IL: Open Court Publishing, 1987).

   Antoine Chrysostome Quatremère de Quincy was perhaps the most important figure contemporary with Wagner and Schelling who attempted to give such terminology theoretical heft, primarily in three important theoretical works: *Essai sur la nature, le but et les moyens de l'imitation dans le beaux-arts* (Paris: Imprimerie de Jules Didot L'Ainé, Imprimeur du Roi, 1823); *Essai sur l'idéal dans ses applications pratiques aux oeuvres de l'imitation propre* (Paris: Libraire d'Adrien le Clere et Cie., 1837); and the work of greatest importance to Schelling himself, *Le Jupitier Olympien, ou, L'Art de la Sculpture Antique considéré sous un nouveau point de vue* (Paris: De l'Imprimerie de Firmon Didot, 1815). I will have much more to say about this last work, since it figures prominently in Schelling's notes and appendices.

9. RUPRECHT'S NOTE: The reference here is to Ennio Quirino Visconti (1751–1818), the author of a massive catalogue of the sculptural treasures in the Vatican Museums, *Il Museo Pio-Clementino* (Roma, 1785–1807). Visconti moved to Paris and notoriously curated these same treasures in their new (if only temporary) home in Paris, where he became good friends with Quatremère de Quincy. Quatremère offered an effusive eulogy to his friend at the Royal Academy of Fine Arts on February 9, 1818, *Funérailles de M. Le Chevalier Visconti* (Paris: De l'Imprimerie de Firmin Didot, Imprimeur du Roi et de l'Institut, Rue Jacob, no 24).

   For more on Ennio Quirino Visconti's work in Rome and Paris, see Daniela Gallo, "Originali Greci e Copie Romane secondo Giovanni Battista ed Ennio Quirino Visconti," *Labyrinthos* 21–24 (1992–93): 215–51; Daniela Gallo, "I Visconti: Una Famiglia Romana al Servizio di Papi, della Repubblica e di Napoleone," *Roma moderna e contemporanea* 2, no. 1 (1994): 77–90; and Francis Haskell and Nicholas Penny, *Taste and the Antique: The Lure of Classical Sculpture, 1500–1900* (New Haven, CT: Yale University Press, 1981), 106–113, with the authors' important nod to the long reach of Winckelmann's foundational ideas.
10. RUPRECHT'S NOTE: This is the first of many places in which Schelling will apply developments in contemporary philosophy (which is what he seems to mean by *Forschung* here) to brilliant art historical effect. The essential background text here is Hegel's 1807 *Phenomenology of Spirit*, in which a number of tried-and-true dichotomous hierarchies are called into question, with revolutionary implications: man and woman, Creon and Antigone, master and slave. In each of these cases, Hegel first presents the dichotomy, followed by the expected description of the relevant social roles and norms. In each case, Hegel uses ambiguous phrasing to suggest that the former (*jene*) character and the latter (*diese*) occupy the relevant role with their implicit social norms. Since he has been deliberately indeterminate in his phrasing, referring simply to "this and that," Hegel's subtle verbal ambiguity enables the reader to see that these implicit roles are as much reversible as they are self-evident . . . most dramatically in the case of the master, who ironically appears to need the slave (for "recognition") far more than the slave needs the master, whose full recognition will never be forthcoming.

    Hegel is pointing the way toward *mutual recognition* as the determinative social and historical reality that such rigidly dichotomous systems have rendered invisible. Schelling will use this same strategy, and this same language, here to suggest that we ought not view either the Greeks or the Egyptians in the role of teacher and/or student. His purpose is to view Mediterranean antiquity "as a whole."

    For more on the implications of the ambiguities of this language and its philosophical purpose, see my "This, That and the Other: A Note on Hegelian Diction" (forthcoming). See also appendix 4.
11. RUPRECHT'S NOTE: The citation is from Antoine Chrysostome Quatremère de Quincy (1755–1849), *Le Jupitier Olympien, ou, L'Art de la Sculpture Antique considéré sous un nouveau point de vue* (Paris: De l'Imprimerie de Firmon Didot, 1815), a text that was enormously important to Schelling's thinking at this time:

    > *Or, il est dans la nature de tous les commencements, d'être ou de paraître uniformes entre eux, et de la même manière que tous les germes d'une même plante se ressemblement beaucoup plus que les plantes qui en proviennent.* (1)

> Now this is in the nature of all beginnings that are or appear to be the same, in much the same way that the seeds from the same plant resemble each other far more than the plants which later grow up from them.

Quatremère tells us that he had been working on *Le Jupiter Olympien* for thirty years (i), ever since his first trip to Rome inspired his classical sentiments. He had also been mulling over this horticultural analogy for that long, it would appear.

We meet it in the text that first earned Quatremère notoriety in Paris, *De l'état de l'architecture Égyptiennes*, considérée dans son origine, ses principes et son goût, et comparée sous les mêmes rapports à l'Architecture Greque. Dissertation qui a remporté, en 1785, le Prix par l'Académie des Inscriptions et Belles-Lettres (Paris: Chez Barrois l'aîné e Fils, Libraires, rue de Savoye, no. 23, An XI—1803). Quatremère first submitted this as an essay to the Academy of Inscriptions and Literature for a contest in 1785, addressing the question "What was the state of architecture among the Egyptians, and what did the Greeks appear to borrow from it?" (*Quel fut l'état de l'architecture chez les Égyptiens, et ce que le Grecs paraissent en avoir emprunté*?; taking advantage of new materials gathered during the failed Napoleonic mission to Egypt, he revised the essay for publication in 1803. He was elected to the restructured French Academy in the following year.

The text is divided into three parts. The first part utilizes an analogy from language: all human beings have language, but these languages differ so fundamentally that there is no such thing as a simple, universal grammar. Nonetheless, generalizations can be ventured and various languages may still be meaningfully compared. So too with architecture, the science and art of human shelter, decoration, and worship:

> *Ce germe, tout informe qu'il peut paroître, porte déjà certains caractères qu'il ne perdra plus, et qu'on reconnoîtra dans son plus haut point d'accroissement.* (17)

> This seed determines everything that may appear, and already contains certain characteristics which it will never lose, and which we may still recognize even in the highest points of its later development.

Quatremère then refers to Egyptian and Greek architecture as "two distinct species with an essential structure" (*deux espèces distinctes dans leur conformation essentielle*, 19).

The third part takes up the question of the relationship between Egyptian and Greek art and architecture most explicitly (203–66). Famously referring to architecture as an "ocular music" (*musique oculaire*, 215), Quatremère is not coy in admitting the astonishing range of items (tonalities, perhaps?) that the Greeks appear to have borrowed from Egypt: columns, "Corinthian" capitals, labyrinths, monumental funerary forms, sphinxes, interior temple design, animal and hybrid sculptural figures. While insisting that all art and architecture is the product of a particular social and cultural location ("there is no such thing as human architecture," 226), Quatremère distinguishes the Greek way of borrowing (*emprunt*) other cultural forms from, say, the Roman manner of imitating (*imitation*) them. The Greeks appropriated, actively interpreting and changing what they borrowed, making such things into their own, distinctively hybrid forms. It is at this point that several interesting biological metaphors appear again, among them:

> *Et comme ces développemens naissent de leur propre fonds, comme ils ne sont pas empruntés d'ailleurs, mai sont comme des branches sorties d'une seule e unique tige, c'est-à-dire des parties d'un tout homogène; l'unité s'y trouve dans la variété, et la variété dans l'unité.* (245)
>
> And as these developments were born of their own distinct background—not borrowed from elsewhere, but more like branches on a single, unique stem—they are, so to say, parts of a seamless whole. Unity is to be found in the variety, and variety in the unity.

That gesture toward *a pluralistic unity* of Greek and Egyptian art clearly resonated with the ideas that concern Schelling in this discussion.

For more on Quatremère's important and forward-looking early text, see Sylvia Lavin, *Quatremère de Quincy and the Invention of a Modern Language of Architecture* (Cambridge, MA: The MIT Press, 1992), 18–61; my *Classics at the Dawn of the Museum Era: The Life and Times of Antoine Chrysostome Quatremère de Quincy* (New York: Palgrave Macmillan, 2014), 54–60, as well as appendix 4.

12. RUPRECHT'S NOTE: This privileging of ancient origins, as preserving the purest religious forms of humanity, received close attention in Schelling's lecture on the Samothracian deities one year prior to his work on this book [see appendix 3], and would culminate in the sociological theories of Emile Durkheim, most notably his 1912 classic, *The Elementary Forms of Religious Life*, Joseph Ward Swain, trans. (New York: Free Press, 1995).

13. RUPRECHT'S NOTE: The passage comes in a description of some important oldest sites in Asia Minor, and reads as follows:

> [T[wo temples (ναοὺς) in Ionia were burned down by the Persians, the one of Hera in Samos and that of Athena at Phocaea. Damaged though they are by fire, I found them a wonder (θαῦμα). You would be pleased as well with the sanctuary of Herakles (Ἡρακλείῳ) at Erythrae and with the temple (ναῷ) of Athena at Priene, the latter on account of its statue (ἀγάλματος) and the Herakleion on account of its antiquity (ἀρχαιότητα). The statue (ἄγαλμα) is neither like the so-called Aeginetan (οὔτε τοῖς καλουμένοις Αἰγιναίοις), nor yet like the most ancient Attic images (οὔτε τῶν Αττικῶν τοῖς ἀρχαιοτάτοις); it is precisely Egyptian (ἀκριβῶς ἐστιν Αἰγύπτιον), if ever there was such a thing. (*Guide to Greece* VII.5.5, translation emended)

Schelling has mistakenly read this as a reference to the image of Herakles at Erythrae (which Pausanias does not discuss specifically) rather than referring to that of the Athena at Priene, which makes the remark even more relevant to the discussion of the Aeginetan Marbles, whose Athena was the largest statue to be found and one of the preeminent ones.

14. RUPRECHT'S NOTE: The passage comes in a description of an ancient Temple to Apollo at Megara, near Athens, and reads as follows:

> The ancient temple (ναός) of Apollo was made of brick, but the Emperor Hadrian later re-built it with white marble. The Apollo called Pythian and the

> other one called Dekatephoros are very similar to Egyptian wooden images (ξοάνοις), but the one they called Archegetes is similar to Aeginetan works. (Αἰγινητικοῖς ἔργοις ἐστιν ὅμοιως, *Guide to Greece* I.42.5)

15. RUPRECHT'S NOTE: As I have already suggested, this subtle conception of "mutuality" is one of the most creative and fruitful of Schelling's many contributions to this *Report.* It demonstrates how artfully he was able to translate complex and technical philosophical notions from idealist philosophy into clear art historical terms. Whereas a traditional progressive account of artistic development posited early stages of art, like the Egyptian or Aeginetan, that were superceded by later stages, such as the Athenian, Schelling cautions his readers that the dividing lines between such stylistic and cultural stages is not nearly so clear. Better, he suggests, to speak of various Mediterranean cultures *mutually influencing one another's* artistic development and expression.

    In short, one needs the other to constitute the self; that insight lay at the heart of idealism's attempt to overcome the excessive subjectivity of modern philosophy culminating in Kant. Schelling makes much of this issue in his lectures *On the History of Modern Philosophy*, Andrew Bowie, trans. (Albany, NY: SUNY Press, 1994), 42–43, 94–114.
16. RUPRECHT'S NOTE: The chapter in question offers a description of some of the Dodecanesian islands off the coast of Asia Minor, and focuses on the island of Samos with its very ancient sanctuary dedicated to Hera. The passage in question reads as follows:

> That this sanctuary (ἱερὸν) is very ancient (ἀρχαῖον) may be inferred mainly by attending to the statue (ἀγάλματι). It is the work of an Aeginetan man, Smilis the son of Eucleides. This Smilis was a contemporary of Daedalus (ἡλικίαν κατὰ Δαίδαλον), though not of equal fame (δόξης). (*Guide to Greece* VII.4.4, translation emended)

17. RUPRECHT'S NOTE: The citation is from Christian Gottlob Heyne (1729–1812), *Opvscvla Academica Collecta et Animadversionibvs Locvpletata* in six volumes (Gottingae: Apud Henricvm Dieterich, 1785–1802). In an essay entitled "*Antiqvior artivm inter Graecos historia ad tempora sva probabiliter revocata*" (V: 338–91), we read the following account of some of the most famous, and the most ancient, Greek monuments from Crete, Laconia, Rhodes, Samos, Argos, and Olympia. The relevant point Heyne emphasized is that the Heraion on Samos was an Ionian monument built well after the Trojan War:

> Antequam vlterius progrediar, mihi nonnulla omnino monenda sunt. Fama antiquissimorum operum, quae quidem Pausaniae vel innotuerant vel visa fuerant, aut ab aliis memorata sunt, ad certa tantum templa antiqua spectat, in quibus illa feruata fuerunt, eoque etiam ad certas vrbes. Praeter Cnossum Cretae, Amyclas Laconicae, Lindum Rhodi, fuere inprimis Samos et Argos; tum Olympia; vetustis operibus celebratae. Templi quidem Iunonis Samiae vtinam superesset disertior historia; in eo enim reconditum fuit plurimum antiqui operis, omnis generis; nam etiam picturae antiquissimae in eo templo fuisse

memorantur. Samos Iones incolas nacta est non nisi post profectionem Ionum in Asiam, quae non ante annum CXXX a capta Troia exordia habuit. Itaque nec templum Iunonis Samiae nec signa in eo, si quidem a Graecis elaborata fuere, ad antiquiora tempora recte referri possunt; vnde etiam apparet, nomen Smilidis eiusque aequalium ad tempora antiquiora perperam reuocari. Poterant tamen vel sie in templo eo, vt in aliis, opera antiqua rudis artis et ingenii ex antiquioribus temporibus seruari; nam ante Iones tenuere insulam Cares et Leleges; potuit quoque templum vetustius ab iis conditum esse; diuersa tamen illa esse debuere ab Hellenum conatibus, quandoquidem hos ferius immigrasse constat. Cum sacra Iunonis Samiae et Argiuae communem religionem et antiquitatem haberent, disceptatum est inter Samios et Argiuos, vtri ab alteris et sacrum et signum Iunonis accepissent: qua de re locus copiosus est apud Athenaeum. (V: 343–45, notes from Athenaeus, Clement of Alexandria, Diodorus Siculus, Pausanias, Proclus, and Strabo omitted)

An English translation, for which I am most grateful to Professor Michael B. Lippman for his assistance, is as follows:

Before proceeding further, I should make a few things absolutely clear. The good repute of the most ancient works, those that were known to Pausanias in particular, or those which had been seen or described by others, belong for the most part to certain ancient temples, the ones in which these primitive items existed, as well as in specific cities. Aside from Knossos in Crete, Amyclae in Lakonia, and Lindus in Rhodes, first and foremost were Samos and Argos, then Olympia, all of them filled to overflowing with celebrated works of ancient art. If only we had a thorough history of the Temple of Juno at Samos, in which was housed a tremendous amount of ancient art of every type, including the most ancient paintings which were said to have been in that temple. Samos received Ionian settlers only after the departure of the Ionians into Asia, which is not thought to have occurred until 130 years after Troy was captured. And so neither the temple of Samian Juno nor the statues within it—if they were indeed erected by Greeks—may be properly considered among the most ancient of such remains. It appears as if the name of Smilis was invoked incorrectly in much the same way in antiquity. Even so, in that temple, as in many others, ancient works of raw art and talent were to be seen, since before the Ionians settled the island there were Carians and Lelegians there; it is possible that there was an even older temple built by them. These older temples were likely very different from those built by the Greeks, and of inferior quality. Since the rituals for Juno at Samos and at Argos share common elements and the same claim to antiquity, there was a disagreement between the Samians and Argives as to which of the two of them had the greater claim to the original form of worship and the original image of Juno. On this subject, there is abundant evidence in Athenaeus. (Book V, 343–45)

Heyne was a prominent classical scholar and professor in Göttingen, known as well for his two-volume critical edition of the Iliad, *Homeri Ilias, cum Brevi Annotatione*

(Lipsiae: In Libraria Weidmannia, 1804), and his published lectures, *Akademische Vorlesungen über die Archäologie der Kunst des Alterthums, inbesondere der Griechen und Römer* (Braunschweig: bei Friedrich Vieweg, 1822).

Heyne's eulogy on Winckelmann was translated into French and printed in *Lettres Familieres de M. Winckelmann* (Amsterdam: Chez Couturier fils, Libraire, Quai & près les Grands Augustins, au Coq, 1781), ix–xxxiv (together with Winckelmann's letters to Heyne, which may also be found at I: 143–97), and would presumably have been known to Quatremère de Quincy.

18. RUPRECHT'S NOTE: The citation is from Quatremère de Quincy's *Le Jupitier Olympien, ou, L'Art de la Sculpture Antique considéré sous un nouveau point de vue*, 175.

Quatremère cites multiple ancient sources from various periods (Pausanias, Callimachus, and Clement of Alexandria) to suggest that Smilis, while doubtless an ancient representative of ancient sculpture, should not be considered a contemporary of Daedalus, who was a relatively prominent character in the Homeric poems. Quatremère observes that the island of Samos was never mentioned in these epics, and was believed to have been inhabited more than a century after the destruction of Troy; he owes this latter point to Heyne. The actual quotation [with his footnote citations included in brackets] is as follows:

> M. Heyne [*Opuscul.* tom. V, p. 344] a déja prouvé qu'on avait beaucoup trop reculé l'époque de Smillis d'Égine, réputé faussement l'auteur de cette statue de Junon à Samos, apportée, disait-on, d'Argos dans cette île par les Argonautes. Ce Smillis, selon Pausanias, était contemporain de Dédale, ἐστὶν ἡλικίαν κατὰ Δαίδαλον. Mais si l'on compare, à ce que dit Pausanias [*Pausan.* lib. VII, cap. 4], les écrits [*Fragment. Callimachi* CV] de Callimaque, et ceux que Clément de Alexandrie [*Clement. Alex.* lib. 1] a tirés des auteurs Samiens, on voit que l'opinion du premier est tout-à-fait inadmissable. Samos à la vérité était habitée avant la guerre de Troie, mais elle ne fut civilisée qu'après la prise de cette ville. Homère n'en en a fait aucune mention; et, selon les historiens de Samos, dans Clément d'Alexandrie, la statue de Junon n'avait été érigée que cent quarante ans après la prise de Troie. Par conséquent Smillis, en le supposant auteur de l'antique idole de Junon, n'a pas pu être contemporain de Dédale. Mais si, comme je le pense, le sculpteur des figures des Heures en ivoire, dont on parlera au paragraphe VIII (*voy.* ci-après), et dont le nom s'écrit ̎ Εμιλος d'Égine, est le même que Σμίλλις d'Égine, ce sera une raison de plus pour révoquer en doute cette haute antiquité, que ferait encore supposer l'exécution de l'ancienne idole de Samos: car le travail de l'ivoire en statue ne put être pratiqué avant le perfectionnement de l'art de mouler, dont on verra qu'il dépend, et qui fut dû nécessairement à Théodore et Rhæcus.

An English translation is as follows:

> Mr. Heyne has already proven that the age of Smilis of Aegina was grossly exaggerated, since he was falsely reputed to have been the creator of this statue of Juno on Samos, which was said to have been taken from Argos to this island

> by the Argonauts. This Smilis, according to Pausanias, was a contemporary of Daedalus. But if we compare what Pausanias says to the writings of Callimachus and to those passages which Clement of Alexandria takes from the Samian authors, then we see that the opinion of the former is entirely unacceptable. Samos was in fact inhabited before the Trojan War, but it did not achieve a level of civilization until after the destruction of that city. Homer never mentioned it; according to the historians of Samos, which we find in Clement of Alexandria, the statue of Juno was not constructed until one hundred forty years after the destruction of Troy. As a result Smilis, the supposed creator of this ancient idol of Juno, could not have been a contemporary of Daedalus. But if, as I believe to be the case, the sculptor of the Hours in ivory, which will be discussed in paragraph viii (see below), and which bears the name of *Emilos* of Aegina, is in fact this same *Smillis* of Aegina, then this will be one more reason to place in grave doubt the great antiquity which continues to be assigned to the execution of the ancient idol of Samos. For the working of ivory for making statues was not practical before the perfection of the art of molding on which it depends, and which necessarily belonged to the age of Theodore and Rhaecus.
> [notes omitted]

Quatremère includes a luscious polychrome reconstruction of the statue of Juno/Hera from Argos at page 326; the Hours and the Three Graces are discussed at pages 206, 298, and 329.

Quatremère's other supporting passages are: first, from *Callimachus*, edited by C. A. Trypanis and Thomas Gelzer, and translated by Cedric Whitman (Cambridge, MA: Loeb Classical Library of Harvard University Press, 1978), 74–75:

> The well-carved work (ἔργον εὔξοον) of Skelmius was not yet made,
> but according to ancient custom you were an uncarved (ᾄξοος) plank,
> for this was the way they rendered gods then. Much like the Athena
> which Danaos set up so simply in Lindos . . . (Fragment 100)

As well as,

> A vine-branch runs around the hair of the Samian Hera (Fragment 101), and second, from Clement of Alexandria's "Exhortation to the Greeks," in *Clement of Alexandria*, G. W. Butterworth, trans. (Cambridge, MA: Loeb Classical Library of Harvard University Press, 1979), 102–03:

> It is said that men rendered statues with the human form (ἀγάλματα ἀνδρείκελα) out of stone and wood, that is, out of matter (ὕλην), and in so doing they transformed the pious into sycophants of truth (ἐπιμορφάζετε εὐσέβειαν συκοφαντοῦντες τὴν ἀλήθειαν). . . . Now everyone knows that the Olympian Zeus and Athena Polias at Athens were made of gold and ivory by Pheidias; and Olympichus in his Samian History relates that the image (ξόανον) of Hera in Samos was made by Smilis the son of Eucleides. (translation emended)

19. RUPRECHT'S SUPPLEMENT: The passage reads as follows:

> In the course of this summer the Athenians also expelled the Aeginetans from Aegina, together with their wives and children, making it their main charge against them that they were responsible for (αἰτίους) the war in which they were involved; besides Aegina lay close to the Peloponnesus, and it was clearly a safer policy to send colonists (ἐποίκους) of their own to occupy it. And indeed soon afterwards, they sent their own settlers (οἰκήτορας) there. As for the Aeginetan refugees, the Lacedaimonians gave them Thyrea to live in and its territory to cultivate, moved to do this not only by the hostility of the Aeginetans toward the Athenians but also because the Aeginetans had done them a service at the time of the earthquake and the revolt of the Helots (τὸν σεισμὸν καὶ τῶν Εἰλώτων τὴν ἐπανάστασιν). Now the region of Thyrea is the border country between the Argolid and Lakonia, extending down to the sea. Some of the Aeginetans settled there, while others were scattered over the rest of Greece (Ἑλλάδα).

For the text of Thucydides, I am using C. F. Smith's four-volume edition, *Thucydides* (Cambridge, MA: Loeb Classical Library of Harvard University Press, 1928), I: 308–09, translation slightly emended.

20. RUPRECHT'S NOTE: Pausanias begins his description of Aegina by noting its geographical location adjacent to Epidaurus. After rehearsing the main lines of the island's mythic founding by Aiakos, Pausanias turns to this latter episode in Aeginetan history:

> Such was the line (γένη) of the so-called Aiakidai (family of Aiakos), but they departed from the beginning (ἀπ' ἀρχῆς) to other lands. Subsequently a division of the Argives who, under Deïphontes, had seized Epidauros, crossed over to Aegina and, settling among the old Aeginetans (Αἰγινήταις τοῖς ἀρχαίοις γενόμενοι σύνοικοι), established Dorian manners (ἔθη) and the Dorian dialect (φωνὴν) on the island. Although the Aeginetans rose to great power, so that their navy was superior even to that of Athens, and in the war with the Persians they supplied more ships than any place after Athens, still their happiness was not lasting. When they were made exiles (ἀνάστατοι) by the Athenians, they settled in Thyrea in the Argolid, which the Spartans ceded to them. They recovered their island when the Athenian triremes were destroyed at the Hellespont, but they never achieved their former level of wealth and power. (*Guide to Greece* II.29.5, translation emended)

21. RUPRECHT'S SUPPLEMENT: Since Schelling had never been to Greece, it is unclear what formed the basis of this assured judgment, other than the enthused description of men like Cockerell and Hallerstein. It does not appear that Wagner visited the island during his time in Athens.

22. RUPRECHT'S NOTE: In a description of the religious architecture at Troezen, Pausanias makes the following observation:

> On the akropolis is a temple (ναός) to Athena, called Sthenias. The wooden image (ξόανον) of the goddess was made by Kallon of Aegina. Kallon was a

student of Tektaeus and Angelion, who made the statue (ἄγαλμα) of Apollo for the Delians. Angelion and Tektaeus in turn were taught by Dipoenus and Scyllis. (*Guide to Greece* II.32.5, translation emended)

23. RUPRECHT'S NOTE: This text once again is Antoine Chrysostome Quatremère de Quincy, *Le Jupitier Olympien, ou, L'Art de la Sculpture Antique considéré sous un nouveau point de vue*, arguably the definitive work on polychrome and chryselephantine Greek sculpture in the nineteenth century. The reproduction of the sketch by Louis François Sébastien Fauvel (1753–1838), the French consul in Athens, may be seen at the lower half of the last page of Quatremère's preface (xxv). Schelling's observation as to its limited art historical value is well taken.
24. RUPRECHT'S NOTE: The question of how many statues had in fact been removed from the Temple of Aphaia on Aegina was exceedingly difficult to answer. A great many fragments were found in addition to the larger pieces (as this *Report* makes abundantly clear), and the task of reassembly—of determining what parts belonged together—was a matter of interpretive guesswork as much as it was archaeological science; everyone from Charles Cockerell, to Carl Haller von Hallerstein, to Bertel Thorvaldsen, to Wagner himself vouched an opinion in sketches. We may recall that the original description of the find in the *Allgemeine Zeitung* (December 5, 1811) mentioned eighteen statues in total, and that a great many years later, Charles Cockerell recalled them to be "no less than sixteen" in *The Temples of Jupiter Panhellenius at Aegina and of Apollo Epicurius at Bassae near Phigalia in Arcadia* (London: John Weale, 1860), 51–52. Wagner's own elaborate sketch reconstruction placed all fifteen figures in a single pediment.

    When the collection finally went on public display at the Glyptothek Museum in 1830, they were reassembled as fifteen: ten in one pediment and five in the other. See Leo von Klenze, with Ludwig Schorn, *Beschreibung der Glyptothek Sr. Majestät des Königs Ludwig I von Bayern* (München: J. G. Cotta'schen, 1830), 45–68.
25. RUPRECHT'S NOTE: The lettering system that Wagner uses throughout this chapter comes from his own sketches, which were designed to offer an interpretative reconstruction of how the [one or two] pedimental groups were arranged in antiquity. I include reproductions of these sketches for the reader to consult in this chapter. Wagner and Thorvaldsen arrived at one such reconstruction, Cockerell and Hallerstein at another. Later archaeological discoveries at the Aeginetan site, including the pedimental bases, have significantly advanced our understanding of the composition of the pediments, which may be clearly seen in their current display.
26. RUPRECHT'S SUPPLEMENT: This note concludes with the letters "A.d.H.," which I take to mean "Note from the Editor" (*Anmerkung des Herausgebers*).

    Winckelmann observes the following in note 850 from the second 1767 edition of his *History of the Art of Antiquity*:

    > Nicht viel später dürfte der Kopf einer Minerva, ohngefähr lebensgroß, in der Florintinischen Gallerie verfertigt seyn, welcher unter allen alt Griechischen Denkmalen den meisten Fleiß, die größte Sorgfalt in der Ausfuhrung erfahren und wohl erhalten ist. Die Augen sind groß und senken sich ein wenig gegen die Nase; der Schnitt der Augenbraunen hat gleiche Richtung und und steht hoch über den Augen. Diese liegen wenig vertieft; auch springen die Augenlieder

> nicht weit vor; der geschlossene Mund zieht sich in den Winkeln etwas aufwärts; die Vertiefung zwischen der Unterlippe und dem Kinn ist nur geringe, daher erscheint dieses flach und hängt etwas nieder. Die Ohren stehen sehr hoch; eine horizontale Linie vom unterersten Theil des Ohrläppschens gezogen, würde ohngefähr auf die Hälfte der Nase treffen. Um Hals ist der Apfel stark angedeutet, eben so die beyden großen Sehnen, welche den Kopf wenden; das Halsgrübchen hingegen und die Schlüßelbeinen sind kaum sichtbar. Man erblickt noch dem Anfang eines kraus, doch dabey flach gefalteten Gewandes, welches bis auf ein Paar Finger breit nehe an den Hals heran tritt, aber selbst auch nicht breiter ist, und vom Untergewand dasjenige Stück zu seyn scheint welches über dem Brustharnisch sichtbar wurde. Denn ohne Zweifel war dieser Kopf ursprünglich einer Figur eingefügt. Die Haare treten unter dem Helme etwa Fingersbreit hervor; anliegend verbreiten sie sich wellenförmignach den Schläfen zu, neben welche breiten flache Locken herunterhängen, die an ihren Enden oder Spitzen umbebogen sind. Zwar ist nur die Anfang dieser Locken antik und das übrige ergänzt; allein man bemerkt neben den Ohrläppchen die Stelle wo sie an der Wange angelegen. Hinter den Ohren fallen längere Haarlocken, deren Enden ebenfalls ergänzt worden, bis auf die Schultern herab, und im Nacken kommen sie unter dem Helme hervor; sie sind aber wieder zurückgenommen. Der Helm an sich ist rund, an den Kopf anschließend, ohne Vorsprung und hat über der Stirne einen schön ausgearbeiteten Rand. Oben auf dem Helme kann man noch acht Spuren zählen, wo Füße von Pferde-Figuren gefessen; an den Seiten sind noch ein Paar Greife übrig geblieben. Andere Zierratchen scheinen durch modernes Ueberarbeiten weggenommen, als der fehlende Helmbusch ergänzt wurde. Allein das Gesicht hat, außer an der Nase, deren Spitze ergänzt ist, nicht gelitten. (527–28)

The so-called Weimar edition to which Schelling refers was edited by Heinrich Meyer and Heinrich Schulze as *Winckelmann's Geschichte der Kunst des Alterthums* (Dresden: In der Walterschen Hofbuchhandlung, 1812), which may be accessed online at http://goobipr2.uni-weimar.de/viewer/image/PPN645178659/1/LOG0004/.

I am grateful to Nedda Ahmed of the Georgia State University Library for making me aware of this link. An English version of this note is as follows:

> Probably not much later than this is a nearly lifesize head of Minerva now in the Florentine Gallery, which of all such Greek monuments demonstrates the greatest diligence [*Fleiß*] and care [*Sorgfalt*] in its execution, and is probably the best preserved. The eyes are large and slightly reduced nearer to the nose; the carving of the eybrows is in the same direction but is raised high above the eyes. They are not deeply incised and the eyelids do not stand out; the closed mouth is slightly upturned at the corners. The carving between the lower lip and the chin is in low relief, such that it appears flat and hangs slightly downwards. The ears are unusually high; a horizontal line drawn from the lower part of the earlobes would meet roughly at the midpoint of the nose. The Adam's apple is sharply drawn, as are the two tendons that turn the head; the clavicle and

collarbones are barely visible. We note the beginning of the curve of a flat folded robe that comes within two fingers-width to the neck, but no more, and the undergarment appears to be the one piece that was visible above the breastplate. Thus this head was doubtless originally inserted onto a sculpted figure. Locks of hair extend about a fingers-width below the helmet, and frame her temples beautifully; in addition broad, flat curls hang down lower and are curved at their ends or tips. Although only the beginnings of these locks are ancient and the rest are restored [*ergänzt*], one notices alongside the earlobes the place where they lay upon her cheeks. There are longer locks behind the ears which go as far as the shoulders, the ends of which are entirely restored [*ergänzt*], and her hair extends from beneath the helmet to her neck, but is now lost. The helmet itself is round and attached to the head without elevation, with a beautifully rendered border at her brow. There are eight holes on top of the helmet where the feet of small horse figurines were attached and a pair of griffins are visible to the sides. Other details appear to have been lost to modern work when the helmet's plume was restored [*ergänzt*]. Only the face is intact, save for the tip of the nose, which was restored [*ergänzt*].

27. RUPRECHT'S NOTE: The text in question was published by Wilhelm Tischbein, the director of the Royal Academy of Painting at Naples, not written by him. The bilingual (French and English) text was written by William Hamilton, *Collection of Engravings from Ancient Vases Mostly of Pure Greek Workmanship Discovered in Sepulchres in the Kingdom of the Two Sicilies but Chiefly in the Neighborhoods of Naples during the Course of the Years 1784 and 1790 now in the Possession of Sir. W.m Hamilton, His Brittanic Majesty's Envoy Extr.y and Plenipotentiary at the Court of Naples with Remarks on Each Vase by the Collector* (Naples: William Tischbein, 1791), in four volumes. To date, I have only been able to locate the first volume. It is unclear what citation from this volume Wagner has in mind. Page 1 reads as follows:

> In consequence of His Sicilian Majesty's having lately taken off the Prohibition to search for Antiquities, which prohibition had long subsisted in this Kingdom, several Excavations have been made by the Proprietors of Land in the neighborhood of Nola, S. Agata de Goti, Trebbia, S. Maria di Capua (the spot on which the ancient city of Capua flourished), in Puglia, and in other parts of the Two Sicilies, and many Sepulchres have been discoverd [sic] containing Earthen Vases of beautifull [sic] forms, with Elegant figures, either drawn, or painted on them, of the sort that have been usually called Etruscan Vases, although there now seems to be little doubt of such monuments of Antiquity being truly Grecian.

28. RUPRECHT'S NOTE: Wagner frequently associates hairstyles with pasta, noodles, and macaroni. While odd-sounding, and even humorous, to a contemporary reader, I suspect that these references served a more serious purpose for him: they were a subtle reminder to Wagner's audience that he lived in Rome, enjoying (in addition to the pasta) the authority and inspiration born of such close proximity to the visual remains

of the classical world. The noodles associated with his native Franken were another thing entirely, both in form and texture.

29. RUPRECHT'S SUPPLEMENT: Herodotus's *Histories* I.7 describes the descendants of Herakles (a possible stand-in for the Persian sun god, and a noted archer) and an enslaved woman, who became the ruling family in Lydia for 505 years, prior to the advent of the legendarily wealthy King Croesus (who succeeded the ill-starred Candaules, after the famous affair reported in the Ring of Gyges episode). There is no explicit mention of archery in the passage.

    Herodotus's *Histories* V.49 describes an embassy from the Ionian Greek colonies to Sparta, in which the following observation is offered: "And for their fashion of fighting, they carry bows and short spears [τόξα καὶ αἰχμὴ βραχέα]; and they go into battle with breeches on their legs and turbans on their heads; so they are easy to overcome."

    Herodotus's *Histories* VII.61 describes the battle array of Xerxes's army on the Greek mainland and begins as follows: "Those that served in the army were as I will now show. Firstly, the Persians; for their equipment they wore on their heads loose caps called tiaras, and on their bodies sleeved tunics of diverse colors, with scales of iron like fish-scales in appearance, and breeches on their legs; for shields they had wicker bucklers, their quivers hanging beneath these; they carried short spears [αἰχμὰς δὲ βραχέας], long bows [τόξα δὲ μεγάλα], reed arrows, and daggers that hung from the girdle on the right thigh."

    Perhaps most moving is Herodotus's explanation of his interest in the Persian case (I.5): "For small and great cities are similar [ὁμοίως σμικρὰ καὶ μεγάλα ἄστεα]. Many states that were formerly great have now become small; those that were great in my time were small before. Knowing therefore that human happiness [εὐδαιμονίην] never lasts in the same way, I will make mention of both kinds alike."

    I am using the Loeb edition of *Herodotus*, translated and edited by A. D. Godley, in four volumes (Cambridge, MA: Loeb Classical Library of Harvard University Press, 1920–1925) I: 6–11, III: 52–53, and III: 374–77.

30. RUPRECHT'S NOTE: The citation from William Hamilton, *Collection of Engravings from Ancient Vases*, appears to refer to a description of the fourth vase in the collection (at pages 56–58); I see nothing of relevance on page 4 specifically, though the surrounding discussion does gesture to the historical value of the images on these vases:

    > Ten years after the first war against Thebes, the Epigones, that is to say the Children of the Generals, who had been killed in that war, resolved to attack that City again. The Oracle promised them victory, if Alcmaon was at the head of the Expedition. This Hero declined the command until he should have punished his mother; but however changed his mind afterwards. His repugnance to the command of the Army, and then his acceptance of the command without any apparent motive according to Apollodorus, is probably the subject in this plate. A young Warriour is seen in a state of deliberation, and seems to be decided at last by the impulse of heaven. The shield on which there is a serpent, is a circumstance common to many Warriours, but Alcmaon wore such a shield on his expedition against Thebes, and Pindar speaks of it in Ode VIII. of his Pythicks. . . .
    >
    > The Divinity, who offers him the helmet, may be Iris the messenger of Juno, indicated by the Caduceus. As Alcmaon meditated an action, the end of which

was to punish the perfidy of his mother toward her husband, it was natural that it should be executed under the auspices of Juno the avenger of conjugal transgressions. Such an action, in which the first Goddess took so great an interest, could not fail of immediate success, unless she had judged otherwise.

The case was such as to render it necessary that the punishment should be delay'd, as Alcmaon was immediately after the Matricide to be deliver'd up to te [sic] fury of the Eumenides, which would have ruin'd the project of the Epigones: it was therefore absolutely necessary that Juno should send Iris to persuade him to grant their request.

31. RUPRECHT'S NOTE: This reference is to Tischbein's engraved illustrations in William Hamilton's *Collection of Engravings for Ancient Vases*. Plate 38 of volume I depicts four figures (three women and one satyr in what Hamilton describes as an initiatory Bacchic ceremony). The women are all wearing tied hairpieces that end in two fillets that trail down their backs and are decorated with three small balls.
32. RUPRECHT'S NOTE: This may well seem an odd observation to a contemporary viewer. Even Wagner admits that this figure is "one of the most excellent in the collection," but we should hardly agree that his rendering suggests fat or the weakness of age. The balletic leanness of the Aeginetan figures is one of their most striking characteristics. I suspect that Wagner is here indulging one of the neoclassical artifices of his day: namely, an insistence on physical perfection in the name of the ideal. It thus subjects the judgment of physical beauty to an unattainable standard of perfection.
33. RUPRECHT'S NOTE: Subsequent excavation has confirmed Wagner's hunch here, with the continued discovery of a great many more sculptural fragments and more significant pieces of pedimental statuary. For the relevant discussion and images, see: Adolf Furtwängler, *Die Aeginetan der Glyptothek König Ludwigs I nach den Resultaten der neuen Bayerischen Ausgrabung* (München: A Buchholz, 1906), 38–41; Adolf Furtwängler, ed., *Aegina: Das Heiligtum der Aphaia* (München: Verlag der K. B. Akademie der Wissenschaften, 1906), "Die Marmorskulpturen," Volume I, ii–iii and 174–365, esp. 256–74; Dieter Ohly, *Aegina: Tempel und Heiligtum* (München: Verlag C. H. Beck, 1978), 23–34; Dieter Ohly, *Die Aegineten I: Die Ostgiebelgruppe* (München: Verlag C. H. Beck, 1976); Dieter Ohly, *Die Aegineten II: Die Westgiebelgruppe* (München: C. H. Beck, 2001), but especially the accompanying images assembled posthumously by Martha Ohly-Dumm in *Die Aegineten III* [Die Gruppen auf dem Altarplatz (Tafeln ##163–91), Figürliche Bruchstücke (Tafeln ##192–98), Akrotere (Tafeln ##199–234), Aus der Tempelcella (Tafeln ##235–38), Die Klassizistische Restaurierung der Aegineten (Tafeln ##239–50)] (München: C. H. Beck, 2001); Dieter Ohly, *The Munich Glyptothek: Greek and Roman Sculpture*, Helen Hughes-Brock, trans. (München: Verlag C. H. Beck, 1974), 47–66 [this is a translation of Ohly's *Glyptothek München: Griechische und römische Skulpturen* (München: Verlag C. H. Beck, 1972)]; and Martha Ohly-Dumm and Martin Robertson, "Aegina, Aphaia-Temple XII. Archaic Marble Sculpture Other than Architectural," *Archäologischer Anzeiger* 103, Heft 3 (1988): 405–21.
34. RUPRECHT'S NOTE: To recall, Quatremère's main thesis in that book was that gold and ivory were not exceptional Greek media, nor were images made of such material to be thought of as kitsch exceptions: "Almost always we have looked upon these sculptural

monuments in gold and ivory as exceptional works [*ouvrages d'exception*], as accidental and occasional [*productions de caprice*]. I had to prove that this taste reigned supreme for twelve centuries, and I have reproduced a series of artworks in support of my research," he tells us. (*Presque toujours on a regardé les monuments de la statuaire en ivoire come des ouvrages d'exception, comme des productions de caprice. J'ai eu en vue de prouver que le goût pour ces ouvrages avait régné pendant douze siècles, et j'ai produit une série de monuments à l'appui de mes recherches. Le Jupiter Olympien*, xx–xxj). Clearly, Quatremère believed that an older "classical" image of Greek art, best symbolized by pure white marble, would have to be seriously altered. The passage to which Schelling refers may actually be found at page 308n4:

> Cette pratique semble avoir été fort commune. . . . . Depuis l'impression de l'article qui regarde la Minerve du Parthénon, j'ai reçu de M. Fauvel, consul à Athènes, un renseignement qui confirme cette opinion. Dans les fouilles faites l'an passé au temple d'Égine, et dont j'ai parlé page 24, on a trouvé un oeil d'ivoire de 5 pouces de long "dont la prunelle," dit M. Fauvel, était de rapport. La convexité est trés-légère, elle n'est que de 8 lignes; "ce qui me ferait croire que cet oeil pourrait bien avoir été un oeil votif." Le peu de convexité dont parle M. Fauvel, n'est pas une raison de rejeter l'idée que cet oeil aura appartenu au colosse d'or et d'ivoire placé dans le temple d'Égine. L'ivoire étant une matière flexible a pu perdre un peu de sa courbure; mais ce nouvel exemple d'une prunelle de rapport dans un oeil d'ivoire, montre que l'usage n'en fut pas rare. [ellipsis in original]

An English translation is as follows:

> This practice seems to have been quite common. . . . Since the publication of the article that examines the Parthenon Minerva, I have received information from Mr. Fauvel, the Consul at Athens, which confirms this opinion. In the excavations made last year at the Temple on Aegina (which I discuss at page 24), an eye made of ivory and 5 inches in length was discovered, "including the pupil," as Mr. Fauvel reports. The curvature is very slight, less than 8 degrees; "this causes me to believe that this eye may have been a votive eye." The slight curvature of which Mr. Fauvel speaks is no reason to reject the idea that this eye was part of a colossal statue of gold and ivory placed within the Temple on Aegina. Ivory is a flexible material that might have lost some of its curvature. But this new example of a pupil incised on an ivory eye suggests that it was not uncommon.

35. RUPRECHT'S NOTE: Recall that Wagner and Schelling assumed this to be a temple dedicated to Zeus, thus perhaps warranting a colossal chryselephantine dedicatory statue of some kind. A temple to Aphaia might not have warranted such a thing, and thus Schelling's analogizing from Athens (and Olympia) loses much of its interpretive power to convince.
36. RUPRECHT'S NOTE: As noted briefly in note 3, the Frenchman Jacob (or Jacques) Spon (1647–1685) traveled with the English antiquarian and collector, Sir George

Wheler (1650–1723), to Italy, Greece, Constantinople and the Levant in 1675–76. Spon published his memoir two years later as *Voyage d'Italie, de Dalmatie, de Grèce et du Levant, fait aux années 1675 & 1676 par Iacob Spon Docteur Medecin Aggregé à Lyon, & George Wheler Gentilhomme Anglois* (Lyon: Chez Antoine Cellier le fils, 1678), in three volumes. Wheler published his memoir four years after that, as *A Journey Into Greece in Company of Dr. Spon of Lyons* (London: William Cademann, Robert Kettlewell, and Awnsham Churchill, 1682).

For more on the two men and their travels, see Roland Etienne, *Jacon Spon, un humaniste lyonnais du XVIIme siecle* (Lyon: Bibliothèque Salomon-Reinach, 1993); Eftirpe Mitsi, "Travel, Memory and Authorship: George Wheler's *A Journey Into Greece* (1682)," *Restoration* 30, no. 1 (2006): 1–15; and Robert Ramsey, "Sir George Wheler and His Travels in Greece, 1650-1724," in R. W. Chapman, ed., *Essays by Divers Hands*, Transactions of the Royal Society of Literature XIX (1942), 1–39. The last of these essays offers interesting biographical information about Wheler's evolving religious attitudes, as well as certain features of Greek travel that remained in place a century later when the Aegina Marbles were discovered. Zante (Zakynthos) was directly accessible by boat from Corfu, boasting a significant British presence and extended business interests already in Spon and Wheler's day.

37. RUPRECHT'S NOTE: It is unclear whether Schelling has in mind the more famous classical Parthenon, or the Archaic Athenian temple that preceded it, one that was destroyed by fire during the Persian invasion of 480/479 BCE. Parallels with older temples are more suggestive, though it is unclear how much Schelling would have known about them.

    For more on the similarities between these two Archaic temples, see my *Afterwords: Hellenism, Modernism and the Myth of Decadence* (Albany, NY: SUNY Press, 1996), 36–43. For more on the excavation history of this earlier temple to Athena Polias, see Mary Beard, *The Parthenon*, rev. ed. (Cambridge, MA: Harvard University Press, 2003), 23–48 and 103–109.

38. RUPRECHT'S SUPPLEMENT: Pliny the Elder's most extended discussion of the history of Greek painting and sculpture appears in his *Natural History*, Book XXXV, and Book XXXVI, chapters 4–15, 21–24, respectively; a great deal of his attention is consumed with the manufacture of pigments and other natural artistic materials, especially marble. In fact, Pliny begins with the observation that "painting, an art that was formerly illustrious, . . . has been entirely ousted by marbles, and indeed finally also by gold" (XXXV.1.2), referring both to statuary and to decorative marble panels. "In the halls of our ancestors," he continues, "it was otherwise; portraits were the objects displayed to be looked at, not statues by foreign artists, nor bronzes nor marbles, but wax models of faces were set out each on a separate side-board, to furnish likenesses to be carried in procession at a funeral of the clan" (XXXV.2.6). There is a sort of golden age primitivism lying behind many of his observations in these books, describing a time before "morals had already lost the battle" to Roman luxury (XXXVI.2.5).

    Pliny makes no mention of the Aeginetan School in these books, though earlier Pliny credited the legendary figure Aiakos of Aegina (along with Erichthonius of Athens) with the discovery of silver (VII.56.197), and credited the island of Aegina with a distinctive mode of bronze-making, which was deemed to produce bronze superior to all others, save that of the bronze from Delos (XXXIV.5). We have already examined the several passages in which Pausanias praises the Aeginetan School of sculpture in its various media.

39. RUPRECHT'S NOTE: This phrase concerning "the imitation of nature" seems the most direct reference to Winckelmann's highly influential account of neoclassicism in the previous generation. I will make note of Wagner's and Schelling's dramatic and repeated use of this phrase throughout this chapter.

In his first essay from 1755—what really amounts to an art historical manifesto—Winckelmann offered his *Reflections on the Imitation [Nachahmung] of Greek Artworks in Painting and Sculpture*. What he suggests there is that the Greeks were unsurpassed in their imitation *of nature*, and therefore the best that the modern artist could hope to achieve would be accomplished through an imitation *of Greek art*. In the early nineteenth century, and especially under the aegis of German aesthetics, this interest in imitation generated fascinating further discussion of the relationship between the real and the ideal, which is apparently what Wagner is grappling with in this difficult paragraph.

Winckelmann distinguished between individual and ideal beauty as follows in his 1764 opus, *History of the Art of Antiquity*:

> The appearance of beauty is either *individual*, that is, tending toward the singular, or a selection of beautiful parts from many individuals and their combination into one, which we call *ideal*. . . .
>
> Nevertheless, the nature and build of the most beautiful bodies is rarely without fault, and they have forms or parts that can be found or imagined more perfectly in other bodies. Accordingly, this experience led these wise artists to proceed like a skilled gardener, who grafts different shoots of a noble species onto one stem. And as a bee gathers from many flowers, so their concept of beauty was not limited to the individual attributes of a single beauty. . . . (*History of the Art of Antiquity*, 196, 198)

It appears as if Wagner wishes to congratulate the Aeginetan artists for their attention to particulars, as opposed to a generic idealizing in their rendition of the human form; it is possible that he wishes to distinguish these Aegina Marbles from the thoroughly idealized sculptures of the Athenian Parthenon which had, by then, been transferred to London. Making precisely such a distinction becomes an ever-more prominent concern for Schelling in his later annotations to this study.

40. RUPRECHT'S NOTE: Some more recent scholarly discussion of these pedimental groups has tended to assume that there was a temporal gap of some ten to twenty years between the completion of the two pediments, based (like Wagner's hypothesis) on primarily stylistic assessments of the various statues. I am agnostic on this issue, primarily because it is hard to account for such a time delay in the creation of decorative statuary for a single temple, and also because Wagner's acknowledgment of the varying quality of various pieces might be easily explained by the variety of artists (and their varying skills) who were working on the commission. If the sculptural groups belonged to two different temples this might be more easily explained, but then the fact that they are so close to one another temporally raises more questions.

41. RUPRECHT'S NOTE: The relevant quotation is as follows:

> There are similar differences in statuary. The work of Callon and Hegesias was stiff, very like the Tuscanic work (*duriora et Tuscanicis proxima*), that of Calamis less so, and Myron's more fluid (*molliora*) than any of those. Polyclitus had more craftmanship and grace (*diligentia ac decor*) than the rest; most critics award him the palm, but, in order to find some fault with him, judge that he lacks "weight" (*pondus*), because, while he gave the human form (*humanae formae*) a beauty transcending the reality (*supra verum*), he seems not to have given adequate expression to the authority of the gods (*deorum auctoritatem*). He is also said to have avoided portraying the mature adult, never venturing beyond smooth cheeks.
>
> What Polyclitus lacked, Phidias and Alcamenes are allowed to have possessed. . . .

Quintilian, *The Orator's Education*, Donald A Russell, ed. and trans. (Cambridge, MA: Loeb Classical Library of Harvard University Press, 2001), XII.10.7–8, pages 284–87.

What immediately follows this passage is Quintilian's observation that Pheidias's work was of such surpassing perfection that *it had actually added something to the received religion*, an observation on the relationship between visual culture and religion that would have an enormous influence on Quatremère de Quincy.

> Pheidias is thought more skillful at representing gods than men; in ivory (*ebore*) he would be far and away without a rival, even if he had produced nothing but the Athena at Athens and the Olympian Zeus at Elis, the beauty of which is said to have added something to the traditional religious conception of the god (*cuius pulchritudo adiecisse aliquid etiam receptae religioni videtur*), so perfectly did the majesty of the work match its divine original.

42. RUPRECHT'S NOTE: Quatremère observes that the elaborate robing of such figures is best attributed to a *caprice des artistes*, and that its "bizarre" extremities represent *a stylistic convention*, not an *imitation* of actual Greek fashion. If such robes were imitative in any way, he suggests, then they would most likely have been modeled on the thick folds of the robes that the Greeks customarily created to clothe their most venerated statues, not actual people. The next paragraph reads as follows:

> Mais autant il répugne à toutes les sortes de vraisemblance d'admettre un tel style de draperies, comme ayant été l'imitation d'un mode d'habillement social et effectif, autant on trouve probable que ce genre bizarre et contraint aurait appartenu à la méthode de plis artificiels dont on mannequinait les statues primitives en bois. Si ce genre parait faux, postiche, et hors de nature dans le premier cas, il semble avoir dans le second une vérité naturelle et une propriété spécial; c'est-à-dire qu'on ne peut rien imaginer qui convienne mieux que des draperies guindées et artificiellement rangées, à des figures que nous appelerions des *poupées*: or, c'est bien là ce qu'étaient à la rigueur de la lettre les anciens simulacres de bois avec leurs étoffes réelles. (*Le Jupiter Olympien*, 21)

An English translation is as follows:

> But as repellant as it is to suggest an actual resemblance to any real style of drapery here, of its having been the imitation of an actual mode of social attire or actual dress, so it is likely that this bizarre and confining genre of dress should rather be assigned to the dressing of primitive wooden statues, almost as if they were mannequins. If this genre seems false and artificial in the former case, in the latter case it suggests a truthfulness and particular propriety. That is to say, we may more suitably imagine these stiff robes, so artificially arranged, as appropriate for figures we call *dolls*. Gold: this is literally what these ancient simulations of wood with their real fabric were intended to represent.

43. RUPRECHT'S NOTE: Quatremère cites the phrase *Duriora et tuscanicis proxima* from Quintilian's *Institutes of Oratory* (XII.10) at *Le Jupiter Olympien*, 23.
44. RUPRECHT'S NOTE: The relevant general description of Egyptian temples appears to be the following, at Strabo, *Geography* XVII.1.28:

> The plan of the construction of the temples (τῶν ἱερῶν) is as follows. . . . On either side of the pronaos project the wings (πτερά), as they are called. These are two walls equal in height to the naos, which are at first distant from one another a little more than the breadth of the foundation of the naos, and then, as one proceeds onward, follow converging lines as far as fifty or sixty cubits; and these walls have figures of large images (μεγάλων εἰδώλων) cut in low relief, like the Tyrrhenian images and the very old works of art (τοῖς ἀρχαίοις) among the Greeks.

See *The Geography of Strabo*, H. L. Jones, trans. (Cambridge, MA: Loeb Classical Library of Harvard University Press, 1982) in eight volumes; here VIII, 80–83.

45. RUPRECHT'S NOTE: Winckelmann's observation is as follows:

> In the earlier style of drawing the nude has clear and tangible characteristics that differ not only from the drawings of other peoples but also from the late Egyptian style. These characteristics exist and can be defined as much in the outline, or in the delineation and the contouring of the figure as a whole, as in the drawing and appearance of each particular part. The general and most prominent characteristics of drawing the nude in this style is the straight line, or the delineation of figures with slightly outwardly swelling and moderately curved lines. We find this style also in their architecture and in their decorations; their figures therefore lack grace (the Graces were deities unknown to the Egyptians) and painterliness, as Strabo says about their buildings. (*History of the Art of Antiquity*, 131)

Winckelmann cites Strabo's *Geography* XVII.1.27 in a note.

46. RUPRECHT'S NOTE: That is, to help clarify the specific character of the Aeginetan School.

47. RUPRECHT'S NOTE: The relevant comment from Demetrius of Phaleron, *On Style*, 14 is the following:

> That is why there is something that distinguishes the ancient style, such as ancient statuary, the art of which possessed simplicity and sobriety (ἡ συστολὴ καὶ ἰσχνότης). The style of later works resembled the works of Pheidias in matters large and small.

For the Greek text of Demetrius, I have used Pierre Chiron, *Démétrios Du Style* (Paris: Les Belles Lettres, 1993), 7.

48. RUPRECHT'S NOTE: Winckelmann's observation is as follows:

> Die Ursache, warum wir jene zwey sitzenden Figuren im Museo Pio-Clementino in Hinsicht ihre Alters dem Basrelief des Callimachos nachsetzen, ist keine andere, als weil man in diesen Figuren den nach außen aufwärts gezogenen Augen- und Mund-Winkel nicht mehr gewart; ein Merkzeichen, welches, wenn mir nicht irren, für die Denkmale aus dem höhern Alterthum entscheidend ist. Hätten Augen und Mund die aufwärts gezogene Richtung, so würden wir kein Bedenken tragen, diese beiden Figuren in noch ältere Zeiten hinaufzusetzen, weil die zuerst genannte, gleich den allerältesten für Griechisch erkannten Werken, in ihren Zügen einige Aehnlichkeit mit den Egyptischen Denkmalen hat. Die andere zeigt neben sehr vielem Fleiß eine höchst alterthümliche Rohheit, Unbeholfenheit und Steifheit in der Arbeit. (taken from the 1812 edition of Winckelmann's *Geschichte der Kunst des Alterthums*, 531)

An English translation is as follows:

> The reason why we associate those two seated figures in the Pio-Clementine Museum [at the Vatican] with the bas-relief by Callimachos in terms of their age is none other than the upward and outward angle to the lips and mouth in these figures, a characteristic which, if I am not mistaken, distinguishes monuments of the very greatest antiquity. If the eyes and mouth were to have this same direction, we would have no hesitation in assigning both figures to an even greater antiquity, since the features of the first aforementioned figure, like those figures recognized as the very oldest Greek works, bear a similarity to Egyptian monuments. The other figure demonstrates, in addition to great diligence, an utterly antique rawness, awkwardness and stiffness in the rendering.

49. RUPRECHT'S NOTE: While Schelling does not provide a citation here, the source is obviously *Le Jupiter Olympien*. Building on the developmental theories of Winckelmann, Quatremère compares "the savage and the infant," who are "affected by imitation in the same way, to the same degree, and by the same means" (*Le sauvage et l'infant sont affectés par l'imitation, de la même manière, dans la même mesure, et sous les mêmes rapports*, 2). The larger purpose of Quatremère's study is to describe the very gradual perfection of the techniques of idealizing imitation culminating in the School of Pheidias, where the

excellence of execution finally catches up to the sophistication of the religious imagination of a people.

> En tout genre d'inventions, d'arts et de connaissances, l'esprit humain suit une marche uniforme. Rien ne croit subitement. Un chef-d'ouevre n'est autre chose que le prix s'un nombre infini d'essais. . . . Ces siècles qu'on dit être les siècles de l'invention, ont simplement recueilli l'héritage de ceux qui les précédèrent. . . . Phidias, l'homme le plus éminent de l'époque la plus brillante de l'art en Grèce, confirme cette théorie, lorsqu'on le considère à la place qu'il occupe a milieu d'une longue suite d'artistes, et non ainsi qu'on le fait ordinairement. . . . (211)
>
> In every type of creation, art, or knowledge, the human spirit displays a uniform development. Nothing comes suddenly. A masterpiece is nothing more than the reward of an infinite number of previous attempts. Those centuries which one thinks of as the truly inventive ones are simply heir to the centuries that preceded them. . . . Pheidias, the preeminent man from the most brilliant period of art in Greece, confirms this theory, if we consider the place he occupied in a long line of artists who preceded him, and not as he is usually described. . . .

50. RUPRECHT'S NOTE: If this discussion begins to seem like special pleading on behalf of the Aeginetan School, and on behalf of the unique aesthetic quality of these sculptures, then it probably is. We should note the real thrust of Schelling's suggestion here. In an age still enamored of Winckelmann's neoclassicism and Pheidias's Parthenon Marbles, with their privileging of Greek naturalism, to suggest that the Aeginetan School was actually the inspiration for all later Greek naturalism was to grant the highest place of honor to the Aeginetan School. Since, as I have suggested, the gunpowder empires had taken their rivalries in a new aesthetic direction, competing for what were deemed to be the best classical collections, it is also clear that Munich's museum collection was claiming pride of place over its main rival, in London. Schelling's subsequent remarks make this contrast even clearer.
51. RUPRECHT'S NOTE: The passage proceeds from Pausanias's description of two altars outside of Tegea, one dedicated to Pan and the other to Zeus, which he relates to a more famous image of Artemis, "the Lady of the Lake" (Λιμνάτιδος): "the style of the workmanship is what the Greeks call Aeginetan" (*Guide to Greece* VIII.53.11).
52. RUPRECHT'S NOTE: This is a large claim, with a great deal of philosophical argument lying behind it, as Jason M. Wirth has brought to my considered attention. For Schelling to claim, on Pausanias's authority no less, that an actual work of art, a physical expression of artistic intention, is also "the more spiritual type," is to enact a curious kind of idealism. Whereas earlier Schelling utilized Quatremère's distinction between the execution of an artwork and its imaginative idea, here he introduces a third term: the actual, concrete work of art. This is an important glimpse of his turn, in these same years, to *particular case studies* in order to develop a more complete philosophy of art. For more on this turn, see appendix 3.
53. RUPRECHT'S NOTE: Put another way: as Germania was to Italia, so Aegina was to Athens; the former is realist, the latter idealist. The connections of Spirit have thus become

surprisingly ambiguous. What, after all, had been more "idealist" than German aesthetics? Schelling is thus very subtly announcing his own contribution to a new kind of idealism.

54. RUPRECHT'S NOTE: This passage from Quatremère's *Le Jupiter Olympien*, citing the elimination of Aegina's political independence and the dispersion of its artworks, nonetheless suggests that the island's distinctive style remained famous for its workshops, its metalwork and especially for its candelabras. Echoes of Aeginetan bronzework appear again in the misnamed "Etruscan" marble sculpture from the same period. The passage reads as follows:

> L'histoire des écoles d'art de la Grèce a reçu jusqu'ici peu de lumiéres. Il reste par exemple beaucoup de passages relatifs aux statuaires de l'école d'Egine; mais il n'est pas facile de dire si ces ouvrages sont d'une date antérieure ou postérieure à l'événement qui déstruisit la puissance de cet état. Toutefois on peut conclure du caractère qui faisait, au temps de Pausanias, distinguer ses ouvrages de ceux des autres écoles, que ce caractère s'était perpétué dans tous ses travaux, indépendamment des modifications que le temps avait dû y apporter. Du reste, que cette île ait continué d'avoir des ateliers célèbres, c'est ce que nous apprendra dans la suite le passage où Pline vante ses fonderies, son alliage, et ses fabriques de candélabres. Peut-être même serait-il permis de conclure de ce grand nombre de candélabres en marbre parvenus jusqu'à nous, où se trouvent si fréquemment des figures appelées improprement étrusques, que ces ouvrages sont des copies faites d'après les bronzes d'Egine; . . . La manière éginète (ἐργασία Αἰγιναία) se reconnaissait jadis aussi sur des statues de marbre. Dans le temple de Diane Dictymée, à Ambrisse, en Phocide, on voyait un simulacre de marbre noir fait dans le goût de l'école d'Egine (23–24).

An English translation is as follows:

> The history of the Greek schools of art has thus far received little illumination. For example, there remain many passages related to statues from the School of Aegina, but it is not at all easy to say whether these works should be dated before or after the events that destroyed the power of that city. Nonetheless we may assess its character in the time of Pausanias, who distinguished its works from those of the other schools, a character preserved in all of its works, regardless of the changes wrought by time. In addition, that this island continued to possess celebrated workshops may be concluded from passages in Pliny where he boasts of her foundries, her alloys, and her manufacture of candelabras. We might even conclude from the large number of marble candelabras that have come down to us, and which are frequently misnamed Etruscan, that these works are actually copies made from bronze Aeginetan originals; . . . The Aeginetan style was previously recognized in marble statues. At the temple of Dictynnian Artemis at Ambrossus in Phokis, we find a simulation in black marble rendered in the style of the Aeginetan School.

Quatremère is referring to a passage from Pausanias's *Guide to Greece* X.36.5.

55. RUPRECHT'S NOTE: The passage from *Guide to Greece* is as follows:

> The he-goats are no bigger than those found elsewhere, but their shape is that of the wild ram which an artist would carve in the Aeginetan style (ὁποῖον ἐν πλαστικῇ τις ἂν τῇ Αἰγιναίᾳ ποιήσειεν), except that their breasts are too shaggy to liken them to Aeginetan art (πρὸς Αἰγιναίαν τέχνην). (X.17.12)

56. RUPRECHT'S NOTE: Schelling has altered Wagner's phrasing considerably here, which reads:

> From them, it becomes clear to us what road art took from its childhood in order to achieve its highest fulfillment in the works of Pheidias and his contemporaries, works that move us to such wonder today. It is clear that these great masters had merely to take a further step along the paths laid out so clearly for them by their predecessors. (page 3)

57. RUPRECHT'S NOTE: The sympathetic reader of Friedrch Nietzsche's *The Birth of Tragedy Out of the Spirit of Music* (1872) cannot fail to be struck by the way these observations anticipate so many of Nietzsche's most striking and provocative claims by more than fifty years. For more on that connection, see Jason M. Wirth, *The Conspiracy of Life*, 146–51.

58. RUPRECHT'S NOTE: This is one of the places where Schelling utilizes Wagner's concrete descriptions as a means with which to illustrate and to ground some of his own most creative contributions to aesthetic theory. As Jason M. Wirth has emphasized, Schelling is out to describe nothing less than the process whereby art becomes nature (and a very rarified type of nature, at that). Schelling first gestured toward this idea in another one of his important public lectures in Munich: an 1807 address entitled "The Relation of the Plastic Arts to Nature" [*Über das Verhältnis der bildenden Kunst zu der Natur*]. Framed as an intervention in the long tradition of philosophical reflection on *mimesis* (imitation), Schelling there distinguished between *dead* (or servile) imitation (imagined as a mere aping of an original, such as what Kandinsky would later condemn as the essence of all neoclassical *mimesis*) and *living* imitation (imagined as the attempt to become like nature which, through a more thoroughgoing embrace of the creative process, enables new forms of life to emerge). The essential point seems to lie with what Wirth calls "the productive creativity or coming into being of form" (xvi). In short, the productive artistic imagination is being upheld as the uniquely human capacity that mediates between the world of nature and the world of art. It is a small step from this claim, I think, to Quintilian's magisterial belief that a work of visual representation might actually add something to received religion, a claim with which Schelling (like Quatremère) was much intrigued.

Schelling's 1807 lecture, which focused primarily on sculpture fittingly enough, as well as the larger theoretical context of Schelling's thinking at this time, are developed with great subtlety and insight by Jason M. Wirth in *Schelling's Practice of the Wild*, 125–39. The concluding chapter offers Wirth's decisive analysis of the role of the imagination in the development of Schelling's mature aesthetic viewpoint (especially at 151–60), and culminates in a stunning rendition of the philosophical depths in *Moby*

Dick. This, we are now able to see more clearly, is (the) wild. But many of these moves are anticipated in Wirth's earlier book, *The Conspiracy of Life*, 10ff.

59. RUPRECHT'S NOTE: The imperial-cum-cultural special pleading here takes on a striking aesthetic and spiritual dimension.
60. RUPRECHT'S SUPPLEMENT: For an excellent summary of the three-month hearing in the British House prior to the purchase of the so-called Elgin Marbles, see Arthur H. Smith, "Lord Elgin and His Collection," *Journal of Hellenic Studies* 36 (1916): 163–372.
61. RUPRECHT'S NOTE: It bears mention that Wagner here presupposes what is arguably the greatest revolution in art history and aesthetics after Winckelmann, namely, the declaration of independence of modern art from inherited religion. For some reflection on the implications of this not-quite-secular form of institutional detachment, see my *Classics at the Dawn of the Museum Era*, 9–16, and *Winckelmann and the Vatican's First Profane Museum*, 95–108.
62. RUPRECHT'S NOTE: This quotation comes from the famous exchange between Just and Unjust Argument in Aristophanes's *Clouds*, ll. 977–78, as part of a debate in which the length of the hair, the form(s) of legitimate sexuality, and their relation to acceptable forms of masculinity were to be—then as now—significant markers in the culture wars:

> ἀρχαῖά γε καὶ Διπολιώδη, καὶ τεττίγων ἀνάμεστα,
> καὶ Κηκείδου-καὶ Βουφονίων . . .

The loose translation by William Arrowsmith renders it this way:

> Ugh, what musty, antiquated rubbish. It reeks of golden grasshoppers,
> all gewgaws and decaying institutions!

[*Aristophanes: The Clouds*, translated by William Arrowsmith (New York: New American Library, 1962), 88]

Aristophanes's specific reference is to the Bouphonion, or ox sacrifice, an essential part of the ancient, midsummer Attic rite of the Dipolieia, a festival dedicated to Zeus, Protector of the City. In the Athenian version of this rite, a group of working oxen were led to the Akropolis before an altar laden with grain; the first ox to begin eating the grain was deemed to have selected itself for sacrifice. It was summarily butchered, and the wielder of the axe abandoned the weapon at the scene and fled. The axe was then tried for murder. Such a ritual demonstrates a deep ambivalence about blood sacrifice that would eventually lead to the abandonment of such practices entirely centuries later. So we appear to be witnessing *the dawning self-consciousness* about religious rites that will necessarily call these same rites into question—a matter of profound interest to post-Kantian (idealist) philosophy in Germany, as Schelling knew well. For more on this rite, see Pausanias, *Guide to Greece* I.24.4.

It is striking that Schelling's reading of Aristophanes is as one-sided as it appears to be. After all, when such religious rites have come to a certain level of cultural self-consciousness, as it were, then the old arguments for old-fashioned virtue necessarily lose much of their rhetorical power. You simply cannot believe what you no longer believe. . . .

63. RUPRECHT'S NOTE: Thucydides's *Peloponnesian War* I.6 reads as follows:

> Indeed, all of Greece (ἡ Ἑλλὰς) used to carry arms because the places where they lived were unprotected, and their social interactions with each other were unsafe; in general they went about armed, just as the barbarians did. And the fact that these districts of Greece still retain this custom is evidence that at one time their way of life was similar everywhere (πάντας ὁμοίων). The Athenians were among the very first to lay aside their arms and, adopting a mellower way of life, to adopt more luxurious customs. And indeed owing to this fastidiousness, it was not long ago that their older men of the wealthier class gave up wearing linen tunics (χιτῶνάς τε λινοῦς) and tying up their hair in a knot fastened by a golden grasshopper as a brooch; and this same dress obtained for a long time among the elderly men of the Ionians as well, owing to their kinship with the Athenians. A more moderate mode of dress such as we have now was first adopted by the Lakedaimonians. . . . (C. F. Smith, trans., *Thucydides*, 10–11, translation emended)

The reference to grasshopper brooches explains the reference that William Arrowsmith had in mind in his translation of Aristophanes's *Clouds,* which I cite at note 62. Thucydides goes on to report that the Lakedaimonians were also the first to exercise in the nude, a custom that he also feels distinguished Greeks from barbarians significantly in his own day.

64. RUPRECHT'S NOTE: "Denn alles, ist mit einer solchen Naivetät, Sorgfalt, Eigenthümlichkeit und Unschuld gemacht, dass ich unmöglich glauben kann, es sei ein Werk der Nachahmung."

I have been unable to locate the source of this quotation from Wagner's works; it may well come from one of Wagner's letters to Schelling, which were lost in the war (many of Schelling's letters to Wagner, by contrast, are preserved in Würzburg).

65. RUPRECHT'S NOTE: I have utilized a significant portion of this important passage as the frontispiece to this book.

66. RUPRECHT'S NOTE: In Diodorus's *Library of History* IV.61, he relates the story of how King Minos of Crete called down a curse of drought on the city of Athens and the entire region of Attica as retribution for the killing of his son, Androgeos. When the Athenians consulted the oracle as to what should be done about this curse, they were advised to seek Aiakos's aid, who might then intervene with Zeus on their behalf. The Athenians did so, and the drought was lifted everywhere but in the city of Athens itself. They once again consulted the oracle and were directed to provide Minos with seven boys and seven girls, once every nine years, for the Minotaur to devour. Diodorus then relates the well-known story of Theseus's eventual slaying of the Minotaur.

67. RUPRECHT'S NOTE: In Diodorus's *Library of History* IV.76, we read the following about Daedalus:

> By nature he far surpassed all other men in the arts of building (τεκτονικὴν), making statues (τῶν ἀγαλμάτων κατασκευὴν) and carving stone (λιθουργίαν). . . . In the carving of statues (τῶν ἀγαλμάτων κατασκευὴν) he so far excelled all other

> men that later generations invented the story (μυθολογῆσαι) about him, that the statues of his making were entirely like (ὁμοιότατα) their living models; they could see, they said, and walk and, in a word, preserved so well the characteristics of the entire body that the beholder thought that the image made by him was a being endowed with life (ἔμψυχον ζῷον). And since he was the first to represent the eyes open, and to fashion the legs separated in a stride, and the arms and hands as extended from the body, it was a natural thing that he should have received the wonder of mankind; for the artists before his time had carved their statues with the eyes closed and the arms and hands hanging and attached to the sides.

I am using the edition of Diodorus, *The Library of History*, translated by C. H. Oldfather (Cambridge, MA: Loeb Classical Library of Harvard University Press, 1939, 1993), III: 56–57, translation emended.

Diodorus goes on to relate the very strange story of Daedalus's killing of his nephew out of jealousy at the boy's inventiveness, and his subsequent exile to Crete.

68. RUPRECHT'S NOTE: Pausanias's comment is as follows:

> This Callimachus . . . although not of the first rank of artists, was yet of unparalleled cleverness (σοφίᾳ), so that he was the first to drill holes through stones, and gave himself the title of Refiner of Art (κατατηξίτεχνον), or perhaps others gave him the title and he adopted it as his own. (*Guide to Greece* I.26.7)

69. RUPRECHT'S NOTE: In describing the Temple of Zeus at Olympia, Pausanias notes the following:

> The tiles are not of baked clay (κέραμος), but of Pentelic marble cut into the shape of tiles (κεράμου τρόπον λίθος). The invention is said to be that of a man from Naxos named Byzes, who they say made the images (ἀγάλματα) in Naxos on which is the inscription (ἐπίγραμμα):
>
> To the offspring of Leto was I dedicated by Euergus,
> A Naxian, son of Byzes, the first to make tiles of stone (λίθου κέραμον).
>
> This Byzes lived about the time of Alyattes the Lydian, when Astyages, the son of Cyaxeres, reigned over the Medes. (*Guide to Greece* V.10.3, translation emended)

70. RUPRECHT'S NOTE: The reference here is to Johann Joachim Winckelmann's last work, and the only one he published in Italian, *Monumenti Antichi Inediti*, spiegati ed illustrati da Giovanni Winckelmann, Prefetto delle Antichità di Roma (Roma: Marco Pagliarini, 1767). Plate 17 depicts a fragmentary statue with one of these neck straps, whereas plate 109 depicts a naked warrior holding a shield with an inner strap. The texts read as follows:

> Dalla parte di dentro questo scudo ha come due anse dette già da' greci ῎Οχανον, ed Οχάνη, l'una e la più grande nel mezzo, per imbracciarlo, e l'altra verso l'orlo per tenerlo e reggerlo con la mano. Sebbene la riferita parola ῎Οχανον, ed

' Οχάνη non trovasi in Omero; anzi questo poeta non fa veruna mensione di anse; onde credesi, che gli scudi a' tempi della guerra di Troja fossero privi del comodo d'imbracciarli; perciò, secondo che ho notato al Num. 17 portavansi legati al collo per mezzo d'un corame detto Πόρπαξ; sicchè pendessero, allor che non si era in atto d'adoprarli, sul petto, e in marciando, dietro la schiena, e nell'atto di usarne si potessero altresì rivolgare sopra il braccio. (144)

and

Stimabilissima è la statua di Pallade nella villa dell'Eminentissimo Alessandro Albani, al Num. 17. . . . Questa Pallade, in atto di combattere, probabilmente contro i Titani, porta l'egide squammosa orlata di biscie e legata al collo, nella guisa stessa nella quali i Greci in tempo della guerra di Troja si legarono lo scudo con un laccio di corame, detto Πόρπαξ al collo, non essendosi per ancora pensato al comodo del corame dalla parte di dentro (' Οχάνη) per mettervi il braccio. (18)

An English translation is as follows:

On the interior of this shield there are two such loops called *Ochanon* and *Ochane* by the Greeks: the one larger and located in the middle to be used for attachment; the other closer to the edge to be used to hold and secure it with the hand. Since these terms, *Ochanon* and *Ochane*, do not appear in Homer—indeed this poet makes no mention at all of these loops—we may conclude that shields in the time of the Trojan War lacked these forms of attachment. Therefore, as I noted in Number 17, they could be tied at the neck by a leather cord called *Porpax*, such that when they were not in the act of combat it could be worn suspended, and when marching it could be slung behind the back, and when it was in actual use it could be returned to the arm. (144)

and

Of the highest quality is the statue of Pallas Athena in the villa of the Most Eminent Alessandro Albani, No. 17. . . . This Pallas, depicted in the act of combat (probably with the Titans) wears the aegis fringed with waving serpents and fixed at the neck, and in the manner which the Greeks used in the time of the Trojan War, the shield is fixed to the neck with a leather strap, called *Porpax*, since they had not yet thought of a more convenient interior leather strap (*Ochane*) to fix the shield at the arm. (18)

71. RUPRECHT'S NOTE: Herodotus's comment (*Histories* I.171) is as follows:

Three things they invented in which they were followed by the Greeks: it was the Carians who first taught the wearing of crests on their helmets and devices on their shields, and who first made for their shields holders (ὄχανα); until then all who used shields carried them without these holders (ἄνευ ὀχάνων), and guided them with leather baldries which they slung around the neck and over the left shoulder. (A. D. Godley, trans., *Herodotus*, 212–15, translation emended)

72. RUPRECHT'S NOTE: Pliny's story begins with this phrase, as follows:

> The very first men to make a name as sculptors in marble were Dipoenus and Scyllis, who were born on the island of Crete (*geniti in Creta insula*) while Media was still a great power and Cyrus had not yet come to the throne of Persia. Their date falls approximately in the 50th Olympiad. They made their way to Sicyon, which was for a long time the fatherland (*patria*) of all such industries (*officinarium omnium talium*). The men of Sicyon had given them a contract for making images of the gods (*deorum simulacra*). . . . (*Natural History* XXXVI.4.9, translation emended)

73. RUPRECHT'S NOTE: Pausanias's comment is actually a good deal more conditional than Schelling suggests:

> Here there is a sanctuary of Athena (ἱερὸν Ἀθηνᾶς), and the image (ἄγαλμα) is a work (τέχνη) of Scyllis and Dipoenus. Some hold them to have been the students of Daedalus, but others say that Daedalus took a wife in Gortyn, and that Dipoenus and Scyllis were his sons by this woman. (*Guide to Greece* II.15.1, translation emended)

74. RUPRECHT'S NOTE: The passage from *Le Jupiter Olympien* is as follows [with notes in brackets]:

> Les ouvrages de ces artistes [Dipoene et Scyllis] étaient très-nombreaux en Grèce. Ambracie, Argos et Cléonée, dit Pline [lib. XXXVI, cap. 5], en étaient remplies. Les statues de leur école ou de leurs élèves ont été décrites par Pausanias, et l'époque qu'il assigne à plusieurs d'entre eux, tels que Tecteus et Angelion [Pausan. lib. II, cap. 32; lib. VII, cap. 18], et postérieure à la 50.e olympiade. (*Le Jupiter Olympien*, 179)

An English translation is as follows:

> The works by these artists [Dipoinis and Skyllis] were quite numerous in Greece. Ambracia [Arta], Argos and Cleonae are often mentioned by Pliny. The statues produced by their school, or else by their students, were described by Pausanias, and he assigns a date to several of them, like Tectaeus and Angelion, after the 50th Olympiad.

75. RUPRECHT'S NOTE: Pausanias's comment is as follows:

> The image (ἄγαλμα) at Olympia dedicated by the Greeks was made by Anaxagoras of Aegina. The name of this artist is omitted by the historians of Plataea. (*Guide to Greece* V.23.3).

Pausanias does not in fact specify what god the statue represented; given the Panhellenic nature of the offering, Schelling assumes it to have been Zeus.

76. RUPRECHT'S NOTE: The relevant report in Pausanias is as follows:

> Opposite the offerings I have enumerated are others in a row; they face towards the south, and are very near to that part of the precinct (τοῦ τεμένους) that is sacred to Pelops. Among them are those dedicated by the Maenalian Phormis. He crossed to Sicily from Maenalus to serve Gelon the son of Deinomenes. Distinguishing himself in the campaigns (τὰς στρατείας) of Gelon and afterwards of his brother Hieron, he reached such a pitch of prosperity that he dedicated not only these offerings at Olympia, but also others dedicated to Apollo at Delphi. The offerings at Olympia are two horses and two charioteers, a charioteer standing by the side of each of the horses. The first horse and man are by Dionysius of Argos, the second are the work of Simon of Aegina. (*Guide to Greece* V.27.1–2)

77. RUPRECHT'S NOTE: Pausanias's comment is as follows:

> As for the chariot of Gelon, I did not come to the same opinion about it as my predecessors, who hold that the chariot is an offering of Gelon who became tyrant in Sicily. Now there is an inscription (ἐπίγραμμα) on the chariot that it was dedicated by Gelon of Gela, son of Deinomenes, and the date of the victory of this Gelon is the seventy-third Olympiad. But the Gelon who was tyrant of Sicily took possession of Syracuse when Hybrilides was archon at Athens, in the second year of the seventy-second Olympiad, when Tisicrates of Croton won the foot race (στάδιον). Plainly, therefore, he would have announced himself as of Syracuse, not Gela. The fact is that this Gelon must be a private person (ἰδιώτης), of the same name as the tyrant, whose father had the same name as the tyrant's father. It was Glaukias of Aegina who made both the chariot and the portrait statue (τὴν εἰκόνα) of Gelon. (*Guide to Greece* VI.9.4–5, translation emended)

78. RUPRECHT'S NOTE: Pausanias's comment, as cited earlier, is as follows:

> On the akropolis is a temple (νάος) of Athena, called Sthenias. The wooden image (ξόανον) itself of the goddess was made by Kallon of Aegina. Kallon was a student (μαθητὴς) of Tectaeus and Angelion, who made the image (ἄγαλμα) of Apollo for the Delians. Angelion and Tectaeus were trained in the school of Dipoenus and Scyllis. (*Guide to Greece* II.32.5)

79. RUPRECHT'S NOTE: Pausanias's comment is as follows:

> The image represents her in the guise of a huntress (τὸ μὲν σχῆμα τοῦ ἀγάλματος θηρεύουσά ἐστιν); it is made of ivory and gold, and the artists were Menaechmus and Soïdas of Naupactus, who, it is inferred, lived not much later than Kanachus of Sicyon and Kallon of Aegina. (*Guide to Greece* VII.18.10)

80. RUPRECHT'S NOTE: The quotation is actually from Pliny's *Natural History* XXXIV.19.50: "In the 95th Olympiad flourished Naucydes, Dinomenes, Canachus and Patroclus . . ."
81. RUPRECHT'S NOTE: The quotation is from Cicero's *Brutus*, G. L. Hendrickson, trans. (Cambridge, MA: Loeb Classical Library of Harvard University Press, 1962), 66–67:

> What critic who devotes his attention to the lesser arts (*minora*) does not recognize that the statues of Canachus are too rigid (*signa rigidiora*) to reproduce the truth of nature (*imitentur veritatem*)? The statues of Calamis again are still hard (*dura*), and yet more lifelike than those of Canachus. Even Myron has not yet fully attained naturalness, though one would not hesitate to call his works beautiful (*non dubites pulchra dicere*). Still more beautiful (*pulchriora*) are the statues of Polyclitus, and indeed in my estimation quite perfect (*pulchriora etiam Polycliti et iam plane perfecta, ut mihi quidem videri solent*). The same development may be seen in painting (*in pictura*).

Schelling has omitted Cicero's casual qualification, "to me, in any case" *(ut mihi quidem videri solent . . .*). I am grateful to Mary Grace Dupree for bringing this to my attention.
82. RUPRECHT'S NOTE: The full quotation from Quintilian's *The Orator's Education* XII.10.8 is as follows:

> There are similar differences in statuary. The work of Callon and Hegesias was stiff (*duriora*), very like the Tuscanic work, that of Calamis less rigid (*minus rigida*), and Myron's more fluid (*molliora*) than any of these. Polyclitus had more craftmanship and grace (*diligentia ac decor*) than the rest; most critics award him the palm, but, in order to find some fault in him, judging that he lacks "weight" (*pondus*), because, while he gave the human form a beauty transcending the reality (ut *humanae formae addiderit supra verum*), he seems not to have given adequate expression to the authority of the gods (*deorum auctoritatem*). He is said also to have avoided portraying the mature adult, never venturing beyond smooth cheeks (*nihil ausus praeter leves genas*).
>
> What Polyclitus lacked, Phidias and Alcamenes are allowed to have possessed. Phidias is thought more skillful at representing gods than men (*Phidias tamen dis quam hominibus effigendis melior artifex creditur*); in ivory (*ebore*) he would be far and away without a rival, even if he had produced nothing but the Athena at Athens (*Minervam Athenis*) and the Olympian Zeus at Elis (*Olympium in Elide Iovem*), the beauty of which is said to have added something to the traditional religious concept of the god (*cuius pulchritudo adiecisse aliquid etiam receptae religioni videtur*), so perfectly did the majesty of the work match its divine original (*adeo maiestas operis deum aequavit*).

The latter observation, about a novel visual image actually having the capacity to add something to the received, traditional religion was the focus of considerable theoretical attention by Quatremère de Quincy, as I have noted previously. See my *Classics at the Dawn of the Museum Era: The Life and Times of Antoine-Chrysostome Quatremère de Quincy* (New York: Palgrave Macmillan, 2014), 68, 91, 183, 195.

83. RUPRECHT'S NOTE: The epigram by Antipater of Sidon, *On Statues of the Muses*, reads as follows:

> Three are we, the Muses who stand here; one bears in her hands a flute, another a harp, and the third a lyre. She who is the work of Aristocles holds the lyre, Ageladas's Muse the harp, and Canachus's the musical reeds. The first is she who rules tone, the second makes a melody of color, and the third invented skilled harmony.

See W. R. Paton, *The Greek Anthology* in five volumes (Cambridge MA: Loeb Classical Library of Harvard University Press, 1979) V, 290–91.

84. RUPRECHT'S NOTE: Pausanias's comment is as follows:

> Next to Pantarces is the chariot of Cleosthenes, a man from Epidamnus. This is the work (ἔργον) of Ageladas, and it stands behind the Zeus dedicated by the Greeks from the spoils of the battle of Plataea. Cleosthenes's victory occurred at the sixty-sixth Olympiad, and together with the image (εἰκόνα) of his horses he dedicated one of himself and one of his charioteer. . . . This Cleosthenes was the first of those who bred horses in Greece to dedicate his image (εἰκόνα) at Olympia. (*Guide to Greece* VI.10.6–8)

85. RUPRECHT'S NOTE: Pausanias's comment is as follows:

> The things worth seeing (θέας ἄξια) in Amyclae include a victor in the pentathlon, named Aenetus, on a stele. The story is that he won a victory at Olympia, but died while the crown was being placed on his head. So there is the image (εἰκὼν) of this man; there are also bronze tripods. The older ones are said to be a tithe from the Messenian war. Under the first tripod stood a statue (ἄγαλμα) of Aphrodite, and under the second an Artemis. The two tripods themselves and the reliefs are the work of Gitiadas. The third was made by Kallon of Aegina, and under it stands a statue (ἄγαλμα) of the Maid, daughter of Demeter. (*Guide to Greece* III.18.7–8, translation emended)

86. RUPRECHT'S NOTE: The phrase is actually from Pliny's *Natural History* XXXIV.19.49:
An almost innumerable multitude of artists have been rendered famous by statues and figures of smaller size (*minoribus simulacris*); but before them all stands the Athenian Pheidias, celebrated for the statue of the Olympian Zeus, which in fact was made of ivory and gold (*facto ex ebore quidem et auro*), although he also made figures in bronze (*sed et ex aere signa fecit*). He flourished in the 83rd Olympiad, about the 300th year of our city, at which same period his rivals were Alcamenes, Critias, Nesiotes and Hegias; and later, in the 87th Olympiad there were Hagelades, Callon and the Spartan Gorgias, and again in the 90th Olympiad Polycleitus, Phradmon, Myron, Pythagoras, Scopas and Perellus.

87. RUPRECHT'S NOTE: It is noteworthy that the later excavator at the Temple to Aphaia on Aegina and Glyptothek director, Adolf Furtwängler, published an essay on

the literary attestations to Kalamis in the year he died, one designed to counter the thesis that there were in fact two artists by that name, whose careers were separated by centuries. See "Zu Pythagoras und Kalamis," *Separat-Abdruck aus den Sitzungsberichten der philos.-philol. und der histor. Klasse der Kgl. Bayer. Akademie der Wissenschaften* (1907): Heft II: 157–69.

88. RUPRECHT'S NOTE: Schelling seems to be thinking of two separate passages here:

> On the offering of the Thasians at Olympia there is an elegiac couplet:
> Onatas, son of Micon, fashioned me,
> He who has his dwelling in Aegina.
>
> This Onatas, though belonging to the Aeginetan school of sculpture (καὶ τέχνης ἐς τὰ ἀγάλματα ὄντα Αἰγιναίας), I shall place below none of the successors of Daedalus or of the Attic school. (*Guide to Greece* V.25.13, translation emended)

and the second passage, which I cited earlier:

> The offerings at Olympia [by Hieron] are two horses and two charioteers, a charioteer standing by the side of each of the horses. The first horse and man are by Dionysius of Argos, the second are the work of Simon of Aegina. (*Guide to Greece* V.27.2)

89. RUPRECHT'S NOTE: The passage reads as follows:

> When the Phigalians heard the oracle (μάντευμα) that was brought back, they held Demeter in greater honor than before, and particularly they persuaded Onatas of Aegina, son of Micon, to make them a statue (ἄγαλμα) of Demeter at a price. The Pergamenes have a bronze Apollo made by this Onatas, a marvelous wonder both for its size (μεγέθους) and artistry (τέχνῃ). This man then, about two generations after the Persian invasion of Greece, made the Phigalians a statue (ἄγαλμα) of bronze, guided partly by a picture or copy of the ancient wooden image (γραφὴν ἢ μίμημα τοῦ ἀρχαίου ξοάνου) which he discovered, but mostly (so goes the story) by a vision he saw in dreams (κατὰ ὀνειράτων ὄψιν). As to the date, I have the following evidence to produce. At the time when Xerxes crossed over into Europe, Gelon the son of Deinomenes ruled Syracuse and the rest of Sicily besides. When Gelon died, the kingdom devolved on his brother Hieron. Hieron died before he could dedicate to Olympian Zeus the offerings (ἀναθήματα) he had vowed for his victories in the chariot-race, and so Deinomenes his son paid the debt for his father. These too are works (ποιήματα) by Onatas, and there are two inscriptions at Olympia. . . . Onatas was a contemporary with Hegias of Athens and Ageladas of Argos. (*Guide to Greece* VIII.42.7–10)

90. RUPRECHT'S NOTE: Pausanias describes a curious gilded wooden statue in the Temple to Athena Areia, as well as two paintings by different artists:

> It is a wooden statue gilded with gold (ἄγαλμα ξόανόν ἐστιν ἐπίχρυσον), but the face, hands and feet are of Pentelic marble. In size it is slightly smaller than the bronze Athena on the Akropolis, the one which the Athenians also erected as first-fruits of the battle of Marathon; the Plateans too had Pheidias for the maker of their statue (τὸ ἄγαλμα ποιήσας) of Athena. In the temple are paintings (γραφαὶ): one of them, by Polygnotus, represents Odysseus after he has killed the suitors; the other, painted by Onasias, is the former expedition of the Argives, under Adrastus, against Thebes. (*Guide to Greece* IX.4.2)

91. RUPRECHT'S NOTE: Schelling's translation of the passage from Pausanias is as follows: *Diesen Onatas aber, der ein Aeginet ist, werden wir keinem derjenigen nachsetzen, die sowohl vom Dädalus als von der attischen Werkstatt herkommen.*

Jones's and Ormerod's English translation of this passage is instructive, given its reference to the Aeginetan School rather than the island of Aegina: "This Onatas, though belonging to the Aeginetan school of sculpture, I shall place after none of the successors of Daedalus or of the Attic School."

Pausanias's language at *Guide to Greece* V.25.13 refers to Onatas as ὄντα Αἰγιναίας (the full phrase is καὶ τέχνης ἐς τὰ ἀγάλματα ὄντα Αἰγιναίας); Schelling is correct to argue that this phrasing pretty clearly referred to a school or workshop rather than simply to the island as this artist's home.

92. RUPRECHT'S NOTE: The passage in question speaks well to the ambiguity of this phrase, "of Aegina":

> The image represents her in the guise of a huntress (τὸ μὲν σχῆμα τοῦ ἀγάλματος θηρεύουσά ἐστιν); it is made of ivory and gold, and the artists were Menaechmus and Soïdas of Naupactus, who, it is inferred, lived not much later than Kanachus of Sicyon and Kallon of Aegina (τοῦ Αἰγινήτου Κάλλωνος, *Guide to Greece* VII.18.10).

93. RUPRECHT'S NOTE: This seems slightly to misrepresent Quatremère's intention in this passage. Quatremère is arguing for the evidence concerning a distinction already evident in the ancient world: that between the Daedalean or Attic School on the one hand, and the Aeginetan School on the other, however blurry the lines between one school and its successors or rivals may be. One of the central contributions of this book lay in its explication of what the author imagines as constituting the features of such a "school": "a certain method, a particular way of seeing, of feeling and of manufacture." The full passage reads thus:

> Du reste, il ne faut pas s'imaginer que dans le cours naturel des choses, et lorsque l'art se développe de lui-même, sans le secours de modèles étrangers, les changements de style et de manière arrivent par des transitions brusques et tranchantes. Le goût de ce qu'on appela l'école de Dédale, et aussi de l'ancienne école attique, se perpétua sans aucun doute dans beaucoup de parties, sous l'école suivante. C'est ainsi que la manière de Giotto est encore sensible dans les ouvrages du

quinzième siècle, quoique les peintres de ce siècle soient fort supérieurs à ceux du treizième. On doit conclure à-peu-près la même chose d'une réflexion faite par Pausanias, sur le compte d'Onatas d'Egine, dont l'âge bien connu ne peut guère être porté plus haute que la 70e olympiade [Pausan., lib. VIII, cap. 42], mais dont le style, ainsi que celui de ses contemporains Callon et Égésias [Quintil., lib. XII, cap. 10], tenait encore à la manière de l'école antérieure. Après avoir parlé d'un Hercule colossal en bronze, qu'on voyait de cet artiste à Olympie, l'écrivain voyageur ajoute, qu'il ne jugeait Onatas [Pausan., lib. V, cap. 25] inférieur à aucun de ceux qui suivirent l'école de Dédale et l'école attique (sans doute l'ancienne): οὐδενὸς ὕστερον θήσομεν τῶν ἀπὸ Δαιδάλου τε καὶ ' Εργαστηρίου τοῦ ' Αττικοῦ. Il est clair qu'ici le mot *Dédale* n'est qu'une dénomination fictive qui signifiait l'ancienne école de sculpture.

École n'est donc qu'un mot qui désigne en général une certaine méthode, une façon particulière de voir, de sentir et de faire. (*Le Jupiter Olympien*, 176)

An English translation is as follows:

Moreover, we must not imagine, in the natural course of things, as art itself develops without recourse to foreign models, that changes in style and mannerism come through sharp and sudden transitions. The taste to which we assign the name of the School of Daedalus, much like the Ancient Attic School, is perpetuated without a doubt in various ways by subsequent schools. So it is that the mannerism of Giotto is still perceptible in the works of the fifteenth century, although the painters of that century were far superior to those of the thirteenth. One may conclude much the same thing from a remark made by Pausanias in his account of Onatas of Aegina, whose dates are well known to have been not later than the 70th Olympiad, but whose style, like his contemporaries Callon and Hegesias, still maintained the style of the preceding school. After discussing a colossal bronze Heracles by this artist which he saw at Olympia, the travel writer adds that he deemed Onatas in no way inferior to those followers of the School of Daedalus or the Attic School (no doubt the Ancient Attic School): οὐδενὸς ὕστερον θήσομεν τῶν ἀπὸ Δαιδάλου τε καὶ ' Εργαστηρίου τοῦ ' Αττικοῦ. It is clear that the name of Daedalus was a fictitious name signifying an ancient sculptural school.

Thus *School* is simply a word designating a certain method, a particular way of seeing, of feeling and of manufacture.

94. RUPRECHT'S NOTE: As we have already seen, the fuller quotation is this:

When the Phigalians heard the oracle (μάντευμα) that was brought back, they held Demeter in greater honor than before, and particularly they persuaded Onatas of Aegina, son of Micon, to make them an image (ἄγαλμα) of Demeter at a price. The Pergamenes have a bronze Apollo made by this Onatas, a marvelous wonder both for its size (μεγέθους) and artistry (τέχνῃ). This man then, about two generations after the Persian invasion of Greece, made the Phigalians an image (ἄγαλμα) of bronze, guided partly by a picture or copy of the ancient wooden image (γραφὴν ἤ μίμημα τοῦ ἀρχαίου ξοάνου) which he discovered, but mostly (so goes the story) by a vision he saw in dreams (κατὰ ὀνειράτων ὄψιν). (*Guide to Greece* VIII.42.7)

95. RUPRECHT'S NOTE: As I have noted previously, this passage was a favorite of Quatremère de Quincy's:

> What Polyclitus lacked, Phidias and Alcamenes are allowed to have possessed. Phidias is thought more skillful at representing gods than men (*Phidias tamen dis quam hominibus effigendis melior artifex creditur*); in ivory (*ebore*) he would be far and away without a rival, even if he had produced nothing but the Athena at Athens (*Minervam Athenis*) and the Olympian Zeus at Elis (*Olympium in Elide Iovem*), the beauty of which is said to have added something to the traditional religious concept of the god (*cuius pulchritudo adiecisse aliquid etiam receptae religioni videtur*), so perfectly did the majesty of the work match its divine original (*adeo maiestas operis deum aequavit*).

[Quintilian, *The Orator's Education* XII.10.8]

96. RUPRECHT'S NOTE: The chapter in question offers a laudatory description of Smyrna and of the virtues of Ionian art in general. The passage Schelling has in mind is probably the same one he has discussed previously: "The image (ἄγαλμα) is like neither the Aeginetan, as they are called, nor yet the most ancient Attic images; it is absolutely Egyptian, if any statue ever were." (*Guide to Greece* VII.5.5)
97. RUPRECHT'S NOTE: The relevant passages are as follows:

> The residence of Daedalus with Minos at Knossus secured for the Cretans a reputation for the making of wooden images (ξοάνων) also, which lasted for a long period; . . . and about seven stades farther on is a sanctuary (ἱερὸν) of Artemis, surnamed Lady of the Lake, with an image (ἄγαλμα) made of ebony. The style (τρόπος) of the workmanship is what the Greeks call Aeginetan (Αἰγιναῖος καλούμενος). (*Guide to Greece* VIII.53.8 and 11)

98. RUPRECHT'S NOTE: The relevant passage is as follows:

> The road to Anticyra is at first up-hill. About two stades up the slope is a level place, and on the right of the road is a sanctuary (ἱερόν) of Artemis surnamed Dictynnaean, a goddess worshiped with great reverence by the citizens. The image is of Aeginetan workmanship (ἀγάλματι ἐργασία τέ ἐστιν Αἰγιναία), and made of black stone. (*Guide to Greece* X.36.5)

99. RUPRECHT'S NOTE: The extended discussion of this chronological dating may be found in Quatremère, *Le Jupiter Olympien*, 180–82.
100. RUPRECHT'S NOTE: Already by 1830, this identification had apparently been called into question. The first guide to the Glyptothek collection notes that these statues

belonged *either* to the pediments of the Temple to Athena described by Herodotus (*Histories* III.59), *or else* to the Temple of Panhellenic Zeus briefly mentioned by Pausanias (*Guide to Greece* II.30.4). Curiously, the Guide mentions a recently discovered inscription linking the finds to the Temple of Zeus (whereas subsequent excavation brought inscriptions to light clearly identifying the Temple as dedicated to Aphaia, see note 6).

See Leo von Klenze with Ludwig Schorn, *Beschreibung der Glyptothek Sr. Majestät des Königs Ludwig von Bayern* (München: J. G. Cotta'schen, 1830), 48.

101. RUPRECHT'S NOTE: The question of how many statues had been discovered by the four men who first "excavated" them at Aegina, not to mention how they should be assembled, proved to be a very difficult question to resolve; it hinged on matters of interpretive reconstruction, and thus on the complex type of "restoration" ventured by Thorvaldsen.

As I noted in the introduction, one of the first German language descriptions of these discoveries in the *Allgemeine Zeitung* (December 5, 1811) listed the number of statues as eighteen, not seventeen. Near the end of his life, Charles Cockerell recalled them to be "no less than sixteen" in *The Temples of Jupiter Panhellenius at Aegina and of Apollo Epicurius at Bassae near Phigalia in Arcadia* (London: John Weale, 1860), 51–52. The Museum guide published in 1830, the year in which the Glyptothek Museum opened to the public, described fifteen pedimental statues: five from the east pediment [Hercules, Laomedon, Telamon, a fallen warrior, and an advancing figure]; and ten from the west pediment [Minerva, Patroklus, Telamonian Ajax, Teucer, the Lesser Ajax, a wounded Greek, Hektor, Paris, Aeneas, and a wounded Trojan]); the remaining two female figures (Damia and Auxesia) were displayed separately, along with an akroterion, a sphinx, a Doric capital, twenty-nine fragments of the pediment and thirty-one fragments of statuary. See Leo von Klenze with Ludwig Schorn, *Beschreibung der Glyptothek*, 45–68.

Charles Cockerell suggested a reconstruction of the west pediment with eleven figures; Carl Haller von Hallerstein suggested a reconstruction of nine figures in the west and six in the east. Wagner, as we have seen, artistically imagined all fifteen figures in a single sketched pediment, though he explains that he envisioned the actual arrangement at the temple much as Haller had done (namely, with nine figures and six respectively). It is unclear how he might have imagined the arrangement of "thirty statues" in all—divided between fifteen in each pediment, perhaps. For a comparative view of these various sketched reconstructions, see Raimond Wünsche, *Kampfe um Troja: 200 Jahre Ägineten in München, Ausstellungskatalog* (München: Kunstverlag Josef Fink, 2011), 76, 83, 107–111, 120, and 124.

The discovery of so many indeterminate fragments, coupled with the discovery of many more sculptural finds in subsequent excavations at the Aegina site, significantly complicated interpretation of these groups. The current consensus view seems to be that we have remains from three distinct pedimental groups, rather than two, each comprised by ten figures (the current Glyptothek display imagines ten figures in each of the two temple pediments). Such an unusual circumstance raises new interpretive questions and challenges, all of this complicated further by significant differences in dating estimates for the construction of the Temple to Aphaia based on the distinctive stylistic features of the statues versus the apparent dating of the pottery fill in the temenos wall and foundations of the temple.

One theory suggests that we have remains from two different temples here: one pedimental group from an earlier temple that was destroyed by fire, and two pedimental groups from the later temple that replaced it. Another theory asserts that all three groups were produced at roughly the same time in a sculptural contest possibly funded by the Aeginetan share of spoils from the Persian Wars: the first- and second-prize submissions were placed in the temple pediments themselves, whereas the third-place submission was displayed at ground level under cover to the southeast of the temple proper, as a sort of amplification to the altar. A contrasting theory imagines that the two pedimental groups were produced at different times, the first around 510 BCE and the second around 480 BCE; for some reason, the elder of the two groups was later replaced. For a helpful summary of these theories, see Rene Frederiksen, "Aphaia in Aegina," *The Encyclopedia of Ancient History* (John Wiley & Sons, Inc., 2012) online version.

For analysis of the significant archaeological evidence for a Bronze Age sanctuary of some sort on the site (most of which was recovered only in 1976), and for the likelihood that the site was dedicated to a goddess, see Korinna Pilafidis-Williams, *The Sanctuary of Aphaia on Aigina in the Bronze Age* (München: Hirmer Verlag GmbH, 1998), esp. 1–4, 121–46.

An excellent summary of the evidence for dating the entire Aphaia temple complex to 480 BCE (if not later still) rather than 510 BCE (based on strictly archaeological rather than stylistic grounds), see David W. J. Gill, "The Temple of Aphaia on Aegina: The Date of the Reconstruction," *The Annual of the British School in Athens* 83 (1988): 169–77, and "The Temple of Aphaia on Aegina: Further Thoughts on the Date of the Reconstruction," *The Annual of the British School in Athens* 88 (1993): 173–81. The situation remains puzzling, to put it mildly.

102. RUPRECHT'S NOTE: The reconstruction of the original position of the Aeginetan pediments has been subject to continued revision since the publication of Wagner's *Report.* As I have noted, subsequent German excavations have supplied significant new evidence for the missing pieces to which Wagner alludes, as well as the floor slabs whose foot cuttings provide important additional evidence for the actual sculptural arrangement of the pediments.

For an early argument that the two pediments almost certainly contained symmetrically equal numbers of figures in both, see Duncan Mackenzie, "The East Pediment Sculptures of the Temple of Aphaia at Aegina," *Annual of the British School at Athens* XV (1908–1909): 274–307, esp. 306. For a summary of the current state of thinking about the arrangement of the two pediments, see Raimund Wünsche, *Kampfe um Troja: 200 Jahre Ägineten in München, Ausstellungskatalog*, "Deutung der Giebelgruppen," 205–221.

103. RUPRECHT'S NOTE: The reader is once again directed to Wagner's informative sketch reconstruction of the two pedimental groups (see image 22).

104. RUPRECHT'S NOTE: Two things are striking about this paragraph. First, Wagner almost casually refers to his own eyewitness observations at the Parthenon, when he was given his tour of the antiquities by Fauvel, the French consul. Second, Wagner seems as comfortable *equating* these Aeginetan and Athenian works of art as Schelling seems intent on emphasizing the *superiority* of the Aeginetan works from the standpoint of their naturalism.

105. RUPRECHT'S NOTE: It will be born in mind that this same subject provided the theme for Wagner's highly influential monumental canvas, completed in 1807, "Der Rat der Griechen vor Troja."

106. RUPRECHT'S SUPPLEMENT: The source for this is Pausanias's *Guide to Greece* V.25.10: "This is one of the many works of wise (σοφοῦ) Onatas/The Aeginetan, who was the son of Micon" (translation emended).

107. RUPRECHT'S NOTE: The passage is as follows:

> There are also offerings (ἀναθήματα) dedicated by the whole Achaean race (ἔθνους) in common; they represent those who, when Hector challenged any Greek to meet him in single combat, dared to cast lots to choose the champion. They stand, armed with spears and shields, near the great temple (ναοῦ τοῦ μεγάλου). Right opposite, on a second pedestal, is a figure of Nestor, who has thrown the lot of each into the helmet. The number of those casting lots to meet Hector is now only eight, for the ninth, the statue of Odysseus, they say that Nero carried to Rome, but Agamemnon's statue is the only one of the eight to have his name inscribed upon it; the writing is from right to left. (*Guide to Greece* V.25.8–9)

Pausanias does not give the name of the sculptor of this group here, if there were just one.

108. RUPRECHT'S NOTE: Wagner has slightly garbled the Greek text. While his summary of Pausanias's description is accurate and complete, they are identified by Pausanias as sculptures executed by Lycius, the son of Myron (ταῦτά ἐστιν ἔργα μὲν Λυκίου τοῦ Μύρωνος), not by Myron of Lykia. Pausanias also mentions that they were dedicated at Olympia by the city of Apollonia on the Ionian Sea, citing an inscription to that effect. (*Guide to Greece* V.22.2–3)

109. RUPRECHT'S NOTE: Pausanias's comment is worth quoting at greater length here:

> Herakles and Apollo are holding on to the tripod and are preparing to fight (ἐς μάχην) about it. Leto and Artemis are restraining Apollo's rage (τοῦ θυμοῦ), and Athena is restraining Herakles. This too is an offering (ἀνάθημα) of the Phocians, dedicated when Tellias of Elis led them against the Thessalians. Athena and Artemis were made by Chionis, the other statues (ἀγάλματα) are works shared by (ἐν κοινῷ) Diyllus and Amyclaeüs. They are said to be Corinthians. The Delphians say that when Herakles the son of Amphitryon came to the oracle, the prophetess (πρόμαντιν) Xenocleia refused to give a response on the ground that he was guilty of the murder of Iphitus. Whereupon Herakles took up the tripod and carried it out of the temple. Then the prophetess said:
>
> Then there was another Herakles, of Tiryns, not the Canopian.
>
> For before this the Egyptian Herakles had visited Delphi. On the occasion to which I refer the son of Amphitryon restored the tripod to Apollo, and was told by Xenocleia all he wished to know. The poets adopted the story, and sing about a fight (μάχην) between Herakles and Apollo for a tripod. (*Guide to Greece* X.13.7–8, translation emended)

110. RUPRECHT'S SUPPLEMENT: The text by Charles R. Cockerell, *La celebrattissimi statue rappresentati la favola di Niobe* (n.p., 1816) consists of a single incised print page (58.5cm × 95cm) with Cockerell's imaginative reconstruction of the pedimental group

which was discovered in 1583 and was then housed in the Villa Medici in Florence, as well as a reconstruction of the temple itself. The narrative analysis to which Wagner refers, composed in Italian, cites the main sources that Wagner and Schelling also use (Pausanias, Diodorus Siculus, and Pliny), in addition to more recent discoveries of pedimental groups from the Parthenon and Theseion in Athens, the Temple of Zeus at Olympia, as well as two Aeginetan sites ("*Nei templi di Minerva, e di Giove Panellenio in Egina*"), to assist in his reconstruction of the Niobe pediment with its hypothetical arrangement of thirteen (not fourteen) separate statues. Cockerell was living in Florence or Rome at the time of this publication, which was likely circulated privately. I have examined a copy of this text from the Vatican Library's Cicognara collection [XII.M-85]; the aesthetic effect of the print is quite striking.

111. RUPRECHT'S NOTE: This is a somewhat strange-sounding claim. A contemporary observer is most struck by the kneeling figure of Herakles, with the identifying mark of his lion's head helmet. At the time of Wagner's writing, this was apparently not taken as a given, though there was near unanimity concerning the identity of the "Phrygian archer" as Paris, ever since the French consul in Athens, Fauvel, first proposed it.

112. RUPRECHT'S SUPPLEMENT: Pausanias's discussion is brief and suggestive:

> A drought (αὐχμὸς) had for some time afflicted Greece, and the god sent no rain either beyond the Isthmus or in the Peloponnesus, until at last they sent envoys to Delphi to ask what was the cause (τὸ αἴτιον) and to beg for deliverance from the evil (λύσιν τοῦ κακοῦ). The Pythian priestess bade them to propitiate Zeus, saying that he would not listen to them unless the one to supplicate him were Aiakos. And so envoys came with a request to Aiakos from each city. By sacrifice and prayer (θύσας καὶ εὐξάμενος) to Panhellenic Zeus, he caused rain to fall upon the earth, and the Aeginetans made these likenesses (εἰκόνας) of those who came to him. Within the enclosure (τοῦ περιβόλου) are olive trees that have grown there from of old, and there is an altar (βωμός) that is raised only slightly above the ground. That this altar is also the tomb (μνῆμα) of Aiakos is told as a holy secret (ἐν ἀπορρήτῳ). (*Guide to Greece* II.29.7–8, translation emended)

The story as recounted by Isocrates in the *Evagoras* is as follows:

> In the first place Aiakos, son (ἔκγονος) of Zeus and ancestor (πρόγονος) of the family of the Teuceridae, was so distinguished that when a drought (αὐχμῶν) visited the Greeks and many persons had perished, and when the magnitude (μέγεθος) of the calamity had exceeded all bounds, the leaders of the cities came as suppliants to him; for they thought that, by reason of his kinship (συγγενείας) with Zeus and his piety (εὐσεβείας), they would most quickly obtain from him the god's relief from the evils (κακῶν) that afflicted them. Having gained their desire, they were saved and built in Aegina a temple (ἱερὸν) to be shared by all the Greeks (κοινὸν τῶν Ἑλλήνων) on the very spot where he had offered his prayer. During his entire stay among men he ever enjoyed the finest and most glorious reputation, and after his departure from life it is said that he sits by the side of Pluto and Kore and enjoys the very highest honors (μεγίστας τιμᾶς).

[*Isocrates*, in three volumes, Larue van Hook, trans. (Cambridge, MA: Loeb Classical Library of Harvard University Press, 1954), III: 10–13, translation emended]

Pausanias has a second drought-related story of equal interest:

> The Panhellenic Mount, except for the sanctuary of Zeus (Διὸς τὸ ἱερόν), had nothing else worthy of mention. This sanctuary (ἱερόν), they say, was made by Aiakos for Zeus. The story of Auxesia and Damia, how the god did not send rain to the Epidaurians, how in obedience to an oracle (ἐκ μαντείας) they had these wooden images (τὰ ξόανα) made of olive wood that they received from the Athenians, how the Epidaurians left off paying to the Athenians what they had agreed to pay, on the ground that the Aeginetans had the images (τὰ ἀγάλματα), and how the Athenians perished who crossed over to Aegina to fetch them—all this, since Herodotus has described it accurately and in great detail, I have no intention of relating, because the story has been well told already; but I will add that I saw the images (τὰ ἀγάλματα), and sacrificed to them (ἔθυσά σφισι) in the same way as is customary to sacrifice at Eleusis. (*Guide to Greece* II.30.4, translation emended)

Herodotus's account, which he describes as "the beginning of the long-standing animosity between Athens and Aegina," is as follows. The citizens of Epidaurus consulted the Delphic oracle in order to deal with their lands' sterility. They were directed to set up images of Damia and Auxesia and to make them of olive wood, rather than bronze or marble. They commissioned olive wood from Athens since it was deemed holiest, and agreed to pay an annual sacred tithe to the city thereafter. The island of Aegina was at that time subject to Epidaurus, but after building a large navy the island revolted from the city's control, stole the statues and brought them to their island. The city of Epidaurus ceased its annual payments to Athens, the Athenians protested, and upon hearing what had been done, demanded of the Aeginetans that they restore the statues to Epidaurus; the Aeginetans refused. At this point the accounts of the Athenians and Aeginetans vary, but this much is agreed. The Athenians sent forces to the island to recoup the statues and were slaughtered; only one man returned to Athens alive to report the loss. Strangely, Herodotus then tells us that the widows of the slain soldiers, resenting his lone survival, stabbed him to death with their brooches, resulting in a law limiting the size of Athenian brooch pins and mandating a change in female dress from the Doric to the Ionian/Carian style. (*Histories* V.82–88)

It is interesting that, in the original layout of the Glyoptothek Museum in 1830, the half-lifesize female figures were identified as Damia and Auxesia; see Leo von Klenze with Ludwig Schorn, *Beschreibung der Glyptothek,* 60–61.

113. RUPRECHT'S NOTE: This hitherto worthy assumption was abandoned when further German excavation at the temple under Adolf Furtwängler, brought inscriptions to light that identified the temple as Aphaia's. The discovery of the pedimental statue base also resulted in significant revision of the assumed relation between the various sculptural figures.

See Adolf Furtwängler, *Aegina: Das Heiligtum der Aphaia* (München: Verlag de K. B. Akademie der Wissenschaften, 1906), Volume 1, 1–9, 316–41, 366–69.

114. RUPRECHT'S NOTE: This conjecture by Wagner is a fascinating one. Contemporary scholars are more inclined to see the theme of these pedimental sculptural groups—installed in a temple dedicated to a local goddess, not to Zeus—as the two generational campaign of assembled Greeks against Troy. The first was in the generation of Telamon and Peleus and Herakles (who is now taken to be one of the kneeling archers); the second was the generation of their sons, Ajax and Achilles (and, most likely, the Greek archer Teucer, another blood relation to Aiakos).

For a recent summary of the history of interpretation of the two pedimental groups and the best contemporary guesses (with all due deference to Wagner's initial proposals), see Raimond Wünsche, *Kampfe um Troja: 200 Jahre Ägineten in München, Ausstellungskatalog*, "Deutung der Giebelgruppen," 205–221.

115. RUPRECHT'S SUPPLEMENT: What Schelling has in mind in the first citation is not immediately apparent, and in any case, neither Thucydides nor Herodotus are discussing the Battle of Salamis in these passages. Thucydides, *Peloponnesian War* VI.93, reports on developments in Sparta, where Alcibiades convinced the Spartan Assembly to assist the Syracusans against the Athenian invasion of Sicily, while at the same time the Athenian generals in Sicily sent a trireme back to Athens with a request for more "money and horses" (the Greek text actually reads ἐπί τε χρήματα καὶ ἱππέας). Apart from the general necessity to transport items between islands by boat, it is unclear what Schelling's interest in this passage might be.

Herodotus, *Histories* V.80, describes the fascinating way in which the citizens of Thebes became convinced that a highly ambiguous oracle was intended to direct them to solicit Aeginetan support in their conflict with Athens.

> This was how they thought it over, and then someone understood and said, "I think I understand what the oracle (τὸ μαντήιον) wants to say to us. The story is that Asopus had two daughters, Thebe and Aegina. They were sisters, and I think that the god is telling us to beg the Aeginetans to help us take vengeance." There did not seem to be any better opinion (ἀμείνων γνώμη) than this put forward, and so they at once made their request of the Aeginetans, begging them to help them according to the terms of the oracle, since "they were our nearest." In response to this request, the Aeginetans said they were sending the Aiakidoi (τοὺς Αἰακίδας) to help them. [Herodotus, *The Histories*, David Grene, trans. (The University of Chicago Press, 1987), 389–90]

This ambiguous reference to the Aeginetans' consent in sending the "Aiakidoi," or "sons of Aiakos," as a form of assistance is the central interpretive challenge this passage presents. The question turns on whether images of the Aiakidoi or their actual ashes were sent.

Petrus Wesseling (1692–1764) was a notable philologist and the author of the seven-volume *Herodoti Musae, Sive Historiarum* (Argentorati et Parisiis: apud Treuttel et Würtz, 1816); a copy from the Princeton University Library is available online at http://catalogue/hathitrust.org/api/volumes/oclc/4373878.html.

Wesseling's notes to Herodotus V.80 focus on the terms μαντήιον (oracle) and Αἰακίδας, identifying the ambiguous latter term as referring to *images* of "the sons of Aiakos" (at Volume VII, 84):

10. τοὺς Αἰακίδας συμπέμπειν ἔφασαν) Etsi haec priscae superstitionis pars in densa sit caligine, συμπείθειν *Med.* et *Ask.*, docte a celeb. Viro expositum, recepto non antepono. Spartanorum Locrensibus responsum apud *Zenobium*, de quo superius, [And. Ad c. 75, 12] τοὺς δὲ Διοσκούρους αὐτοὺς ἐπιπέμψουσιν, stat contra istos Codices: tum, quod continuo subsequitur, τοὺς μὲν Αἰακίδας σφι ἀπεδίδοσαν, eosdem, quo tandem cunque modo, accepisse innuit Thebanos. Accedat *Philostrati* illud, Heroic. lib. XIX. p.743. ἐπειδὴ ναῦς ἐς Σαλαμῖνα ἐξ Αἰγίνης ἔπλευσεν, ἄγουσα ἐπὶ συμμαχίᾳ τοῦ ʼΕλληνικοῦ τὸν τῶν Αἰακιδῶν οἶκον. Advexit itaque ea navis suppetias Graecis *Aeacidas*. Atque hoc est, quod lib. VIII, 64. perscribitur, missam tum fuisse navem ἐπὶ Αἰακὸν και [sic] τοὸς ἄλλους Αἰακίδας in Aeginam, quam reducem dabit c. 84. Hoc amplius; Locri Italiotae Aiacem, Oilei F., impetrarunt ab Opuntiis apud *Pausaniam* lib. III. 19. simili consilio; cui quidem cum in instructa acie χώρην κενὴν, *vacuum locum*, Locri reliquerint, teste *Conone* Narrat. XVIII. utique probabile accidit, arcessitos hos supplicationibus Heroas fuisse et in speciem abductos, ut omen praelio et spem praesidii praeberent. *Plutarchus* certe pugna Salaminia Aeacidas παρακεκλημένους εὐχαῖς πρὸ τῆς μάχης ἐπὶ τὴν βοήθειαν in Themist. p. 119. E. perhibit, propositis auctoritatem concilians. Hinc ἐπεκαλέοντο Αἴαντα τὸν Τελαμῶνος lib. VIII. 64. et ἐπίκλητοι Tyndaridae supra c. 75 h.e. σύμμαχοι, *Hesychio* interprete.

I am grateful to Michael B. Lippman of the University of Nebraska for helping me make sense of this very difficult passage, made more difficult by non-standardized abbreviations and dated language; an English summary is as follows:

> There is a manuscript variant in this passage from Herodotus, which replaces συμπέμπειν with συμπείθειν. This would alter the meaning of the passage, from "they said they were sending the Aiakidoi" to "they said they persuaded the Aiakidoi"; the idea appears to be that Schelling, by wondering exclusively whether the Aeginetans possessed the ashes or actual images of the Aiakidoi, ignores a third possibility—namely, that the Aiakidoi came on their own when bidden and appeared in the skies over Salamis. Despite a prominent contemporary scholar's preference for this reading, Wesseling rejects it, and Schelling appears to concur. Wesseling also imagines them to have been actual statues, citing a great many ancient sources, some of them obscure, to bolster this reading. "Although this part of an ancient superstition [*superstitionis*] is lost in the haze of time," Wesseling concludes, "and while we may not know exactly what practices were alluded to here, it was a common enough practice to solicit the help of ancient heroes prior to battle. That is clearly what was happening here, as many passages attest, and as Philostratus makes clearest, by saying (then the ship sailed from Aegina to Salamis, bearing the house of Aiakos [τὸν τῶν Αἰακιδῶν οἶκον] to the Greek allies."

Wesseling's Latin translation of the passage from Herodotus (at II, 476–77) is as follows:

> Ita dum hi inter se disceptant, postremo aliquis, re audita, ait: *Ego mihi videor intelligere quid velit oraculum. Asopi dicuntur filiae fuisse Thebe et Aegina: hae*

> *quum sint sorores, puto iubere nos Deum ab Aeginetis auxilia petere.* Et Thebani, quum nulla ex sententiis, quae dicebantur, hac potior esse videratur, protinus ad Aeginetas miserunt, ex oraculi mandato auxilia ab illis petentes, ut qui sibi essent proximi. Petentibus Aeginetae tradentes Aeacidaru imagines, responderunt, *se eis Aeacidas auxilio mittere.*

116. RUPRECHT'S NOTE: Schelling is simply paraphrasing Pausanias here, as we may recall:

> . . . in the most conspicuous part of the city what is called the shrine to Aiakos (τὸ Αἰάκειον καλούμενον), a quadrangular enclosure (περίβολος) of white marble. Wrought in relief at the entrance are the envoys whom the Greeks once dispatched to Aiakos. . . . Within the enclosure (τοῦ περιβόλου δὲ ἐντός) are olive trees that were planted long ago and an altar (βωμός) that is raised only slightly above the ground. That this altar is also the tomb (μνῆμα) of Aiakos is reported in secret (ἐν ἀπορρήτῳ). (*Guide to Greece* II.29.6–8)

117. RUPRECHT'S NOTE: Pausanias's description of the Treasuries at Olympia appears in book VI, chapter 19 (not chapter 9). In the Sicyonian treasury he reports seeing the following:

> There is also a bronze-plated shield, adorned with paintings on the inside (γραφῇ τὰ ἐντὸς πεποικιλμένη), and along with the shield are a helmet and greaves. An inscription on the armor says that they were dedicated by the Myanians as first-fruits to Zeus. Various conjectures have been made as to who these Myanians were. (*Guide to Greece* VI.19.4)

118. RUPRECHT'S SUPPLEMENT: A note on *Lawsonia inermis* as a hair-coloring agent in Greece appears at the back of Wagner's Greek *Reisebuch*, in a concluding eleven-page section of scattered notes, addresses, and observed details such as this. It is the first such entry.
119. RUPRECHT'S SUPPLEMENT: Schelling has here identified one of Quatremère's most consistent and recurrent concerns: namely, that the three major plastic arts be more fully integrated, and that state sponsorship is a necessary precondition for such art to maintain its public place and so most effectively to play its important social, cultural, and spiritual roles. It is also worth recalling that the Glyptothek Museum, which King Ludwig commissioned in Munich for the express purpose of housing this new collection, was envisioned as precisely such a *Gesamtkunstwerk*, creating a unified architectural, painterly, and sculptural effect. Moreover, the topic chosen for the Glyptothek's own pedimental decoration was a unified depiction of all the visual arts, including one image of a painter decorating a statue. It is noteworthy, the way in which so many of these early modern museums imitated and recalled classical temples. A *mouseion*, after all, is literally a "shrine to the Muse." I discuss this further in the translator's afterword and appendix 5.
120. RUPRECHT'S NOTE: The reference here is to the school, or atelier, of Pheidias. Another major aspect of Quatremère's overall purpose in *Le Jupiter Olympien* was to

establish the existence and the preeminence of this school (211–312), whose existence and stature had first been suggested by Winckelmann.

121. RUPRECHT'S NOTE: It is striking here how comfortable Wagner appears to be in asserting the supremacy of the Parthenon and the Elgin Marbles, in contrast to Schelling's suggestive elevation of the superior type of Aeginetan "naturalism" he perceived in these novel pieces bound now for Munich. We should bear in mind that Wagner observed the Athenian Akropolis firsthand, when he was given a tour by the French consul Fauvel, and it left a deep impression on him. By contrast, he never saw the mountaintop temple at Aegina that housed the artworks to which he devoted so much care.

122. RUPRECHT'S NOTE: Pausanias's remarkable story is as follows:

> Hera, they say, was for some reason or other angry with Zeus, and had retreated to Euboea. Zeus, failing to make her change her mind, visited Cithaeron, at that time despot in Plataea, who surpassed all men for cleverness (σοφίαν). So he ordered Zeus to make an image of wood (ἄγαλμα ξύλου), and to carry it, wrapped up, in a bullock wagon, and to say that he was celebrating his marriage with Plataea, the daughter of Asopus. So Zeus followed the advice of Cithaeron. Hera heard the news at once, and at once appeared on the scene. But when she came near the wagon and tore away the dress from the statue (τοῦ ἀγάλματος), she was pleased at the deceit, on finding it a wooden image (ξόανον) and not a bride, and was reconciled to Zeus. To commemorate this reconciliation they celebrate a festival (ἑορτὴν) called Daedala, because the men of old gave the name of *daedala* (δαίδαλα) to wooden images (ξόανα). (*Guide to Greece* IX.3.1–2)

123. RUPRECHT'S NOTE: This remark appears to be an anticipation of the construction and eventual opening of the Glyptothek Museum in Munich. Ludwig had already announced a competition among architects for the design of a museum specifically intended to house the Aegina collection after its restoration by Thorvaldsen and its publication by Wagner and Schelling. One senses the pieces slowly falling into place. And we can see how crucial it was to Wagner's way of seeing and thinking, this ability to *walk around* the statues, and so to see them from all angles.

124. RUPRECHT'S NOTE: Winckelmann makes this observation near the beginning of part 2:

> Wenn man auf das Alter der Aeginitischen Schule von dem berühmten Smilis, aus dieser Insel, schließen dürfte, so würde sie ihre Stiftung von den Zeiten des Dädalus herführen. Daß sich aber schon in ganz alten Zeiten eine Schule der Kunst in dieser Insel angefangen habe, bezeugen die Nachrichten von so vielen alten Statuen in Griechenland, die im Aeginetischen Stil gearbeitet waren. Ein gewisser Aeginetischer Bildhauer ist nicht dem Namen nach, sondern durch die Benennung des Aeginetischen Bildes bekannt. Die Einwohner dieser Insel, welche Dorier waren, trieben großen Handel und Schiffarth, wodurch sich die Künste daselbst empor brachten; so daß sogar ihre Gefäße von gebrannter Erde gesucht und verschicket wurden, die vermuthlich gemalt waren; sie waren mit einem wilden Widder gemerket. Pausanias redet von der Schiffarth derselben

> schon in den ältesten Zeiten, und sie waren den Atheniensern zur See überlegen, welche so, wie jene, vor dem Persischen Kriege nur Schiffe von funfzig Rudern und ohne Verdeck hatten. Die Eifersucht zwischen ihnen brach endlich in einen Krieg aus, welcher beygelegt war, da Xerxes nach Griechenland kam. Aegina, welche vielen Antheil an dem Siege des Themistocles über die Perser hatte, zog viele Vortheile aus demselben: denn die reiche Persische Beute wurde dahin gebracht und verkauft, wodurch diese Insel, wie Herodotus meldet, zu großen Reichtum gelangte. In diesem Flor erhielt sich diese Insel bis zur acht und achtzigsten Olympias, da die Einwohner von den Atheniensern, weil es jene mit den Lacedämoniern gehalten, verjaget wurden. Die Athenienser besetzten diese Insel mit ihren Colonien, und die Aegineter begaben sich nach Thyräa in der Argolischen Landschaft. Sie kamen zwar von neuem zum Besitze ihres Vaterlandes, konnten aber nicht zur ehmaligen Macht wieder gelangen. (I take this from the 2002 critical edition of Winckelmann's *Geschichte der Kunst des Alterthums*, 610–613.)

An English translation is as follows:

> If we could deduce the age of the School of Aegina from the famous Smilis who came from this island, we would conclude that it was founded in the time of Daedalus. In any event, the reports of so many ancient statues in Greece fashioned in the Aeginetan style bear witness to a School of Art existing on this island even in very ancient times. A certain Aeginetan sculptor is known, not by his name, but by the designation "Aeginetan Image-maker." The inhabitants of this island, who were Dorian, carried on extensive commerce and shipping, such that the arts flourished there. Pausanias speaks of their shipping as existing even in earliest times, and at sea the Aeginetans were superior to the Athenians, who, like the Aeginetans, had only fifty-oared vessels without decks prior to the Persian Wars. The jealousy between the states of Athens and Aegina eventually erupted in war, which halted when Xerxes invaded Greece. Aegina, which contributed much to the victory of Themistocles over the Persians, drew many advantages from this: the rich spoils from the Persians were brought to Aegina and sold there, whereby this island acquired great wealth, as Herodotus relates. The island continued to prosper until the 88th Olympiad, when its inhabitants were banished by the Athenians because they had sided with the Lacedaemonians. The Athenians occupied the island with their colonies, and the Aeginetans emigrated to Thyrea in the Argolid. Later they regained possession of their native land, but they never again achieved their former power. (*History of the Art of Antiquity*, 301–302, translation emended)

The following sentence was added to the second (1767) edition of Winckelmann's text:

> Es mögen diejenigen, die Münzen von Aegina gesehen haben, deren Gepräge auf der einen Seite den Kopf der Pallas, und auf der andern den Dreyzack des Neptunus hatten, urtheilen, ob man in der Zeichnung gedachten Kopfs einen besonderen Stil der Kunst erkennen könne.

> Those who have seen the coins of Aegina, which boast the head of Pallas on one side and the trident of Neptune on the other, may judge whether one may discern a specific style of art in the rendering of these heads.

125. RUPRECHT'S NOTE: The German text, as Schelling quotes and italicizes it, reads as follows:

> Schulen lassen sich nicht eher denken, als bis die Kunst zu einer gewissen Vollkommenheit gelangt ist, bis die Meister nach festen Grundsätzen, und zwar *jeder nach seinen eigenen*, zu arbeiten anfangen.

The quotation comes from Lessing's "Notes on Winckelmann's History of the Art of Antiquity" (*Anmerkungen zu Winckelmanns Geschichte der Kunst des Altherthums*), which appears in Gotthold Ephraim Lessing, *Vermischte Schriften* (Berlin: In der Vossischen Buchhandlung, 1792), Volume 10, 252–53, and appears to have been significantly emended by Schelling. The full quotation (with the missing passages included in brackets) is as follows:

> [Denn] Schulen [in dem beygebrachten Verstande] lassen sich [überhaupt] nicht eher denken, als bis die Kunst zu einer gewissen Vollkommenheit gelangt ist, bis die Meister nach festen Grundsätzen, und zwar Jeder nach seinen eigenen, zu arbeiten anfangen. [Werke vor dieser Zeit hießen also bey den Griechen äginetische, oder attischer, oder ägyptische Werke; wie aus der Stelle des Pausanias (L. VII. p. 533) erhellt, die der lateinischer Uebersetzer aber nicht verstanden zu haben scheint.]

An English translation is as follows:

> We cannot think of Schools in the general understanding of the term until art attains a certain degree of perfection, that is, until the masters begin to work according to established principles and each according to his own. Works prior to this period were referred to as Aeginetan, or Attic, or Egyptian by the Greeks, as the passage from Pausanias establishes (B. VII, page 533), a passage which the Latin translator appears not to have understood.

126. RUPRECHT'S NOTE: The German text, as Schelling quotes it, reads as follows:

> durch die Benennung des äginetischen Styls nur gewisse alte Werke unterschieden habe, die lang [sic] vor der Stiftung aller Schulen gemacht worden.

The paragraph in its entirety is relevant to Schelling's argument and reads as follows (*Vermischte Schriften* X, 252):

> W. glaubt S. 321., daß sich schon in ganz alten Zeiten eine Schule der Kunst auf der Insel Aegina angefangen habe, wegen der Nachrichten von so vielen alten Statuen in Griechenland, im äginetische Style gearbeteitet. Es ist wahr,

> Pausanias gedenkt αιγινητικων ἐργων, er gedenkt eines Styls, ὁ αιγινητικος καλουμενος ὑπο ' Ελληνων. Aber dem ungeachtet kann man nicht berechtigt seyn, hieraus eine besondere Schule zu machen, wenn man nicht das Zeugniß des Plinius ganz umstoßen will. Man muß vielmehr den Pausanias mit dem Plinius zu vergleichen suchen: welches am Besten geschehen kann, wenn man annimmt, daß man durch die Benennung des äginetischen Styls nur gewisse alte Werke unterschieden habe, die lange vor der Stiftung aller Schulen gemacht worden.

And an English translation is as follows:

> W[inckelmann] believes (page 321) that a School of Art had already been established on the island of Aegina in the most ancient times, on account of the numerous descriptions throughout Greece of ancient statues worked in the Aeginetan style. It is true that Pausanias understood *aiginetikwn ergwn* ("Aiginetan works"), and he understood *ho aiginetikos kaloumenos hypo Hellenwn* ("the Aeginetan so-called by the Greeks") to refer to a style. But one is not justified in turning this vague term into the name of a specific School, if one does not wish to contradict the testimony of Pliny completely. One must rather seek to harmonize Pausanias with Pliny: and this is best accomplished when one accepts that the naming of an Aeginetan style was used simply to distinguish certain ancient works which had been made long before the establishment of any Schools.

127. RUPRECHT'S NOTE: We will recall the relevant phrasing:

> The image (ἄγαλμα) is neither like the so-called Aeginetan (τοῖς καλουμένοις Αἰγιναίοις), nor yet the most ancient (ἀρχαιοτάτοις) Attic images; it is precisely Egyptian (ἀκριβῶς ἐστιν Αἰγύπτιον), if ever there was such a thing. (*Guide to Greece* VII.5.5)

This passage does not refer to "schools," of course, but seems to assume a fairly clear and concise differentiation in sculptural styles, however much they may overlap or bleed into one another. The essential question Schelling is pursuing is whether we should associate schools of art with people ("masters") or with places (like Aegina).

This was also a central concern for Quatremère de Quincy in *Le Jupiter Olympien*. His solution was essentially to overcome the distinction, utilizing the modern example of Raphael, about whom he also wrote a book: *Histoire de la vie et des ouvrages Raphaël*, 2 Edition (Paris: Adrien le Clere et C.ie Imprimeurs-Libraires, Quai des Augustins, no. 35, 1833); the book was translated by William Hazlitt in *Lives of the Italian Painters* (London: David Bogue, Fleet Street, 1846), 191–461. Quatremère saw Raphael both as the product of a local Tuscan artistic tradition and as the founder of a school, or atelier. For Quatremère, then, one can (and should) speak of both an Aeginetan and a Pheidian school in classical antiquity.

128. RUPRECHT'S NOTE: This claim is perplexing. As noted above, Lessing's own words suggest his clear understanding of the confusion between the Greek and Latin versions of this passage:

Works prior to this period were referred to as Aeginetan, or Attic, or Egyptian by the Greeks, as the position of Pausanias establishes (B. VII, page 533), *a passage which the Latin translator appears not to have understood* (italics mine).

129. RUPRECHT'S NOTE: The German text as Schelling quotes it is this:

> Alle neueren Entdeckungen alter Denkmale, alle angestellten Vergleichungen haben den Forschern bis jetzt noch immer nocht zur genauen Kenntniß von dem eigentlichen Unterschiede der Kunstschulen verholfen. Daß aber, in Werken der Malerey wie der Plastik, ein solcher Unterschied statt gefunden, und von geübten Augen wahrzunehmen gewesen, ist vermöge der nachrichten, *und vermöge der strengen Sonderung in Sitten, Gebräuchen, Sprache und Lebensart-zwischen dem ionischen und dorischen Stamme* keinem Zweifel unterworfen.

I have been unable to locate this note from the Weimar edition of Winckelmann's *Art History*.

130. RUPRECHT'S NOTE: The claim is this:

> In Aegina, as you go toward the mountain of Zeus, God of all the Greeks, you reach a sanctuary of Aphaia (' Αφαίας ἱερόν), in whose honour Pindar composed an ode for the Aeginetans. (*Guide to Greece* II.30.3)

It is ironic to note that this temple for Aphaia was actually the one from which these statues had been removed.

131. RUPRECHT'S NOTE: Pindar's Fifth Nemean Ode was commissioned to celebrate the victory of Pytheas of Aegina, in the Youths' Pankration in 485 or 483 BCE. It begins thus:

> I am not a sculptor (ἀνδριαντοποιός) who fashions motionless
> statues that stand still on their bases.
> Rather, on board every ship
> and boat, my sweet song (γλυκεῖ ' ἰοιδά),
> sails forth from Aegina with the news that
> Lampon's son, Pytheas, was awarded
> the crown at Nemea for the Pankration. . . .

Pindar, in two volumes, William H. Race, trans. (Cambridge, MA: Loeb Classical Library of Harvard University Press, 1997), II: 46–47. Note that, in contrasting motionless statues to moving song, Pindar uses a word that suggests a similarity between the images (*andrianta*) and the men (*andros*) they are intended to represent. I develop the importance of this term in *Classics at the Dawn of the Museum Era*, 1–2.

132. RUPRECHT'S NOTE: This is taken from Pausanias's description of the Temple of Zeus at Olympia: "The temple is in the Doric style (τοῦ ναοῦ δὲ Δώριος μὲν ἐστιν ἡ ἐργασία), with a peristyle all around it" (*Guide to Greece* V.10.3).

133. RUPRECHT'S NOTE: This is taken from Pausanias's description of the Temple of Hera inside the Altis at Olympia: "The temple is in the Doric style (ἐργασία μὲν δή ἐστι τοῦ ναοῦ Δώριος), with columns (κίονες) placed all around it" (*Guide to Greece* V.16.1).

134. RUPRECHT'S NOTE: The passage appears in Strabo's description of the religious architecture of Ephesus, but there are manuscript variations, some bearing the phrase Σκόπα ἔργα (works of Skopas) and others the phrase σκολιὰ ἔργα (crooked or twisted works, an odd term whose meaning Winckelmann and Schelling both were attempting to discern); one manuscript actually combines the two terms (σχολιὰ σκόπ ' ἔργα):

> There are several temples (πλειόνων ναῶν) in the place, some ancient (ἀρχαίων) and some built later (ὕστερον); in the ancient temples there are ancient wooden images (ἀρχαῖά ἐστι ξόανα), whereas in the newer temples there are works of Skopas/twisted works. (XIV.1.20)

The Geography of Strabo, H. L. Jones, trans. (Cambridge, MA: Loeb Classical Library of Harvard University Press, 1929), VI, 222–23. Jones takes the phrase to be Σκόπα ἔργα, "works of Scopas."

135. RUPRECHT'S NOTE: I have been unable to locate this reference in the first edition of Winckelmann's *Art History*. According to the pagination available in the critical edition of Winckelmann's *Art History* (*Geschichte der Kunst des Alterthums*, 148), this corresponds to his discussion of Etruscan female deities, but nothing in that discussion refers to the apparent rigidity of the figures.

136. RUPRECHT'S NOTE: Winckelmann's comment on part 1, chapter 1 is as follows:

> . . . un dieses war der Stil, den die angeführten Scribenten mit dem Hetrurischen vergleichen, und welcher, wie es scheinet, der Aeginetischen Schule eigen blieb: denn die Künstler dieser Insel, welche von Doriern bewohnet war, scheinen bey dem ältesten Stil am längsten geblieben zu seyn. Das Uebertriebene im Stande und der Handlung der Figuren, die die allerälteste Form verlassen hatten, scheinet Strabo durch das Wort Σκολιος, verdrehet, anzuzeigen. Denn wenn er berichtet, daß zu Ephesus viele Tempel so wohl aus der ältesten als folgenden Zeit gewesen, und daß in jenen sehr alte Statuen von Holze (αρχαια ξοανα) gestanden, in den andern Tempeln aber Σκολια εργα, hat dieser Scribent vermuthlich hier nicht sagen wollen, daß die Statuen der Tempel, die nach der ältesten Zeit erbauet worden, schlecht und tadelhaft gewesen, wie es Casaubonus verstanden, welcher Σκολιος mit *pravus* übersetzet; dieses hätte Strabo vielmehr von den ältesten Bildern sagen sollen.
>
> Das Gegentheil von Σκολιος scheinet das Wort Ορθος anzudeuten, welches wo es von Statuen gebrauchet wird, wie beym Pausanias von einer Statue des Jupiters von der Hand des Lysippus durch die Uebersetzer von einem geraden Stande erkläret wird, da es vielmehr eine Figur anzeigen soll, die einen ruhigen Stand ohne Action hat. (*Geschichte der Kunst des Alterthums*, 17–19).

An English translation is as follows (it does not appear in the Potts edition with the Mallgrave translation, since that translation is of the first edition of Winckelmann's 1764 opus, not the much-expanded 1767 edition):

> . . . and this was the style which the aforementioned writer associated with the Etruscan style and which, it appears, remained the style of the Aegineten School,

since the artists of this island, who were Dorian, appear to have maintained the most ancient style for the longest period of time. The exaggerated postures and movements of those figures which had departed from the most ancient form, Strabo intended to denote with the word Σκολιος. For when he reports that there were many temples in Ephesus from the most ancient as well as later times, and that they all contained ancient wooden statues (αρχαια ξοανα), whereas other temples held Σκολια εργα, then this scholar probably did not want to say that the statues in the temples that were built after the oldest ones were bad or ugly, as Casaubon understood the matter when he translated Σκολιος as *pravus*. Strabo should rather have said this about the very oldest works.

The opposite of Σκολιος appears to be the word Ορθος, which was used in relation to statues such as when Pausanias describes a statue of Jupiter from the hand of Lysippus, and which the translator explains as denoting a figure with rigid posture, when in fact it is far more likely that it referred to a figure in a calm state without motion.

137. RUPRECHT'S NOTE: Jones's translation of this passage is somewhat different:

> On the same coast, slightly above the sea, is also Ortygia, which is a magnificent grove of all kind of trees, of the cypress most of all. It is traversed by the Cenchrius River, where Leto is said to have bathed herself after her travail (μετὰ τὰς ὠδῖνας). For here is the mythical scene of the birth (λοχείαν), and of the nurse Ortygia, and of the holy place (ἄδυτον) where the birth (λοχεία) took place, and of the olive tree near by, where the goddess is said first of all to have taken a rest after she was relieved from her travails (τῶν ὠδίνων). Above the grove lies Mt. Solmissus, where, it is said, the Kouretes stationed themselves, and with the din of their arms (τῷ ψόφῳ τῶν ὅπλων) frightened Hera out of her wits when she was jealously spying on Leto, and they helped Leto to conceal the birth (λοχείαν) of her children. There are several temples in the place, some ancient and others built in later times; and in the ancient temples are many ancient wooden images, but in those of later times there are works of Scopas [or "twisted works"]: for example, Leto holding a sceptre and Ortygia standing beside her with a child in each arm. (*The Geography of Strabo* XIV.1.20)

138. RUPRECHT'S NOTE: The reference is to Thomas Tyrwhitt (1730–1786) a classical scholar more famous for his five-volume critical edition of Chaucer's *Canterbury Tales*. Tyrwhitt's emendation here has more plausibility than Schelling acknowledges, and has been accepted by some later commentators, including the Loeb translator.
139. RUPRECHT'S NOTE: The quote is as follows: "Pythagoras of Rhegium was the first sculptor to show the sinews and veins (*nervos et venas*), and to represent the hair more carefully (*capillumque diligentius*)" (*Natural History* XXXIV.19.59). Pliny also reports that this same Pythagoras outdid Myron with his depiction of a Pankratiast.
140. RUPRECHT'S NOTE: Pliny's observation is as follows:

> Myron is the first (*primus*) sculptor who appears to have enlarged the scope of realism (*multiplicasse veritatem videtur*), being more prolific in his art

(*numerosior in arte*) than Polycleitus and being more careful in his proportions (*in symmetria diligentior*). Yet he himself so far as surface configuration goes attained great finish, but he does not seem to have given expression to the feelings of the mind (*animi sensus non expressisse*), and moreover he has not treated the hair and the pubes with any more accuracy than had been achieved by the rude work of olden days (*capillum et pubem non emendatius fecisse, quam rudis antiquitas instituisset*). (*Natural History* XXXIV.19.58)

141. RUPRECHT'S NOTE: The quote from Pliny is as follows:

> Among these artists the following remarkable case is not to be left out: the man who ground the colours for the painter Nealces, Erigonus, attained such proficiency on his own account that he actually left behind him a famous pupil, Pasias, the brother of the painter Aeginetas (*fratrem Aeginetae pictoris*). It is also a very unusual and memorable fact that the last works of artists and their unfinished pictures such as the Iris of Aristides, Tyndarus's Children of Nicomachus, the Medea of Tinomachus and the Aphrodite of Apelles which we have mentioned, are more admired than those which are finished (*in maiore admiratione esse quam perfecta*), because in them are seen the preliminary drawings left visible and the artists' actual thoughts, and in the midst of approval's beguilement we feel regret that the artist's hand while engaged in the work was removed by death. (*Natural History* XXXV.40.145)

The line once again has manuscript variants, one describing a man named Aeginetas as *fictoris* (or *fictores*), and another as *pictoris* (or *pictores*). It is important to note that this man is identified as the brother of Pasias (*fratrem Aeginetae*); the reference is clearly not to Aeginetans in general nor to Aeginetan art.

142. RUPRECHT'S NOTE: The quote from Pausanias's description of Sardinia and Corsica is, we will recall, as follows:

> The he-goats are no bigger than those found elsewhere, but their shape is that of the wild ram which an artist would carve in the Aeginetan style (ἐν πλαστικῇ τις ἂν τῇ Αἰγιναίᾳ ποιήσειεν), except that their breasts are too shaggy to liken them to Aeginetan art (πρὸς Αἰγιναίαν τέχνην). (*Guide to Greece* X.17.12)

143. RUPRECHT'S NOTE: Wagner's description was as follows:

> G.G. There are also many more fragments of Greek vases and small figurines in baked clay, which were found in the initial excavation of the temple. Especially noteworthy is the fragment of a cup [*Tazze*] of exceptional beauty. It is regrettable that the foot and [81] also the middle portion of the cup are damaged. On the inner surface there was a Europa, seated on the bull, rendered in color on a white background. Her arm-buckle, necklace, earrings, and the hem of her garment, as well as her diadem, are all set off, gilded and in high relief. The outside of the cup is decorated in the usual way, in red and black, with two winged genii who hold a cup in one hand and a lyre in the other.

144. RUPRECHT'S NOTE: The first reference to the image is this:

> In the reign of Simus, the son of Phialus, the people of Phigalia lost the ancient wooden image (ξόανον) of Black Demeter to fire. This loss proved to be a sign that Simus himself also was soon to meet his end. (*Guide to Greece* VIII.5.8)

The image is described in greater detail later in book VIII. Pausanias relates the local tradition that claims that Demeter, impregnated by Poseidon, had given birth to Persephone, and when the daughter was later raped, she put on black garments and sealed herself in a dark cave. The local Phigalians later erected a strangely posed black wooden image to her in that same cave.

> The image (τὸ ἄγαλμα), they say, was made after this fashion. It was seated on a rock, like to a woman in all respects except for the head. She had the head and hair of a horse, and there grew out of her head images (εἰκόνες) of serpents and other beasts. Her chiton reached all the way to her feet; on one of her hands was a dolphin, and on the other a dove. Why they had the image (τὸ ξόανον) made after this fashion is plain to an intelligent man who is learned in traditions (τὰ ἐς μνήμην δῆλά ἐστι). They say they named her Black (μέλαιναν) because the goddess had black apparel. They cannot relate either who made this wooden image (τὸ ξόανον) or how it caught fire. But the old image (τοῦ ἀρχαίου) was destroyed, and the Phigalians gave the goddess no fresh image (ἄγαλμα ἄλλο), while they neglected for the most part her festivals and sacrifices, until barrenness fell on the land. (*Guide to Greece* VIII.42.4-5, translation emended)

Translator's Historical Afterword

"Mortal"—t'was thus she spake—"that blush of shame
Proclaims thee Briton, once a noble name;
First of the mighty, foremost of the free,
Now honour'd less by all, and least by me:
Chief of thy foes shall Pallas still be found.
Seek'st thou the cause of loathing?—look around.
Lo! Here, despite of war and wasting fire,
I saw successive tyrannies expire.
'Scaped from the ravage of the Turk and Goth,
Thy country sends a spoiler worse than both.
Survey this vacant, violated fane;
Recount the relics torn that yet remain:
These Cecrops placed, this Pericles adorned,
That Adrian rear'd when drooping science mourn'd.
What more I owe let gratitude attest—
Know, Alaric and Elgin did the rest."

Lord Byron, "The Curse of Minerva" (1811)

Happy the nations of the moral North!
  Where all is virtue, and the winter season
Sends sin, without a rag on, shivering forth
  (T'was snow that brought St. Antony to reason);
Where juries cast up what a wife is worth,
  By laying whate'er sum, in mulct, they please on
The lover, who must pay a handsome price,
  Because it is a marketable vice.

Lord Byron, *Don Juan* I §64 (1819)

Byron! how sweetly sad thy melody!

John Keats, "Sonnet to Byron" (1820)

> How many monuments have lost their virtue through their displacement! How many works have lost their real value in losing their use! How many objects are viewed with indifference because they no longer interest the curious viewer! These are the currencies no longer valued save by savants. Thus, as we see every day, they are condemned to the tribute of sterile admiration, all these scattered and mutilated fragments of antiquity—these gods without altars, these altars without worshipers, these symbols of honor emptied of meaning, these bases stripped of their images, these sarcophagi emptied of affection which the antiquarian may examine for scholarly purpose but before which the soul seeks in vain for an emotional response. They are simply too far removed from their original place.
>
> Quatremère de Quincy, *Considérations Morales sur la Destination des Ouvrages de l'Art* (1815), 68–69

Work continued in a relatively systematic but episodic way, both at the Munich Königsplatz and at the Temple to Aphaia on the island of Aegina (as well as at other Greek sites, most notably Olympia), which were primarily excavated under German auspices.[1] Things were to change, swiftly and repeatedly, in the tumultuous course of the twentieth century.[2]

The debate over Bertel Thorvaldsen's "restorations," of which Charles Cockerell had already been critical in 1860, was really joined in 1901, when the director of the Glyptothek, Adolf Furtwängler (1853–1907), discovered the pedimental bases for the Temple of Aphaia, thereby disconfirming some of the errant guesses the sculptor had made. Statues that Thorvaldsen had restored in a supine posture were discovered to have been standing; heads were mismatched to the wrong torsos; several sculptural compositions now seem overdrawn.

After the First World War, the fledgling National Socialist movement enjoyed some of its earliest support in Munich, a city that would later be touted as the capital of the movement.[3] It was in Munich that Hitler staged his abortive "beer hall *Putsch*" in November 1923, and—after a brief imprisonment, during which he penned *Mein Kampf*—it was to Munich that he turned some of his earliest architectural attention, shortly after coming to power as Reichs-chancellor in 1933. In point of fact, Hitler's early career as Chancellor might be viewed as a never-ending commute between his old power base in Munich and the new capitol of the nation, in Berlin. Hitler was to devote significant architectural energy to both cities in these years.[4]

Hitler's interests in art and architecture are now well known and well attested. Like so many of the figures I discussed in the introduction, he too began as an aspiring and largely unsuccessful watercolorist, a youthful artistic type eerily reminiscent of the four men who originally discovered the Aegina

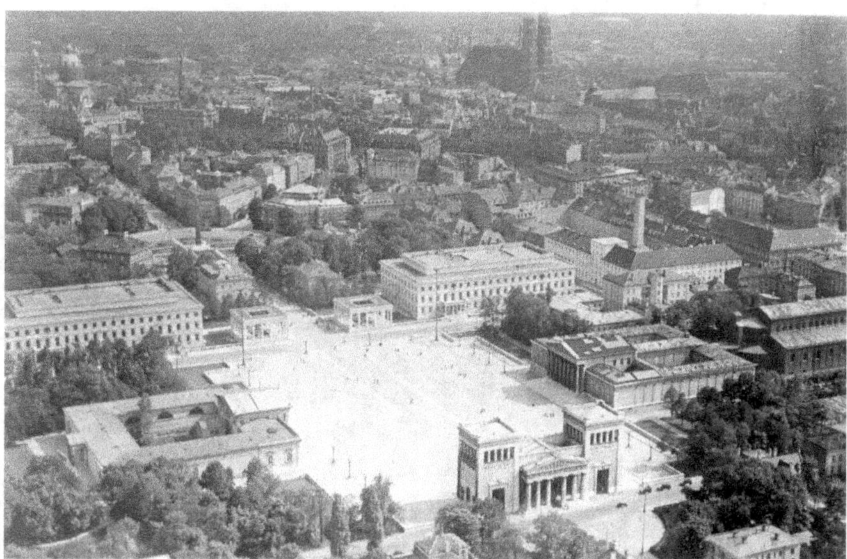

Figure 4.1. Aerial photograph of the Königsplatz from the west, 1936. Printed with permission of the State Archives of Munich (*Stadtarchiv München* Stb-Luft-124).

Marbles. Several of Hiler's earliest important political commissions would be for the construction of monumental new headquarters: both NSDAP party headquarters and his own personal chancellories, in Munich and in Berlin. Albert Speer (1905–1981) handled the Berlin commissions, famously bringing them to completion in record time and, amazingly, under budget. Paul Ludwig Troost (1864–1934) handled the Munich plans, though he failed to see them to completion due to his premature death on January 21, 1934.

The site chosen for the Munich program was the Königsplatz. Since the eastern end of the Platz had remained open, Troost proposed closing off the Platz—and thus, in effect, "completing" it, as another sort of palimpsestic architectural "restoration"—with an impressive array of four new buildings. The cost was enormous—nearly two and one-quarter million *Reichsmark*, by the time it was completed in early 1936—and its reception by the local public was predictably (and likely mandatorily) enthusiastic:

> Paul Ludwig Troost, the Führer's greatest architect, has provided this fine memorial with the proper form—with a purity and a clarity that has nothing to do with the Classical nostalgia of Ludwig's era, but is founded instead on

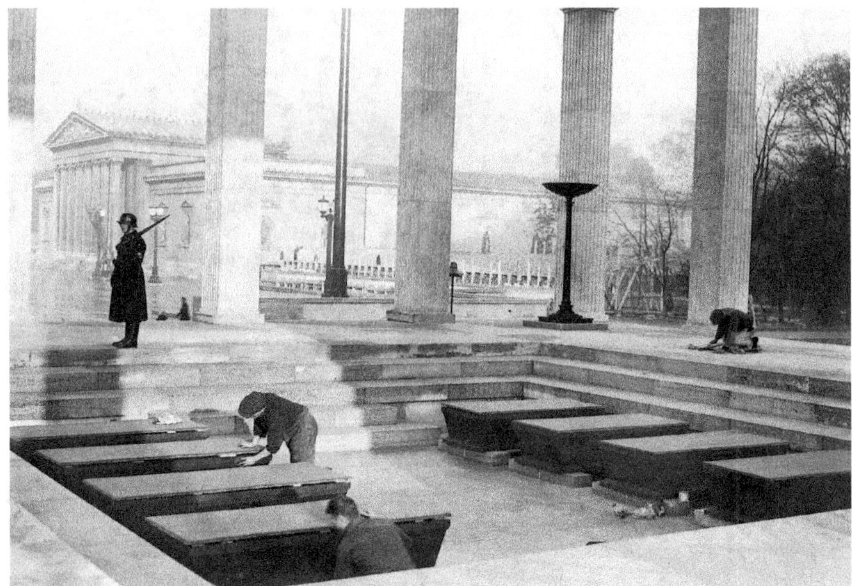

Figure 4.2. Bronze sarcophagi inside the Ehrentempel with the Glyptothek in the background, 1935. Printed with permission of the "South-German News," Munich (*Süddeutsches Zeitung*, Munich, REF82292).

> the independent and secure foundation of modern ideals and engineering. Through this he has achieved a rich cultural and symbolic image, a monumental image, an image that well characterizes the heroic path of a great political movement. . . .
>
> *A cultural continuity and completeness* [Einheit und Geschlossenheit] *now exists that did not exist here before.* A real Platz has been created, a place that finally provides a secure foundation for the Greek temple buildings. So it is that now, for the first time, they stand proudly on the spot, and no longer appear to be accidental architectural bodies cast randomly about the place, as they did before.[5]

No accidents here. The whole idea hinges on a sense of programmatic integrity and completeness. Two smaller structures were to flank the new entrance to the Königsplatz. These were the *Ehrentempeln*,[6] or "temples to the heroes": square, open-aired, *faux*-Doric shrines in which the exhumed bodies of the martyrs of the failed 1923 *Putsch* were to be reinterred in bronze sarcophagi.

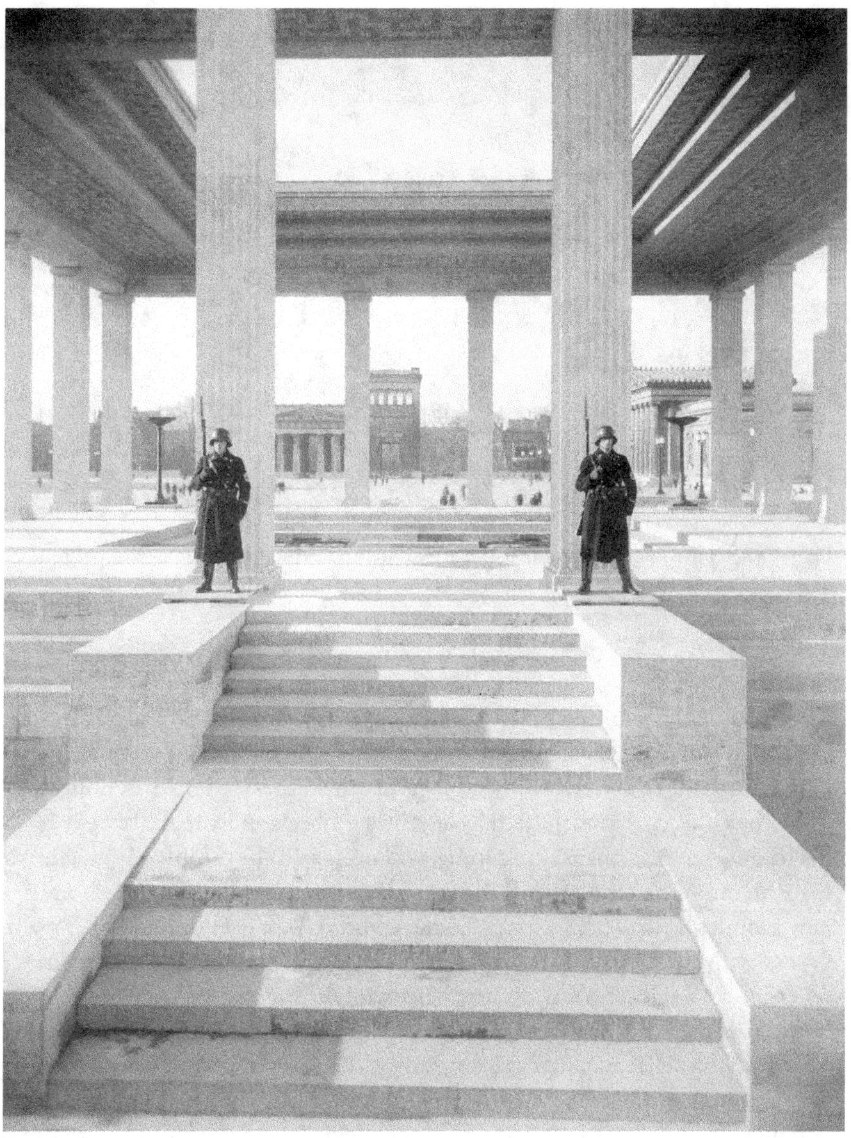

Figure 4.3. Guards stationed at the Ehrentempel, 1936. Printed with permission of the "South-German News," Munich (*Süddeutsches Zeitung*, Munich, REF84072).

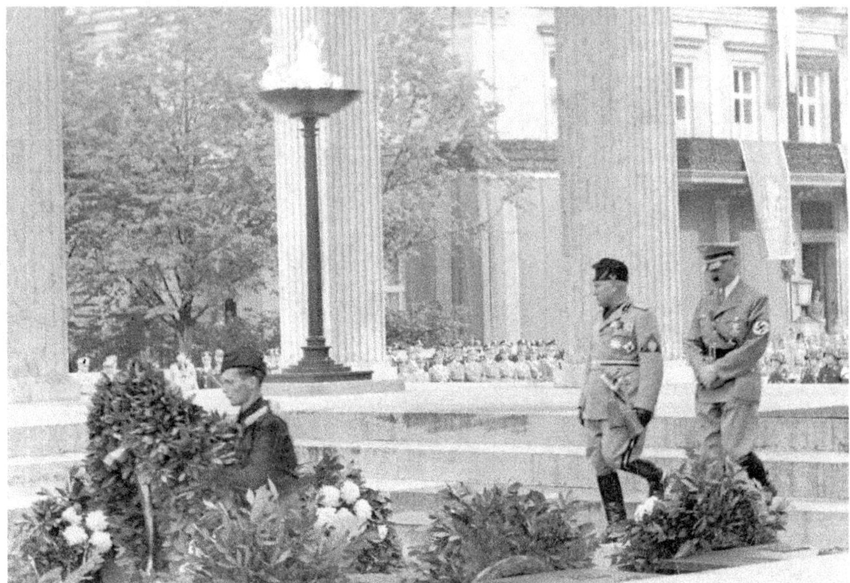

Figure 4.4. Hitler and Mussolini visiting the Ehrentempeln, 1937. Printed with permission of the "South-German News," Munich (*Süddeutsches Zeitung*, Munich, REF9566).

The site quickly became a place of pilgrimage, as well as a source of fascist statecraft. It is noteworthy that sixteen dead bodies were linked, architecturally and spiritually, to sixteen restored Aeginetan statues: stones and bones were to be the chief currency in such a romantic museum culture. Hitler expressed his intention to be buried here in his will, either in the temples or in a nearby mausoleum.[7] The two larger buildings placed to the north and south of these new temples were the *Führerbau*, Hitler's Munich chancellory, and the *Verwaltungsbau*, Munich party headquarters of the NSDAP. As I have argued elsewhere, Greek statues have proven to be magnets for some very strange energy in the past two centuries; that is a significant subtext to this entire book.[8]

Munich was damaged most severely by the Allies during three continuous days of aerial bombardment in late July 1944. The Glyptothek itself was badly damaged by a direct hit; fortunately, the Aegina Marbles had been removed for safekeeping long before then. Most of Schelling's handwritten manuscripts, however, including two versions of "The Ages of the World," which had just been rediscovered in 1939 and were also housed in Munich, were destroyed by fire during this bombing campaign. (Similarly, when Allied bombers turned

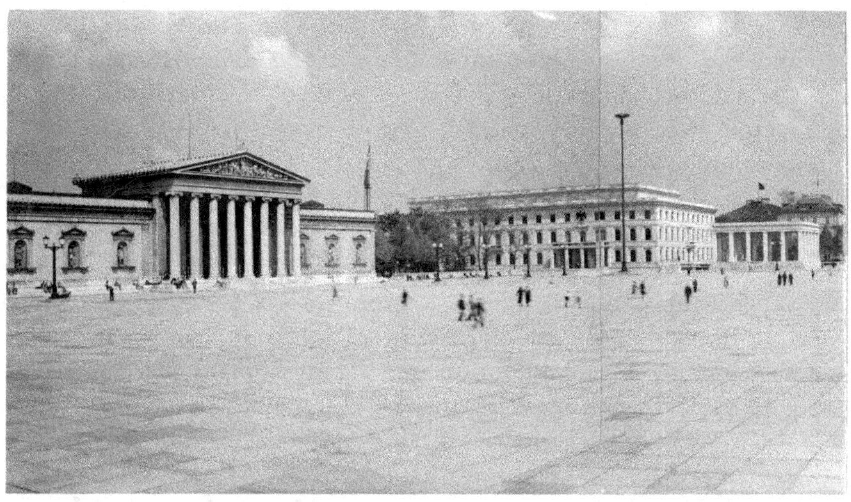

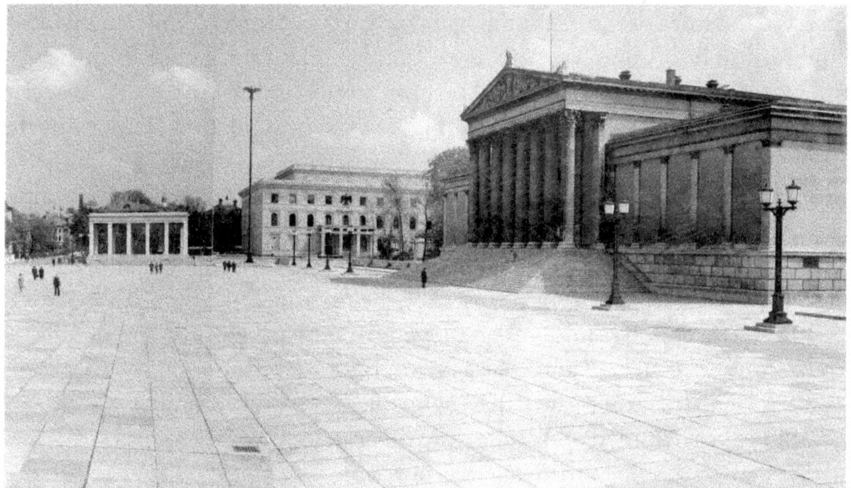

Figure 4.5a–4.5b. The Ehrentempeln on the Königsplatz, 1936. Printed with permission of the State Archives of Munich (*Stadtarchiv München* HB-II-b-0252a, and HB-II-b-0252b).

their sites on Würzburg in mid-March of 1945, some, though not the majority, of Wagner's personal papers were destroyed.) But Hitler's *Ehrentempeln*, party headquarters, and the chancellory emerged largely unscathed from the war. German residents in Munich consented[9] to the dynamiting the *Ehrentempeln* in 1947, after the bodies had been removed and entombed again.[10] It has never been clear since then what should be done with such a fraught architectural site and, until very recently, the site and its memory had been literally buried. The concrete foundations of the *Ehrentempeln* were abandoned to overgrowth so that they were relatively invisible; there was no indication as to what they had been not so very long before.

This was changed in a most moving and dramatic way by the city of Munich in May of 2015. Just a few yards to the east of the one exposed foundation line of the northern *Ehrentempel*, the city has opened the Munich Documentation Center for the History of National Socialism (*NS-Dokumentationszentrum München*). It is a museum designed specifically to counter any such architectural and political amnesia. A white modernist structure designed to be discontinuous with the other buildings on the Königsplatz, and with a vague architectural gesture to the demolished *Ehrentempeln,* the center is intended to make explicit what time tends to erase—namely, inconvenient local histories. It is a four-story structure organized to tell discrete parts of the story of the rise and fall of the Nazis in Munich. The fourth, third, and second floors tell a story in a way quite similar to that told at the nearby memorial of Dachau: the political turmoil created by the First World War and its aftermath (1918–33); the astonishingly rapid consolidation of power by the new regime (1933–39); and the cataclysmic course of the war (1939–45). The first floor, however, is altogether novel, surprising and courageous. It attempts to describe the confused attempts to remember and to commemorate the Nazi era in Munich, as well as to chronicle the periodic eruptions of anti-Semitic and neo-Nazi sentiment in the city. For the first time, the public is explicitly reminded that all the buildings on this side of the Königsplatz were significant Nazi constructions . . . and that as many as sixty or more buildings nearby were as well. This story is worthy of consideration and comment.

In the years immediately following the war, the two larger Nazi structures were adapted to some surprising new purposes. The *Führerbau* was to become *Amerika-Haus*, a site that did double duty as headquarters of the American occupation as well as a cultural center of sorts, designed to promote the democratic virtues deemed necessary for the reestablishment of free political parties, and some short years later, free elections.[11] Later, this building was to house the reading room of the Bavarian State Library. The *Verwaltungsbau* was first used as a clearinghouse for the attempted repatriation of international art that had been systematically looted under the Nazi protocols for occupation of conquered territories.[12] In other words, it was where the story described by the recent film *Monuments Men* was first institutionalized and warehoused. Today, the *Führerbau* houses the State University of Munich's School of Music

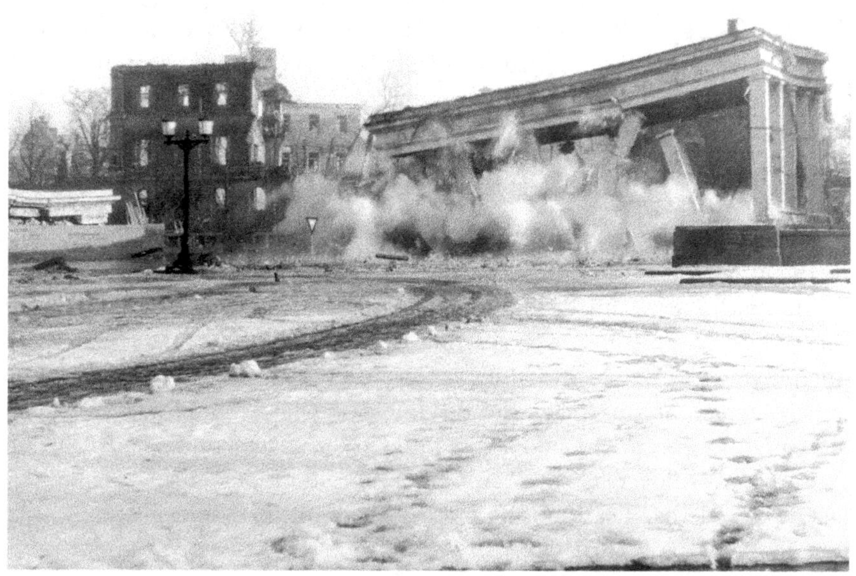

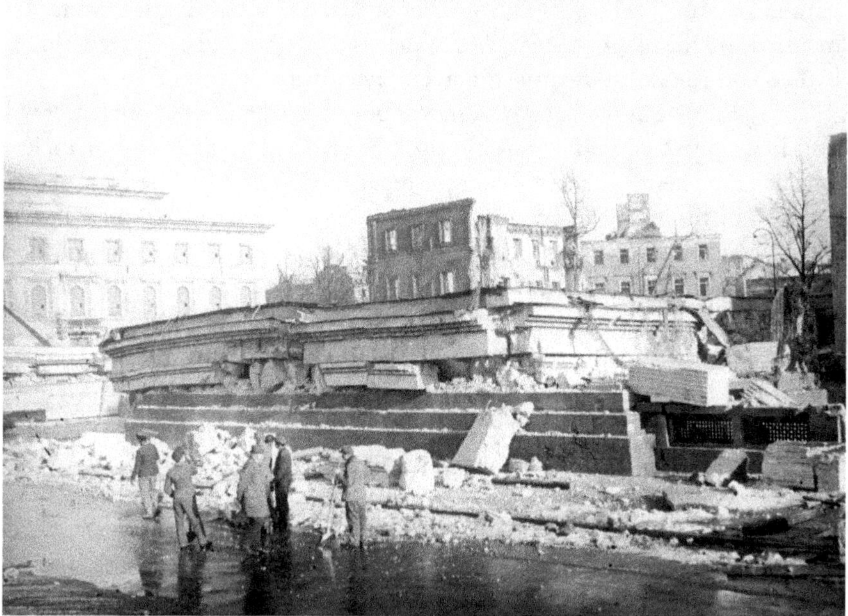

Figure 4.6a–4.6b. Dynamiting of the Ehrentempeln, 1947. Printed with permission of the "South-German News," Munich (*Süddeutsches Zeitung*, Munich, REF60090110; *Süddeutsches Zeitung*, Munich, REF 60090111).

and Theater; the *Verwaltungsbau* houses, among other things, the University's Institute for Egyptology, its Center for Art History, and its Archaeology Seminar. The latter also houses materials from the state's print collection, as well as offices for the Antikensammlung and Glyptothek museums themselves.

Since the Glyptothek needed to be rebuilt virtually from the ground up, and since its elaborate, nineteenth-century interior was already lost, then-director of the Glyptothek Museum Dieter Ohly (1911–1979) deemed it time to revisit Thorvaldsen's restorations. He thus would call for the "de-restoration" of the Aeginetan collection, along lines similar to the de-Nazification of the Königsplatz itself. This dismantling of Thorvaldsen's work was undertaken from 1962 to 1966, and in 1972, the Munich Glyptothek was reopened to the public just prior to the Munich Olympics . . . with a very different and much simpler interior design more in line with what Johann Martin Wagner had originally proposed, and a very different arrangement of the Aeginetan pedimental sculptures. Connecting the "de-restoration" of the Aegina statues to the "de-nazification" (*Entnazifizierung*) of the Königsplatz, in 1988, the "re-greening" (*Wiederbegrünung*) of the Königsplatz was undertaken, whereby the granite paving stones that the Nazis had installed to create a parade ground (and postwar Müncheners used as a parking lot) were dismantled and the plaza was returned to the original level and design envisioned by Leo von Klenze in the mid-nineteenth century

Images, as we know, can possess great power and emotional impact. It will not do simply to erase the Nazi hiccup at the Königsplatz in favor of ancient marbles and their nineteenth-century recuperation. In fact, the Nazi appropriation of the Königsplatz and, by cruel implication, the Aegina Marbles themselves, may remind us of other inconvenient realities. The religious decoration of the Temple to Aphaia at Aegina displayed two scenes of lethal violence and warfare, with dead and dying men lying before their killers, all of this presided over by the cool detachment of an Olympian goddess (Athena). Greek religious art was almost theatrical in its deployment of violence, however beautifully rendered such violent deaths may appear; we might make the same observation about the Homeric poems. What is remarkable is that these statues, which have not changed in two and one-half millennia, or more, came to be seen in so many different ways: as pagan idols, as fine art, as instantiations of supreme beauty, as national treasure, as cultural patrimony, as archaeological evidence, and even as world heritage. The public art museum emerged in the nineteenth century as the means with which to house some of the more powerful and persistent ways of seeing the classical tradition anew. There is a line that links nineteenth-century Romanticism to twentieth-century fascism; it is not the only path Romanticism took, nor the only link, but there is a link. Such museums have survived repeated changes of regime, violent conflicts, and more.[13] What we may observe here is that material culture has a strange way of inspiring spiritual activity, in this and every age. The nature of the activity continually changes; the energy, it would seem, does not fade so fast. It appears to me that it has not faded in Munich at all. In tracing the long, strange course taken by somewhere between fifteen and twenty (or more) Greek statues—from Aegina, to Athens, to Corinth, to Patras, to Zakynthos, to Malta, to Rome, to Munich—a number of important aspects of nineteenth-century classicism and neo-Hellenism may be perceived in somewhat sharper detail.

Most of the men I mentioned in the introduction were amateurs, most of them were quite young, most were aspiring artists of one sort or another, and all of them operated with what seems to us now like an outrageous sense of aristocratic privilege. They loved what they took, and took what they loved. They were inventing new disciplines, like art history and archaeology, modeling them on other "human sciences," loosely so-called. They were instrumental in designing important new public monuments and museums as well. Viewing their activities through the lens of a modern "museum culture," we can see how much of the "rediscovery" of the classical world was bound up in a revaluation and a refashioning of the *European* identity. The so-called Great Powers were instrumental in setting Greece's political and military destiny; Greece's first king was in fact Ludwig I's son, Otto. But neo-Hellenism was also responsible for the simultaneous looting and restoration of countless Greek archaeological sites. As Thorvaldsen's work illustrates with singular poignancy, there are no gains without commensurate losses. That has ever been the strange paradox lying at the heart of the neoclassical vision.

Here, cloaked in the rhetoric of classical taste and defined within a newly emerging European order, Hellenism was being subtly redefined—as scholarly discipline, as romantic idyll, and as a cultural alternative to what was often perceived to be a dying Christian civilization. It is this romantic tenor, with these alternatively somber and luminous bass notes, that one may hear echoed in some of our finest classical museums still today. I am grateful to count the Munich Glyptothek, and the remarkable Königsplatz of which it is a part, among them.

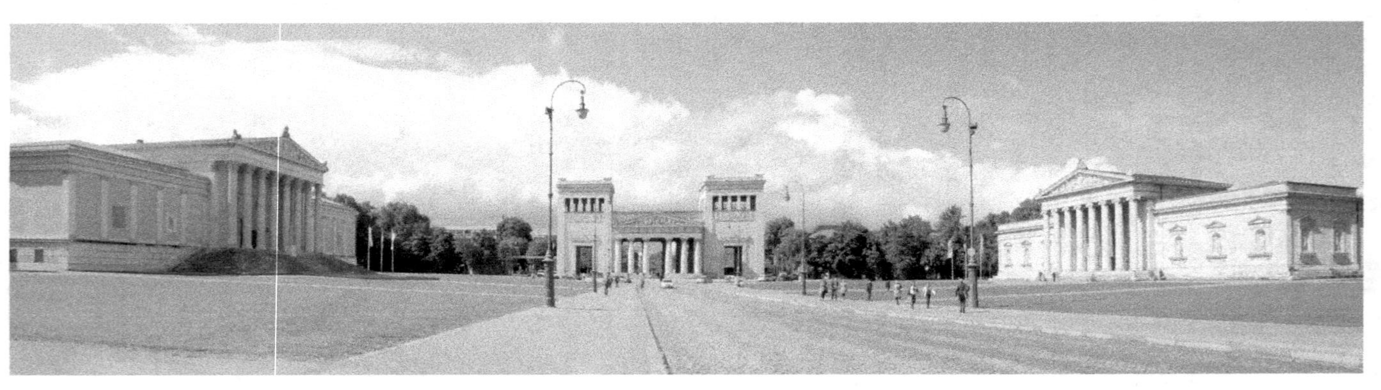

Figure 4.7. The Munich Königsplatz today. Photograph by Renate Kühling. Printed with permission of the Munich State Collection of Antiquities and Glyptothek (*München Antikensammlung und Glyptothek* K+,nigsplatz_gesamt_RK).

ENDNOTES TO THE TRANSLATOR'S AFTERWORD

1. There is a large bibliography on Aeginetan archaeology and the Temple of Aphaia in particular. The site was excavated briefly by Greek archaeologists in 1894, and then more systematically under the auspices of the German School in Athens. See B. Σταης, "Περὶ τῶν ἐν Αἰγίνῃ ἀνασκαφῶν," Πρακτικὰ τῆς ἐν ' Αθήναις ' Αρχαιολογικῆς 'Εταιρείας (1894): 17–20.

   Adolf Furtwängler (1853–1907) led the work from 1900 until his death in 1907 (he died of dysentery contracted at the site), and published several important pieces on his new discoveries, most notably, *Aegina: Das Heiligtum der Aphaia*, mit Ernst R. Fiechter und Hermann Thiersch (München: Verlag der K. B. Akademie der Wissenschaften, 1906), in two volumes.

   Dieter Ohly (1911–1979) returned to the site in 1966 and worked there until his death in 1979; he too published several important studies of the new finds, including *Die Aeginetan: die Marmorskulpturen des Tempels der Aphaia auf Aegina* (München: C. H. Beck, 1976), in four volumes.

   Ernst Ludwig Schwandner and Martha Ohly supervised the remaining German work at the Aphaia Temple through 1989. The Bayerische Akademie der Wissenschaft's *Aegina-Kommission* published eighteen serial articles relating to the site, all of them entitled *Alt-Aegina* (and dating 1970–98). These are:

   Dieter Ohly with Ernst Ludwig Schwander, "Aegina, Aphaia-Temple I. Die südliche Stützmauer der Temenosterasse," *Archäologischer Anzeiger* 85, Heft 1 (1970): 48–71;

   ———, "Aegina, Aphaia-Temple II. Untersuchungen in der spätarchaischen Tempelsterasse," *Archäologischer Anzeiger* 86, Heft 3 (1971): 505–38

   Hansgeorg Bankel, "Aegina, Aphaia-Temple III. Die Kurvatur des spätarchaischen Tempels" *Archäologischer Anzeiger* 95, Heft 2 (1980): 171–79;

   Dyfri Williams, "Aegina, Aphaia-Temple IV. The Inscription Commemorating the Construction of the First Limestone Temple and Other Features of the Sixth Century Temenos," *Archäologischer Anzeiger* 97, Heft 1 (1982): 55–68;

   Dyfri Williams, "Aegina, Aphaia-Temple V. The Pottery from Chios," *Archäologischer Anzeiger* 98, Heft 2 (1983): 155–86;

   Michael Maaß, "Aegina, Aphaia-Temple VI. Neue Funde von Waffenweihungen," *Archäologischer Anzeiger* 99, Heft 2 (1984): 263–82;

   Hans Georg Bankel, "Aegina, Aphaia-Temple VII. Geraupten Metopen," *Archäologischer Anzeiger* 100, Heft 1 (1985): 1–13;

   Mary B. Moore, "Aegina, Aphaia-Temple VIII. The Attic Black-Figured Pottery," *Archäologischer Anzeiger* 101, Heft 1 (1986): 51–93;

   Henry R. Immerwahr, "Aegina, Aphaia-Temple IX. An Archaic Abacus from the Sanctuary of Aphaia," *Archäologischer Anzeiger* 101, Heft 2 (1986): 195–204;

Ingo Pini, "Aegina, Aphaia-Temple X. Die Steinsiegel," *Archäologischer Anzeiger* 102, Heft 3 (1987): 413–33;

Dyfri Williams, "Aegina, Aphaia-Temple XI. The Pottery from the Second Limestone Temple and the Later History of the Temple," *Archäologischer Anzeiger* 102, Heft 4 (1987): 629–80;

Martha Ohly-Dumm and Martin Robertson, "Aegina, Aphaia-Temple XII. Archaic Marble Sculpture Other than Architectural," *Archäologischer Anzeiger* 103, Heft 3 (1988): 405–21;

Alan W. Johnston, "Aegina, Aphaia-Temple XIII. The Storage Amphorae," *Archäologischer Anzeiger* 105, Heft 1 (1990): 37–64;

Donald M. Bailey, "Aegina, Aphaia-Temple XIV. The Lamps," *Archäologischer Anzeiger* 106, Heft 1 (1991): 31–68;

Thomas Schäfer, "Aegina, Aphaia-Temple XV. Becken und Ständer aus Marmor und Kalkstein," *Archäologischer Anzeiger* 107, Heft 1 (1992): 7–37;

Kees Neeft, "Aegina, Aphaia-Temple XVI. Corinthian Alabastra and Aryballoi. Mit 61 Abbildungen," *Archäologischer Anzeiger* 108, Heft 4 (1993): 543–69;

Dyfri Williams, "Aegina, Aphaia-Temple XVII. The Laconian Pottery," *Archäologischer Anzeiger* 108, Heft 4 (1993): 571–98; and

Michael Maaß and Imma Kilian-Dirlmeier, "Aegina, Aphaia-Temple XVIII. Bronzefunde außer Waffen. Mit 19 Abbildungen," *Archäologischer Anzeiger* 113, Heft 1 (1998): 57–104

In addition, the following volumes are noteworthy:

Hansgeorg Bankel, *Der spätarchaische Tempel der Aphaia auf Aegina* (Berlin: Walter de Gruyter, 1993); Thomas J. Figueira, *Aegina and Athens in the Archaic and Classical Periods: A Socio-Political Investigation* (Ph.D. Dissertation, University of Pennsylvania, 1977); Charles Garnier, *Le temple de Jupiter Panhellénien à Égine; restauration exécutée en 1852* (Paris: Firmin-Didot et cie, 1884); Maximillian von Groote, *Ägineten und Archäologen : eine Kritik* (Berlin: Heitz & Mundel, 1912); Otto Jahn, *Beschreibung der Vasensammlung König Ludwigs in der Pinakothek zu München* (München: Jos. Lindauer'sche Buchhandlung, 1854); Sonia di Neuhoff, *Aegina*, 3rd Edition (Athens: Apollo Editions, 1978); Korinna Pilafidis-Williams, *The Sanctuary of Aphaia on Aegina in the Bronze Age* (München: Hirmer Verlag, 1998); Hans Walter, *Aegina: Die archäologische Geschichte einer griechischen Insel* (Deutscher Kunstverlag, 1993); Elena Walter-Karydi, *Die äginetische Bildhauerschule : Werke und schriftliche Quellen* (1987); and Anne Yannoulis, *Aegina* (Athens: Lykabettos Press, 1974, 1983).

I am indebted to Lucia Carbone of Columbia University, and Nedda Ahmed of the Georgia State University Research Library, for much of this bibliography.

2. The essential resource for this is *Der Königsplatz, 1812–1988* (München: Staatliche Antikensammlungen und Glyptothek, 1991).
3. See David Clay Large, *Where Ghosts Walked: Munich's Road to the Third Reich* (New York: W. W. Norton & Company, 1997), esp. 278–83, on the Munich building program I describe here.
4. See Albert Speer, *Inside the Third Reich*, trans. Richard and Clara Winston (New York: Macmillan, 1970), 3–79.

5. This passage from the *Süddeutsche Monatshefte* (December 1935) is quoted in *Der Königsplatz, 1812–1988*, 44–45; translation and italics are mine.
6. Lines of influence can be difficult to draw, but this same term was used by Frederick Kohlrausch in his *Die Deutschen Geschichte für Schulen bearbeitet*, a text first published for school use in 1816, and expanded through sixteen editions by 1875, in specific reference to Tacitus's *Germania*. The English version may be found at *History of Germany: From the Earliest Period to the Present Time*, James D. Haas, trans. (New York: D. Appleton and Company, 1889), 17:

   > His deep feeling for simplicity of manners, and healthy energy of nature, had made him a warm friend towards the German natives; and it appeared to him that a faithful description of the German nation would be a work worthy of his pen, so that, when placed before his corrupted countrymen, it should present to their view a picture which might bring many of those whose minds were as yet not quite unsusceptible, to acknowledge their own unnatural condition. For this purpose he collected all that he could obtain from the earlier authors, from the oral information of the Romans who had been in Germany, and from the Germans who were in the Roman service. Thus arose this invaluable book, which may be called a temple of honor to the German nation [*Ehrentempel des deutschen Volkes*], and which illuminates, like a bright star, the commencement of their otherwise obscure path.

   I am indebted to Martin A. Ruehl, "German Horror Stories: Teutonomania and the Ghosts of Tacitus," *Arion, Third Series* 22, no. 2 (2014): 129–89, for this reference.

   The rival account of which Ruehl is justly critical is Christopher B. Krebs, *A Most Dangerous Book: Tacitus's Germania from the Roman Empire to the Third Reich* (New York: W. W. Norton & Company, 2011), esp. 182–91.
7. See *Der Königsplatz, 1812–1988*, 10–11, 42–43, 56–59, as well as William J. Diebold, "The Politics of Derestoration," *Art Journal* 54.2 (1995): 60–66, esp. 62 and note 20.

   Diebold's article is not only a wonderful source of information and exquisite detail, but it also offers a remarkably creative thesis: namely, that since the aesthetic interest in "totalization" and "completion" (executed through a peculiar sort of time-dilation) were shared by Romantics like Thorvaldsen and Nazis like Troost and Speer, the "denazification" of the *Königsplatz* naturally led to the "de-restoration" of the Aegina Marbles. My one caveat is this: Diebold seems so concerned with the erasure of the nineteenth-century layer to this complex archaeological history that he fails to note the erasure of antiquity enacted by Thorvaldsen's work. That seems to me more the problem that postwar scholars and curators alike were trying to redress . . . or rather, to *un*dress.
8. See my earlier articulations of this idea in: *Afterwords: Hellenism, Modernism and the Myth of Decadence* (New York: SUNY Press, 1996), 23–63, esp. 43–52; *Was Greek Thought Religious? On the Use and Abuse of Hellenism, From Rome to Romanticism* (New York: Palgrave Macmillan, 2002), 77–91; as well as *Winckelmann and the Vatican's First Profane Museum* (New York: Palgrave Macmillan, 2011) and *Classics at the Dawn of the Museum Era: The Life and Times of Antoine Chrysostome Quatremère de Quincy* (New York: Palgrave Macmillan, 2014).

Special attentions can have manifold outcomes, of course. The German occupation of Greece in the Second World War was an especially barbaric one. See Mark Mazower, *Inside Hitler's Greece: The Experience of Occupation, 1941–1944* (New Haven, CT: Yale University Press, 1993), and Violetta Hionidou, *Famine and Death in Occupied Greece, 1941–1944* (New York: Cambridge University Press, 2006).

9. Who made the actual decision concerning the destruction of the *Ehrentempeln* is not entirely clear. Certainly, it could not have been done without the consent and oversight of the American forces of occupation, but this was precisely the kind of Nazi monument that possessed an historical valence that the majority of the war's survivors wished to disown. I am indebted to Regina Höschele of the University of Toronto for pointing out this ambiguity to me. She also shared her grandfather's eyewitness account of the destruction; that he happened upon the site at the moment of detonation suggests that the decision was not widely publicized in Munich. A film record of the destruction may be viewed at https://www.youtube.com/watch?v'-47LAmbC-EQ, and is currently on display at the new NS-Dokmentationszentrum München, about which more will be said below.

10. See Jay W. Baird, *To Die for Germany: Heroes in the Nazi Pantheon* (Indianapolis: Indiana University Press, 1992), 41–72: "the bodies of the fallen were buried yet again in several Munich cemeteries" (72), at the time of the destruction of the *Ehrentempeln.*

    I am grateful to Dr. Elisabeth Kraus of the *NS-Dokumentationszentrum* in Munich for this reference, as well as for the relevant text of the *Stadtkronik* for January 9, 1947:

    > Already in June of 1945, the remains of the dead were returned to their original resting places; the sacrophagi were melted down. The foundations of the Ehrentempel are still there today. (translation mine)

    One interesting feature of this account is the suggestion that only one *Ehrentempel* was initially destroyed. The *New York Times* referred to the abandoned "Temple of Honor" (in the singular) on May 1, 1945; reported on the destruction of "one of the twin temples of honor" on January 10, 1947; and announced the decision that "both monuments will now be razed by order of the Allied Control Council" on March 25, 1948.

11. Surprisingly, if not to say inexplicably, the only significant change to the building was the removal of the Nazi war-bird from the front façade and its replacement with the red, white, and blue insignia of the American eagle. American forces also used the Königsplatz as a parade ground for occupation forces, much as the Nazis had done. One may well wonder how such performative and architectural echoes were received by the local population at the time.

12. For more on this remarkably systematic and bureaucratic program of art acquisition, see Russell Chamberlin, *Loot! The Heritage of Plunder*, 149–87. Soviet armies proceeded to loot Germany after the war, under the aegis of recovering and repatriating their lost national treasures. Europe had seen this kind of thing before, with the French looting of the Vatican Museum and the recovery of the Vatican treasures during Canova's mission in 1822. We have seen it many times since then. See Elazar Barkan, *The Guilt of Nations: Restitution and Negotiating Historical Injustices* (New York: W. W. Norton & Company, 2000), 65–87.

13. Not always. Recent developments in Iraq and Syria provide a grievous counterexample to the story of the Glyptothek Museum.

APPENDIX ONE: THE CHRONOLOGY OF CHARLES COCKERELL'S GRAND TOUR (1810–1817)

April 19, 1810: Cockerell departs from Plymouth, armed with dispatches for Sir Robert Adair, British ambassador to the Sublime Porte. The ship calls at Gibraltar and Malta en route.

June 6, 1810: Arrival in Constantinople.

June 7, 1810: Cockerell's first meeting with Byron and Hobhouse.

Late June 1810: Cockerell first meets John Foster Jr.

July 14, 1810: Byron and Hobhouse depart from Constantinople. Cockerell presents Hobhouse with a new journal as a parting gift.

September 9, 1810: Cockerell and Foster depart for Greece in the company of Sir William Amcotte Ingelby.

September 19, 1810: Landfall at Salonika (Thessaloniki).

October 6, 1810: Cockerell, Foster, and Ingleby depart by boat for Athens.

October 7, 1810: Zagora.

October–November 1810: Visits to the islands of Tinos, Delos (scene of their first "excavations"), and Kea.
Ingelby leaves them at Kea. Cockerell and Foster continue on to Athens.

Winter 1810/11: The grand winter in company with Byron, et al.

April 22, 1811: Byron departs for England.
Cockerell, Haller, Linkh, and Foster depart for Aegina.
Final farewells on the fantail of HMS *Hydra* at dusk.

April/May 1811: Excavations at the Temple of Aphaia on Aegina.

Late May 1811: The party returns with the Aegina Marbles to Athens.

June/July 1811: Initial reassembly of the fragmentary Aegina collection.
Gropius, the Austrian consul, is appointed as the four men's agent.

July 30, 1811: The first batch of Aegina Marbles is moved to Zante, passing through Porto Germano, the Gulf of Corinth and Patras.

August 18, 1811: The four men depart together from Athens.

August–September 1811: The four men make an excursion through the Peloponnese: Pyrgos, Olympia, Kalamata, Kardamyli, and the Mani.
Haller and Cockerell "discover" the Temple of Apollo Epikourius at Bassae.

October 1811: The four men return to Athens.

November 28, 1811: Captain Perceval arrives in Piraeus Harbor aboard the brig-o-war *Paulina*. Arrangements for the Aegina Marbles to be shipped from Zante to Malta for safekeeping.

December 1811–May 1813: Cockerell plans to visit Crete, Egypt, Turkey, Malta, Sicily, and Italy.

December 1, 1811: Cockerell departs for Crete in company with Lord Guilford, Frederick Douglas, and John Foster Jr.

December 3, 1811: Arrival at Xania.

Mid-December 1811: Residence in Herakleion.

December 24, 1811: Lord Guilford departs for the island of Dia.

December 25, 1811: The party gathers on Dia.

January 1812: The island of Siphnos.

Lord Guilford abandons plans for the trip to Egypt as too dangerous.

The party moves to the island of Chios.

Frederick Douglas returns to England. Lord Guilford remains on Chios.

Cockerell and Foster continue to Smyrna (Izmir).

February 1812: Foster falls in love with the daughter of the Russian consul, Mary Maraccini.

April 1812: Cockerell tours Anatolia alone. Unexpectedly he meets Lord Guilford again on the island of Rhodes. The two men tour Asia Minor, Malta, and Italy together.

November 1, 1812: Auction of the Aegina Marbles on Zante.

The British representative, Taylor Coombe, is on Malta with the marbles. Mr. McGill, Gropius's agent on Malta, assures him that the auctioneer will come to him there.

On Zante, the French bid 160,000 francs (£4,000).

Johann Martin Wagner bids 10,000 sequins (£4,500) on behalf of Crown Prince Ludwig of Bavaria.

March 1813: Cockerell learns of the auction's results while on Sicily and is incensed.

May 1813: Cockerell returns to Athens. Haller and Stackelberg have already begun excavating at Bassae. Cockerell and Haller move into lodging outside of Athens, at Patissia.

August 22, 1813: Cockerell falls seriously ill. Hallerstein personally nurses him to recovery.

September 1813: Cockerell is well enough to travel again.

September 23, 1813: Otto von Stackelberg departs from Athens for Vienna. He travels from Euboea to Xalkis and Xerochori, where he hires a *trabakalo*.

He is kidnaped by Albanian *klephts*. Haller arranges his ransom for £500.

Stackelberg is returned to Athens and nursed back to health until March 1814.

October 29, 1813: Thomas Smart Hughes and R. Townley Parker arrive in Athens.

They lodge in the home of Theodora Makri, made famous by a poem from Lord Byron ("Maid of Athens, Ere I Part"). They fall into the circle of Cockerell, now fully recovered, and Haller, now famous for the Stackelberg affair.

November 29, 1813: Cockerell, Hughes, Parker, and General Davies, the quartermaster of British Mediterranean forces, arrange an excursion to Albania.

They pass the Fortress of Phyle.

November 30, 1813: Mount Parnes and Thebes.

December 1–10, 1813: Livadhia; Hughes falls ill.

Mid-December 1813: Chaironea, Delphi, Scala Salona, Galaxidi.

The party returns to General Davies's gunboat and sails to Patras and Levkas (Lefkada).

General Davies falls ill and dies that winter on Zante.

December 27, 1813: Prevesa.

January 6–26, 1814: Ioannina. Cockerell, Hughes, and Parker are all housed with Nicolo Argyri, Byron's and Hobhouse's host.

Athanasios Petrides Psalidas condemns Cockerell for his "excavations" at Aegina very publicly at a dinner party.

Cockerell stays with Ali Pasha until January 14.

January 27, 1814: Cockerell sets out alone for Athens over the Pindus Mountains.

March 1814: Residence in Athens. John Oliver Hanson arrives from Smyrna with Stephen Maltass (former British consul at Alexandria) and a Mr. Grabau of Hamburg.

Thomas Burgon and John Foster Jr., both recently married, also arrive.

Gropius, Haller, and Linkh are all still in Athens as well.

April 1814: Excursions to Zante, in anticipation of the auction of the Phigalian frieze from the Temple of Apollo Epikourius at Bassae.

Hanson, Maltass, and Brabau arrive on April 15.

Cockerell, the Burgons, the Fosters, Haller, and Linkh arrive on April 20.

Gropius and Masson arrive on April 23.

Napoleon abdicates.

May 1, 1814: Auction of the Phigalian Marbles. They are purchased by General Sir James Campbell on behalf of the Prince of Wales for approximately $60,000.

May 3, 1814: Hanson, Grabau, and Stackelberg depart on a Greek ship for the Adriatic and home.

July 11, 1814: Cockerell returns to Athens, seriously ill once again.
John Spencer Stanhope, an old school friend, and Thomas Allason join him there.

Summer 1814: The three men make excursions to Marathon, Tanagra, Aulis Eretria, and Euboea.

Mid-October 1814: Cockerell falls ill again, and is finally taken to Eleusis for "a change of air."

November 1814: Cockerell's last trip to Aegina, to correct and revise his drawings of the Aegina Temple.

January 15, 1815: Italy is reopened to British travelers.
Cockerell departs from Athens with Linkh and a man named Tupper. The three men make a final tour through the Peloponnese then pass over to Italy, lodging primarily in Naples, Rome, and Florence.
Cockerell will remain in Italy for two years, meeting old friends in Naples, Rome, (Canova, Thorvaldsen) and Venice (Stackelberg).

Spring 1817: Cockerell finally departs by ship for England.

October 5, 1817: Carl Haller von Hallerstein dies in the Tempe Valley in Greece, near Delphi, and is buried in Athens.

APPENDIX TWO: ITINERARY OF JOHANN MARTIN WAGNER'S GREEK JOURNEY (1812–1813)[1]

July 21, 1812: Wagner receives a letter from Crown Prince Ludwig of Bavaria, asking him to make a trip to Greece.

Wagner protests that he cannot locate a map (*charte*), but Ludwig is insistent.

Wagner eventually hires an assistant, Pacifico Storani, and prepares for his journey.

DEPARTURE FROM ITALY

September 8, 1812: Wagner and Storani depart from Rome in a *vetterin* bound for Naples.

September 9, 1812: The two men spend their second night in Terracina. Storani adopts a dog he refers to as their "good genius" and names it Fundi.

September 11, 1812: The two men arrive at Capua, but are required to return without their luggage to secure further permissions from the French consulate.

September 12, 1812: Naples again. Wagner remains here for one week, to arrange credit with bankers here and in Greece.

September 19, 1812: The Feast of Saint Januarius. The two men depart Naples in the evening.

September 20, 1812: Passing through Avellino ("not a bad spot in the Appenine hills"), the two men stay at Aviano, and sightsee the next day.

September 21, 1812: Ordona.

September 22, 1812: St. Cassiano, in the plain of Puglia and in sight of the Adriatic Coast. Wagner wishes to depart from Barletta, but cannot find a boat to take him to Corfu, as everyone is fearful of the British naval blockade.

Otranto is recommended as the closest, and likeliest, point of departure.

September 25, 1812: The two men take a *fuhrman* (a type of carriage Wagner had previously seen on Malta, with glass on three sides and "with room for two, if they're not fat"). Barletta-to-Andria, after passing through Molfutta with Bari visible off to the right.

September 26, 1812: Midday arrival at Mola. The two men arrive at Monopoli in the evening, a small seaside town with especially good local Puglian wine.

September 27, 1812: Midday arrival at Ostuni. The two men arrive at St. Vito in the evening.

September 28, 1812: The coast of Brindisi comes into view.
They stop in Cellino at midday ("awful") then arrive at Lecce by nightfall (Wagner calls this city "another world").

September 29, 1812: Midday arrival at Garrano. The two men arrive at Otranto in the evening.
The French consul is very helpful, and arranges Wagner's transport.
Wagner hears the sounds of a British cannonade close by during the night.

THE CROSSING

September 30, 1812: The two men board a Neapolitan *sciabeko* [or *spironera*] at sunrise under the direction of Captain Saverio Castagnola.
The vessel departs with four other boats at dusk; Wagner judges theirs to be the best of the group.
Wagner immediately becomes seasick, and the Captain keeps an all-night lookout for British warships.
The four ships arrive at the island of Fanno (also called Fanoo, it is now called Othoni), which houses a French battery.

October 1, 1812: The two men depart from Othoni at midday, and arrive at the "Canal von Corfu" at 11:00 p.m. that same evening.

PROBLEMS OF GUNPOWDER DIPLOMACY

October 2, 1812: The *Festungs Commandant* is General Lanzalotte, and the *Ordinateur General* is the Chevalier Thieboult, who receives his papers from Naples.
The Police Directeur Fouchier did all he could to assist Wagner's passage.
The problem was that Wagner had permission for travel to Patras, Prevesa, and Athens on the Greek mainland, but not to the island of Zante.

"Things went as well as I could have hoped," Wagner comments, "better perhaps than I expected."

October 2–10, 1812: Wagner is stuck on Corfu, seeking passage to Zante. Unable to pass from French to British territory, the two must pass through the Ottoman-controlled coast first.

October 10, 1812: Wagner takes ship from Corfu bound for Cephallonia.

October 11, 1812: They stop on an unnamed island off the Albanian coast.

October 12, 1812: Their ship departs but is forced to return, harboring on another vaguely "Turkish" island.

October 13, 1812: The party is unable to depart due to adverse winds.

October 14, 1812: Morning departure, they land at the harbor of Barga (now Parga), which is administered by both French and Greek officials.

October 15, 1812: Early morning departure from Barga. The ship gets as far as Regnossa, but is forced back by British corsairs and retires to the harbor of Fanari. Wagner suffers through supper aboard ship.

October 16, 1812: Uncertain of the possibility of a passage by sea, the two men send their luggage ahead with two Greeks, Tomassio Tavesi of Patras and Andre Zornarello of Zephalonia (Cephallonia).

They stay in a Turk's home near the sea, and sleep outside near the fire under a full moon.

October 17, 1812: The two men visit the ruins of Nicopolis, founded by Augustus after his victory at the Battle of Actium off this same coast. They pass through Artea Actium and arrive at Prevesa, where they secure food and wine.

Wagner searches for the French consul, but finds a "lousy Greek" instead. The Greek official arranges lodging with an elderly widow across the street from his own quarters.

October 17–26, 1812: Stuck in Prevesa, Wagner is unable to arrange papers that will enable his free passage to Zante. Eventually he hires passage to Santa Maura *without* the proper permissions.

October 26, 1812: Departure from Prevesa for Santa Maura at midday. Two British soldiers take him to the *Platzcommandant*, a native-born Italian by the name of Aratta. He takes note of Wagner's Roman residence, and the purpose of his trip, and makes Wagner's arrangements.

The two men talk for an hour and Aratta informs Wagner that Ali Pasha reported the news (he heard it in Vienna) that Moscow was soon to be burned by the French. The British were especially despondent at the news.

Wagner is taken to the British General Campbell, who is also friendly and helpful. He feeds him, then accompanies him to his boat for Zante.

Wagner falls asleep as soon as the boat departs.

October 27, 1812: Wagner wakes up back in the harbor of Santa Maura. The Greek captain had returned in the night and Wagner, nearly out of time, is furious.
They leave again at midday. A bad storm comes up in the afternoon, and they put in at Mekanisi for the night. They are drenched by the rains and drink "a kind of salve made of talc mixed with rum" to say warm.
October 28, 1812: Passage on to Fermecolo (also called Felsen).
October 29, 1812: Good winds blowing straight in the direction of Zante.

LANDFALL AT ZANTE

October 30, 1812: Gropius makes an appearance. Wagner, in quarantine, meets with Haller, Linkh, Stackelberg, Bronstadt, and Luz. Only Gropius is unknown to him. Gropius informs Wagner that he is the only representative who has yet arrived for the auction, which is scheduled to be held in two days. The men all agree that these statues would be best housed in Bavaria since London is too "inaccessible." Wagner learns only now that the statues have been removed to Malta, but his Bavarian colleagues assure him of the quality of the pieces. Wagner remains uncertain how to proceed.
November 1, 1812: Wagner agrees to purchase the Aegina Marbles in the name of His Royal Highness Ludwig of Bavaria. The deal, involving all the statues listed in the manifest, is conditional upon Wagner's actually seeing the collection. Given the difficulties of sea travel to Malta, the men propose a visit to Athens, where Wagner may inspect the Aeginetan pieces and plaster casts still in the possession of the French consul, Fauvel.
November 2–27, 1812: Wagner remains for the month of November on Zante with Gropius, Haller, Linckh ("from Constatt"), Stackelberg ("an artist and friend of the arts"), Bronstadt ("an archaeologist from Denmark"), and Luz (a Swabian tutor hired by the Danish consul on Zante).

THE GREEK MAINLAND TO ATHENS

November 28, 1812: With Gropius and his servants, Wagner and his men take ship from Zante for the coast of the Morea.

November 29, 1812: They arrive at the Peneus River. Wagner sets out on foot with Gropius to Gastuni, near ancient Elis. The two take lodgings with a local doctor while they wait for their luggage and Gropius attempts to arrange an engagement with the daughter. They press on to Antrovitti (Andravida) and Legonoo (Lechaina).

November 30, 1812: A day of sightseeing, they arrive in the evening at Bali Agaja (Ano or Kato Achaia), near the site of ancient Dyme.

December 1, 1812: The two men arrive in Patras at 10:00 a.m.
This is Wagner's first experience with Ottoman Turks, whom he considers far more civilized than the others nearby. He enjoys a Turkish bath "for 30 *para*, some 10 or 12 *bajucchi* in Roman money."
They stay three days while Gropius works with the British consul (Mr. Strange), the French consul (Ercole Rioussel), and the American consul (Mr. Contoquri), the financial liaisons for the sale of the Aegina Marbles.

December 4, 1812: Wagner, Gropius, and Storani depart Patras by boat. With the wind very light, they pass Epakta (Naupaktos) and Vostizza (Aegium), then spend the evening on the island of Trifonia.

December 6, 1812: With the wind virtually nonexistent, the party lands at Scala Von Salona for lunch, and explores ancient Krisa, where they take lodging.

December 7, 1812: There is rain in the morning and the *scirocco* winds return. They explore Krisa again, examining the cylopean walls, boustrophedon inscriptions, and visual designs. They move on to Mount Parnassus and Delphi, explore the Castalian Spring, and spend the night at Arachova.

December 8, 1812: They pass through Cisma (where Oedipus killed Laius), Platanos, and Chaironea (site of the victory of Philip and Alexander of Macedonia over an alliance of Greek cities). They return to Livathia in the evening.

December 9, 1812: They remain in Livathia while Gropius continues his marriage negotiations (*Heyrathsspeculationen*). Wagner explores ancient ruins on his own.

December 12, 1812: Everyone but Gropius departs, passing on to Thebes, where they camp outside on Mount Cithairon.

December 13, 1812: Wagner explores the ruins of Thebes at dawn, before the party departs at around 8:00 a.m. With Roman aqueducts lining their route, they pass the Fortress of Phyle, bordering the regions of Boeotia and Attica. Wagner enjoys his first sight of the Akropolis in the distance.

ATHENS

December 14, 1812: Eager to arrive, the party leaves very early and arrives in Athens at 3:00 p.m. They are required to wait at the gates, since reports have arrived that three Turks have just died of plague (*Pest*) in Thebes. Wagner requests an audience with his consul—in this case the French consul, since Wagner is a Roman resident and Rome is still occupied by the French. He forwards his letter of introduction from the French consul of Patras, Rioussel, to the consul of Athens, Louis-François Sébastien Fauvel.

Wagner is lodged in a hovel, outside the city walls.

December 15, 1812: After a terrible breakfast, Wagner explores the outside circuit of city walls while he waits on Fauvel, who moves him into excellent quarters inside the city.

Fauvel holds some excellent casts of the Aegina Marbles, and they exceed Wagner's expectations. Judging them Archaic (*altklassische*) and singularly naturalistic, Wagner deems this to be the finest example of ancient art he has ever seen. The bodies alone confirm "the heretofore unknown gifts of the Aeginetan School."

Wagner confirms the Zante contract, and arranges for a payment, through Gropius, to Cockerell, Haller, Linkh, and Foster.

Next they begin negotiations for the cost of transport of the marbles from Malta and Athens to Rome.

December 15, 1812–March 15, 1813: Wagner in residence in Athens at the Capuchin hostelry. There is a long battle over the manner and costs of transport. Wagner suspects Gropius of trying to make a profit on this part of the deal and protests to the French consulate, whose officer, Nicola Giograsso, assists him.

Wagner spends most of his time sightseeing with Fauvel, whom he admires. He also finds the Ottoman Turks to be more like Germans than anyone he has met thus far in his travels.

RETURN TO ROME

March 15, 1813: Wagner departs from Athens with Giograsso and Luz. They take ship in the Piraeus harbor past Salamis and Megara to Corinth.

March 17–18, 1813: Lodging in Corinth.

March 23, 1813:Crossing overland to the Gulf of Corinth.

March 24, 1813: Departure by boat to Patras.
March 25, 1813–April 19, 1813: Final arrangements in Patras.
April 20–21, 1813: Wagner travels from Patras to Zante. He reconfirms the conditions of the contract with Gropius, but this time with the witness of lawyers, governors, and a man named Friedrich Nord.
April 21–May 5, 1813: Wagner remains in Zante through Greek Easter, until the arrival of a British fleet.
May 5, 1813: Wagner returns from Zante to Patras.
May 5–29, 1813: Preparations for final transport of some marbles from Patras.
May 29, 1813: Departs Patras for the final time.
June 9, 1813: Landfall at Ancona.
June 13, 1813–July 10, 1813: Wagner is quarantined at Lazareth.
July 25, 1813: Wagner returns to Ancona.
July 30, 1813: Overland departure from Ancona.
August 4, 1813: Wagner arrives in Rome.

APPENDIX THREE: SCHELLING'S 1815 LECTURE "ON THE DEITIES OF SAMOTHRACE" AS THE PRELUDE TO HIS WORK ON THE AEGINA MARBLES

> The artist who has the marble before himself from which a work of art is to emerge does not *see* this work of art; but if he did not have the belief, i.e., the confidence that what he cannot now see could become visible via his effort, via a sequence of actions which he carries out with the marble, he would never put his hand to it. Belief always presupposes a goal which is present in *every* activity which wishes to achieve something specific. Columbus *believed* in the existence of a part of the world which was unknown at his time and steered boldly westwards. Would we be able to say Columbus *believed* in this part of the world if he had never *left* the Spanish coast? Hence there is no belief where there is not *wanting* and *doing* at the same time. . . . If belief is a necessary element of all goal-directed activity, then it is also an essential element of the true philosophy. *All* science only arises in belief. . . . Those who separate knowledge and belief, indeed oppose them, therefore belong to the class of people, who these days are unfortunately extremely numerous, who do not themselves know what they want: the saddest thing which one can ever encounter in any being endowed with reason.
>
> Schelling, *Lectures on the History of Modern Philosophy*, 178

This remarkable passage appears in the context of Schelling's criticism of Theosophy, as developed in the later work of Friedrich H. Jacobi (1743–1819); Jacobi had earlier criticized Schelling in print, in January of 1812, so the challenge was personal. But it was not only this. I begin with this passage not only because it offers such a striking interpretation of the creative agency of the sculptor, but also because it helps to counter a common misunderstanding of the allegedly mystical and mythological—not to say deeply religious—dimension to Schelling's later thought. If Schelling is suggesting that no truly scientific inquiry may be undertaken without some belief, then he is not saying that science is just another kind of faith. Quite the contrary. By linking wanting and doing, Schelling draws the surprising conclusion that belief, much like sculpting marble or examining the heavens, is a matter of doing every bit as much as it is a matter of heart or mind.

Echoing the Epistle of James ["just as the body (σῶμα) without spirit (χωρὶς πνεύματος) is dead, so faith (πίστις) without works (χωρὶς ἔργων) is dead also,"

2:26], Schelling appears to question whether the customary division between these two imaginative modes of coming to know—through rational inquiry and through belief—can be maintained. One-sided rationalism, like one-sided fideism, is to be avoided. Schelling, as we have seen, is attempting to think dialectically, not dualistically. And he specifically invoked the plastic arts in this regard. For most of the philosophers working within the idealist tradition with which Schelling identified (however ambivalently), art and religion and philosophy were viewed together as works of the (collective) human spirit. Differences there assuredly were, but there were deep connections between these creative modes of human speculation as well. Schelling was preeminently a philosopher of connections, imaginative connections.

It is important to emphasize that the Aeginetan works of art that inspired Ludwig's acquisitive tastes, and Wagner's enthusiastic descriptions, as well as Schelling's historical and philosophical ruminations, were religious images designed to decorate and to amplify a sanctuary sacred to a Greek god or goddess. By 1815, Schelling had determined to apply his primary philosophical energies to the close study of such religious artifacts—to Greek case studies, if you will. In doing so, he wished to hold the artistic (doing), the religious (believing), and the speculative (inquiring) modes of human activity together. To this end, he applied himself first to an important sanctuary on the Greek island of Samothrace, and then again here to an important temple on the island of Aegina. In this appendix, I would like to offer some further context for this dramatic shift in Schelling's scholarly interests and approach.

Schelling was five years junior to his roommates in the theology program at the *Tübinger Stift*: Georg Wilhelm Friedrich Hegel (1770–1831) and Friedrich Hölderlin (1770–1843), whom he joined one year after their arrival in 1789. This is among the most remarkable moments of philosophical synergy in the history of modern thought. As George Steiner puts it:

> The complicity of ideals, the reciprocity of heuristic energies, which marked the intimacy of these three young men, were to have an effect on European thought and sensibility which it is not easy to exaggerate. Enthusiasts for the French Revolution, in its dawn stages, acolytes of Kantian Idealism as seen through the eyes of Schiller's poetry and aesthetic essays, equally determined to restore to the enlightened soul what Hölderlin called "that golden age of truth and beauty which was Greece," Hegel, Hölderlin, and Schlegel [sic] turned to identical imperatives and models of radiance. We cannot reconstruct the exact motion of symbiosis, but Hölderlin's cult of Sophocles and Schelling's conviction that tragedy was the essential discourse of being

> probably derived, in the first instance, from Hegel. As early as July 1787, Hegel had attempted to translate Sophocles, notably the *Oedipus at Colonus*. This text would refer him to the incomparable pathos of Antigone. He communicated the vital encounter to his two companions with ardour. Even across subsequent polemics and silences, the *Antigone* was to remain a bond between the three men. Severally, they were to set it at the pivot of consciousness.[1]

It is telling that the three friends were drawn to modern revolutions on the one hand, and to ancient Greek ideals on the other, establishing the essential link between ancient and modern forms of creative independence. Freedom lay at the heart of their common passion: freedom from political domination, freedom of inquiry, freedom of religion. Freedom of religion was essential to these three seminary students, in part (as I suggested in the introduction) because it was the necessary condition from which they might explore the important *connections* between Christian and pre-Christian forms of spiritual life—no crude dualisms, here. Greek tragedy, the three were to conclude collectively, lay at the heart of both.

Hegel would stage a decisive reading of the *Antigone* in the Spirit section of his *Phenomenology of Spirit*, a reading whose influence and vast appeal extends to the present day. Hölderlin turned to a psychologically daunting mode of translation of the *Antigone* in the months prior to his final collapse; while Goethe famously condemned the work, Heidegger would lend this text enormous importance in his later turn to a philosophy of language. And Schelling would return to Greek tragedy in many of his occasional writings and lecture courses; Greek drama makes several important appearances in this text, as we have seen, echoing some of the dramatic observations more commonly credited to Nietzsche.

There is little doubt as to Hegel's influence on his immediate circle of friends, to say nothing of the later world of German thought and letters. Yet to overplay Hegel's power and influence is to underplay Schelling's virtuoso performances on many of these same themes. Of the three men, Schelling was the real prodigy, in any case, which makes his alleged later silence all the more compelling, romantic, and mysterious. Schelling published four significant works before his twenty-second year was ended, and so, in 1797 he was called to his first professorial posting at Jena. (By contrast, Hegel did not publish his first book until 1807, at the age of thirty-eight.) Schelling published another major book in 1800, a significant article on "Philosophy and Religion" in 1804 (to which I will return), and arguably his most famous work, the *Philosophical Investigations on the Essence of Human Freedom* in 1809, another text that Heidegger did much to popularize afresh.[2] And then, so goes the story, Schelling went mysteriously silent.

Now, on the one hand, the publication of this book gives the lie to the idea of Schelling's sudden silence. And if there is no silence, then there is no mystery to resolve. Thus the central issue before us is rather this: that Schelling opted to publish *differently*, and in a highly conscious way, not to avoid publishing at all. That is the shift I would like to sketch out, at least in outline, here.

In order to do so, I would like to walk through Schelling's curriculum in slightly more detail, in order to discern the lineaments of a different story concerning his philosophical career and a different way of assessing its importance. Like his fellow seminarians, Schelling wrote a great deal on ancient Greek themes in Tübingen; a long essay on Plato's *Timaeus* in 1794 is especially relevant to contemporary Heideggerian and Derridean readings of this same text, as John Sallis and Jason Wirth have recently shown.[3] Schelling published his first major work in 1794, "On the Possibility of a Form of Philosophy in General" [*Über die Möglichkeit einer Form der Philosophie überhaupt*], then followed this with three more significant works: "On the I as a Principle of Philosophy" [*Von Ich als Prinzip der Philosophie* (1795)]; "Philosophical Letters on Dogmatism and Criticism" [*Philosophische Briefe über Dogmatismus und Kritizismus* (1795)]; and "Ideas Toward a Philosophy of Nature" [*Ideen zur einer Philosophie der Natur* (1797)]. It was then that he received the call to Jena. Two works of even greater significance came next: the "System of Transcendental Idealism" [*System des transzendentalen Idealismus*] in 1800; and the "Philosophical Investigations on the Essence of Human Freedom" [*Philosophische Untersuchungen über das Wesen der menschlichen Freiheit*] in 1809. Then, so we have heard, he stopped.

What happened? If we assume that Schelling did indeed fail to publish anything else of significance in his lifetime, then we may be inclined to one kind of explanation. Schelling's wife, Caroline, died on September 7, 1809; her husband's grief was immense and lasting. It was during this period that Johann Martin Wagner returned to his German homeland, and he spent six weeks with Schelling then[4]; the visit, the sharing of grief and vulnerability, sealed their friendship as a lifetime of epistolary intimacy, and this book, both make clear.

But Schelling, in actual fact, was very shortly involved in a major new project: *The Ages of the World* [*Die Weltalter*], which he revised with enormous energy and attention through three successive drafts that differ quite dramatically; they are dated to 1811, 1813, and 1815. The second 1813 version was translated into English by Judith Norman (in 1997)[5] and is accompanied by an important essay on the text by Slavoj Zizek; the third 1815 version was translated by Jason Wirth (in 2000),[6] with a very insightful introductory essay that has been of great value to me in the preparation of this manuscript. But Schelling himself never saw the book into print. His son, Karl Friedrich August, included the third 1815 version in his father's *Collected Works* in 1861 (in Volume 8); the first and second drafts lay dormant until they were rediscovered in the Library of Munich in 1939 and were published by Manfred Schröter in 1946.[7]

To return to our central question: Why *The Ages of the World*, and why was it never completed? These are not easy questions to answer, in part because *The Ages of the World* is a very difficult text to read. It is just the second major text that Schelling attempted after the publication of Hegel's *Phenomenology of Spirit* and it is aimed in part against aspects of Hegel's approach. Hegel had notoriously (and unfairly) characterized Schelling's aesthetic and intuitionist practices as "the night in which all cows are black"; everything, in other words, remained indeterminate, thus invalidating the approach in its entirety, as unable to deliver that to which it aspired. Schelling was offended, not least because the phrase was his, issued as a cautionary word against the misuse of this same approach, some four years earlier.[8] It was, at best, an uncharitable criticism from the pen of a close personal friend.

Still, Schelling was as interested as Hegel was in the major trajectories of contemporary philosophy: in the aftermath of the French Revolution, with its descent into a spiral of self-consuming violence; and in the aftermath of Kantian philosophy, with its descent into the excesses of subjectivity or fideism. Schelling agreed with Hegel that the task of a truly modern and a truly critical philosophy was to split the difference between dogmatism and skepticism; he agreed that freedom was the *sine qua non* of human existence, and that its authentic embodiment was far from simple; he agreed that the French Revolution had gone awry to the degree that it had misunderstood the form of freedom it was called upon to promote; he agreed that art and religion were essential resources for revolutionary and philosophical inquiry alike; and he agreed, perhaps most of all, on the determinate significance of the ancient Greeks.

This provides the complex intellectual environment in which *The Ages of the World* must be read. When read this way, it seems to me that the project is essentially an attempt to read the first three chapters of Genesis—exegetically, and dramatically, and philosophically, all at once—informed both by Greek drama and the crucial new openings in philosophy managed in the wake of the Kantian critical system. In other words, this is a philosophical account of a Creator who freely creates things out of nothing, and of the free creatures whose freedom is nonetheless constrained by the fact that they did not, and cannot, create themselves. (Recall here that one of Schelling's first major pieces was on Plato's *Timaeus*.) Jason Wirth calls *Ages of the World* "a philosophical poem,"[9] recalling Lucretius's *De Rerum Naturum*. We might also call it a cosmic tragedy, a meditation on freedom and constraint offered in the wake of his wife's recent death. It is, then, a meditation on time and fragility and flux.

And it never succeeded to Schelling's satisfaction. How could it have?, one wonders. It was an ambitious attempt to combine the philosophy of nature with the subjective turn in modern thought as well as a robust exploration of the power of creation, both human and divine. It was virtually a philosophy of Everything, and it put a premium both on artistic creativity and the power of the imagination. The sculptor may not see the statue in the marble, but he or she imagines something, something that does not yet exist . . . but will.

Schelling had come to these ideas as early as 1804, some time after he began lecturing on the philosophy of art, and published his important essay on "Philosophy and Religion."[10] In that essay, he distinguished for the first time between "negative philosophy," which he felt characterized what he had produced up to then, and "positive philosophy," which is what he now intended to offer as a necessary supplement. Jason Wirth has referred to this as "the descending history of the Ideal, or Freedom, among the Real."[11] Andrew Bowie notes that "[t]he goal of positive philosophy was to come to terms both with the fact that things are and with the contingencies of the historical emergence and development of thinking. The ultimate aim of positive philosophy was to derive a philosophically viable religion from a reinterpretation of the historical development of Christianity."[12] In his later "Lectures on the History of Modern Philosophy," Schelling himself called it "the philosophy which relates to existence," and observes that "it took some time before philosophy became clear to itself about this, for all progression of philosophy only happens slowly."[13] He associated negative philosophy most closely with Hegel's *Logic*[14] and, by implication, held up his own approach as the positive alternative. Let me offer a suggestion on what is at stake here, and how it helps explain Schelling's work on the Aeginetan Marbles.

We are probably all familiar with Raphael's canonical contrast of Plato and Aristotle in "The School of Athens" housed at the Vatican Palace. Plato, the philosopher of the forms, holds the *Timaeus* in one hand and points toward the heavens with the other; Aristotle, the philosopher of the particulars, holds the *Ethics* in one hand and points toward the ground with the other. In like manner, Schelling is suggesting that Hegel held his hand aloft, attempting to reveal the logical structures that made sense of the world and made the world make sense. Schelling, by contrast, wishes to hold philosophy accountable to the world as it is, in its radically contingent process of historical becoming. The only way to reinterpret Christianity in a way that makes sense is to study its historical coming-to-be, and that historical process necessarily includes the pre-Christian, Greek culture out of which this new religion emerged. The only way to reveal the philosophical meaning of historical developments is thus through case studies. Such is a more "positive" philosophy.

Schelling may have finally set aside *The Ages of the World* in 1815, though this is not at all clear. He clearly never abandoned the idea, and his interest in it never waned. In fact, he offered a systematic lecture-course on the idea of *Die Weltalter* as late as 1827–28 in Munich.[15] But the focus of Schelling's energies had clearly shifted; it seems as if he realized that he needed to lay a more secure foundation before he could erect the edifice he imagined as the *Weltalter* project. And this is when Schelling turned decisively to several Greek case studies, case studies that he himself referred to as "supplements" (*Beilage*). He offered an enormously important lecture (important to him) entitled "The Deities of Samothrace" at the Bavarian Academy of Sciences in Munich on October 12, 1815; he had been preparing this lecture for quite some time.[16] He devoted the following year to the preparation of his notes and appendices for Wagner's book on the Aegina Marbles, which was published in early 1817. He would devote the rest of his professional life to working on precisely these kinds of narrower case studies, which he presented serially in lectures on the "Philosophy of Art," the "Philosophy of Mythology," and the "Philosophy of Revelation." He did so in later years, ironically enough, from Hegel's Chair of Philosophy in Berlin to which he was called in 1841, one decade after his friend's demise.

"The Deities of Samothrace" thus offers a marvelous window that opens onto some of the new methodological approaches that also inform Schelling's supplements to Wagner's text, I think. I would like briefly to rehearse his complex analysis in that lecture, an argument that relies heavily on dazzling flights of philological fancy. I am using the English translation by Robert F. Brown, which was published in 1974,[17] though I eagerly await a new critical edition of the lecture which will be edited by Jason Wirth and David Krell, and which will restore the extensive notes Schelling appended to the lecture (most, but not all, of which Brown eliminated). I include the pagination from Brown's translation parenthetically here.

Schelling begins with the island of Samothrace as a physical location, a context, a volcanic island rising dramatically from out of the northern

Aegean Sea. It stood in between Greece and Asia Minor, symbolically linking east and west. It was even called "the Thracian Samos" in antiquity, linking it decisively to the Dodecanesian island of Samos just off the coast of Asia Minor and home to one of the most ancient of all Greek sanctuaries, the Heraion of Samos (which receives significant discussion in this text). "A mysterious polytheism was established there in indeterminable antiquity" (15), Schelling observes. If the Ionian island of Samos were famous for its native son, Pythagoras, who contributed to communal religion aimed at the elevation of humanity, then Samothrace was renowned for "the cult of the Cabiri, the most ancient in all of Greece" (15). It was a mystery cult, and an initiatory cult, one where "Greece first received from the forests of Samothrace the belief in a future life" (15).

Who, then, were these Cabiri? Schelling develops a complex philological answer to that question. He asserts that they were linked in Greek mythology to Demeter, Dionysus, Hermes, and more obliquely, to Zeus himself. The evidence Schelling marshals to his purpose is obscure, to say the least. He turns to a note written by a scholiast named Mnaseas and appended to the margins of one manuscript (the Parisiana) of Apollonius of Rhodes's *Argonautika* I: 917.[18] It is, to say the least, a Gnostic-seeming foundation for a philosophical argument of this historical complexity.

Mnaseas suggests that the name Cabiri is neither Greek, nor Egyptian, nor Indian, but rather Hebrew-Phoenician (17); Mnaseas also noted that these Cabiri were three in number: Axieros (whom he associated with Demeter), Axiokersa (whom he associated with Persephone), and Axiokersos (whom he associated with Hades). Schelling later mentions a fourth figure, Kasmilos (21), whom he associated with Hermes. By hypothesizing the meaning of these names from their Phoenician roots, Schelling associated Axieros with yearning or desire, the feminine power lying behind the act of creation itself (18). And then, through some dazzling sleights of philological hand, Schelling eventually concluded that "the first three Samothracian gods form the very same sequence and chain in which we everywhere find Demeter, Persephone, and Dionysos" (21).

Schelling's reconstruction faces a grave problem, as he readily admits: the traditional number of the Cabiri "is given quite definitely as seven, with which an eighth is associated" (22). His solution to this numerical inconsistency is to hypothesize an original trinity of higher Cabiri, with a second group of four, all of whom were "served" by Hermes, the liminal deity who bridges the higher and lower orders; Schelling, however, associated Kadmilos/Hermes with that higher order, lending a balance of four deities each, above and below, mirror images of the creative ages of the world, as it were (22–23).

Schelling's interest in this complex and comparative cosmology ultimately lies with the desire to make better sense of what he refers to as "natural monotheism," and its specific relation to polytheistic cosmologies such as the one identified here on Samothrace. The gods (plural) in this view are not best imagined as "emanations" from one primal divinity, but are better seen as steps along the way toward an ever-more complex and *pluralistic monotheism*.

> The ascending series now reads as follows. The lowest is Ceres, whose essence is hunger and seeking. . . . The next, Proserpina, is the essence of the fundamental origin of the whole [external] nature. Then comes Dionysos, lord of the spirit world. Over nature and the spirit world is Kadmilos or Hermes who has both subordinate to him. . . . Beyond all of these is the demiurge, the god who stands over against the world.
>
> Thus the Cabiri doctrine was a system ascending from subordinate personalities or nature deities up to a highest personality ruling them all, a transcendent god. (24)

We can see the lengths to which Schelling is prepared to go to *systematize* mythology, to make philosophical sense of the most ancient of religious ideas. He concludes that a true monotheism is a *pluralistic* monotheism, "not that so-called monotheism which is not derived from the Old or New Testaments but is perhaps Mohammedan" (25).[19] That is to say, a truly pluralistic monotheism, even in its later polytheistic expressions, possesses the traces of its origin which may also provide, Ariadne-like, the guiding thread with which to find our way back to such an originally pluralistic conception of deity. These traces we find especially clearly in Greek myth, "which, of all paganism, is the purest and closest to the truth" (29). Thus the paths from and to these explicitly polytheist frameworks must not be foreclosed.

Not only is Greek mythology the purest and closest to truth, for Schelling, but it is also closest to the originary Hebrew monotheism, whose primary (and therefore "original") name for the deity was in fact a plural, *Elohim* (27–28, with notes 113, 118). The Etruscans too utilized divine names in the plural (as *Consentes* and *Complices*, 28). In each such polytheistic case, these deities were envisioned in male-female pairs, presided over by the Supreme Being. Thus, Schelling concludes, on Samothrace we should imagine three divine pairs, with Zeus presiding over all (which six gods, exactly, Schelling curiously does not say). This, in any case, is the philosophical meaning of the cult, *a pluralist unity of the Godhead*, and somehow this revelation of originary pluralism held the key to the Samothracian intimation of immortality (30).

The island of Aegina makes a brief appearance in Schelling's lecture, near the beginning:

> Now that more than ever public attention is again directed to ancient Greece, if this almost forgotten island would be investigated throughly like the others perhaps the yield of such research would not be the value of the art works, *as in that incomparable discovery on Aegina*, but instead monuments of the most ancient belief, even more important than the former for the entire history of our species. (16, italics mine)

It is a stunning mode of argumentation. Both Aegina and Samothrace are incomparably beautiful and incomparably old Greek islands. Each bears significant secrets about human origins. And here is the key: as *art* is to Aegina, so *religion* is to Samothrace . . . over them both presides modern philosophy which, when sufficiently scientific *and historical* in its approach (29–30), can make the fullest sense of each.

One of the most striking assertions in this Aeginetan text is that great age granted great authority. Schelling had already gestured in that direction in *The Ages of the World*. Beginnings were uniquely revelatory, or at least they could be. It was the very antiquity of the Samothracian cult that established its relevance (and revelatory value) from an archaeological and a religious point of view. It was the very antiquity of the Aeginetan School that established its value from a naturalistic and art-historical point of view. These claims represented a profound challenge to the then-emerging progressivist view of human history.

And thus they also posed anew the question concerning the relationship of older Egyptian to more recent Greek art.

APPENDIX FOUR: THEORIES ON THE RELATIONSHIP BETWEEN EGYPTIAN AND GREEK, OR AEGINETAN, ART

Thereupon one of the [Egyptian] priests, who was of a very great age, said, "O Solon, Solon, you Greeks are always children, and there is not an old man among you."

Solon asked him what he meant.

"I mean to say," he replied, "that in mind you are all young. . . ."

Plato, *Timaeus* 22b [4th century BCE]

Among the Egyptians, art did not advance much beyond its earliest style, and it could not easily have attained the heights it did among the Greeks. The reasons for this lay partly in their physical appearance, partly in their way of thinking, and just as much in their customs and laws, especially those relating to religion.

Johann Joachim Winckelmann, *History of the Art of Antiquity*, 128 [1764]

It is clear that the name of Daedalus was a fictitious name signifying an ancient sculptural school.

Thus *School* is simply a word designating a certain method, a particular way of seeing, of feeling and of manufacture.

Antoine Chrysostome Quatremère de Quincy, *Le Jupiter Olympien*, 176 [1815]

We can easily see the problem in general terms: How to account for the alleged superiority of Greek art over its highly influential Egyptian predecessor? What made Greek art exemplary, and what accounts for the longevity of its appeal? Winckelmann, who was arguably the first to develop an historical template, and a genealogy, for looking at ancient art in a comparative manner, was not coy about the matter. The Greeks, he suggested, were superior to the Egyptians in appearance, in philosophical temperament, in democratic commitment, and in spiritual discernment. Democracy, in fact, provided the foundation of freedom upon which the Greeks were to build their revolutionary edifice, the elective affinity they established between the visual arts, tragedy, and philosophy, all of them aiming at fuller religious insight.

So Egyptian art *gave way* to Greek art, which *surpassed* it in all its particulars. Now—despite the obvious Orientalist excess, the way in which Egypt often serves merely as a placeholder for "Eastern" culture and its inferiority to "Western" European forms as first embodied in Greece herself—loosely speaking, we know what Winckelmann had in mind. The essential contrasts span the fields of architecture, sculpture, and religion. Egyptian architecture was massive, granite, and designed to be overwhelming; no modern building had yet surpassed the Great Pyramids in height in Winckelmann's, Quatremere's, and Schelling's day. And this was all a monument to imperial state religion. Greek religious architecture was elegant, marble, and designed on a human scale; it was taken to be a monument to Greek democracy. Egyptian sculpture was rigid in every sense of the term: fully forward-facing, blocklike in design, without the intentional display of movement, never altering its limited repertoire of forms across two millennia. Greek sculpture was, from the outset, rendered in the nude, and quite early on it placed those nudes in motion, developing with astonishing rapidity in the course of just two centuries. Egyptian conceptions of divinity combined human and animal forms in a manner Winckelmann could only see as monstrous, whereas Greek art imagined the divine anthropomorphically, and established the human form as the canonical measure of both beauty and excellence. Like most such generalizations, there is a kernel of insight here, combined with a deliberate avoidance of all the counterevidence that might complicate this general picture. Of course Egyptian art developed and changed significantly, like every other artistic tradition, but the image of a *static* Eastern world juxtaposed to the dynamism and revolutionary ethos of the West enjoyed a long afterlife, and was rendered canonical in Hegel's "Lectures on the Philosophy of World History," which he offered throughout the 1820s, as Greece was involved in its long war of independence against the Ottoman Empire.

Tellingly enough, Quatremère de Quincy's academic career actually *began* with this question of the relationship between Greek and Egyptian art. Breaking free of his father's mercantile interests even as he aspired to an academic career, Quatremère made two important trips to Italy in order to cultivate his art historical knowledge and aesthetic tastes. The first trip lasted more than three years (1776–1780) and was important, among other things, for the friendship he developed there with the French artist, Jacques Louis David (1748–1825). The second, far briefer visit in 1783 produced an even more important and more lasting friendship with the neoclassical Venetian sculptor, Antonio Canova (1757–1822). Under the influence of Winckelmann's inspired ruminations on the classical world, most all of them written in Rome—and inspired both by the political use David made of neoclassical forms, as well as the spiritual use Canova made of these same forms—Quatremère was determined to lend his services to the same revolution in morals, spirituality and aesthetic taste. It was a bit early for Romanticism, but these ideas were very much in the air.

Distinguishing Greek art emphatically from its Egyptian predecessor was the route that Quatremère pursued to achieve fairly early academic success. Quatremère enjoyed his first taste of the severe Doric style at Paestum, and then again when he visited Sicily in 1779. The Temple of Zeus at Agrigento had by then been restored according to its description in the account of Diodorus Siculus, and was to be the subject of Quatremère's first essay, written at the age of twenty-five.[1] The idea of using ancient literary sources (Diodorus in this case) to assist in the reconstruction of ancient monuments would be a recurrent theme throughout Quatremère's long scholarly career;[2] both Wagner and Schelling participate in this same extensive scholarly practice, as we have seen.

But first came Egypt. When Quatremère returned to Paris in 1784–85, he was determined to stay and determined to make his living through scholarly pursuits. In the previous year, the Academy of Inscriptions and Literary Arts, to which Quatremère would devote much of his later professional life, proposed the following topic for its celebrated *Prix Caylus:*[3] "What was the state of architecture among the Egyptians, and what do the Greeks appear to have borrowed from it?" (*Quel fut l'état de l'architecture chez les Égyptiens, et ce que le Grecs paraissent en avoir emprunté*). Quatremère was awarded the prize for his submission, which won him early notice at the French Academy, as well as a stipend for further research. But he did not return to the topic for nearly twenty years, and when he did, he took surprisingly little notice of the new acquisitions installed in Paris after the abortive French expedition to Egypt under Napoleon in 1799. It was as if his own views were to be as rigid and unchanging as the Egyptian art he wished to analyze.

The book was finally published in 1803 as *De l'état de l'architecture Égyptiennes, considérée dans son origine, ses principes et son goût, et comparée sous les mêmes rapports à l'Architecture Greque.*[4] The very specificity of the topic posed by the French Academy in 1785, clearly weighted in favor of Greek things, had enabled Quatremère to display his Hellenic credentials, but it also invited him to a fairly dismissive view of the Greeks' Egyptian predecessors. He was not entirely seduced by this progressive viewpoint, as the passages Schelling quotes with such appreciation make clear. There is a great deal in this book that seems crudely Orientalist to us now, but two things distinguished this first ambitious and even ambidextrous work by Quatremère de Quincy.

First, Quatremère devoted extraordinarily close attention to the various materials—stones, gems, woods, clays, and pigments—used by the Egyptians and the Greeks, respectively. Second, Quatremère devoted himself with at least as much passion to Greek and Egyptian architecture as he later would to sculpture in the round. Now, on the one hand this is unsurprising; the question posed by the French Academy specifically mentioned architecture. But Quatremère made the question very much his own. He famously referred to architecture as "an ocular music" (*une musique oculaire*, 215), and already in 1788 he was invited by a prominent bookseller and personal friend, Charles-Joseph Pancoucke, to edit an ambitious *Dictionary of Architecture*, the first volume of which appeared in Quatremère's name.[5]

A superb study of Quatremère's early work on Egypt was published by Sylvia Lavin in 1992,[6] and offers a fascinating interpretation of Quatremère's achievement as something that goes well beyond an expression of the accepted wisdom concerning the Greek's artistic exceptionalism. Lavin focuses on Quatremère's novel idea that architecture might be meaningfully compared to human language, since both were conventional, socially meaningful, and the product of human artifice. She identifies three related trajectories that Quatremère was able to develop through this analogizing of architecture to language: the *origins* of architectural forms; the *evolution* of architectural forms; and the *social use* of such forms. Quatremère proposed what became a highly influential idea: that the original "type" (or typology) for Egyptian architecture was the cave, whereas Chinese architecture was inspired by the tent, and ancient Greek architecture by the hut. Trees, in the Greek case, may thus be read as a primitive "type" of the architectural column. By the same logic, pyramids were vast caverns designed as eternal and unchanging sepulchers for the deceased.

It is striking, when the text is read this way, how *comparative* Quatremère's approach really was, in our contemporary sense of the term. He was not merely interested in demonstrating that Greek art was comparatively superior to Egyptian art. Rather, he was interested in appreciating artistic diversity for its own sake, for what it has to teach us about the sheer variety of human visual expression. The work was at least as *primitivist* as it was Orientalist, aiming to uncover the very oldest evidence of human artistic expression in architecture and design. Such primitivism, and the "epigenetic view of mankind" it assumed, also demonstrated how "Egypt" was a shifting scholarly register, no longer serving scholarly interests in biblical studies and biblical history alone, so much as it was to be repurposed for the emerging new interest in *classical* historiography and antiquarianism.[7]

It is here that Schelling offered an important intervention with far-reaching humanistic consequences. We have already seen how he rejected the crudely progressive strand of Enlightenment thought, with its confident belief that human social and cultural endeavors evolve forward and advance in the direction of nearly continuous improvement. Rather, Schelling was attracted to a kind of primitivism that also informed his interest both in Samothracian cult and in Aeginetan art.

I mentioned in the introduction that Schelling was unusually eloquent and clear-minded in describing what the shift from dualistic to dialectical thinking would entail, from an (art) historical standpoint. Here, in this text (and especially in the notes to the first chapter), we see how this idea cashes out in practical terms. Whereas his friend Wagner seemed content to assume the standard progressivist view—that Greek art surpassed and replaced Egyptian art—Schelling cautions us to imagine the nature of such cross-cultural contact and influence more carefully. It is too simplistic to speak of Egyptian art and Greek art as entirely separate entities. Such a view is what Schelling calls *einseitige*, "one-sided," presupposing as it does that one "side," the *Greek* side, simply trumped its artistic predecessor.

Schelling invited a more subtle, and far more sophisticated, perspective on the past, involving what he calls a *gegenseitige* perspective that imagines *mutual* lines of influence and cross-fertilization, the two-way flow of all genuine artistic creativity. On this view, it will not do to speak of Greek art surpassing Egyptian art; rather, the two art forms *mutually influenced* one another in the creation of what we might better imagine as a new whole: ancient Mediterranean art that was necessarily influenced most by classical and Hellenistic Greek forms after Alexander the Great's conquests. I recall the determinative passage from Schelling here:

> Moreover, the generally accepted rule concerning the relationship between the Egyptians and the Greeks—according to which the former is presented as the teacher and the latter as the pupil—ought to be called into doubt, as should the term "borrow," and also the idea of material exchange or communication as the most suitable model for this relationship. Thus it is far more the interpretation and explanation of this relationship, rather than the relationship itself, that may well appear most objectionable from the standpoint of contemporary German research.
>
> Since it is precisely among us that the entire world of antiquity is viewed more and more as a *whole*, as a self-contained and integrated world, and since every day we appear to be more convinced that Greek religion and culture represents the most vital development of all . . . because of this, the soil in which Greek culture grew and the ground in which it ripened—namely the

> religions and the cultures of other peoples—must be studied. Why should we not view Egyptian and Greek art in a living relationship, indeed in one and the same line of development? The whole culture of Egypt bears the marks of a great reversal, of the violent inhibition and postponement of a mighty principle in the course of its development. In the face of such repressive inhibition, must not the overflow of great cultural energy seek relief in the terrible, even in the desire to create the monstrous? And this same principle in Greece, beginning so to speak for a second time, but tending toward a freer, gentler and less repressed form of development, was it not able to achieve its highest possible perfection through an inner necessity?
>
> It is indisputable, and even necessary, that the most independent and contrasting forms, the ones that come to be most different in the end, are in their first beginnings really quite similar. As Mr. Quatremère'de'Quincy has charmingly observed, the seeds of a plant look much more similar than the plants which develop from them. The application of this general observation will be even more determinative in the present case, if we remind ourselves that it really was one and the same principle striving toward realization in both Egyptian and in Greek art, only it was pressed much further in the Greek case. Furthermore, whoever would comprehend the unity of cultural power, will he not most likely discover that this unlimited, continuous and irresistible drive already appears in the first mighty movement of the human spirit, that which the oldest religious beliefs of the people produce?

I hope it is clearer now just how radical was the view that Schelling proposed, and what some of its far-reaching implications actually were. His reference to Quatremère is instructive in this regard. We will recall that Winckelmann first referred to "schools" of art: Egyptian, Etruscan, Aeginetan, and Attic. He tended to arrange them in a hierarchy, a developmental hierarchy culminating in the high point of classical Athenian art in the generation of Pheidias. Quatremère devoted a great deal of energy in *Le Jupiter Olympien* to the attempt to comprehend what we should understand by the appeal of such "schools." His conclusion, as the quotation above makes abundantly clear, is that a "school" simply refers to *a style*, a style that can persist as distinctive and recognizable alongside of and even after the appearance of other styles. In this case the Egyptian style, and still more the Aeginetan style, were not replaced by the classical Athenian style; rather, all of these styles served as tributaries flowing into the mighty stream that was to be Greek art in the age of Pheidias. Pheidias simply represents the culmination of a process of religious representation initiated by the Egyptians and a process of naturalism initiated by the Aeginetans. The supreme moment of culmination in the monumental chryselephantine statue of Zeus at Olympia, also represents the moment when art quite literally crosses over into religion.

Schelling is thus interested in *both* Egyptian and Greek art, *both* Aeginetan and Athenian art, *both* the origins and their culminations. Why the culmination matters is made clear by the startling observation from Quintilian that left such a lasting impression on Quatremère and, through him, on Schelling as well.

> What Polyclitus lacked, Phidias and Alcamenes are allowed to have possessed. Phidias is thought more skillful at representing gods than men; in ivory he would be far and away without a rival, even if he had produced nothing but the Athena at Athens (*Minervam Athenis*) and the Olympian Zeus at Elis (*Olympium in Elide Iovem*), the beauty of which is said to have added something to the traditional religious concept of the god (*cuius pulchritudo adiecisse aliquid etiam receptae religioni videtur*), so perfectly did the majesty of the work match its divine original (*adeo maiestas operis deum aequavit*).

Pheidias's sculptural group—populated by an uncanny number of additional hybrid figures on Zeus's throne, his sandals, and his scepter, all of them brilliantly colored, glittering in gold and ivory, surrounded by a hydrating bath of olive oil—is not the standard image of classical Greek art most of us have inherited. It was as massive as its Egyptian counterparts, and as brilliantly polychrome as anything to be found on Aegina. And that massive, hybrid, multicolored image is what actually managed to enhance the received religion of the Greeks.

Art, to say it plainly, had become the new religion.

APPENDIX FIVE: ON POLYCHROMATIC GREEK ART

> Almost always we have looked upon these sculptural monuments in gold and ivory as exceptional works [*ouvrages d'exception*], as accidental and occasional [*productions de caprice*]. I had to prove that this taste reigned supreme for twelve centuries, and I have reproduced a series of artworks in support of my research.
>
> *Presque toujours on a regardé les monuments de la statuaire en ivoire come des ouvrages d'exception, comme des productions de caprice. J'ai eu en vue de prouver que le goût pour ces ouvrages avait régné pendant douze siècles, et j'ai produit une série de monuments à l'appui de mes recherches.*
>
> A. C. Quatremère de Quincy, *Le Jupiter Olympien*, xx–xxj

One of the many ways in which these Aeginetan sculptures caused a stir when they were first unearthed had to do with the fact that they had long been buried underground—unlike their Parthenon counterparts, which had been exposed for millennia to sun, wind, and rain. As a result, most of the Aeginetan fragments bore clear evidence of the paint that had originally graced their surfaces. The idea that "classical" Greek art should have been a riot of brilliant color, rather than composed of simple and serene white marble, generated a great deal of discussion at the time; Wagner chose to tackle this prickly topic in the last chapter of his *Report.*

It was an idea whose time had come, and the Aeginetan evidence was not unique in any case. The Aegina Marbles were simply the latest, and in some ways the loveliest, examples of painted Greek marbles yet known. And they provided further evidence of the degree to which the Greeks were comfortable with, and even appeared to have expected, bright colors on their most important religious images as well as on the temples themselves. Wagner, for his part, did not shy away from all the trappings that might have made the statues as he imagined them altogether kitsch to his contemporaries: painted eyes, painted lips, elaborately painted clothing and military dress, coiled lead bangles imitating hair, large bronze weapons attached to most every one of the military figures, even gemstone inlaid inside a colossal ivory eyeball. All of this was quite startling.

In 1815, while Wagner was consumed with his trip to Malta, arranging for the transport of the Aegina Marbles to Rome—where he could observe them at his leisure while Bertel Thorvaldsen began the work on their restoration and rearrangement—Antoine Chrysostome Quatremère de Quincy (1755–1849) published what was to be his magnum opus and, at the time, the definitive work on polychrome Greek art in the round. Schelling had time to work through this impressive volume, *Le Jupiter Olympien*, as Wagner did not; this is why Quatremère is one of the most recurrent, and certainly the most important, supplement that Schelling's notes and appendices provide to Wagner's *Report.*

As the quote from the preface makes clear, Quatremère's overarching purpose in this copious reconstruction of polychrome Greek visual art was to demonstrate that this was not an occasional taste, nor one confined to certain types of cult image; the Greeks, he insisted, preferred to work in multiple media and had a surprisingly wide range of colors on their palette. This deliberate combination of metals with marble, combined with the riotous decoration of that same marble, might make Greek art from the high classical period seem in rather poor taste to a modern observer schooled on a certain neoclassical ideal. Quatremère was out to combat that prejudicial judgment as well. Along the way, he offered incisive judgments as to the relations among the various schools in the pre-classical Greek world, and elevated the artistic production of Pheidias and his atelier to that of such a school.

Le Jupiter Olympien made its case in six long chapters. The first chapter marshaled the literary and material evidence to confirm this ancient taste for polychrome three-dimensional images. The second provided primarily philological evidence for the "toreutic" style in the ancient world, a style characterized by the creative juxtaposition of various materials in a single work of art. The foremost example of such a style was chryselephantine (gold and ivory) sculpture, much of it enormous. Three chapters were devoted to such chryselephantine sculpture, arranged chronologically: before the age of Pericles, in the age of Pheidias, and then after Pheidias, from the age of Polycleitus through the reign of Alexander the Great. A final chapter examined the mechanics of producing such enormous works through the assemblage of ivory and gold plates, many of them formed by elaborate molding. Quatremère's striking conclusion, that "this taste reigned supreme for twelve centuries," took the reader from the Homeric period all the way to the Christian age of Constantine. But two works above all others confirmed the virtue and the importance of this style: Pheidias's monumental statues of Athena inside the Athenian Parthenon and his Zeus at Olympia, the latter of which was deemed one of the genuine wonders of the ancient world.

Yvonne Luke suggests[1] that Quatremère intended his massive study to inspire contemporary French artists to move beyond the monotony of monochromatic white marble. If the Revolution and its Napoleonic aftermath were coming to an end, then so too might a monochromatic promotion of that Revolution. Quatremère had long been involved in the sponsorship and state patronage of contemporary arts in the early years of the Revolution (especially at the French Pantheon, from 1790–94), and then again when he was recalled to service after the general amnesty of 1803. The polis-sponsored atelier of Pheidias, as he understood it, provided him with a conceptual model for the France of his day.

If the sculpture and friezework from the Parthenon was becoming quite literally the gold standard for neoclassical art historical judgments,[2] then the way in which Wagner and Schelling, but mostly Schelling, elevated this Aeginetan collection to a position of equal grace (and greater naturalism) with Pheidias's masterpieces is quite striking. Wagner's relatively underappreciated genius may be seen most clearly here, in his meditation on the painting of the Aegina Marbles.

As a working artist, and in a manner quite similar to Quatremère's work, which he had not read, Wagner locates the primary explanation for this apparently un-classical practice within a longer history of the *materiality* of religious and artistic production. Most all of the earliest statues, and the temples that housed them, were made of wood, Wagner reminds his reader. As such, and for a variety of intersecting reasons, they were elaborately painted. When stone of various kinds, and eventually even the finest Aegean marble, was dedicated to the same purposes, then the religious traditions of inherited visual form dictated that the stone, too, should be painted. Color and form were the two primary instruments with which ancient artists and religious visionaries communicated their devotion and their ideas of the divine. More recent archaeological work at the site of the Aphaia temple on Aegina suggests that the Archaic predecessor-temple at this site was also elaborately painted.[3] So color as well as form were decidedly placed in the service of ancient religion. Kandinsky could not have said it any better, in his reflections on "the spiritual in art."[4]

The contemporary Glyptothek has gone in for color in a big way. The last publication of the previous Glyptothek director, Raimond Wünsche, makes this very plain. Like Wagner, whose work Wünsche very much admires,

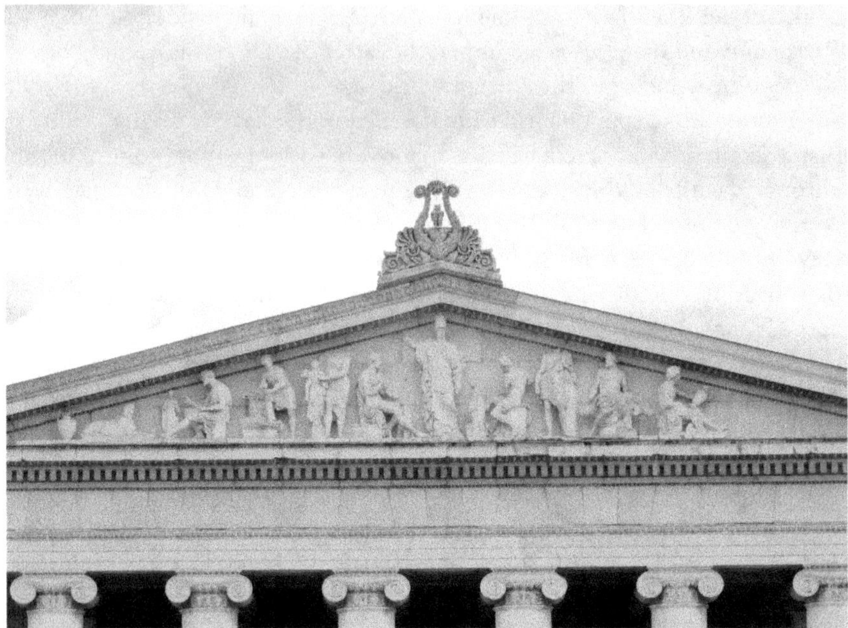

Figure A.1. The Glyptothek's Modern Pedimental Group. Author's photograph.

he devotes the last chapter of his book to the question of painted marble statuary.[5] The history Wünsche lays out in compelling detail is really quite fascinating. As we see in Wagner's final chapter, by 1817 the fact of Greek polychrome was indubitable, and Wagner defended the practice as an example of the Greeks' good taste. Schelling concurred, regretting the relative absence of color in modern architecture and sculpture. As work began on the Glyptothek design, and its conception as a *Gesamtkunstwerk* (combining all of the artistic elements to a single purpose) was established, then the design selected for the museum's own pediment included images of an artist painting an Archaic-seeming statue reminiscent of the Aegina Marbles; this idea too was Wagner's.[6]

Not long after completing the Glyptothek, Leo von Klenze was experimenting with polychrome neoclassical architecture (he completed his first such venture in 1836). In 1842, Ludwig commissioned his residence ("Walhalla") in Regensburg, which also boasted polychrome architectural elements. Back from his extended Grand Tour, Charles Cockerell was promoting the same idea in England, where the sculptor John Gibson (1790–1866) displayed

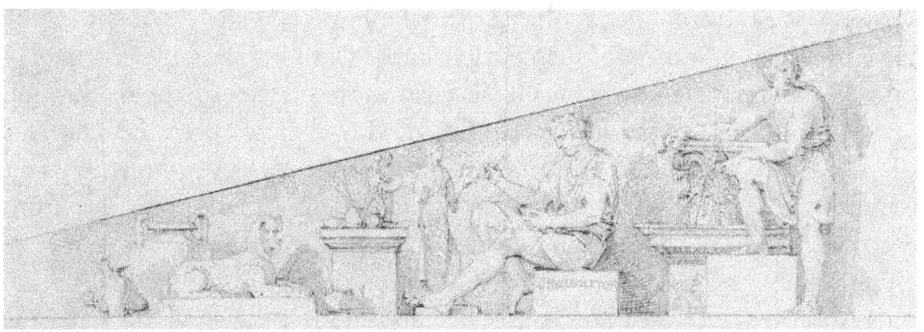

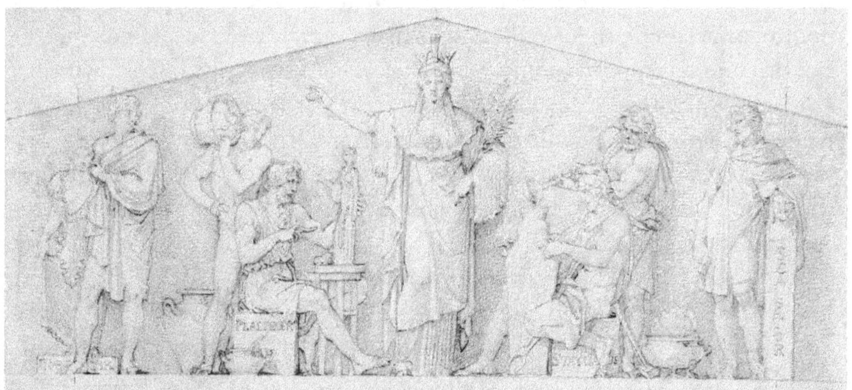

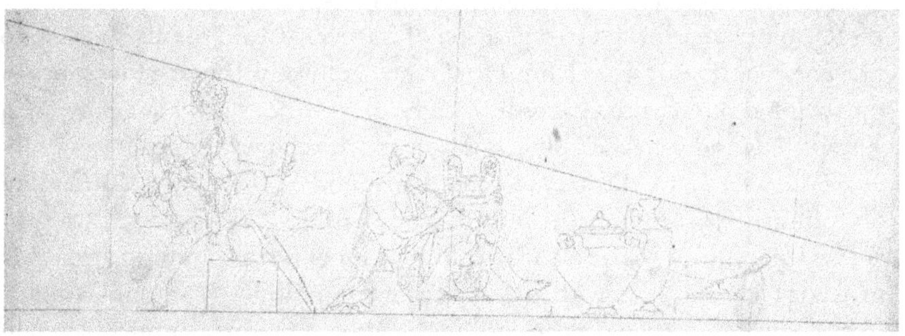

Figure A.2a–A.2c. Martin Wagner's sketch proposal for the Glyptothek's Modern Pedimental Group, 1817. Printed with permission of the Martin von Wagner Museum, Würzburg (*Martin von Wagner Museum*: Prints HZ-3666_1167_frei, and HZ-3667_1166_frei, and HZ-3672_1169_trans).

his "Tinted Venus" in 1856. Just four years later, as we have seen, Cockerell finally published his own polychrome reconstruction of the Aegina Temple.[7] By then the technology of colored lithograph was sufficiently advanced that it made the publication of such designs more feasible and more affordable.

And there was more. New Greek excavations on the Athenian Akropolis (1885–91) revealed a treasure trove of painted Archaic statuary, the Koroi and Korai, which are still on prominent display in the New Akropolis Museum. These discoveries inspired Adolf Fürtwangler to publish his own polychrome reconstruction of the Aegina Marbles in 1906.[8] "It was," says Wünsche, "the high point of polychrome theories."[9]

And then, just as suddenly as it had appeared, it vanished. Between 1918 and 1970, there was virtually nothing said about Greek polychrome. While dominant aesthetic theories like formalism, which were suspicious of excessive ornamentation, and dominant political ideologies like fascism were hard at work "whitening" the classical heritage, another technological development really serves to explain the shift: photography. Strictly black and white, in the early twentieth century photography rapidly replaced lithography as the means with which art history and archaeology dispensed their images. The colors were quite literally erased from view. Ironically enough, after 1970, when Greek polychrome began to reemerge as a topic of scholarly enquiry, new forms of photography were central to making the case: UV photography and UV florescence. These new technologies enabled a new examination of the Aegina Marbles, for instance, and revealed far more extensive and complex patterning on the clothing, shields, and helmets.

So color has returned to our vision of classical art and the classical world. But essential questions remain. How much color was there? How much of the sculpted surface was painted? Which colors were used? Wagner had seen vibrant reds and softer sky blue, but how much yellow and green was also in use? And what kind of patterns were to be found on the clothes? What kind of clothing were the figures imagined to be wearing? Greek vase painting provides some clues as to the elaborate decoration of Greek clothing, even their martial attire, and so new theories continue to multiply. Raimond Wünsche offers a superb overview of various theories, but in the end nothing is conclusive. "It is a mystery to us," he concludes. "And it will likely remain a mystery to us."[10]

In the English language, the contemporary scholar who has perhaps done most to advance our understanding of chryselephantine and other polychromatic examples of ancient art, in Greece and elsewhere, is Kenneth D. S. Lapatin (curiously, Wünsche did not mention him). His exhaustive 2001 study,

Chryselephantine Statuary in the Ancient Mediterranean World[11] provides a stunning visual tour of the practice throughout the Mediterranean basin and beyond. Lapatin explicitly relates his work to Quatremère's groundbreaking book, but whereas Quatremère had only ancient literary testimonia, coins, gems, and statuettes to consult, Lapatin exploits the nearly two hundred statues and fragments that have come to light since "the advent of systematic archaeology in the nineteenth and twentieth centuries."[12] Most of this new material is quite old, deriving from the Aegean Bronze Age, a time period virtually unavailable to Quatremère. Gold and ivory, Lapatin reminds us, were not native Greek materials. Rather, "[t]hese literally exotic materials and ideas first reached the Aegean long before the rise of classical civilization."[13] Exotic it may have been, but we should recall that Aegina enjoyed extensive trade relations with Egypt.

Lapatin, like Quatremère, organizes his book for the most part chronologically, but with seven chapters instead of six. The second chapter examines the "exotic" materials themselves and how they could be worked most malleably and effectively. The third chapter introduces the Bronze Age evidence unavailable to Quatremère. The fourth chapter explores the evidence for the reintroduction of this sculptural practice after the Greek Dark Ages (c.1100–800 BCE), and the fifth describes its culmination in "the Pheidian revolution." Lapatin argues that agonistic rivalry with this exemplary Pheidian form generated tremendous new aesthetic energy, and a great deal of new chryselephantine work, in the fifth and fourth centuries BCE; he describes this in the sixth chapter. Chapter seven then surveys later artistic use of these same materials in the Hellenistic and Roman periods. Some of the chief virtues of this book, and there are many, are the extensive lists of all the ancient literary testimonia, of all the recently discovered statues and fragments, as well as a generous body of luscious print images.

While evidence for statuary in gold and/or ivory in the Bronze Age Aegean is what distinguishes Lapatin's work most conspicuously from Quatremère's, Lapatin avoided discussion of unprovenanced "Minoan" pieces from Bronze Age Crete for the most part. He preferred to deal with that material separately in the very next year, when he published *Mysteries of the Snake Goddess.*[14] The book offers a humorous supplement to the painstaking and serious work evidenced by both Quatremère and Lapatin in their exhaustive volumes on chryselephantine sculpture culminating in the "revelatory" work of Pheidias at Olympia. Lapatin tells the fascinating story of the so-called Boston Snake Goddess, a 16.1 cm statuette seemingly worlds away from that massive Olympian Zeus. He traces the mysterious history of this gold and ivory statuette, allegedly acquired by the Boston Museum of Fine Arts (MFA) in 1914, evidently restored along the lines of what Thorvaldsen did to the Aegina Marbles, and featured as one of the centerpieces of the new Aegean Bronze Age gallery of the MFA in 1994. The problem is that this piece lacked provenience entirely (an account of the when and where of its actual *discovery*), and its provenance (the history of who *owned* it when, and where) was similarly obscure. It is most likely a modern forgery, created when Arthur Evans's discoveries at Knossos first established the Minoan civilization of Bronze Age Crete in the public mind . . . and tempted modern Cretan forgers to flood the market with such items. Building on his scholarly interest in chryselephantine sculptural techniques, Lapatin here offers a cautionary work of reception history showing, through its complex curatorial history, how each age develops and then sells the image of antiquity that it wants. This is also profoundly relevant to the historical context lying behind the production of Wagner's book, Schelling's philosophical history, and the polychrome historiography that Raimond Wünsche lays out in *Kampf um Troja.*[15]

Wagner, we may recall, also attempted to bring his reflections into the present day, offering some intriguing comparative reflections on the brilliant coloring and the brilliant stonework on the *Mariankirche* in his native Würzburg. There is, however, one problem with the connections he was attempting to draw, and it has something to do with what may seem like a rather dated matter of cultural geography. Put in the starkest terms, you can get away with riotous experiments in polychromatic design in a more equatorial region with blinding summer light (in Guatemala, let's say, or in Greece and Egypt); anything less, and the colors quite literally wash out. But in the greyer skies of Germany, even southern Germany, things are quite different; here, such pattern and color can indeed appear kitsch in such dim lighting.

And yet. The monumental polychrome statue of Zeus at Olympia was set well inside the massive temple designed to house it; this riot of color was thus situated in semi-darkness. The effect it may have elicited has been brilliantly captured by Roberto Calasso in his remarkable reconstruction of the mythopoetic religious mentality evident in Greek myth and Greek sanctuaries, alike. It all hinges, much as Quatremère's analysis did, on Quintilian's extraordinary evaluation of the statue's significance.

> Climbing the spiral staircase inside the temple took you to the upper galleries, where you could get a closer view of Pheidias's Zeus. To Quintilian's mind, this statue had "added something to the religion of men" (*aggiunto qualcosa alla religione degli uomini*). Its gold and ivory surfaces were broken only by

gems, except on the throne, which also had some ebony. The drapery was strewn with animals and lilies. Zeus wore a crown of olive twigs and in his right hand held a Nike, goddess of victory, with a ribbon and a crown. Beneath each of the throne's four feet were other small Nikes, like dancing elves. But something else was going on among those feet: winged Sphinxes carried off Theban youths in their claws, and Apollo and Artemis loosed their arrows at Niobe's children again. And as it grew accustomed to the teeming dark, the eye would make out one new scene after another, sculpted on the cross-struts: the Amazons, Heracles with his escort, Theseus. A boy is adjusting a ribbon on his forehead: is it Pantarches, Pheidias's young lover (*il giovane amante di Fidia*)? You can't go right up to the throne, because of the painted barriers, which again show Theseus and Heracles, and then Peirithous, Ajax, Cassandra, Hippodamia, Sterope, Prometheus, Penthesilea, Achilles, two Hesperides. Other beings sprout from the top of the throne: three Charites [Graces] and three Hours. Then the eye moves back down to Zeus's footstool and finds still more figures: Theseus yet again, and again the Amazons and golden lions. As one looks down even farther, at the base that supports the huge Zeus and his parasites (*l'immane Zeus e i suoi parassiti*), other scenes become apparent: Helios climbs into his chariot, Hermes advances as Hestia follows, Eros greets Aphrodite as she rises from the waves and Peitho crowns her. Nor has the sculptor forgotten Apollo and Artemis, Athena and Heracles, Amphitryon and Poseidon, and Selene on a horse. A seated giant encrusted with creatures (*incrostato di creature*), Zeus was reflected in a floor of shiny black stone where oil flowed in abundance to preserve the ivory.

No other statue was so beloved by the Greeks (*ammirata dai Greci*), nor even by Zeus himself, who hurled an approving thunderbolt down on the black paving when Pheidias finished the job and asked the god for a sign. Olympia's chryselephantine Zeus was destroyed in a palace fire in Byzantium in the fifth century. All that remains are some Elean coins showing the statue, and the words of those who, like Callimachus and Pausanias, saw it and were enamored (*ammirati*). Paulus Aemilius claimed that Pheidias had given form to Homer's Zeus.

The moderns have been cowed and confused (*timorosi e perplessi*) by these descriptions. Too many colors (*troppo colori*), too much Oriental pomp (*troppo fasto orientale*), the suspicion of a lapse of taste (*una mancanza di gusto*). Could Pheidias, they wonder, in this, his most ambitious project, have tossed aside all the qualities so beloved (*ammirano*) in the Parthenon frieze? The mistake of the moderns (*L'errore dei moderni*) is to think of Pheidias's Zeus as a statue, in the sense in which Praxiteles's Hermes is a statue. For

> it was something else (*E invece era altro*). Shut away and sparkling in the temple's cella, Pheidias's Zeus was closer to a dolmen, to a bethel, to a stone fallen from heaven, to which other gods and heroes clung in order to live. The gold and ivory seethed like an ants' nest. Zeus did not exist except (*Zeus non sussisteva se non*) as a support for animals and lilies, arches and drapes, old scenes forever repeated. But Zeus was more than just the motionless guardian seated on his throne: Zeus was all of those scenes, those deeds, muddled and shuffled about, rippling his body and throne in tiny shivers. Without meaning to (*senza volerlo*), Pheidias had illustrated that Zeus cannot live alone: without meaning to (*senza volerlo*), he had represented the essence of polytheism (*l'essenza del politeismo*).[16]

We have returned to the subject of Schelling's lecture on the Deities of Samothrace, it would seem. If Pheidias managed to display the clear connection between art and religion, then the religion he served appears to have been precisely that *pluralist monotheism* defined and defended by Schelling in his 1815 lecture. It is also very much in line with the image of creative divinity that Schelling portrayed in all three versions of *The Ages of the World*. The god who creates cannot, or at least would not care to, exist alone. To represent this god, then, requires the necessary theological supplements—of companions, lovers, friends, and the history of their coming together, their endless coming to be.

ENDNOTES TO THE APPENDICES

Appendix Two

1. For this itinerary I am indebted primarily to Reinhard Herbig, "Johann Martin Wagners Beschreibung seiner Reise nach Griechenland (1812–1813)," *Würzburger Studien zur Altertumswissenschaft* 13 (1938): 1–46.

   Thanks to the generosity of the administration of the Martin von Wagner Museum and the Department of Art History at the University of Würzburg, I was able to consult Wagner's little travel book for his "Griechische Reise," a small red notebook (#20 in his collection). The book has five separate sections, divided by blank pages of varying lengths. These include: first, a seven-page section of disordered notes on some costs of his preparations in June/July 1812, a list of some foreign words, and a list of general payments and foreign exchanges; second, a four-page section with detailed notes from the complicated stretch of island travel he attempted on October16–29, 1812, landing finally on Zante, with a final page list of five to-do items, all checked off; third, a thirty-page narrative account of the trip, which appears to be the part Herbig edited; fourth, a fascinating six-page list of the letters Wagner received and wrote on the road, including, most notably, the Crown Prince Ludwig, who followed his trip with close interest; a fifth and final section of eleven pages with random observations on local customs, a list of important payments, as well as the names and addresses of the various representatives through whom he needed to arrange his transit.

   In short, Wagner was required to navigate no fewer than five different currencies (Italian scudi, Neapolitan ducats, French francs, Spanish Thaler and the Ottoman piaster . . . as well as the Venetian zecchini, in which currency the purchase of the Aegina Marbles would be made) and four languages (Italian, French, English, and German), not to mention the ever-shifting political landscape of the regions through which he was traveling. All in all it is a most impressive organizational achievement.

Appendix Three

1. George Steiner, *Antigones* (New York, NY: Oxford University Press, 1984), 7–8.
2. Martin Heidegger, *Schelling's Treatise on the Essence of Human Freedom*, Joan Stambaugh, trans. (Athens: Ohio University Press, 1985).
3. John Sallis, *The Verge of Philosophy* (University of Chicago Press, 2008), and Jason Wirth, ed., *Schelling Now: Contemporary Readings* (Indianapolis: Indiana University Press, 2005).
4. Guntram Beckel, "Johann Martin von Wagner," *Fränkische Lebensbilder* 8 (1978): 238–39 and Jason M. Wirth, ed., *Schelling Now*, 29.
5. F. W. J. Schelling, *The Abyss of Freedom/Ages of the World*, Judith Norman, trans. (Ann Arbor: University of Michigan Press, 1997).

6. F. W. J. Schelling, *The Ages of the World*, Jason Wirth, trans. (Albany, NY: SUNY Press, 2000).
7. Schelling, *The Ages of the World*, Jason Wirth, trans., vii–viii.
8. Schelling, *The Ages of the World*, Wirth, trans., 133–134n7.
9. Schelling, *The Ages of the World*, Wirth, trans., x, xv–xx.
10. Schelling, *Philosophie und Religion* (Tübingen: In der J. G. Cotta'schen Buchhandlung, 1804). The Getty Foundation has made a digitalized version of this ninety-eight-page text available at Google books.
11. Schelling, *The Ages of the World*, Wirth, trans., ix; see also Wirth's *The Conspiracy of Life*, 12–23.
12. F. W. J. Von Schelling, *Lectures on the History of Modern Philosophy*, Andrew Bowie, trans. (New York: Cambridge University Press, 1994), 3.
13. Ibid., 133.
14. Ibid., 134ff.
15. F. W. J. Schelling, *System der Weltalter: Münchner Vorlesung 1827–28*, Siegbert Peetz, ed. (Frankfurt am Mein: Vittorio Klostermann, 1990). I am indebted to Jason M. Wirth for this reference.
16. See Jason M. Wirth, *The Conspiracy of Life*, 221–22.
17. *"The Deities of Samothrace": A Translation and an Interpretation*, Robert F. Brown, trans. (Missoula, MT: Scholars Press, 1974).
18. The full passage, as translated by Peter Green, is as follows:

> Toward evening, at Orpheus's behest, they beached their vessel
> on the island of Atlas's daughter Elektra, that by learning
> those secret rites, with their benign initiations,
> they might steer in greater safety across the chilling deep.
> Of such rites I say no more, but bid farewell to
> the island itself and its indwelling deities, whose
> are the mystery cults, which here we may not mention.
>
> *The Argonautika by Apollonius Rhodios*, Peter Green, trans. (Berkeley, CA: University of California Press, 1997), I: 915–21 (pages 66–67).

19. While somewhat jarring to modern ears, "Mohammedan," it would seem, is a placeholder in Schelling's thinking here for an extreme and one-sided monotheism that is aggressively anti-polytheist, anti-materialist, and iconoclastic. In short, it is a rigidly dualistic religion, not a dialectical one.

Appendix Four

1. Joseph Daniel Guigniaut, *Notice historique sur la vie et les travaux de M. Quatremère de Quincy* (Paris: Typographie de Firmin Didot Frères, Fils et Cie, 1866), 367.
2. See the especially relevant examples in my *Classics at the Dawn of the Museum Era*, 92–100, and 118–22.
3. In fact, the academy's annual *Prix Caylus* was called the *Prix St. Martin* in 1785 because the award was announced that year on the feast day of St. Martin.

4. Dissertation qui a remporté, en 1785, le Prix par l'Académie des Inscriptions et Belles-Lettres (Paris: Chez Barrois l'aîné e Fils, Libraires, rue de Savoye, No. 23, An XI—1803).
5. *Encyclopedie Méthodique: Architecture, dédiée et présentée a Monseigneur de Lamoignon, Garde des Sceaux de France &c.* (Paris: Chez Pancoucke, Libraire, hôtel de Thou, rue des Poitevins, 1788).
6. Sylvia Lavin, *Quatremère de Quincy and the Invention of a Modern Language of Architecture* (Cambridge, MA: MIT Press, 1992).
7. See Lavin, *Quatremère de Quincy and the Invention of a Modern Language of Architecture*, x–xii, 18, 74–79, 88–89, 120, and 147.

Appendix Five

1. "Quatremère de Quincy's Role in the Revival of Polychromy in Sculpture," published in 1996 by the Centre for the Study of Sculpture to accompany "The Colour of Sculpture" at the Henry Moore Institute (December 12, 1996–April 6, 1997).
2. Quatremère himself inclined to this view after he saw the so-called Elgin Marbles first-hand in London in 1816. His public letters to Canova in support of this view, *Lettres écrites de Londres à Rome, et adressées à M. Canova; sur les Marbres d'Elgin, ou les Sculptures du Temple de Minerve à Athènes* (Rome, n.p., 1818), have recently been translated into English as *Letters to Miranda and Canova on the Abduction of Antiquities from Rome and Athens*, Chris Miller and David Gilks, trans., with David Poulot (Los Angeles: Getty Research Foundation, 2012), 126–67.
3. See Ernst-Ludwig Schwandner, *Der Ältere Poros-tempel der Aphaia auf Ägina* (Berlin: Verlag Walter de Gruyter & Co., 1985), 130–40, with frontispiece.
4. Wassily Kandinsky, *Concerning the Spiritual in Art*, Michael T. H. Sadler, trans. (Boston: MFA Press, 2006), 54:

   > Painting has two weapons at her disposal:
   > 1. Color.
   > 2. Form.
   >
   > Form can stand alone as representing an object. . . . Color cannot stand alone.

5. Raimond Wünsche, *Kampfe um Troja: 200 Jahre Ägineten in München, Ausstellungskatalog* (München: Kunstverlag Josef Fink, 2011), "Die Farbigkeit der Ägineten," 223–61.
6. See Adrian von Buttlar and Bénédicte Savoy, "Glyptothek and Alte Pinakothek, Munich: Museums as Public Monuments," in Carole Paul, ed., *The First Modern Museums of Art: The Birth of an Institution in 18th- and Early-19th-Century Europe* (Los Angeles: The J. Paul Getty Museum, 2012), 305–26, esp. 308.
7. Charles R. Cockerell, *The Temples of Jupiter Panhellenius at Aegina and of Apollo Epicurius at Bassae* (London: John Weale, 1860).
8. See Adolf Furtwangler, *Aegina: Das Heiligtum der Aphaia* (München: Verlag des K. B. Akademie der Wissenschaften, 1906); the second volume contains the relevant colored plates (Tafeln ##48, 61, 62), as well as an interesting model reconstructing the west pediment with thirteen painted figures and the east pediment with eleven painted figures (Tafel #106). Ernst-Ludwig Schwandner also offers a polychrome reconstruction of the earlier Archaic temple to Aphaia in the frontispiece to *Der Ältere Porostempel der Aphaia*

auf Aegina, Deutsches Archäologisches Institut, Band 16 (Berlin: Verlag Walter de Gruyter & Co., 1985), as does Hansgeorg Bankel in *Der Spätarchaische Tempel der Aphaia auf Aegina,* Deutsches Archäologisches Institut, Band 19 (Berlin: Walter de Gruyter, 1993).

9. "*Es war die große Zeit der Polychrometheorien*," Wünsche, *Kampf um Troja*, 228.
10. "*Sie ist uns ein Rätsel. Und dieses Rätsel wird uns wohl bleiben*," Wünsche, *Kampf um Troja*, 261.
11. *Chryselephantine Statuary in the Ancient Mediterranean World* (New York: Oxford University Press, 2001).
12. Lapatin, *Chryselephantine Statuary in the Ancient Mediterranean World*, 1.
13. Lapatin, *Chryselephantine Statuary in the Ancient Mediterranean World*, 1.
14. *Mysteries of the Snake Goddess: Art, Desire and the Forging of History* (Boston: Houghton Mifflin, 2002).
15. In 2008, Lapatin worked with Roberta Pantanelli and Eike D. Schmidt on *The Color of Life: Polychromy in Sculpture from Antiquity to the Present* (Malibu, CA: The Getty Trust, 2008). That work, building on a museum show that the three curated, extends his longstanding interest in polychrome images, much as the title suggests, to the postclassical, medieval, and contemporary worlds.
16. Roberto Calasso, *Le nozze di Cadmo e Armonia* (Milano: Adelphi Edizioni, 1988), 196–98, translated by Tim Parks as *The Marriage of Cadmus and Harmony* (New York: Vintage Books, 1993), 170–71, translation slightly emended.

BIBLIOGRAPHY

Allen, Susan Heuck. 1999. *Finding the Walls of Troy: Frank Calvert and Heinrich Schliemann at Hisarlik* (Berkeley: University of California Press, 1999).

Angelomatis-Tsougarakis, Helen. *The Eve of the Greek Revival: British Travellers' Perceptions of Early Nineteenth-Century Greece.* (London: Routledge, 1990).

Apollonius Rhodius. *The Argonautica.* Translated by Peter Green (Berkeley: University of California Press, 1997).

Athanassoglou-Kallmyer, Nina M. *French Images from the Greek War of Independence, 1821–1830* (New Haven, CT: Yale University Press, 1989).

"'Auf nach Hellas' heil'ger Erde: Johann Martin von Wagners Reise nach Griechenland 1812/1813," Exhibition Katalog bei Tilman Kossatz. Martin von Wagner Museum (Würzburg, Feb. 12–May 31, 1989).

Bac, Ferdinand. *Le Favori du Cardinal Albani: Jean-Joachim Winckelmann "le Père de l'Archéologie" 1717–1768* (Paris: Louis Conard, 6 Place de la Madeleine, 1927).

Bailey, Donald M. "Aegina, Aphaia-Temple XIV: The Lamps." *Archäologischer Anzeiger* 106, Heft 1 (1991), 31–68.

Baird, Henry M. *Modern Greece: A Narrative of a Residence and Travels in that Country* (New York: Harper & Brothers Publishers, 1856).

Baird, Jay W. *To Die for Germany: Heroes in the Nazi Pantheon* (Indianapolis: Indiana University Press, 1992).

Bankel, Hansgeorg. "Aegina, Aphaia-Temple III. Die Kurvatur des spätarchaischen Tempels." *Archäologischer Anzeiger* 95, Heft 2 (1980), 171–79.

———. "Aegina, Aphaia-Temple VII. Geraupten Metopen." *Archäologischer Anzeiger* 100, Heft 1 (1985), 1–13.

———. *Der Spätarchaische Tempel der Aphaia auf Aegina.* Deutsches Archäologisches Institut, Band 19 (Berlin: Walter de Gruyter, 1993).

Barroero, Liliana, and Stefano Susinno. 2000. "Arcadian Rome, Universal Capital of the Arts." In *Art in Rome in the Eighteenth Century.* Edited by Edgar Peters Bowron and Joseph J. Rishel (Philadelphia: Philadelphia Museum of Art, 2000), 17–38.

Baumstark, Reinhold. "Klenzes Museen." In *König Ludwig I. von Bayern und Leo von Klenze: Symposion aus Anlaß des 75. Geburtstags von Hubert Glaser.* Edited by Franziska Dunkel, Hans-Michael Körner, und Hannelore Putz (Münich: C. H. Beck, 2006), 1–20.

Beach, Edward Allen. *The Potencies of God(s): Schelling's Philosophy of Mythology* (Albany: State University of New York Press, 1994).

Beard, Mary. *The Parthenon,* rev. ed. (Cambridge, MA: Harvard University Press, 2003).

Beckel, Guntram. "Johann Martin von Wagner." *Fränkische Lebensbilder* 8 (1978): 228–56.

Belting, Hans. *Likeness and Presence: A History of the Image Before the Era of Art.* Translated by Edmund Jephcott (Chicago: University of Chicago Press, 1994).

Bergau, Richard. "Briefe an und von Carl Haller von Hallerstein." *Zeitschrift für bildende Kunst* 12 (1877): 190–96.

Bergquist, Birgitta. "The Archaic Greek Temenos: A Study of Structure and Function." *Skrifter Utgivna av Svenska Institutet i Athen* 40, 13 (1967): 1–136, with 28 plates.

Black, Barbara J. *On Exhibit: Victorians and Their Museums* (Charlottesville: University of Virginia Press, 2000).

Blakely, Sandra. "The Anthropology of an Island Cult: Samothrace and the Science of Man in the Nineteenth Century" (forthcoming).

———. "Daimones in the Thracian Sea: Mysteries, Iron and Metaphor." *Archiv für Religionsgeschichte* 14, no. 1 (2013): 155–82.

———. "Human Geography, GIS Technology and Ancient Mysteries: A Case Study from the Island of Samothrace." *Getty Research Journal* 7 (2015): 133–41.

———. "Kadmos, Jason and the Great Gods of Samothrace: Initiation as Mediation in a North Aegean Context." *Electronic Antiquity* 11, no. 1 (2010).

———. "Madness in the Body Politic: Kouretes, Korybantes and the Politics of Shamanism." In *The Archaeology and Anthropology of Madness, Disability and Social Exclusion, Part 2 of Mind and Body in Society*. Edited by J. Hubert (New York: Routledge, 2000), 119–27.

———. "Maritime Risk and Ritual Responses: Sailing with the Gods in the Ancient Mediterranean." In *Oceanides.* Edited by C. Buchet and P. De Souza (Paris: Association Oceanides, forthcoming).

———. "Toward an Archaeology of Secrecy: Power, Paradox and the Great Gods of Samotrace." *Beyond Belief: The Archaeology of Religion and Ritual, Archaeological Papers of the American Anthropology Association*. Edited by Y. Rowan, et al. 2, no. 1 (2012): 49–71.

Boardman, John. "The Elgin Marbles: Matters of Fact and Opinion." *International Journal of Cultural Property* 9, no. 2 (2000): 233–62.

Bordeleau, Anne. *Charles Robert Cockerell, Architect in Time: Reflections around Anachronistic Drawings* (Surrey, UK: Ashgate Publishing Ltd., 2014).

Borghese, Maria. *L'Appassionata di Byron: con la lettere inedite fra Lord Byron e la Contessa Guiccioli* (Rome: Garzanti, 1949).

Bouldrey, Brian, ed. *Traveling Souls: Contemporary Pilgrimage Stories* (San Francisco: Whereabouts Press, 1999).

Bouvier, Nicholas. *L'Usage du Monde* (Genève: Librairie Droz S. A., 1999).

———. *The Way of the World.* Translated by Robyn Marsack, with an introduction by Patrick Leigh Fermor (New York: New York Review Books, 2009).

Bowie, Andrew. *Aesthetics and Subjectivity: From Kant to Nietzsche*, rev. ed. (Manchester: Manchester University Press, 1990, 2003).

———. *From Romanticism to Critical Theory: The Philosophy of German Literary Theory* (New York: Routledge, 1997).

———. *Schelling and Modern European Philosophy: An Introduction* (London and New York: Routledge, 1993).

Bracken, Charles P. *Antiquities Acquired: The Spoliation of Greece* (London: David & Charles, 1975).

Brewer, David. *The Greek War of Independence: The Struggle for Freedom from Ottoman Oppression and the Birth of the Modern Greek Nation* (New York: The Overlook Press, 2001).

Brodie, Neil, Jennifer Doole, and Colin Renfrew, eds. *Trade in Illicit Antiquities: The Destruction of the World's Archaeological Heritage* (McDonald Institute for Archaeological Knowledge, 2001).
Brown, Robert F. "Schelling's Treatise on 'The Deities of Samothrace.'" *AAR Studies in Religion* 12 (Missoula, MT: Scholars Press, 1974, 1977).
Brunn, Heinrich. *Beschreibung der Glyptothek König Ludwig's I. zu München* (Münich: In Commission bei Theodor Ackermann, 1868).
———. *Beschreibung der Glyptothek König Ludwig's I. zu München*, Zweite Auflage (Münich: In Commission bei Theodor Ackermann, 1870).
———. *Beschreibung der Glyptothek König Ludwig's I. zu München* , Fünfte Auflage (Münich: In Commission bei Theodor Ackermann, 1887).
Calasso, Roberto. *The Marriage of Cadmus and Harmony*. Translated by Tim Parks (New York: Vintage Books, 1993).
———. *Le nozze di Cadmo e Armonia* (Milan: Adelphi Edizioni, 1988).
Carp, Richard M. "Art, Education and the Sign(ification) of the Self." In *Semiotics and Visual Culture: Sights, Signs, and Significance*. Edited by Debbie Smith-Shank (Reston, VA: National Art Education Association, 2004), 132–37.
Carpenter, Rhys. *Greek Sculpture* (Chicago: University of Chicago Press, 1960).
Chamberlin, Russell. *Loot! The Heritage of Plunder* (London: Thames on Hudson, 1979).
Chandler, Richard. *The History of Ilium or Troy, Including the Adjacent Country and Opposite Coast of the Chersonesus of Thrace* (London: Nichols and Son, 1802).
———. *Travels in Greece* (Oxford: Clarendon Press, 1776).
———. *Travels in Asia Minor, and Greece, or, An Account of a Tour Made at the Expense of the Society of Dilettanti*, 3rd ed., 2 vols. (London: Joseph Booker, 1857).
Chassebouf, Constantin François, comte de Volnay. *Travels through Syria and Egypt, in the Years 1783, 1784, and 1785: Containing the Present Natural and Political State of those Countries, their Productions, Arts, Manufactures, and Commerce; with Observations on the Manners, Customs, and Government of the Turks and Arabs*, 2 vols. (London: G. G. J. & J. Robinson, 1787).
Clairmont, Christoph W. *Fauvel: The First Archaeologist in Athens and His Philhellenic Correspondents* (Zurich: Akanthus Verlag für Archäologie, 2007).
Cocker, Mark. *Loneliness and Time: The Story of British Travel Writing* (New York: Pantheon Books, 1992).
Cockerell, Charles R. *The Temples of Jupiter Panhellenius at Aegina and of Apollo Epicurius at Bassae* (London: John Weale, 1860).
———. *Travels in Southern Europe and the Levant*. Edited by Samuel Pepys Cockerell (London: Longmans, Green & Co., 1903).
———. "Lettre de M. Cockerell à M. Avramiotti, sur le Parthenon (Avril 1814)." *Académie de Rouen, Classe des Belles-Lettres* (n.d.): 110–116.
———. *La celebrattisimi statue rappresentati la favola di Niobe* (1816): n.p.
———, with John S. Harford. *Illustrations, Architectural and Pictorial, of the Genius of Michael Angelo Buonarroti* (London: Colnaghi and Co., and Longman and Co., 1857).
Cole, Juan. *Napoleon's Egypt: Invading the Middle East* (New York: Palgrave MacMillan, 2007, 2008).
Cook, R. M. "The Dating of the Aegina Pediments." *Journal of Hellenic Studies* 94 (1974): 171.

Cooper, Artemis. *Patrick Leigh Fermor: An Adventure* (New York: New York Review Books, 2012).

Cousin, Victor. *Cours de Philosophie: Introduction générale a l'histoire de la philosophie* (Paris: Didier, Libraire-Éditeur, Quai des Augustins 47, 1828).

Cuno, James B. *Museums Matter: In Praise of the Encyclopedic Museum* (Chicago: University of Chicago Press, 2011).

———. *Who Owns Antiquity? Museums and the Battle Over Our Ancient Heritage* (Princeton: Princeton University Press, 2008).

———, ed. *Whose Culture? The Promise of Museums and the Debate over Antiquities* (Princeton: Princeton University Press, 2009).

———, ed. *Whose Muse? Art Museums and the Public Trust* (Princeton: Princeton University Press, 2003).

Davis, Whitney. "Winckelmann Divided: Mourning the Death of Art History." *Gay and Lesbian Studies in Art History* 27, no. 1/2 (1994): 141–59.

Demakopoulou, Katie, ed. *Troy, Mycenae, Tiryns, Orchomenos: Heinrich Schliemann, the 100th Anniversary of His Death* (Athens: Ministry of Culture of Greece, 1990).

Deona, W. *Dédale, ou la style de la Grèce archaïque,* 2 vols. (Paris: E. De Boccard, Éditeur, 1930).

Diebold, William. "The Politics of Derestoration." *Art Journal* (Summer, 1995): 60–66.

Dodwell, Edward. *A Classical and Topographical Tour through Greece During the Years 1801, 1805, and 1806*, 2 vols. (London: Rudwell and Martin, 1819).

Duncan, James, and David Gregory, eds. *Writes of Passage: Reading Travel Writing* (New York: Routledge, 1999).

Dunkel, Franziska, Hans-Michael Körner, and Hannelore Putz, eds. *König Ludwig I. von Bayern und Leo von Klenze: Symposion aus Anlaß des 75. Geburtstags von Hubert Glaser* (Münich: Verlag C. H. Beck, 2006).

Durkheim, Emile. *The Elementary Forms of Religious Life*. Translated by Joseph Ward Swain (New York: Free Press, 1995).

Eisner, Robert. *Travelers to an Antique Land: The History and Literature of Travel to Greece* (Ann Arbor: University of Michigan Press, 1991).

Erinnerung an Dieter Ohly (Münich: des Vereins der Freunde und Führer der Glyptothek und der Antikensammlungen, Jahresgabe, 1980).

Essex, Karen. *Stealing Athena* (New York: Random House, 2008).

Etienne, Roland. *Jacon Spon, un humaniste lyonnais du XVIIme siècle* (Lyon: Bibliothèque Salomon-Reinach, 1993).

Fagan, Brian M., ed. *Eyewitness to Discovery: First-Person Accounts of More than Fifty of the World's Greatest Archaeological Discoveries* (New York: Oxford University Press, 1996).

Farago, Claire, and Donald Preziosi, eds. *Grasping the World: The Idea of the Museum* (London: Ashgate, 2004).

———. *Art is Not What You Think It Is* (Malden, MA: Wiley-Blackwell, 2012).

Felch, Jason, and Ralph Frammolino. *Chasing Aphrodite: The Hunt for Looted Antiquities at the World's Richest Museum* (New York: Houghton Mifflin Harcourt, 2011).

Fermor, Patrick Leigh. *Between the Woods and the Water: The Middle Danube to the Iron Gates* (London: Penguin Books, 1986).

———. *The Broken Road: From the Iron Gates to Mount Athos*. Edited by Colin Thubron and Artemis Cooper (New York: New York Review of Books, 2013).

———. *Mani: Travels in the Southern Peloponnese* (London: John Murray, 1958).
———. *Roumeli: Travels in Northern Greece* (London: Penguin Books, 1966).
———. *A Time of Gifts: From the Hook of Holland to the Middle Danube* (London: Penguin Books, 1977).
Figuera, Thomas J. *Aegina: Society and Politics* (New York: Arno Press, 1981).
———. "Aegina and Athens in the Archaic and Classical Periods: A Socio-Political Investigation." PhD diss. (University of Pennsylvania, 1977).
Fuhrmans, Horst, and Lisolette Lohrer, eds. *Schelling und Cotta Briefwechsel* (Stuttgart: Ernst Klett Verlag, 1965).
Furtwängler, Adolf, ed. *Aegina: Das Heiligtum der Aphaia* (Münich: Verlag des K. B. Akademie der Wissenschaften, 1906), with plates.
———. *Die Aeginetan der Glyptothek König Ludwigs I. nach den Resultaten der neuen Bayerischen Ausgrabung* (Münich: A Buchholz, 1906).
———. *Arianna Dormente e Bacco sopra Cratere Etrusco* (Rome: Coi Tipi del Salviucci, 1878).
———. *Aus Delphi und Athen* (1901), n.p.
———. *Beschreibung der Glyptothek König Ludwig's I. zu München* (Münich: A. Buchholz, 1900).
———. *Führer durch die Glyptothek König Ludwig's I. zu München* (Münich: Kgl. Hofbuchdruckerei Kastner & Lossen, 1899).
———. "Die Giebelgruppen des alten Hekatompedon auf der Akropolis zu Athen." *Separat-Abdruck aus den Sitzungsberichten der philos.-philol. und der histor. Klasse der Kgl. Bayer. Akademie der Wissenschaften* Heft III (1905): 433–66.
———. *Masterpieces of Greek Sculpture: A Series of Essays on the History of Art*. Edited by Eugénie Sellers (London: William Heinemann, 1895).
———. "Neue Denkmäler antiker Kunst," *Separat-Abdruck aus den Sitzungsberichten der philos.-philol. und der histor. Klasse der Kgl. Bayer. Akademie der Wissenschaften* Heft I (1897): 109–145, with plates.
———. "Neue Denkmäler antiker Kunst III: Antiken in den Museen von Amerika." *Separat-Abdruck aus den Sitzungsberichten der philos.-philol. und der histor. Klasse der Kgl. Bayer. Akademie der Wissenschaften* Heft II (1905): 241–79, with plates.
———. "New (German) Excavations at Aegina." *International Monthly* 5 (January, 1902): 10.
———. "Ostgiebel des olympischen Zeustempels." *Separat-Abdruck aus den Sitzungsberichten der philos.-philol. und der histor. Klasse der Kgl. Bayer. Akademie der Wissenschaften* Heft III (1903): 421–38.
———. "Sogenanntes 'Todtenmahl' Relief mit Inschrift—Zur Venus de Milo." *Separat-Abdruck aus den Sitzungsberichten der philos.-philol. und der histor. Klasse der Kgl. Bayer. Akademie der Wissenschaften* (1897): 401–20.
———. "Zu Pythagoras und Kalamis." *Separat-Abdruck aus den Sitzungsberichten der philos.-philol. und der histor. Klasse der Kgl. Bayer. Akademie der Wissenschaften* Heft II (1907): 157–69.
Gidal, Eric. *Poetic Exhibitions: Romantic Aesthetics and the Pleasures of the British Museum* (Lewisburg: PA: Bucknell University Press, 2001).
Gill, David W. J. "The Temple of Aphaia on Aegina: The Date of the Reconstruction." *The Annual of the British School in Athens* 83 (1988): 169–77.
———. "The Temple of Aphaia on Aegina: Further Thoughts on the Date of the Reconstruction." *The Annual of the British School in Athens* 88 (1993): 173–81.

Glaser, Hubert. *König Ludwig I. von Bayern und Martin von Wagner. Der Briefwechsel. Band I: 1809–1815*, bearbeitet von Mathias Hofter and Johanna Selch, Quellen zur Neueren Geschichte Bayerns, no. 5 (Münich: Kommission für Bayerishe Landesgeschichte bei der Bayerische Akademie der Wissenschaften, 2015).

Gleye, Carl Erich, ed. *Aus Stackelbergs Nachlass* (Druck und Verlag Franzen und Grosse, 1859).

———. "Unveröffentliche briefe des archäologen Otto Magnus von Stackelberg." In *Baltische Monatsschrift* Heft 6 (1913): 391–403.

Glyptothek München, 1830–1980 (München: Prestel Verlag, 1980).

Goessler, P. "Jakob Linckh ein Philhellene." In *Münchener Jahrbuch der bildenden Kunst, Neue Folge* 12 (1937–1938): 149.

Greenfield, Jeanette. *The Return of Cultural Treasures* (New York: Cambridge University Press, 1989).

Grünbein, Durs, ed. *Die Götter Griechenlands: Peter Cornelius (1783–1867), Die Kartons für die Fresken der Glyptothek in München aus der Nationalgalerie Berlin* (Berlin and Cologne: SMB-Dumont, 2004).

Guigniaut, Joseph Daniel. *Notice historique sur la vie et les travaux de M. Quatremère de Quincy* (Paris: Typographie de Firmin Didot Frères, Fils et Cie, 1866).

Haller von Hallerstein, Hans. . . . *und die Erde gebar ein Lächeln: Der erste deutsche Archäologe in Griechenland, Carl Haller von Hallerstein, 1774–1817* (Münich: Süddeutscher Verlag, 1983).

Hamilakis, Yannis. *The Nation and Its Ruins: Antiquity, Archaeology and National Imagination in Greece* (New York: Oxford University Press, 2007, 2009).

Hamilton, William. *Antiquités Etrusques, Grecques et Romaines tirées du Cabinet de M. Hamilton Envoyé Extraordinnaire de S. M. Britannique à la Cour de Naples* (Florence: William Tischbein, 1801–08).

———. *Collection of Engravings from Ancient Vases,* 4 vols. (Naples: William Tischbein, 1791).

Hardtwig, Barbara. "Wagner, Johann von Martin." *Nach-Barock und Klassizismus: Vollständiger Katalog* (Münich: Hirmer Verlag, 1978), 377–84.

Haskell, Francis, and Nicholas Penny. *Taste and the Antique: The Lure of Classical Sculpture, 1500–1900* (New Haven, CT: Yale University Press, 1981).

Hegel, Georg W. F. *Lectures on Aesthetics.* Edited and translated by T. H. Knox (New York: Cambridge University Press, 1975).

———. *Lectures on the Philosophy of History.* Translated by Carl Friedrich (New York: Dover Publications, 1956).

———.*Lectures on the Philosophy of Religion,* 2 vols. Edited and translated by Peter C. Hodgson (Berkeley: University of California Press, 1984).

Heidegger, Martin. *Schelling's Treatise on the Essence of Human Freedom.* Translated by Joan Stambaugh (Athens: Ohio University Press, 1985).

Herbig, Reinhard. "Johann Martin Wagners Beschreibung seiner Reise nach Griechenland (1812–1813)." *Würzburger Studien zur Altertumswissenschaft* 13 (1938): 1–46.

Hickey, Dave. *Air Guitar: Essays on Art & Democracy* (Los Angeles: Art Issues Press, 1997).

———. *The Invisible Dragon: Essays on Beauty* (University of Chicago Press, 2009).

Hitchens, Christopher. *The Elgin Marbles: Should They Be Returned to Greece?* (London: Verso, 1997).

Hobhouse, John Cam. *Essay on the Origin of Sacrifices* (London: T. Gillet, 1809).

———. [Right Hon. Lord Broughton, G.C.B.] *Italy: Remarks Made in Several Visits from the Year 1816 to 1854*, 2 vols. (London: John Murray, 1859).

———. *A Journey Through Albania and Other Provinces of Turkey in Europe and Asia to Constantinople during the Years 1809 and 1810*, 2 vols. (London: James Cawthorn, 1813).

———. *Saggio sullo stato attuale della letteratura Italiana di Giovanni Hobhouse, con note dell'Autore*. Translated by M. Pegna (Italia: 1825): n.p.

Hofter, Mathias René. *Die Sinnlichkeit des Ideals: Zur Begründung von Johann Joachim Winckelmanns Archäologie*, Stendaler Winckelmann-Forschungen, Band 7 (Rupholding: Verlag Franz Philipp Rutzen, 2008).

Howard, Seymour. "The Dying Gaul, Aegina Warriors, and Pergamene Academicism." *American Journal of Archaeology* 87, no. 4 (1983): 483–87.

Hüttl, Ludwig. *Ludwig I: König und Bauherr* (Münich/Zurich: Serie Piper, 1986).

Idzerda, Stanley J. "Iconoclasm during the French Revolution." *The American Historical Review* 60, no. 1 (1954): 13–26.

Immerwahr, Henry R. ""Aegina, Aphaia-Temple IX: An Archaic Abacus from the Sanctuary of Aphaia." *Archäologischer Anzeiger* 101, Heft 2 (1986): 195–204.

Invernizzini, Antonio. *I Frontini del Tempio di Aphaia ad Egina* 16, no. 4 (University of Turin: Publicazione della Facoltà di Lettere e Filosofia, 1965).

Jennings, James E. "Aeginetan Trade 650–457 B.C.: A Re-Examination." PhD diss. (University of Illinois at Chicago, 1988).

Johns, Christopher M.S. *Antonio Canova and the Politics of Patronage in Revolutionary and Napoleonic Europe* (Berkeley: University of California Press, 1998).

———. "The Entrepôt of Europe: Rome in the Eighteenth Century." In *Art in Rome in the Eighteenth Century*. Edited by Edgar Peters Bowron and Joseph J. Rishel (Philadelphia Museum of Art, 2000), 39-75.

———. *Papal Art and Cultural Politics: Rome in the Age of Clement XI* (England/New York: Cambridge University Press, 1993).

Johnston, Alan W. "Aegina, Aphaia-Temple XIII: The Storage Amphorae." *Archäologischer Anzeiger* 105, Heft 1 (1990): 37–64.

Jones, H. Stuart. *Select Passages from Ancient Writers Illustrative of the History of Greek Sculpture*. Edited by A. N. Oikonomides (Chicago: Argonaut Inc., Publishers, 1960).

Jørnaes, Bjarne. *Bertel Thorvaldsen: la vita e l'opera dello scultore* (Rome: Edizione De Luca, 1993).

Kandinsky, Wassily. *Concerning the Spiritual in Art*. Translated by Michael T. H. Sadler (Boston: MFA Press, 2006).

Kefallineou, Eugeneia. *Byron and the Antiquities of the Acropolis of Athens* (Athens: The Archaeological Society at Athens Library, 1999), 192.

Klenze, Leo von, with Ludwig Schorn. *Beschreibung der Glyptothek Sr. Majestät des Königs Ludwig von Bayern* (Münich: J. G. Cotta'schen, 1830).

Kohlrausch, Frederick. *Die Deutschen Geschichte für Schulen bearbeitet,* 16th ed. (Berlin: 1816, 1875).

———. *History of Germany: From the Earliest Period to the Present Time*. Translated by James D. Haas (New York: D. Appleton and Company, 1889).

Koliopoulos, John S., and Thanos M. Verenas. *Greece, the Modern Sequel: From 1831 to the Present* (London: Hurst & Company, 2002).

———. *Modern Greece: A History Since 1821* (Chichester: Wiley-Blackwell, 2010).
Der Königsplatz, 1812–1988 (Münich: Staatliche Antikensammlungen und Glyptothek, 1991).
Koppe, Konrad. *Martin von Wagner Museum der Universität Würzburg: Gemäldekatalog* (Würzburg, 1986).
Μανολης Κορρες, Οι πρωτοι χαρτες της πολεως των Αθηνων (Αθηνα: Εκδοτικος Οικος Μελισσα, 2010).
Körner, Hans-Michael. "Paradigmen der Ludwig-I.-Forchung zwischen Kunst und Schönheit, Dynastie und Staat." In *König Ludwig I. von Bayern und Leo von Klenze: Symposion aus Anlaß des 75. Geburtstags von Hubert Glaser*. Edited by Franziska Dunkel, Hans-Michael Körner, and Hannelore Putz (Münich: C. H. Beck, 2006), 21–30.
Köster, Gabriele. "Architektur als Bildträger. Klenze und die Bildausstattung seiner Bauten." In *König Ludwig I. von Bayern und Leo von Klenze: Symposion aus Anlaß des 75. Geburtstags von Hubert Glaser*. Edited by Franziska Dunkel, Hans-Michael Körner, and Hannelore Putz (Münich: C. H. Beck, 2006), 243–71.
Kraeland, P., and M. Nykjer, eds. *Thorvaldsen: L'ambiente l'influsso il mito* (Rome: L'Erma di Brentschneider, 1996).
Kraus, Bettina. "Ludwig I. und seine Kunstberater. Das Beispiel Johann Martin Wagner." In *König Ludwig I. von Bayern und Leo von Klenze: Symposion aus Anlaß des 75. Geburtstags von Hubert Glaser*. Edited by Franziska Dunkel, Hans-Michael Körner, and Hannelore Putz (Münich: C. H. Beck, 2006), 81–104.
Krebs, Christopher B. *A Most Dangerous Book: Tacitus's "Germania" from the Roman Empire to the Third Reich* (New York: W. W. Norton & Company, 2011).
Krell, David Farrell. "God's Footstool: A Note on the Source for Schelling's Description of the Olympian Zeus in the 1811 Draft of *The Ages of the World*." In *Schelling Now: Contemporary Readings*. Edited by Jason M. Wirth (Indianapolis: Indiana University Press, 2005), 101–21.
Kroll, John H. "Dikasts' Pinakia from the Fauvel Collection." *Bulletin de Correspondance Hellénique* 901/2 (1967): 379–96.
Kummer, Stefan, and Ulrich Sinn, eds. *Johann Martin von Wagner: Künstler, Sammler und Mäzen* (Würzburg: Ergon Verlag, 2007).
Lapatin, Kenneth D. S. *Chryselephantine Statuary in the Ancient Mediterranean World* (Oxford: Oxford University Press, 2001).
———. "Journeys of an Icon: The Provenance of the 'Boston Goddess.'" *Journal of Mediterranean Archaeology* 13, no. 2 (2000): 127–54.
———. *Mysteries of the Snake Goddess: Art, Desire and the Forging of History* (Boston: Houghton Mifflin, 2002).
———, with Roberta Pantanelli and Eike D. Schmidt, eds. *The Color of Life: Polychromy in Sculpture from Antiquity to the Present* (Malibu, CA: The Getty Trust, 2008).
Large, David C. *Where Ghosts Walked: Münich's Road to the Third Reich* (New York: W. W. Norton & Company, 1997).
Larrabee, Stephen A. *English Bards and Grecian Marbles: The Relationship Between Sculpture and Poetry especially in the Romantic Period* (Port Washington, NY: Kennikat Press, Inc., 1964).
———. *Hellas Observed: The American Experience of Greece, 1775–1865* (New York: New York University Press, 1957).

Lavin, Sylvia. *Quatremère de Quincy and the Invention of a Modern Language of Architecture* (Cambridge, MA: The MIT Press, 1992).

Leake, William Martin. *Journal of a Tour in Asia Minor* (London: John Murray, 1824).

———. *Researches in Greece: Remarks on the Language Spoken in Greece at the Present Day* (London: John Booth, 1814).

———. *Travels in the Morea with a Map and Plans.* 3 vols. (London: John Murray, 1830).

———. *Travels in Northern Greece.* 4 vols. (London: J. Rodwell, 1835).

Legrand, A., and Ph. E. "Biographie de Louis-François-Sebastien Fauvel. Antiquaire et Consul (1753–1838)." *Revue Archeologique* 30 (1897): 185–201, and *Revue Archaeologique* 31 (1898): 94–103.

Leontis, Artemis, ed. *Greece: A Traveler's Literary Companion* (San Francisco: Whereabouts Press, 1997).

Lessing, Gotthold Ephraim. *Laocoon: An Essay on the Limits of Painting and Poetry*. Translated by Ellen Frothingham (New York: Farrar Straus Giroux, 1961).

Littlewood, Ian. *Sultry Climates: Travel and Sex Since the Grand Tour* (London: John Murray, 2001).

Löhlein, Georg, Horst Pohl, et al. *Archive der Freiherren Haller von Hallerstein in Schloß Gründlach* (Münich: Karl Zink Verlag, 1965).

Luke, Yvonne. "The Politics of Participation: Quatremère de Quincy and the Theory and Practice of 'concours public' in Revolutionary France." *The Oxford Art Journal* 10 (1987): 15–43.

———. "Quatremère de Quincy's Role in the Revival of Polychromy in Sculpture." Supplement to "The Colour of Sculpture" (England: Centre for the Study of Sculpture at the Henry Moore Institute, 1996–1997).

Maaß, Michael. "Aegina, Aphaia-Temple VI. Neue Funde von Waffenweihungen." *Archäologischer Anzeiger* 99, Heft 2 (1984): 263–82.

———. "Nachträgliche Uberlegungen zur Restaurierung der Äginetan." *Athenische Mitteilungen* 99 (1984): 165.

Maaß, Michael, and Imma Kilian-Dirlmeier. "Aegina, Aphaia-Temple XVIII. Bronzefunde außer Waffen. Mit 19 Abbildungen." *Archäologischer Anzeiger* 113, Heft 1 (1998): 57–104.

MacKenzie, Duncan. "The East Pediment Sculptures of the Temple of Aphaia at Aegina." *Annual of the British School at Athens* 15 (1908–1909): 274–307.

Mazzeo, Tilar J., ed. *Travels, Explorations and Empires, Writings from the Era of Imperial Expansion, 1770–1835, Part IV: The Middle East* (London: Pickering and Chatto, 2001).

McNeal, R. A. "Nicholas Biddle and the Literature of Greek Travel." *Classical Antiquity* 12, no.1 (1993): 65–88.

Maiuri, Amedeo. "L'iscrizione del tempio di 'Aphaia' in Egina," with L. Savignoni, "Nuove osservazioni sull'iscrizione e sul tempio di Aphaia" (Rome: Loescher & Co., 1910), 197–220.

Marbach, Gotthard Oswald. *Schelling, Hegel, Cousin und Krug: Erörterungen auf dem Gebiete der Philosophie* (Leipzig: Otto Wigand's Verlags Expedition, 1835).

Marstine, Janet, ed. *The Routledge Companion to Museum Ethics: Redefining Ethics for the Twenty-First Century Museum* (New York: Routledge, 2011).

McCarthy, Mary. *Venice Observed* (New York: Harcourt Brace Jovanovich, 1956, 1963).

Meine-Schwahe, Monika. "Johann Martin von Wagner: 'Die griechischen Helden vor Troja' und Neues zur Kunstlerbiographie." *Aus Weltkunst* 73, no. 6 (2003): 863–64.

Michaelis, Adolf. "Geschichte des Statuenhofs im Vaticanisches Belvedere." *Jahrbuch des Kaisarl. Deutschen Archaologisches Instituts* 5 (1890): 5–72.

———. "Stella della Collezione Capitolina di Antichita." *Romische Mittheilungen* 6 (1891): 3–66.

Miles, Margaret M. *Art as Plunder: The Ancient Origins of Debate about Cultural Property* (New York: Cambridge University Press, 2009).

Minor, Vernon Hyde. *The Death of the Baroque and the Rhetoric of Good Taste* (New York: Cambridge University Press, 2006).

Minta, Stephen. *On a Voiceless Shore: Byron in Greece* (New York: Henry Holt and Company, 1998).

Mitsi, Eftirpe. "Travel, Memory, and Authorship: George Wheler's *A Journey Into Greece* (1682)." *Restoration* 30, no. 1 (2006): 1–15.

Moore, Mary B. "Aegina, Aphaia-Temple VIII. The Attic Black-Figured Pottery." *Archäologischer Anzeiger* 101, Heft 1 (1986): 51–93.

Moret, Stefan. "Wagner als Künstler und Kunstagent in Rom." In *Johann Martin von Wagner: Künstler, Sammler und Maler*. Edited by Stefan Kummer and Ulrich Sinn (Würzburg: Ergon Verlag, 2007), 23–32.

Morritt, John B. S. *A Grand Tour: Letters and Journeys 1794–96* (London: 1914, 1985).

Murphy, Peter. "Architectonics." In *Agon, Logos, Polis: The Greek Achievement and Its Aftermath*. Edited by Johann P. Arnason and Peter Murphy (Stuttgart: Franz Steiner Verlag, 2001).

Napoleon in Egypt: Al-Jabarti's Chronicle of the French Occupation, 1798. Translated by Schmuel Moreh, with an introduction by Robert L. Tignor, and an afterword by Edward W. Said (Princeton: Marcus Wiener Publishing, 1993).

Neeft, Kees. "Aegina, Aphaia-Temple XVI. Corinthian Alabastra and Aryballoi. Mit 61 Abbildungen." *Archäologischer Anzeiger* 108, Heft 4 (1993): 543–69.

Nehamas, Alexander. *Only a Promise of Happiness: The Place of Beauty in a World of Art* (Princeton: Princeton University Press, 2010).

Nerdinger, W. *Leo von Klenze: Architect zwischen Kunst und Hof, 1784–1864* (2000), with CD-ROM.

———, ed. *The Walter Gropius Archive*, 4 vols. Busch-Reisinger Museum, Harvard University (New York: Garland Press, 1990–91).

Noack, Frederick, ed. *Das Deutschtum in Rom: Seit dem Ausgang des Mittelalters* (1927), 2 vols. (Darmstadt: Scientia Verlag Aalen, 1974).

Ohly, Dieter. *Aegina: Tempel und Heiligtum* (Münich: Verlag C.H. Beck, 1978).

———. *Die Aegineten I: Die Ostgiebelgruppe* (Münich: Verlag C.H. Beck, 1976).

———. *Die Aegineten II: Die Westgiebelgruppe* (Münich: C. H. Beck, 2001), with images assembled posthumously by Martha Ohly-Dumm.

———. *Die Aegineten III* [Die Gruppen auf dem Altarplatz (Tafeln 163–91), Figürliche Bruchstücke (Tafeln 192–98), Akrotere (Tafeln 199–234), Aus der Tempelcella (Tafeln 235–38), Die Klassizistische Restaurierung der Aegineten (Tafeln 239–50)] (Münich: C. H. Beck, 2001).

———. *Die Antikensammlungen am Königsplatz in München: Geleitwort für den Besucher* (Waldsassen/Bayern: Stiftland-Verlag, n.d).

———. *Glyptothek München: Griechische und römische Skulpturen* (Münich: Verlag C.H. Beck, 1972).

———. *The Münich Glyptothek: Greek and Roman Sculpture*. Translated by Helen Hughes-Brock (Münich: Verlag C. H. Beck, 1974).

———, with Ernst Ludwig Schwander. "Aegina, Aphaia-Temple I. Die südliche Stützmauer der Temenosterasse." *Archäologischer Anzeiger* 85, Heft 1 (1970): 48–71.

———, with Ernst Ludwig Schwander. "Aegina, Aphaia-Temple II. Untersuchungen in der spätarchaischen Tempelsterasse." *Archäologischer Anzeiger* 86, Heft 3 (1971): 505–38.

Ohly-Dumm, Martha, and Martin Robertson. "Aegina, Aphaia-Temple XII. Archaic Marble Sculpture Other than Architectural." *Archäologischer Anzeiger* 103, Heft 3 (1988): 405–21.

Origo, Iris. *Allegra* (London: Hogarth Press, 1935).

Parkinson, Richard. *Cracking Codes: The Rosetta Stone and Its Decipherment* (Berkeley: University of California Press, 1999).

Pater, Walter. *Greek Studies: A Series of Essays* (London: Macmillan and Co., Limited, 1925).

Paul, Carole. *The Borghese Collections & the Display of Art in the Age of the Grand Tour* (Los Angeles: Getty Research Institute, 2008).

———. *Making a Prince's Museum: Drawings for the Late-Eighteenth Century Redecoration of the Villa Borghese* (Los Angeles: Getty Research Institute, 2000).

———. ed. *The First Modern Museums of Art: The Birth of an Institution in 18th- and Early-19th-Century Europe* (Los Angeles: The J. Paul Getty Museum, 2012).

Pilafidis-Williams, Korinna. *The Sanctuary of Aphaia on Aigina in the Bronze Age* (Münich: Hirmer Verlag GmbH, 1998).

Pietrangeli, Carlo. *I Musei Vaticani: cinque secoli di storia* (Rome: Edizioni Quasar, BAV, 1985).

———. *The Vatican Museums: Five Centuries of History*. Translated by Peter Spring (Rome: Edizioni Quasar, BAV, 1993).

Pini, Ingo. "Aegina, Aphaia-Temple X. Die Steinsiegel." *Archäologischer Anzeiger* 102, Heft 3 (1987): 413–33.

Polinskaya, Irene. "Fifth Century Horoi on Aigina." *Hesperia* 78, no. 2 (2009): 231–67.

———. *A Local History of Greek Polytheism: Gods, People and the Land of Aegina, 800–400 BCE* (E. J. Brill, 2013).

Pölnitz, P. Winfrid Frhr. von O.S.B. *Ludwig I. von Bayern und Johann Martin von Wagner: Ein Beitrag zur Geschichte der Kunstsbestrebungen König Ludwigs I.* Schriftenreihe zur bayerischen Landesgeschichte, Band 2 (Münich: Verlag der Kommission, 1929).

Pommier, Édouard. *Più antichi della luna: Studi su J. J. Winckelmann e A. Ch. Quatremère de Quincy*. Translated by Michela Scolaro (Bologna: Minerva Soluzioni Editoriali srl, 2000).

———. *Winckelmann, inventeur de l'histoire de l'art* (Paris: Editions Gallimard, 2003).

Potts, Alex D. *Flesh and the Ideal: Winckelmann and the Origins of Art History* (New Haven, CT: Yale University Press, 2000).

———. "Political Attitudes and the Rise of Historicism in Art Theory." *Art History* 1, no. 2 (1978): 191–213.

Pratt, Mary Louise Pratt. *Imperial Eyes: Travel Writing and Transculturation* (New York: Routledge, 1992).

Prignitz, Sebastian. *Der Pergamonaltar und die pergamenische Gelehrtenschule* (Berlin: Arenhövel, 2008).

Prott, Lyndel V., ed. *Witnesses to History: A Compendium of Documents and Writings on the Return of Cultural Objects* (Paris: UNESCO, 2009).

Quatremère de Quincy, A. C. *Canova et ses ouvrages, ou Mémoires Historiques sur la vie et les travaux de ce célèbre artiste* (Paris: Adrien le Clere et C.ie Imprimeurs-Libraires, 1834).

———. *Considérations morales sur la destination des ouvrages de l'Art*, ou de l'influence de leur emploi sur la génie et le gout de ceux qui les produisent ou qui les jugent, et sur le sentiment de ceux qui en jouissent et en reçoivent les impressions (Paris: L'Imprimerie de Crapelet, 1815).

———. *The Destination of Works of Art and the Use to Which They Are Applied, Considered with Regard to their Influence of the Genius and Taste of Artists, and the Sentiment of Amateurs*. Translated by Henry Thomson (London: John Murray, 1821).

———. *Dictionnaire historique d'architecture* (Paris: Librairie D'Adrien le Clere et C.ie, Quai des Augustins, no. 35, 1832).

———. *Encyclopedie Méthodique: Architecture, dédiée et présentée a Monseigneur de Lamoignon, Garde des Sceaux de France &c.* (Paris: Chez Pancoucke, Libraire, 1788).

———. *Essai sur l'idéal dans ses applications pratiques aux oeuvres de l'imitation proper* (Paris: Libraire d'Adrien le Clere et Cie., 1837).

———. *Essai sur la nature, le but et les moyens de l'imitation dans le beaux-arts* (Paris: Imprimerie de Jules Didot L'Aîné, 1823).

———. *Essay on the Nature, the End and the Means of Imitation in the Fine Arts*. Translated by J. C. Kent (London: Smith, Elder & Co., Cornhill, 1837).

———. *Histoire de la vie et des ouvrages des plus célèbres architects du XIe jusqu'a la fin du XVIIIe*, 2 vols. (Paris: Jules Renouard, Libraire, 1830).

———. *Histoire de la vie et des ouvrages Raphaël*, 2nd ed. (Paris: Adrien le Clere et C.ie Imprimeurs-Libraires, 1833).

———. *Le Jupiter Olympien*, ou, L'Art de la Sculture Antique considéré sous un nouveau point de vue (Paris: De l'Imprimerie de Firmon Didot, 1815).

———. *Letters to Miranda and Canova on the Abduction of Antiquities from Rome and Athens*. Translated by Chris Miller and David Gilks, with David Poulot (Los Angeles: Getty Research Foundation, 2012).

———. *Lettres au Générale Miranda sur le Préjudice qu'Occasionneraient aux Arts & à la Science le Déplacement des Monuments de l'Art de l'Italie, le Démembrement de ses Écoles, & la Spoliation de ses Collections, Galeries, Musées*, etc. (1796).

———. *Lettres écrites de Londres à Rome, et adressées à M. Canova; sur les Marbres d'Elgin, ou les Sculptures du Temple de Minerve à Athènes* (Rome: 1818).

———. *Lettres sur l'enlèvement des ouvrages de l'art antique a Athènes et a Rome* (Paris: Adrien le Clere et C.ie, 1836).

———. *Life of Raffaelo*. Edited and translated by William Hazlitt (London: David Bogue, Fleet Street, 1846), 191–461.

———. *Restitution du Char Funéraire qui Transporta de Babylone en Egypte le Corps d'Alexandre d'après la description de Diodore de Sicile* (Paris: De L'Imprimerie de T. F. Rignoux, 1827).

———. *Sur la Statue Antique de Vénus Découverte dans l'Ile de Milo en 1820, Transporte a Paris par M. Le Marquis de Rivière, Ambassadeur de France a la Cour Ottomane* (Paris: Chez Debure Frères, Libraires du Roi, 1821).

———. *The True, the Fictive, and the Real: The Historical Dictionary of Architecture of Quatremère de Quincy*. Edited and translated by Samir Younés (London: Andreas Papadakis Publisher, 1999).

Ragaller, Heinrich. "Martin Wagners 'Rat der Griechen vor Troja': Die Entstehungsgeschichte eines klassizistischen Bildes." *Kunst in Hessen und am Mittelrhein* 3 (Darmstadt, 1963): 107–20.

Ramsey, Robert. "Sir George Wheler and His Travels in Greece, 1650–1724." In *Essays by Divers Hands*. Edited by R. W. Chapman (Transactions of the Royal Society of Literature XIX, 1942), 1–39.

Ray, John. *The Rosetta Stone and the Rebirth of Ancient Egypt* (Cambridge, MA: Harvard University Press, 2007).

Reinholdt, Claus, Peter Scherrer, and Wolfgang Wohlmayr. *Aiakeion: Beiträge zur Klassischen Altertumswissenschaft zu Ehren von Florens Felten* (Wien: Phoibos Verlag, 2009).

Revett, Nicolas, and James Stuart. *The Antiquities of Athens, Measured and Delineated*, 3 vols. (London: Society of the Dilettanti, 1762). Arno reprint, 2 vols. (1980).

Ridgeway, Brunhilde S. *The Severe Style in Greek Sculpture* (Princeton: Princeton University Press, 1970).

Ridley, Ronald T. "To Protect the Monuments: The Papal Antiquarian (1534–1870)." *Xenia Antiqua* 1 (1992): 117–54.

Rothenberg, Jacob. *Descensus ad Terram: The Acquisition and Reception of the Elgin Marbles* (New York: Garland Publishers, Inc., 1977).

Rowlands, Thomas F. "Quatremère de Quincy: The Formative Years, 1785–1795." PhD thesis (Northwestern University, 1987).

Roux, Georges. *Karl Haller von Hallerstein: Le Temple de Bassae* (Strasbourg: Bibliothèque Nationale et Universitaire de Strasbourg, 1976).

Rubin, James Henry. "Allegory versus Narrative in Quatremère de Quincy." *The Journal of Aesthetics and Art Criticism* 44, no. 4 (Summer, 1986): 383–92.

Rudenstine, David. "The Legality of Elgin's Taking." International Journal of Cultural Property 8, no. 1 (1999): 356–76.

Ruehl, Martin A. "German Horror Stories: Teutonomania and the Ghosts of Tacitus." *Arion, Third Series* 22, no. 2 (2014): 129–89.

Ruprecht, Louis A., Jr. *Afterwords: Hellenism, Modernism and the Myth of Decadence* (Albany: State University of New York Press, 1996).

———. *Classics at the Dawn of the Museum Era: The Life and Times of Antoine Chrysostome Quatremère de Quincy (1755–1849)* (New York: Palgrave Macmillan, 2014).

———. *Was Greek Thought Religious? On the Use and Abuse of Hellenism, From Rome to Romanticism* (New York: Palgrave MacMillan, 2002).

———. *Winckelmann and the Vatican's First Profane Museum* (New York: Palgrave MacMillan, 2011).

Said, Edward. *Culture and Imperialism* (New York: Vintage Books, 1993).

———. *Orientalism* (New York: Vintage Books, 1978).

Saisselin, Rémy Gilbert. "Neo-Classicism: Images of Public Virtue and Realities of Private Luxury." *Art History* 4, no. 1 (March, 1981): 14–36.

Sallis, John. *Shades–Of Painting at the Limit.* Indianapolis: Indiana University Press, 1998.

———. *Transfigurements: On the True Sense of Art* (Chicago: University of Chicago Press, 2008).

———. *The Verge of Philosophy* (Chicago: University of Chicago Press, 2008).

Schäfer, Thomas. "Aegina, Aphaia-Temple XV. Becken und Ständer aus Marmor und Kalkstein." *Archäologischer Anzeiger* 107, Heft 1 (1992): 7–37.

Schelling, Friedrich W. J. *The Ages of the World* [1815 manuscript]. Translated by Jason Wirth (Albany: State University of New York Press, 2000).

———. *The Ages of the World* [1813 version]. Translated by Judith Norman, with an introduction by Slavoj Zizek (Ann Arbor: University of Michigan Press, 1997).

———. *Clara, or, On Nature's Connection to the Spirit World.* Translated by Fiona Steinkamp (Albany: State University of New York Press, 2002).

———. *"The Deities of Samothrace": A Translation and an Interpretation.* Translated by Robert F. Brown (Missoula, MT: Scholars Press, 1974).

———. *First Outline of a System of the Philosophy of Nature.* Translated by Keith R. Peterson (Albany: State University of New York Press, 2004).

———. *Historical-critical Introduction to the Philosophy of Mythology.* Translated by Mason Richey and Markus Zissilsberger, with a foreword by Jason M. Wirth (Albany: State University of New York Press, 2007).

———. *On the History of Modern Philosophy.* Translated by Andrew Bowie (New York: Cambridge University Press, 1994).

———. *Of Human Freedom.* Translated by James Guttman (Chicago: Open Court Publishing Company, 1936).

———. *Philosophical Investigations into the Essence of Human Freedom.* Translated by Jeff Love and Johannes Schmidt (Albany: State University of New York Press, 2006).

———. *The Philosophy of Art.* Edited and translated by Douglas W. Stott (Minneapolis: University of Minnesota Press, 1989).

———. *Philosophie und Religion* (Tübingen: In der J. G. Cotta'schen Buchhandlung, 1804).

———. *System der Weltalter: Münchner Vorlesung 1827–28.* Edited by Siegbert Peetz (Frankfurt am Mein: Vittorio Klostermann, 1990).

Schliemann, Heinrich. *Troy and It Remains* (1875). Edited by Philip Smith (New York: Dover Publications, 1994).

Schneider, René. *L'Esthétique classique chez Quatremère de Quincy (1805 –1823)* (Paris: Libraire Hachette et C.ie, 1910).

———. *Quatremère de Quincy et son intervention dans les arts (1788 –1830)* (Paris: Libraire Hachette et C.ie, 1910).

Schwandner, Ernst-Ludwig. "Der Altere Aphaiatempel auf Aegina." *Neue Forschungen in Griechischen Heiligtumern* (1974): 103–20.

———. *Der Ältere Porostempel der Aphaia auf Aegina.* Deutsches Archäologisches Institut, Band 16 (Berlin: Verlag Walter de Gruyter & Co., 1985).

Secrest, Meryl. *Duveen: A Life in Art* (New York: Alfred A. Knopf, 2004).

Seidl, Wilhelm. *Bayern in Griechenland: Die Geburt des Griechischen Nationalistaats und die Regierung König Ottos* (Münich: Suddeutscher, 1965).

Sheehan, James J. *Museums in the German Art World from the End of the Old Regime to the Rise of Modernism* (New York: Oxford University Press, 2000).

Shorrock, Robert. *The Myth of Paganism: Nonnus, Dionysus and the World of Late Antiquity* (London: Bristol Classical Press, 2011).

Sieveking, Johannes, and Ludwig Curtius, eds. *Adolf Furtwangler: Kleine Schriften*, 2 vols. (Münich: C. H. Beck'sche Verlagbuchhandlung, 1912).

Smith, Arthur H. "Lord Elgin and His Collection." *Journal of Hellenic Studies* 36 (1916): 163–372.

Spon, Jacob. *Voyage d'Italie, de Dalmatie, de Grèce et du Levant, fait aux années 1675 & 1676 par Iacob Spon Docteur Medecin Aggregé à Lyon, & George Wheler Gentilhomme Anglois,* 3 vols. (Lyon: Chez Antoine Cellier le fils, 1678).

Sprawson, Charles. *Haunts of the Black Masseur: The Swimmer as Hero* (New York: Pantheon, 1994).

St. Clair, William. *Lord Elgin and the Marbles* (New York: Oxford University Press, 1967).

Stackelberg, Otto Magnus von. *Der Apollotempel zu Bassae in Arcadien und die daselbst ausgegrabenen Bildwerke* (Frankfurt am Mein: Gedruckt mit Andreäischen Schriften, 1826).

———. *Costumes et usages des peuples de la Grèce modern* (Paris: 1825): n.p.

———. *Der Gräber der Hellenen* (Berlin: Verlag von G. Reimer, 1837).

———. *La Grèce: vues pittoresques et topographiques* (Paris: I. F. D'Ostervald, 1834).

———. *Trachten und Gebräuche der Neugriechen* (Berlin: Verlag von G. Reimer, 1831 reprint).

B. Σταης, "Περὶ τῶν ἐν Αἰγίνῃ ἀνασκαφῶν," Πρακτικὰ τῆς ἐν 'Αθήναις 'Αρχαιολογικῆς 'Εταιρείας (1894): 17–20.

Steen, Gonda von. *Liberating Hellenism from the Ottoman Empire: Comte de Marcellus and the Last of the Classics* (New York: Palgrave Macmillan, 2010).

Steiner, George. *Antigones* (New York: Oxford University Press, 1984).

Stoneman, Richard. *Land of Lost Gods: The Search for Classical Greece* (London: Hutchinson, 1987).

———. *A Luminous Land: Artists Discover Greece* (Los Angeles: The J. Paul Getty Museum, 1998).

Struys, Jan Janszoon. *The Voiages and Travels of John Struys through Italy, Greece, Muscovy, Tartary, Media, Persia, East-India, Japan, and Other Countries in Europe, Africa and Asia.* Translated by John Morrison (London: Abel Swalle, 1694).

Thorvaldsen in Rom: Aus Wagners Papieren (Würzburg: 20ten Programm zur Stiftungsfeier des von Wagner'schen Kunstinstituts, 1887).

Thorvaldsen's Ancient Sculptures: A Catalogue of the Ancient Sculptures in the Collection of Bertel Thorvaldsen, Thorvaldsens Museum (Copenhagen: Thorvaldsens Museum, 2003).

Tibal, André. *Inventaire des manuscrits de Winckelmann déposés a la Bibliothèque Nationale* (Paris: Hachette et C.ie, 1911).

Tischbein, Jean-Henri Guillaume.*Figures d'Homère Dessinées d'après l'Antique* (Metz: Chez Collignon, Imprimeur-Libraire, 1801).

Tolias, Giorgos, ed. *The Fever of the Marbles* (Athens: Oikos, 1996).

Traill, David. *Schliemann's Troy: Treasure and Deceit* (New York: St. Martin's Press, 1995).

Trelawney, Edward J. *Recollections of Shelley, Byron and the Author* (New York: New York Review Books, 2000).

Tresgakis, Hugh. *Beyond the Grand Tour: The Levant Lunatics* (London: Ascent Books, 1979).

Turner, William. *Journal of a Tour in the Levant,* 3 vols. (London: John Murray, 1820).

Twain, Mark. *The Innocents Abroad, or, The New Pilgrim's Progress* (New York: Airmont Publishing Company, 1967).

Vidler, Anthon. "The 'Art' of History: Monumental Aesthetics from Winckelmann to Quatremère de Quincy." *Oppositions* 25 (1982): 53–67.

Vierneisel, Klaus, with Gotlieb Leinz, eds. *Glyptothek München, 1830–1980: Jubiläumsausstellung zur Entstehungs- und Baugeschichte, 17 September bis 23 November 1980* (Münich: Glyptothek, 1980).

Vierneisel-Schlörb, Barbara. *Glyptothek München: Katalog der Skulpturen*, 2 vols. (Münich: Verlag C. H. Beck, 1979).

Vin, J. P. A. van der. *Travellers to Greece and Constantinople: Ancient Monuments and Old Traditions in Medieval Traveller's Tales* (Istanbul: Niederlands Historisch-Archaeologisch Instituut, 1980).

Vollmer, Hans, ed. *Allgemeins Lexikon der Bildenden Künstler von der Antike bis zur Gegenwart* (Leipzig: Verlag von E. A. Seemann, 1929).

Vrettos, Theodore. *The Elgin Affair: The Abduction of Antiquity's Greatest Treasures and the Passions It Aroused* (New York: Little, Brown and Company, 1997).

———. *A Shadow of Magnitude: The Acquisition of the Elgin Marbles* (New York: G. P. Putnam's Sons, 1974).

Wagner, Johannes Martin. *Bericht über die Aeginetischen Bildwerke im Besitz Seiner Königl. Hoheit des Kronprinzen von Baiern*, mit Kunstgeschichtlichen Anmerkungen von Fr. W. J. Schelling (Stuttgart and Tübingen: T. G. Cotta'schen Buchhandlung, 1817).

Walter-Karydi, Elena. *How the Aeginetans Formed Their Identity*. Translated by Jean Clough (Athens: The Archaeological Society of Athens, 2006).

———. "Das Theaurion von Ägina. Mit 16 Abbildungen." *Archäologischer Anzeiger* 109, Heft 2 (1994): 125–48.

Walter, Hans. *Ägina: Die Archäologische Geschichte einer griechische Insel* (Deutsche Kunstverlag, 1993).

———. *Die Leute im alten Ägina, 3000–1000 v.Chr* (Stuttgart: Verlag Urachhaus, 1988).

———, and Hans-Joachim Weishaar. "Alt-Ägina. Die prähistorische Innenstadt westlich des Apollontempels." *Archäologischer Anzeiger* 108, Heft 3 (1993): 293–97.

Warburg, Aby. *The Renewal of Pagan Antiquity: Contributions to the Cultural History of the European Renaissance*. Translated by David Britt, with an introduction by Kurt W. Forster (Los Angeles: The Getty Research Institute, 1999).

Watkin, David. *The Life and Work of C. R. Cockerell* (London: A. Zwemmer Ltd., 1974).

Welter, G. "Ausgraben in Aegina." *Gnomon* Band 5, Heft 7 (July, 1929): 415.

Wheler, George. *A Journey Into Greece in Company of Dr. Spon of Lyons* (London: William Cademann, Robert Kettlewell, and Awnsham Churchill, 1682).

Will, Frederic. "Two Critics of the Elgin Marbles: William Hazlitt and Quatremère de Quincy." *The Journal of Aesthetics and Art Criticism* 14, no. 4 (1956): 462–74.

Williams, Dyfri. "Aegina, Aphaia-Temple IV. The Inscription Commemorating the Construction of the First Limestone Temple and Other Features of the Sixth Century Temenos." *Archäologischer Anzeiger* 97, Heft 1 (1982): 55–68.

———. "Aegina, Aphaia-Temple V. The Pottery from Chios." *Archäologischer Anzeiger* 98, Heft 2 (1983): 155–86.

———. "Aegina, Aphaia-Temple XI. The Pottery frm the Second Limestone Temple and the Later History of the Temple." *Archäologischer Anzeiger* 102, Heft 4 (1987): 629–80.

———. "Aegina, Aphaia-Temple XVII. The Laconian Pottery." *Archäologischer Anzeiger* 108, Heft 4 (1993): 571–98.

Wilton, Andrew, and Ilaria Bigliamini. *Grand Tour: The Lure of Italy in the Eighteenth Century* (London: Tate Gallery Publishing, 1996).

Winckelmann, J. J. *Essays on the Philosophy and History of Art*,3 vols. Edited by Curtis Bowman (New York: Continuum International Publishing Group, 2005).

———. *Geschichte der Kunst des Alterthums* (Dresden: In der Walterischer Hofbuchhandlung, 1764).

———. *Geschichte der Kunst des Alterthums,* text of the 1764 Dresden and 1776 Vienna editions printed in parallel, 5 vols. Edited by Adolf H. Borben, et al. (Mainz am Rhen: Verlag Philipp von Zabern, 2002).

———. *Histoire de l'Art chez les Anciens*. Translated by d'Hubert (Paris: Chez Bossange, Masson et Besson, 1802).

———. *History of the Art of Antiquity*. Translated by Harry Francis Mallgrave, and edited by Alex Potts (Los Angeles: Getty Research Institute, 2006).

———. *Reflections on the Imitation of Greek Artworks in Painting and Sculpture.* Bilingual German-Spanish ed. Edited by Elfriede Heyer and Roger C. Norton (La Salle, IL: Open Court, 1987).

Wirth, Jason M. *The Conspiracy of Life: Meditations on Schelling and His Time* (Albany: State University of New York Press, 2003).

———, ed. *Schelling Now: Contemporary Readings* (Indianapolis: Indiana University Press, 2005).

———. *Schelling's Practice of the Wild: Time, Art, Imagination* (Albany: State University of New York Press, 2015).

Withey, Lynne. *Grand Tours and Cook's Tours: A History of Leisure Travel, 1750 to 1915* (New York: William Morrow and Company, Inc., 1997).

Wolters, Paul. *A Guide to the Royal Glyptothek at Münich* (Münich: Kgl. Hofbuchdruckerei Kastner & Gallery, 1913).

Woodhouse, C. M. *Modern Greece: A Short History*, 4th ed. (London: Faber and Faber, 1968, 1986).

The Works of Lord Byron (Hertfordshire: The Wordsworth Library, 1994).

Wünsche, Raimund. "'Come nessuno, dai tempi fiorenti dell'Ellada,' Thorvaldsen, Ludovico di Bavaria ed en il restauro dei marmi di Egina." In *Bertel Thorvaldsen: 1770–1841, scultore danese a Roma.* Edited by E. di Majo, B. Jørnaes, and S. Sussino (Rome: 1989), 80–96.

———. *Glyptothek München: Meisterwerke Griechischer und Römischer Skulptur* (Münich: C. H. Beck, 2005).

———. *Kampfe um Troja: 200 Jahre Ägineten in München, Ausstellungskatalog* (Münich: Kunstverlag Josef Fink, 2011).

———, ed. *Il Torso del Belvedere: Da Aiace a Rodin* (Vatican City: Generale Monumenti Musei e Gallerie Pontficie Tipografia Vaticana, 1998).

Yalouri, Eleana. *The Acropolis: Global Fame, Local Claim* (Oxford: Burg Publications, 2001).

Yannoulis, Anne. *Aegina*, 2nd ed. (Athens: Lycabettus Press, 1986).

Zambon, Alessia. *Aux origines de l'archeologie en Grèce: Fauvel et sa method* (Paris: CTHS: Institut National de l'Histoire de l'Art, 2014).

———. "L. F. S. Fauvel (1753 –1838): Les découvertes d'antiquités en Grèce à la fin du XVIIIe et au début di XIXe siècle." PhD diss. (Università degli Studi di Padova and Université Paris I, Sorbonne, 2009).

Zerbst, Arne. *Schelling und die bildende Kunst: Zum Verhältnis von kunstphilosophischem System und konkreter Werkkenntnis* (Münich: Wilhelm Fink Verlag, 2011).

Zimmer, Johann. "Die Aeginetan in Berlin." *Jahrbuch des Berlin Museums* 46 (2004): 7–104.

Zizek, Slavoj. *The Invisible Remainder: An Essay on Schelling and Related Matters* (London: Verso, 1996).

INDEX

www.ingramcontent.com/pod-product-compliance
Lightning Source LLC
LaVergne TN
LVHW020430080826
844660LV00034B/1384

* 9 7 8 1 4 3 8 4 6 4 8 0 0 *